Hollywood Genres:

FORMULAS, FILMMAKING, AND THE STUDIO SYSTEM

Hollywood Genres:

FORMULAS, FILMMAKING, AND THE STUDIO SYSTEM

Thomas Schatz
The University of Texas at Austin

Boston, Massachusetts   Burr Ridge, Illinois
Dubuque, Iowa   Madison, Wisconsin   New York, New York
San Francisco, California   St. Louis, Missouri

McGraw-Hill

*A Division of The **McGraw·Hill** Companies*

HOLLYWOOD GENRES
First Edition

Printed and bound by Book-mart Press, Inc.

22 23 24 25 26 27 28 29   BKM BKM   0 9 8 7 6 5 4 3

Library of Congress Cataloging in Publication Data
Schatz, Thomas, 1948.
    Hollywood genres.
    Bibliography; p.
    Includes index.
    I. Moving-pictures — United States.   I. Title
PN 1993.5.U6S32   791.43′09794′94   80-25699
ISBN 0-07-553623-4

Composed by American-Stratford Graphic Services, Inc.
Photo Research by Christine Pollo
Book Design by Lorraine Hohman
Cover Design by Doug Fornuff

Preface

The central thesis of this book is that a genre approach provides the most effective means for understanding, analyzing, and appreciating the Hollywood cinema. Taking into account not only the formal and aesthetic aspects of feature filmmaking, but various other cultural aspects as well, the genre approach treats movie production as a dynamic process of exchange between the film industry and its audience. This process, embodied in the Hollywood studio system, has been sustained primarily through genres, those popular narrative formulas like the Western, musical, and gangster film, which have dominated the screen arts throughout this century.

Film critics and historians have, of course, recognized the pervasive and popular nature of these formulas, but genre study generally has been overshadowed by more "literary" critical approaches—particularly those treating film "authorship" (usually in terms of the director) and those treating movies as individual, isolated texts. Such critical efforts have been necessary and laudable, but the more we come to understand commercial filmmaking, the more severely limited they seem to be. Movies are not produced in creative or cultural isolation, nor are they consumed that way. Individual movies may affect each one of us powerfully and somewhat differently, but essentially they are all generated by a collective production system which honors certain narrative traditions (or conventions) in designing for a mass market. As such, we cannot examine individual films without first establishing a critical and theoretical framework that recognizes the cinema's production-consumption process as well as the basic conventions of feature filmmaking.

A genre approach provides this framework, because (1) it assumes that filmmaking is a *commercial* art, and hence that its creators rely on proven formulas to economize and systematize production; (2) it recognizes the cinema's close contact with its *audience*, whose response to individual films has affected the gradual development of story formulas and standard production practices; (3) it treats the cinema as primarily a *narrative* (storytelling) medium, one whose familiar stories involve dramatic conflicts, which are themselves based upon ongoing *cultural conflicts*; and (4) it establishes a context in which cinematic *artistry* is evaluated in terms of our filmmakers' capacity to re-invent established formal and narrative conventions.

The focus of my book is the Hollywood studio system's "classic era," the period roughly from 1930 to 1960. The continuance, since then, of genre production, both in filmmaking and in network television, reaffirms the need for a systematic, in-depth inquiry into the nature and function of that production. This book represents an effort to lay the historical and theoretical groundwork for genre study in the American screen arts, encompassing not only literary and filmic concerns, but cultural, socioeconomic, industrial, political, and even anthropological concerns as well.

Hollywood Genres is divided into two parts. Part One is primarily theoretical, concerned in general terms with the essential characteristics and the cultural role of genre filmmaking. This section does not examine any individual genres or genre films, but instead looks at the very concept of what might be termed "genre-ness"—that is, those formal and narrative features shared by all genres and their relationship to the culture at large.

Part Two is composed of six chapters, each of which examines a dominant Hollywood genre: the Western, gangster, hardboiled detective, screwball comedy, musical, and family melodrama. Each chapter is divided into two sections: an historical survey of the genre and a critical analysis of some of its key films. The Western survey is complemented by an analysis of the genre's evolution; it examines four Westerns directed by John Ford in consecutive decades. The gangster chapter incorporates an essay on the impact of the Production Code (a means of industry-based censorship). The hardboiled detective survey is preceded by an analysis of a certain style (*film noir*) and a single film (*Citizen Kane*) that influenced the genre's development. The screwball comedy chapter contains an essay on the collaborative efforts of director Frank Capra and screenwriter Robert Riskin. The musical survey leads directly into an exploration of the genre's "Golden Age" under producer Arthur Freed at M-G-M. And the family melodrama chapter is rounded out with an analysis of three films by the genre's consummate stylist, Douglas Sirk.

These six formulas obviously represent only a limited number of Hollywood genres. But they do include what I believe are the most significant of Hollywood's popular forms. They also provide a convenient historical "fit." For by surveying these genres within the same context, I have been able to develop a critical-historical overview of Hollywood's classic era. The gangster study concentrates on the early-to-mid 1930s, the screwball comedy on the mid-to-late 1930s, the hardboiled detective on the 1940s, the musical on the late 1940s and the early 1950s, the family melodrama on the mid-to-late 1950s, and the chapter on the Western spans the entire studio era.

At the risk of sounding like some gushing recipient at an Academy Awards banquet, I would like to recognize and thank various individuals who contributed, directly or indirectly, to the writing of this book.

My interest in the American cinema and in genre study began—thanks to my mentors there—Rick (Charles F.) Altman, Franklin Miller, Dudley Andrew, Richard Dyer MacCann, and Sam Becker, while I was at the University of Iowa. I am also indebted to my fellow graduate students, especially to Jane Feuer, Joe Heumann, Bobby Allen, Michael Budd, Phil Rosen, and Bob Vasilak. Some of my earliest professors also contributed to this book, although none of us realized it at the time. I am particularly grateful to James Burtchaell, c.s.c., and Carvel Collins of the University of Notre Dame, and to June Levine and Lee Lemon of the University of Nebraska.

It wasn't until I began teaching at the University of Texas that the present book really began to take shape, and I am grateful to Bob Davis and my other colleagues for being so supportive during the past few years. I also am indebted to all of my students at Texas, particularly those graduate students who, whether as students, critics, editors, or friends, contributed to this project. Special thanks to Greg Beal, David Rodowick, Mike Selig, Karol Hoeffner, Louis Black, Jackie Byars, Ed Lowry, and Stephanie Samuel, and David Brown for their advice and encouragement.

Finally, I would like to thank my editors and readers at McGraw-Hill, Inc. who brought this project to fruition. My acquiring editor, Richard Garretson, and my production editor, Marilyn Miller, were of inestimable assistance in supervising the revisions of the text and translating my scholarly language into, what I hope, is readable prose. McGraw-Hill, Inc. also provided a number of excellent readers from my field who reviewed the manuscript and offered constructive criticism, particularly John Cawelti, Frank McConnell, and Rick Altman.

A word about the stills: I had hoped initially that the illustrations in this book would be composed only of frame enlargements—that is, images "lifted" from actual film footage—rather than production stills which generally are not taken from the movie camera's perspective. Due to various problems regarding the quality of frame enlargement reproduction and the less-than-cooperative attitude of most studios, I have had to settle for production stills in most instances. All of the stills selected, however, do serve to illuminate the text and should help refresh the reader's recollection of the films in question.

Austin

August 1980

Contents

6 THE SCREWBALL COMEDY   150

7 THE MUSICAL   186

Hollywood Genres:

FORMULAS, FILMMAKING, AND THE STUDIO SYSTEM

Hollywood Film Genres

PART ONE

The Genius
of the
System

Whenever a motion picture becomes a work of art it is unquestionably due to men. But the moving pictures have been born and bred not of men but of corporations. Corporations have set up the easels, bought the pigments, arranged the views, and hired the potential artists. Until the artists emerge, at least, the corporation is bigger than the sum of its parts. Somehow, although our poets have not yet defined it for us, a corporation lives a life and finds a fate outside the lives and fates of its human constituents.

—Fortune magazine, December 1932[1]

Paradoxically, the supporters of the politique des auteurs* admire the American cinema, where the restrictions of production are heavier than anywhere else. It is also true that it is the country where the greatest technical possibilities are offered to the director. But the one does not cancel out the other. I do, however, admit that freedom is greater in Hollywood than it is said to be, as long as one knows how to detect its manifestations, and I will go so far as to say that the tradition of genres is a base of operations for creative freedom. The American cinema is a classical art, but why not then admire in it what is most admirable, i.e. not only the talent of this or that filmmaker, but the genius of the system.

—André Bazin[2]

---

* The "*auteur* policy," which held that certain film directors should be considered the "authors" of their films.

The studio system

François Truffaut, French critic turned filmmaker, recently suggested that "when a film achieves a certain success, it becomes a sociological event, and the question of its quality becomes secondary"[3] (Truffaut, 1972). The success of a film may or may not depend upon its artistic quality—and this is a bone of critical contention which forever will separate elitists like John Simon from populists like Pauline Kael. But in the final analysis any film's quality, itself based upon subjective critical consensus, is incidental to the *fact* of its social and economic impact. Truffaut's observation would seem to coincide, interestingly enough, with the U.S. Supreme Court's 1915 decision that "the exhibition of motion pictures is a business pure and simple, originated and conducted for profit." Both Truffaut and the Supreme Court have recognized a fundamental tenet of commercial filmmaking: producers may not know much about art, but they know what sells and how to systematically deliver more of the same. If what the producer delivers happens to be evaluated critically as art, so much the better.

Essentially, the function of the Hollywood production companies always has been to create what Truffaut termed sociological events. In their continual efforts to reach as massive an audience as possible, early filmmakers investigated areas of potential audience appeal and, at the same time, standardized those areas whose appeal already had been verified by audience response. In the gradual development of the business of movie production, experimentation steadily gave way to standardization as a matter of fundamental economics. Between 1915 and 1930 the studios had standardized, hence economized, virtually every aspect of film production[4] (Balio, 1976). Because of this heavy regimentation, the studios of Hollywood's "classic" era (roughly 1930 to 1960) have been referred to as *factory* production systems. The analogy is not without basis in actual industry practice: the "studio system" functioned to mass produce and mass distribute movies. This is considerably different from the "New Hollywood," where the studios function primarily as distribution companies—that is, they distribute films which, for the most part, are produced independently.

Until the '50s, the major studios (MGM, Twentieth Century-Fox, Warner Brothers, Paramount, RKO) not only made motion pictures, but they also leased them through their own distribution companies to theaters which they themselves controlled. Although the "majors"—along with significant "minors" like Columbia, Universal-International, Republic, and Monogram—never controlled more than one sixth of all movie theaters in the United States, they did control most of the important "first-run" houses. In the mid-'40s, when Hollywood's audience was at its peak, the five majors owned or controlled the operations of 126 of the 163 first-run theaters in the nation's twenty-five largest cities. Not only did the audiences attending these theaters provide the bulk of revenue for the studios, but they also determined the general trends of studio production and cinematic expression. The U.S. Supreme Court dismantled this monopolistic "vertical structure" in 1948, after ten years of court battles with Paramount. This was one of the key factors, along with the advent of television and other cultural developments, in the eventual "death" of the studio system. By this time, however, Hollywood had read the pulse of its popular audience in developing an engaging and profitable means of narrative cinematic expression—the conventions of feature filmmaking were firmly established.

Thus the artist and the industrialist were cast into a necessary and highly productive relationship—each one struggling with but also depending upon the other for the success of their commercial art. While filmmakers learned to adapt their own and their audience's narrative impulse to the demands of the medium, businessmen learned to exploit the medium's capacity for widespread dissemination and consumption. While filmmakers advanced narrative traditions developed in drama and literature, producers and exhibitors advanced the commercial potential anticipated by previous forms of mass entertainment. So by the time the movie industry had standardized the feature-length narrative film by the late 'teens, the medium's mixed heritage was fairly obvious. The movies had their roots in both classic literature and bestselling pulp romances, in legitimate theater as well as vaudeville and music halls, in traditions of both "serious art" and American "popular entertainment."[5]

The contemporary mass audience, ultimately, is in good part responsible for the development of the studio system—the same audience whose leisure time and spending money became, in social historian Arnold Hauser's words, "a decisive factor in the history of art"[6] (Hauser, 1951, p. 250). By its attraction to the cinema, this audience encouraged mass distribution of movies, as well as an adherence to filmmaking conventions. Feature filmmaking, like most mass media production, is an expensive enterprise. Those who invest their capital, from the major studio to the struggling independent, are in a curious bind: on the one hand, their product must be sufficiently inventive to attract attention and satisfy the audience's demand for novelty, and on the other hand, they must protect their initial investment by relying to some extent upon established conventions that have been proven through previous exposure and repetition.

We should note here that in film production—and in virtually any popular art form—a successful product is bound up in convention because its success inspires repetition. The built-in "feedback" circuits of the Hollywood system ensured this repetition of successful stories and techniques, because the studios' production-distribution-exhibition system enabled filmmakers to gauge their work against audience response. It is as if with each commercial effort, the studios suggested another variation on cinematic conventions, and the audience indicated whether the inventive variations would themselves be conventionalized through their repeated usage.

We should also note that this is a *reciprocal* relationship between artist and audience. The filmmaker's inventive impulse is tempered by his or her practical recognition of certain conventions and audience expectations; the audience demands creativity or variation but only within the context of a familiar narrative experience. As with any such experience it is difficult for either artist or audience to specify precisely what elements of an artistic event they are responding to. Consequently, filmic conventions have been refined through considerable variation and repetition. In this context, it is important to remember that roughly 400 to 700 movies were released *per year* during Hollywood's classic era, and that the studios depended increasingly upon established story formulas and techniques. Thus any theory of Hollywood filmmaking must take into account this essential process of production, feedback, and conventionalization.

The studio system's role in the evolution of narrative filmmaking was considerable, in terms of its national and international popularity and, more importantly, in its systematic honing of filmic expression into effective narrative conventions. The international film market fluctuated throughout the studio era due to the Depression and the war, but conservative estimates indicate that Hollywood products occupied anywhere from 70 to 90 percent of the available screen time in most European and Latin American countries. In addition, the Motion Picture Association of America's "classification of subject matter" for the year 1950 indicates that over 60 percent of all Hollywood productions that year were either Westerns (27%), crime/detective films (20%), romantic comedies (11%), or musicals (4%), and that roughly 90 percent fell into some preestablished classification—mystery/spy, war, etc.[7] (Sterling and Haight, 1978).

The implications of these data are twofold. First, Hollywood's domination of not only national but international production and distribution suggests that its influence extended well beyond the United States. Second, and even more significantly, the Hollywood imprint generally involved not only isolated production techniques and narrative devices, but established story types or "genres" like the Western or the musical. And these genres have in turn traveled well—think of what Italy's "spaghetti Westerns," Japan's samurai films, or the French New Wave's hardboiled detective films owe to genres developed by the Hollywood studio system.

The genre film and the genre director

Simply stated, a genre film—whether a Western or a musical, a screwball comedy or a gangster film—involves familiar, essentially one-dimensional characters acting out a predictable story pattern within a familiar setting. During the reign of the studio system, genre films comprised the vast majority of the most popular and profitable productions, and this trend has continued even after its death. In contrast, non-genre films tended to attract greater critical attention during the studio era—films like John Ford's *The Grapes of Wrath*, Charlie Chaplin's *Monsieur Verdoux*, Billy Wilder's *The Lost Weekend*, and Jean Renoir's *Diary of a Chambermaid*.

These and other non-genre films generally traced the personal and psychological development of a "central character" or protagonist. The central characters are not familiar types whom we've seen before in movies (like the gangster, the music man, the Westerner). Rather, they are unique individuals whom we relate to less in terms of previous filmic experience than in terms of our own "real-world" experiences. The plot in non-genre films does not progress through conventional conflicts toward a predictable resolution (as with the gangster dead in the gutter, the climactic musical show). Instead it develops a *linear* plot in which the various events are linked in a chronological chain and organized by the central character's own perceptual viewpoint. The plot resolution generally occurs when the significance of the protagonist's experiences—of the "plot line"—becomes apparent to that character or to the audience, or to both.

Non-genre films represent a limited portion of Hollywood's productions, and as we might expect, many were directed by foreign-born filmmakers like Wilder and Renoir. But equally significant are those foreign directors who adapted so effectively to Hollywood's genre-based system, as shown, for example, in Fritz Lang's Westerns and crime films, Ernst Lubitsch's musicals and romantic comedies, and Douglas Sirk's and Max Ophuls' social melodramas.

Actually, the dependence of certain premiere American directors upon established film genres is equally significant and just as often overlooked. Whether we discuss Griffith's melodramas, Keaton's slapstick comedy, Ford's Westerns, or Minnelli's musicals, we are treating Hollywood directors whose reputations as artists, as creative filmmakers, are based upon their work within popular genres. As the studio era recedes into American film history, it becomes increasingly evident that most of the recognized American *auteur* directors did their most expressive and significant work within highly conventionalized forms.

The *auteur* policy

Even with this reservation, we certainly cannot dismiss the "*auteur* policy," the single most productive concept in film study over the past quarter century, although we should be aware of its limitations as well as its assets.[8] The notion of directorial authorship—that the director is the controlling creative force and hence *potentially* the "author" of his films—is a necessary and logical critical approach. Anyone who discussed "the Lubitsch touch" in the '30s or anticipated the next "Hitchcock thriller" in the '40s was, in fact, practicing this critical approach.

Originally, the *auteur* approach was formalized by a group of critics—among them François Truffaut, Eric Rohmer, and Jean-Luc Godard—writing for the

French film journal *Cahiers du Cinema*. Working throughout the 1950s under editor André Bazin, the *Cahiers* critics fashioned the "*auteur* policy" (*la politique des auteurs*) as an alternative to content-oriented, plot-theme analyses of movies. Significantly, the *auteur* policy was developed not to treat foreign filmmakers who had a great deal of control over their productions. Rather, the policy was designed to reconsider those Hollywood directors who, despite the constraints of the studio system, were able to instill a *personal style* into their work.

In order to understand the artistry of commercial filmmaking, argued the *auteur* critics, we must complement the dominant critical concern for a film's "subject matter" with more subtle consideration of visual style, camerawork, editing, and the various other factors which make up the director's "narrative voice." Alfred Hitchcock once said that he is "less interested in stories than in the manner of telling them"[9] (Sadoul, 1972, p. 117). *Auteur* analysis is, in effect, a formalized critical response to this particular conception of filmmaking.

As the *auteur* policy was refined and eventually introduced to English and American critics by Andrew Sarris and others, the Hollywood film industry underwent a steady revaluation. The reputations of directors like Hitchcock and Minnelli, who had been dismissed by many American critics because they worked in such lowbrow forms, were substantially reconsidered. In addition, a number of directors, who somehow had escaped the attention of American critics (Howard Hawks is a prime example), now were recognized as major filmmakers, along with many other exceptional stylists who had directed low-budget "B" productions (Sam Fuller, Anthony Mann, and others). Even the esteem of a widely heralded director like John Ford, whose popular and critical reputation had long been established, underwent a critical revaluation that reflected a basic reconsideration of Hollywood filmmaking. *Auteur* critics argued persuasively that Ford's genre films—war movies like *They Were Expendable* and Westerns like *The Searchers* and *The Man Who Shot Liberty Valance*—demonstrated a stylistic richness and thematic ambiguity that made them artistically superior to the calculated artistry and social consciousness of "serious" Ford films like *The Informer* and *The Grapes of Wrath*.

Experience had taught the *auteur* critics that, because of the popular and industrial nature of commercial filmmaking, the serious film artist often comes in through the back door. Too often "serious social drama" in the cinema is less serious, less genuinely social, and certainly less dramatic than the supposed "escapist entertainment" fare of a Ford Western or a Minnelli musical or a Hitchcock thriller. *Auteur* critics, in acknowledging the popular and industrial demands placed upon filmmakers, rejected the artificial distinctions between art and entertainment, and thus they signaled a substantial evolution in the way people—filmmakers, viewers, and critics alike—thought about movies.

In retrospect, it seems quite logical that *auteur* and genre criticism would dominate Hollywood film study. These two critical methods do complement and counterbalance one another in that genre criticism treats established cinematic forms, whereas *auteur* criticism celebrates certain filmmakers who worked effectively within those forms. Both approaches reflect an increased critical sensitivity to the penchant for conventionalization in commercial filmmaking. In fact the *auteur* approach, in asserting a director's consistency of form and expression, effectively translates an *auteur* into a virtual genre unto himself, into a system of conventions which identify his work. And further, the director's consistency, like the genre's, is basic to the economic and material demands of the medium and to his popularity with a mass audience. As John Ford, who himself considered film directing "always a job of work," once suggested: "For a director there are commercial rules that it is necessary to obey. In our profession, an artistic failure is nothing; a commercial failure is a sentence. The secret is to make films that please the public and also allow the director to reveal his personality"[10] (Sadoul, 1972, p. 89).

One of the essential attributes of *auteur* analysis is its structural approach: Its method is to uncover the "deep structure" (the directorial personality) in order to interpret and evaluate the "surface structure" (his or her movies). The socioeconomic imperatives of Hollywood filmmaking, however, indicate that there are a number of deep structures—industrial, political, technical, stylistic, narrative, and so on—which inform the production process. Further, when we consider a director working within an established genre we are faced with another, even "deeper," structure than that of the director's personality. The genre's preestablished cultural significance in effect determines the range and substance of any one director's expressive treatment of that genre.

That one director's treatment is more effective than another's motivates the film critic, who examines the filmmaker's manipulation and variation of formal, narrative, and thematic conventions. Generally, and especially regarding a director working within a well-developed genre, the knowledgeable critic must distinguish between the director's and the genre's contribution to a film's expressive quality. In examining Sam Peckinpah's *The Wild Bunch*, for example, one must be familiar with the history of the Western and with Peckinpah's career in order to determine how he has reinvented the genre's conventions.

Analyzing a genre director's work, which has grown along with a genre, represents an even more difficult critical challenge. Consider John Ford, who began directing silent, two-reel Westerns in 1917 and continued to produce the most popular and significant films within the genre until the early 1960s. And what of a director like Alfred Hitchcock, who in a sense "invented" the psychological thriller and who completely dominated that genre from the late 1920s through the 1960s? We will discuss these issues in later chapters, but for now they can stand as open questions that indicate the complexity involved in criticizing Hollywood genre films.

The studio production system itself, designed for the variations-on-a-theme approach characteristic of genre filmmaking, is at the very heart of this critical dilemma. Because of the practical budgetary problems of set design, scriptwriting, and so forth, the studios encouraged the development of film genres. Obviously, costs could be minimized by repeating successful formulas. Box-office returns alone provided sufficient criteria for continued genre production; the studios clearly need not understand *why* certain narratives appealed to viewers. They only required assurance that the appeal indeed existed and could be exploited financially. Thus, many aspects of studio production were refined to accommodate genre filmmaking: the "stables" of writers and technical crews whose work was limited to certain types of films; the studio sets and sound stages designed for specific genres; even the "star system," which capitalized upon the familiar, easily categorized qualities of individual performers. (Try to imagine, for instance, a passionate kiss between John Wayne and Ginger Rogers. It just doesn't work, essentially because of the close connections between a star's screen persona and his or her status as a generic convention.)

Genre and narrative conventions

As this example indicates, any genre's *narrative context* imbues its conventions with meaning. This meaning in turn determines their use in individual films. In general, the commercial cinema is identifiable by formal and narrative elements common to virtually all its products: the Hollywood movie is a story of a certain length focusing upon a protagonist (a hero, a central character); and it involves certain standards of production, a style of ("invisible") editing, the use of musical score, and so on. The genre film, however, is identified not only by its use of these general filmic devices to create an imaginary world; it is also significant that this world is predetermined and essentially intact. The narrative components of a non-genre film—the characters, setting, plot, techniques, etc.—assume their significance as they are integrated into the individual film itself. In a genre film, however, these components have prior significance as elements of some generic formula, and the viewer's negotiation of a genre film thus involves weighing the film's variations against the genre's preordained, value-laden narrative system.

An example of this process may be seen in a conventional gunfight in a Western film. Everything—from the characters' dress, demeanor, and weapons to their standing in the dirt street of an American frontier community—assumes a significance beyond the film's immediate narrative concerns. This significance is based on the viewer's familiarity with the "world" of the genre itself rather than on his or her own world. As Robert Warshow observed in his analysis of the gangster genre, "it is only in the ultimate sense that the type appeals to the audience's experience of reality; much more immediately, it appeals to the previous experience of the type itself; it creates its own field of reference"[11] (Warshow, 1962, p. 130). It is not their mere repetition which endows generic elements with a prior significance, but their repetition within a conventionalized formal, narrative, and thematic context. If it is initially a popular success, a film story is reworked in later movies and repeated until it reaches its equilibrium profile—until it becomes a spatial, sequential, and thematic pattern of familiar actions and relationships. Such a repetition is generated by the interaction of the studios and the mass audience, and it will be sustained so long as it satisfies the needs and expectations of the audience and remains financially viable for the studios.

Genre as a social force

Any viewer's familiarity with a genre is the result of a *cumulative process,* of course. The first viewing of a Western or musical actually might be more difficult and demanding than the viewing of a non-genre film, due to the peculiar logic and narrative conventions of the genre. With repeated viewings, however, the genre's narrative pattern comes into focus and the viewer's *expectations* take shape. And when we consider that the generic pattern involves not only narrative elements (character, plot, setting) but thematic issues as well, the genre's *socializing* influence becomes apparent.

Moreover, in examining film genres, these popular narratives whose plots, characters, and themes are refined through usage in a mass medium, we are considering a form of artistic expression which involves the audience more directly than any traditional art form had ever done before. There are earlier forms that anticipated this development, especially performative arts such as Greek or Renaissance drama. However, not until the invention of the printing press and then the popularization of dime novels, pulp literature, and Beadle books (named for their publisher, Erastus Beadle) did the social and economic implications of popular narrative formulas begin to take shape. Henry Nash Smith considered these implications in his evocative study of America's "Western myth," entitled *The Virgin Land.* Smith is especially interested in the creative posture assumed by individual pulp writers who produced and reproduced popular Western tales for an eager, impressionable audience. Smith's fundamental thesis is that these authors participated, with their publishers and audience, in the creative celebration of the values and ideals associated with westward expansion, thereby engendering and sustaining the Western myth. He contends that the pulp writer is not pandering to his market by lowering himself to the level of the mass audience, but rather that he or she is cooperating with it in formulating and reinforcing collective values and ideals. "Fiction produced under these circumstances virtually takes on the character of automatic writing," Smith suggests. "Such work tends to become an objectified mass dream, like the moving pictures, soap operas, or comic books that are the present-day equivalents of the Beadle stories. The individual writer abandons his own personality and identifies himself with his readers"[12] (Smith, 1950, p. 91).

There have, of course, been pulp novelists like James Fenimore Cooper and Zane Grey, just as there have been genre directors like John Ford and Sam Peckinpah, who used exceptional formal and expressive artistry in Western storytelling and whose writing seems anything but automatic. In underscoring the relationship of pulp Western novels to a mass audience and hence to American folklore, however, Smith's study adds an important dimension to our discussion. He suggests that these novels were written not only for the mass audience, but *by* them as well. Produced by depersonalized representatives of the collective, anonymous public and functioning to celebrate basic beliefs and values, their formulas might be regarded not only as popular or even elite art but also as *cultural ritual*—as a form of collective expression seemingly obsolete in an age of mass technology and a genuinely "silent majority."

This view of the nature and function of popular narrative artistry has been extended, predictably enough, into the realm of commercial filmmaking, where many of the same principles apply. In fact, André Bazin's "La politique des auteurs" essay was conceived as a warning to *auteur* critics that they look at the many other aspects of filmmaking besides directing that contribute to the authorship of any individual movie. Bazin suggests:

> What makes Hollywood so much better than anything else in the world is not only the quality of certain directors, but also the vitality and, in a certain sense, the excellence of a tradition. Hollywood's superiority is only incidentally technical; it lies much more in what one might call the American cinematic genius, something which should be analyzed, then defined, by a sociological approach to its production. The American cinema has been able, in an extraordinarily competent way, to show American society just as it wanted to see itself.[13] (1968, pp. 142–143)

The basis for this viewpoint is the level of *active but indirect audience participation* in the formulation of any popular commercial form. And that participation is itself a function of the studio system's repeating and handing down, with slight variation, those stories that the audience has isolated through its collective response.

It should be mentioned that because of the narrow range of distribution and the limited audience feedback involved in the nineteenth century, the pulp author's degree of cooperation with his or her audience was quite different from that of the Hollywood filmmaker.* Furthermore, the dime pulp or bestselling novel is the product of an individual consciousness and is communicated through a personal medium of expression. The Hollywood genre film, conversely, is both produced and consumed collectively. We are dealing here with the studio system over a period of sustained and widespread popular success, from the early years of the sound film through the gradual relinquishing, after some four decades, of the studios and their production system to the commercial television industry. These are the years before American filmmakers began to appeal, as they have tended to more recently, to a specialized market or age group. The Hollywood studios and the genre film had their heyday simultaneously—and this is no coincidence—when films were seen as mass entertainment by a general public who regularly (one might even say religiously) went "to the movies" in numbers peaking in the mid- to late-40's at 90 million viewers per week.

---

* Smith mentions this fact.

Before examining genre filmmaking as a form of collective cultural expression, however, we should acknowledge that certain commercial and technological aspects of the cinema qualify this approach. Dwight MacDonald in his "Theory of Mass Culture" posits "the essential quality of Mass, as against High or Folk, Culture: it is manufactured for mass consumption by technicians employed by the ruling class and is not an expression of the individual artist or the common people themselves"[14] (MacDonald, in Rosenberg and White, 1964). From this viewpoint, even Shakespeare is more a technician than an individual artist. Nevertheless, MacDonald's observations do encourage us to avoid any simplistic association of commercial filmmaking with either elite or folk expression.

Just as we must temper our view of the cinematic *auteur* by acknowledging the depersonalizing production system in which he or she works, so too must we temper our view of the genre film as a kind of secular, contemporary cultural ritual. The cinema's commercial feedback system rarely affords the audience any direct or immediate creative input. Rather it allows it to affect future variations by voicing collective approval or disapproval of a current film. Such a response has a cumulative effect, first isolating and then progressively refining a film story into a familiar narrative pattern. As Robert Warshow observes in his study of the gangster genre: "For such a type to be successful means that its conventions have imposed themselves upon the general consciousness and become accepted vehicles of a particular set of attitudes and a particular aesthetic effect. One goes to any individual example of the type with very definite expectations, and originality is accepted only in the degree that it intensified the expected experience without fundamentally altering it"[15] (Warshow, 1962, p. 130).

In a limited sense, any genre film is the original creation of an individual writer or director, but the nature and range of that originality are determined by the conventions and expectations involved in the genre filmmaking process. Thus, any critical analysis of that originality must be based firmly on an understanding of both the genre and the production system in which any individual genre film is generated. Ultimately, we need to complement elitist critical attitudes with a broader, more culturally and industrially responsive approach. In a certain sense, this approach could be dismissed as simply a formulation of a populist "low art" bias to offset elitist "high art" biases in film study. I hope, however, that the value of the ideas developed in this book will be realized in their application, and not in the context of critical debate. Whatever one's objections to *auteurism*, the fact remains that close analysis of certain directors' movies, along with detailed study of their directing methods, does validate the *auteur* policy as something more than merely a critical bias—it does reveal some fundamental truth about filmmaking and film art. So too should a genre approach, when applied sensibly and with care, reveal some essential truths about commercial filmmaking that will enrich our understanding and appreciation of cinematic art.

Film Genres
and the
Genre Film

I really want to go back to film school. . . . Or maybe I'll get my masters in anthropology. That's what movies are about anyway. Cultural imprints.

—Writer-director George Lucas, discussing Star Wars[1]

Thus far, we have been considering those qualities of Hollywood filmmaking which determine its status as a commercial art form. Our consideration of those qualities led us to the hypothesis that popular cinematic story formulas—or film genres—express the social and aesthetic sensibilities not only of Hollywood filmmakers but of the mass audience as well.

In many ways, this view of contemporary commercial art resists the elitist critical assumption that the artwork carries an asocial, terminal value—that the artwork is an end in itself, somehow disengaged from the mundane trappings of its initial sociocultural environment. The academic or scholarly context in which we generally are exposed to the high arts tends to support this bias, simply because we do study traditional artworks with little concern for the social imperatives involved in their creation. We presume that aesthetic objects do in fact "transcend" the culture in which they were produced, primarily because of their significance for us as members of a modern technocratic society. Our appreciation of Homer's epic poetry, Shakespeare's drama, or Dickens' novels is only marginally related, if at all, to the traditions of oral history, of the Elizabethan popular theater, or of the serialized pulp romances in which those works participated. The historical "gatekeeping"

14

function of aesthetic tradition has singled out great works of art for posterity, and thus we have been less sensitive to their sociological qualities than to their formal and aesthetic qualities. We should avoid, however, assuming that we can study and evaluate the products of our own culture from a similar critical and historical distance.

Film critic Robin Wood, in an essay entitled "Ideology, Genre, Auteur," expresses misgivings about these critical oversights in genre study:

> The work that has been done so far on genres has tended to take the various genres as "given" and discrete, and seeks to explicate them, define them in terms of motifs, etc.; what we need to ask, if genre theory is ever to be productive, is less What? than Why? We are so used to the genres that the peculiarity of the phenomenon itself has been too little noted.[2] (Wood, 1977, p. 47)

As Wood suggests, genre study has tended to disengage the genre from the conditions of its production and to treat it as an isolated, autonomous system of conventions. As a result, genre study tends to give only marginal attention to the role of the audience and the production system in formulating conventions and participating in their evolutionary development.

Genre study may be more "productive" if we complement the narrow critical focus of traditional genre analysis with a broader sociocultural perspective. Thus, we may consider a genre film not only as some filmmaker's artistic expression, but further as the cooperation between artists and audience in celebrating their collective values and ideals. In fact, many qualities traditionally viewed as artistic shortcomings—the psychologically static hero, for instance, or the predictability of the plot—assume a significantly different value when examined as components of a genre's ritualistic narrative system. If indeed we are to explain the *why* of Hollywood genres, we must look to their shared social function and to their formal conventions. Once we examine these shared features, we then can address a particular genre and its films.

Genre as system

Perhaps we should begin by noting a basic distinction between film genre study and its predecessor, literary genre study. In the study of literature, generic categories have been virtually imposed on works of fiction (or poetry or drama), representing the efforts of critics or historians to organize the subject matter according to their own subjective criteria. Literary analysts thus have tended to treat their subject in terms that may be irrelevant to those who produce and consume them. Not so with the commercial cinema, however. Because of the nature of film production and consumption, identifying film genres scarcely involves the subjective, interpretive effort that it does in literature. Film genres are not organized or discovered by analysts but are the result of the material conditions of commercial filmmaking itself, whereby popular stories are varied and repeated as long as they satisfy audience demand and turn a profit for the studios.

The significance of this distinction is twofold. First, it indicates that a film genre is a "privileged" cinematic story form—that is, only a limited number of film stories have been refined into formulas because of their unique social and/or aesthetic qualities. Second, as the product of audience and studio interaction, a film genre gradually impresses itself upon the culture until it becomes a familiar, meaningful system that can be *named* as such. Viewers, filmmakers, and critics know what it means to call this film a Western or that one a musical, and this knowledge is based on interaction with the medium itself—it is not the result of some arbitrary critical or historical organization.

To identify a popular cinematic story formula, then, is to recognize its status as a coherent, value-laden narrative system. Its significance is immediately evident to those who produce and consume it. Through repeated exposure to individual genre films we come to recognize certain *types* of characters, locales, and events. In effect, we come to understand the system and its significance. We steadily accumulate a kind of narrative-cinematic *gestalt* or "mind set" that is a structured mental image of the genre's typical activities and attitudes. Thus all of our experiences with Western films give us an immediate notion, a complete impression, of a certain type of behavioral and attitudinal system.

Because it is essentially a narrative system, a film genre can be examined in terms of its fundamental structural components: plot, character, setting, thematics, style, and so on. We should be careful, though, to maintain a distinction between the *film genre* and the *genre film*. Whereas the genre exists as a sort of tacit "contract" between filmmakers and audience, the genre film is an actual event that honors such a contract. To discuss the Western genre is to address neither a single Western film nor even all Westerns, but rather that system of conventions which identifies Western films as such.

There is a sense, then, in which a film genre is both a *static* and a *dynamic* system. On the one hand, it is a familiar formula of interrelated narrative and cinematic components that serves to continually reexamine some basic cultural conflict: one could argue, for example, that all Westerns confront the same fundamental issues (the taming of the frontier, the celebration of the hero's rugged individualism, the hero's conflicts with the frontier community, etc.) in elaborating America's foundation ritual and that slight formal variations do not alter those static thematic characteristics. On the other hand, changes in cultural attitudes, new influential genre films, the economics of the industry, and so forth, continually refine any film genre. As such, its nature is continually evolving. For example, the evolution of Western heroes from agents of law and order to renegade outlaws or professional killers reflects a genuine change in the genre. One could even argue that the term "Western" means something different today from what it did two or three decades ago.

We are most aware of a generic "contract" when it is violated. The violation may involve casting an established performer "against type," as when musical star Dick Powell portrayed private eye Philip Marlowe in Murder My Sweet (even the title was changed from Farewell My Lovely so that audiences wouldn't mistake the film for a musical). Or the violation may simply be a matter of a vehicle (as a car on a Western set) from one genre turning up on the set of another. (Wisconsin Center for Film and Theater Research); (Private Collection)

17

Thus genre experience, like all human experience, is organized according to certain fundamental perceptual processes. As we repeatedly undergo the same type of experience we develop expectations which, as they are continually reinforced, tend to harden into "rules." The clearest example of this process in any culture is in its games. A game is a system of immutable rules (three strikes in baseball) and components determining the nature of play. Yet no two games in a sport are alike, and a theoretically infinite number of variations can be played within the "arena" that the rules provide. Similarly, certain styles of traditional or popular music involve a variations-on-a-theme approach both within and among individual pieces. In folk and blues traditions, for example, most compositions are generated from a very few chord progressions.

The analogies between film genres and other cultural systems are virtually endless. What such examples seem to highlight is the dual nature of any "species" (or "genus," the root for the word *genre*), that is, it can be identified either by its rules, components, and function (by its static deep structure) or conversely by the individual members which comprise the species (by its dynamic surface structure).

Think of a Western movie, or a musical, or a gangster film. Probably you won't think of any individual Western or musical or gangster film, but rather of a vaguely defined amalgam of actions and attitudes, of characters and locales. For as one sees more genre films, one tends to negotiate the genre less by its individual films than by its deep structure, those rules and conventions which render this film a Western and that film a musical. This distinction between deep and surface structures—between a genre and its films—provides the conceptual basis for any genre study. Of all the analogies we might use to better understand this distinction, the most illuminating involves the "deepest" of human structures: language.

The language analogy

What is natural to mankind is not oral speech but the faculty of constructing a language, i.e. a system of distinct signs corresponding to distinct ideas.

—Ferdinand de Saussure[3]

Among other things, the commercial cinema is a communication system—it structures and delivers meaning. Throughout its history, evocative phrases like "the grammar of film" and "the cinematic language system" have suggested that filmic communication is comparable to verbal communication, although the extent and usefulness of that comparison are limited. Most recently, the film-language analogy has undergone renewed interest within the growing field of *semiology* (or *semiotics*), a science that proposes to study human interaction as a vast network of social and interpersonal communication systems. Semiology is itself the brain child of Swiss linguist Ferdinand de Saussure, who suggested that language provides the "master pattern" for the study of cultural signification. According to de Saussure, verbal language is the one sign system shared by all cultures; its basic structure informs every system of social communication.

That language study and its jargon are a metaphor for genre study should be obvious. Through the "circuit of exchange" involving box-office "feedback," the studios and the mass audience hold a virtual "conversation" whereby they gradually refine the "grammar" of cinematic "discourse." Thus a genre can be studied, like a language, as a formalized sign system whose rules have been assimilated, consciously or otherwise, through cultural consensus. Our shared knowledge of the rules of any film genre enables us to understand and evaluate individual genre films, just as our shared knowledge of English grammar enables me to write this sentence and you to interpret it. The distinction between *grammar* and *usage*, closely akin to that between deep structure and surface structure, originates in de Saussure's distinction between *langue* and *parole* in verbal language. For de Saussure, the speaker's and listener's shared knowledge of the grammatical rules that make up the language system (*la langue*) enables them to develop and understand a virtually unlimited range of individual utterances (*la parole*). American linguist Noam Chomsky has described this distinction in terms of *competency* and *performance*; he suggests that we should differentiate between our inherent capacity to speak and interpret on the one hand and our actually doing so on the other[4] (Chomsky, 1964).

If we extend these ideas into genre study, we might think of the *film genre* as a specific grammar or system of rules of expression and construction and the individual genre film as a manifestation of these rules. Of course, film differs from language in that our verbal competence is relatively consistent from speaker to speaker, whereas our generic competence varies widely. If each of us had the same exposure to Hollywood's thousands of genre films, a critical theory would probably be easier to construct. But obviously not everyone has a minimal understanding of even the most popular and widespread genres, let alone the obscure structural delights of such "subgenres" as the beach-blanket movies of the '60s or the car-chase movies of the '70s.

Moreover, although verbal language systems are essentially neutral and meaningless, film genres are not. As a system, English grammar is not meaningful either historically or in socially specific terms. It is manipulated by a speaker to *make* meaning. A film genre, conversely, has come into being precisely because of its cultural significance as a meaningful narrative system. Whereas a verbal statement represents a speaker's organization of neutral components into a meaningful pattern, a genre film represents an effort to *reorganize* a familiar, meaningful system in an original way.

Another interesting aspect of the language analogy concerns the tension between grammar and usage. Grammar in language is absolute and static, essentially unchanged by the range and abuses of everyday usage. In the cinema, however, individual genre films seem to have the capacity to affect the genre—an utterance has the potential to change the grammar that governs it. Even in film technology (the impact of widescreen on the Western, for example, or of technicolor on the musical), we can see that individual usage influences both viewers and other film-makers, and hence encourages them in effect to renegotiate the generic contract. Whether or not some static nuclear deep structure exists, which defines the genre and somehow eludes the effects of time and variation, we cannot overlook the gradual changes (as revealed in individual genre films) in form and substance on the genre's surface. Genres evolve, and they tend to evolve quite rapidly due to the demands of the commercial popular media. But whether this evolution represents mere cosmetic changes in the surface structure (equivalent to fashionable clichés or idioms in verbal language) or whether it reflects substantial changes in the deep structure (the generic system itself) will remain, at least for now, an open question.

Perhaps the ultimate value of the film-language analogy is as a sort of method or methodological model. That is, the similarities between a language and a genre as communication systems should encourage the analyst to approach individual genre films in much the same way that the linguist approaches individual utterances. Like all signifying systems, languages and genres exist essentially within the minds of their users: No single study of English grammar or of a film genre could possibly describe the system completely. In this sense, studying film genre is not unlike going to school as competent six-year-old speakers of English and then being taught English grammar. In each case, we study the system that is the basis for our existing competence.

In all of this, we should not lose sight of the critical, evaluative factor that motivates the genre critic, while it is virtually irrelevant to the linguist. The linguist's concern is the process whereby we verbally communicate meaning; any concern for the *quality* of that communication falls under the domain of rhetoric. As such, the film genre critic must be both linguist and "rhetor"—that is, he or she is concerned with both the process and the quality of any generic communication. The critic develops competence, a familiarity with the system, by watching and interpreting movies and noting similarities. Ultimately, he or she is concerned with recognizing, appreciating, and articulating *differences* among these movies. As critics, we understand genre films because of their similarity with other films, but we appreciate them because of their difference. Therefore an outline of a basic grammar of genre filmmaking should precede any critical analysis of individual films within a genre.

Toward a grammar of film genre

At this stage, we are somewhere "between" the point of departure (watching movies) and the point of arrival (appreciating and articulating difference—i.e., being critical). We can appreciate difference only when we begin to examine films systematically, when we consider the systems whereby an individual film "makes meaning." Thus far, we have considered the commercial and formal systems involved in Hollywood filmmaking from a rather superficial perspective. In narrowing our focus to examine the workings of Hollywood genres, we will begin to understand how commercial and formal systems are realized in actual production. Genre production itself should be addressed on three distinct levels of inquiry: those characteristics shared by virtually all genre films (and thus by all genres), those characteristics shared by all the films within any individual genre, and those characteristics that set one genre film off from all other films.

Our ultimate goal is to discern a genre film's quality, its social and aesthetic value. To do this, we will attempt to see its relation to the various systems that inform it. For example, in examining a film like *The Searchers*, it is not enough simply to isolate the formal characteristics that identify it as belonging to a particular genre. Nor is it enough to isolate the elements that make it superior. Initially we have to discern those traits that make the film—and indeed the Western form itself—generic. To repeat Wood's observation: we are so accustomed to dealing with genres, with familiar filmic narrative types, that we tend to isolate these types from one another, thus overlooking many of their shared social and aesthetic features. Before considering the Western, gangster, musical, and other Hollywood genres as individual narrative systems, then, we will discuss the qualities that identify these forms as genres.

A genre film, like virtually any story, can be examined in terms of its fundamental narrative components: plot, setting, and character. These components have a privileged status for the popular audience, due to their existence within a familiar formula that addresses and reaffirms the audience's values and attitudes. Thus the genre film's narrative components assume a preordained thematic significance that is quite different from non-generic narratives. Each genre film incorporates a specific cultural context—what Warshow termed its "field of reference"—in the guise of a familiar *social community*. This generic context is more than the physical setting, which some genre critics have argued defines the genre as such. The American frontier or the urban underworld is more than a physical locale which identifies the Western or the gangster film; it is a cultural milieu where inherent thematic conflicts are animated, intensified, and resolved by familiar characters and patterns of action. Although all drama establishes a community that is disturbed by conflict, in the genre film both the community and the conflict have been conventionalized. Ultimately, our familiarity with any genre seems to depend less on recognizing a specific setting than on recognizing certain dramatic conflicts that we associate with specific patterns of action and character relationships. There are some genres, in fact, like the musical and the screwball comedy, that we identify primarily through conventions of action and attitude, and whose settings vary widely from one film to the next.

From this observation emerges a preliminary working hypothesis: the determining, identifying feature of a film genre is its cultural context, its community of interrelated character types whose attitudes, values, and actions flesh out dramatic conflicts inherent within that community. The generic community is less a specific place (although it may be, as with the Western and gangster genres) than a network of characters, actions, values, and attitudes. Each genre's status as a distinct cultural community is enhanced by Hollywood's studio production system, in that each generic context is orchestrated by specialized groups of directors, writers, producers, performers, sets, studio lots, and even studios themselves. (Consider Warner Brothers' heavy production of gangster films in the early '30s and MGM's musicals in the late '40s.)

A genre, then, represents a *range of expression* for filmmakers and a *range of experience* for viewers. Both filmmakers and viewers are sensitive to a genre's range of expression because of previous experiences with the genre that have coalesced into a system of value-laden narrative conventions. It is this system of conventions— familiar characters performing familiar actions which celebrate familiar values— that represents the genre's narrative context, its meaningful cultural community.

Iconography: Imagery and meaning

The various generic communities—from the Old West to the urban underworld to outer space—provide both a visual arena in which the drama unfolds and also an intrinsically significant realm in which specific actions and values are celebrated. In addressing the inherent meaning or intrinsic significance of objects and characters within any generic community, we are considering that genre's *iconography*. Iconography involves the process of *narrative and visual coding* that results from the repetition of a popular film story. A white hat in a Western or a top hat in a musical, for instance, is significant because it has come to serve a specific symbolic function within the narrative system.

This coding process occurs in all movies, since the nature of filmic storytelling is to assign meaning to "bare images" as the story develops. In the final sequence of *Citizen Kane*, for example, the symbolic reverberations of the burning sled and the "No Trespassing" sign result from the cumulative effects of the film's narrative process. These effects in *Kane* accumulate within that single film, though, and had no significance prior to our viewing of that film.

A *generic icon*, in contrast, assumes significance not only through its usage within individual genre films but also as that usage relates to the generic system itself. The Westerner's white horse and hat identify a character before he speaks or acts because of our previous experiences with men who wear white hats and ride white horses. The more interesting and engaging genre films, of course, do more than merely deliver the codes intact—as did many of those "B" Westerns of the '30s that almost literally "all look alike"—but instead manipulate the codes to enhance their thematic effect.

Consider the dress code of the principal characters in *The Man Who Shot Liberty Valance* (John Ford, 1962). In this film, Jimmy Stewart portrays Ransom Stoddard,

an Eastern-bred lawyer bent upon civilizing the Western community of Shinbone. Early in the film, Stoddard takes work as a dishwasher (Shinbone then had little need for lawyers) and continually wears a white apron—even during his climactic gunfight with Liberty Valance. Lee Marvin, portraying the archetypal Western antagonist, Liberty Valance, hired by local cattlemen to prevent statehood and the fencing in of their rangeland, wears black leather and carries a black, silver-knobbed whip. Mediating these two opposing figures is Tom Doniphon (John Wayne), a charismatic local rancher who sympathizes with the cause of statehood. Doniphon eventually murders Valance to save Stoddard, thus enabling Stoddard to gain political prominence and to assume the role of community leader. Throughout the film, Doniphon is dressed in various combinations of black and white. His clothing reflects his ambiguous role as murderous purveyor of eventual social order. Of course, director Ford develops Doniphon's tragic role by manipulating a good deal more than the iconography of Western dress, but this example suggests how filmmakers use a genre's established visual codes to create complex narrative and thematic situations.

A genre's iconography involves not only the visual coding of the narrative, but indicates *thematic value* as well (white civilization good versus black anarchy evil, with black-and-white as thematically ambiguous). We distinguish between characters who wear white and characters who wear black in Westerns, or those who sing and dance and those who do not in musicals, and these distinctions reflect the thematic conflicts inherent within these communities. Because visual coding involves narrative and social values, it also extends to certain nonvisual aspects of genre filmmaking. Such elements as dialogue, music, and even casting may become key components of a genre's iconography.

Think, for example, of the appropriateness of the casting in the film just described (Stewart as naive idealist, Marvin as maniacal anarchist, Wayne as stoic middleman), or think of the way certain movie stars are generally associated with specific genres. Katharine Hepburn, Fred Astaire, Joan Crawford, and Humphrey Bogart have become significant components of a genre's meaning-making system. When we think of Bogart as the typical hardboiled detective or of Astaire as the ultimate, spontaneous, self-assured music man, we are thinking not of the particular human being or of any single screen role but rather of a screen *persona*—i.e., an attitudinal posture that effectively transcends its role in any individual film.

A genre's iconography reflects the value system that defines its particular cultural community and informs the objects, events, and character types composing it. Each genre's implicit system of values and beliefs—its *ideology* or world view—determines its cast of characters, its problems (dramatic conflicts), and the solutions to those problems. In fact, we might define film genres, particularly at the earlier stages of their development, as social problem-solving operations: They repeatedly confront the ideological conflicts (opposing value systems) within a certain cultural community, suggesting various solutions through the actions of the main characters. Thus, each genre's problem-solving function affects its distinct formal and conceptual identity.

Character and setting: Communities in conflict

In discussing the grammar (or system of conventions) of any Hollywood film genre, it is important to note that the *material economy*, which motivated the studios to refine story formulas, translates into *narrative economy* for filmmakers and viewers. Each genre incorporates a sort of narrative shorthand whereby significant dramatic conflicts can intensify and then be resolved through established patterns of action and by familiar character types. These dramatic conflicts are themselves the identifying feature of any genre; they represent the transformation of some social, historical, or even geographical (as in the Western) aspect of American culture into one locus of events and characters.

Although the dramatic conflicts are basic to the generic "community," we cannot identify that community solely by its physical setting. If film genres were identified by setting alone, then we would have to deal with an "urban" genre that includes such disparate forms as gangster films, backstage musicals, and detective films. Because the setting provides an *arena* for conflicts, which are themselves de-

termined by the actions and attitudes of the *participants*, we must look to the generic character types and the conflicts they generate in identifying any genre. And
we might consider a generic community and its characters in relation to the system
of values which both define the problem and eventually are appealed to in solving it.

What emerges as a social problem (or dramatic conflict) in one genre is not necessarily a problem in another. Law and order is a problem in the gangster and detective genres, but not in the musical. Conversely, courtship and marriage are
problems in the musical but not in the gangster and detective genres. Individualism is celebrated in the detective genre (through the hero's occupation and world
view) and in the gangster film (through the hero's career and eventual death),
while the principal characters in the musical compromise their individuality in
their eventual romantic embrace and thus demonstrate their willingness to be integrated into the social community. In each of these genres, the characters' identities and narrative roles (or "functions") are determined by their relationship with
the community and its value structure. As such, the generic character is psycholog-

*Consider the complex of imagery at work in each of these stills. The dress, demeanor,
tools, setting, and of course the performers themselves all provide specific generic
information to the viewer.* (Private Collection); (Wisconsin Center for Film and Theater Research)

ically static—he or she is the physical embodiment of an attitude, a style, a world view, of a predetermined and essentially unchanging cultural posture. Cowboy or Indian, gangster or cop, guy or doll, the generic character is identified by his or her function and status within the community.

The static vision of the generic hero—indeed of the entire constellation of familiar character types—helps to define the community and to animate its cultural conflicts. For example, the Western hero, regardless of his social or legal standing, is necessarily an agent of civilization in the savage frontier. He represents both the social order and the threatening savagery that typify the Western milieu. Thus he animates the inherent dynamic qualities of the community, providing a dramatic vehicle through which the audience can confront generic conflicts.

This approach also enables us to distinguish between such seemingly similar "urban crime" formulas as the gangster and detective genres. Usually, both genres are set in a contemporary urban milieu and address conflicts principally between social order and anarchy and between individual morality and the common good. But because of the characteristic attitudes and values of the genre's principal characters, these conflicts assume a different status in each genre and are resolved accordingly. The detective, like the Westerner, represents the man-in-the-middle, mediating the forces of order and anarchy, yet somehow remaining separate from each. He has opted to construct his own value system and behavioral code, which happens (often, almost accidentally) to coincide with the forces of social order. But the detective's predictable return to his office retreat at film's end and his refusal to assimilate the values and lifestyle of the very society he serves ultimately reaffirm his—and the genre's—ambiguous social stance. The gangster film, conversely, displays little thematic ambiguity. The gangster has aligned himself with the forces of crime and social disorder, so both his societal role and his conflict with the community welfare demand his eventual destruction.

All film genres treat some form of threat—violent or otherwise—to the social order. However, it is the attitudes of the principal characters and the resolutions precipitated by their actions which finally distinguish the various genres from one another. Nevertheless, there is a vital distinction between kinds of generic settings and conflicts. Certain genres (Western, detective, gangster, war, et al.) have conflicts that, indigenous to the environment, reflect the physical and ideological struggle for its control. These conflicts are animated and resolved either by an individual male hero or by a collective (war, science fiction, cavalry, certain recent Westerns). Other genres have conflicts that are not indigenous to the locale but are the result of the conflict between the values, attitudes, and actions of its principal characters and the "civilized" setting they inhabit. Conflicts in these genres (musical, screwball comedy, family melodrama) generally are animated by a "doubled" hero—usually a romantic couple whose courtship is complicated and eventually ideologically resolved. A musical's setting may be a South Pacific island or the backstage of a Broadway theater, but we relate to the film immediately by its treatment of certain sexual and occupational conflicts and also by our familiarity with the type of characters played by its "stars."

Thus, it is *not* the musical numbers themselves which identify these films as musicals. Many Westerns and gangster films, for example, contain musical numbers and still aren't confused with musicals (Westerns like *Dodge City* and *Rio Bravo*, for instance, or gangster films like *The Roaring Twenties* and *The Rise and Fall of Legs Diamond*). The frontier saloon and the gangster's speakeasy may be conventional locales within their respective communities, but their entertainment function clearly is peripheral to the central issue. However, in "musical Westerns" like *Annie Get Your Gun*, *The Harvey Girls*, and *Oklahoma!*, the nature and resolution of the dramatic conflicts as well as the characterization clearly are expressed via the musical formula. In *The Harvey Girls*, for instance, the narrative centers around the exploits of several dozen women—including Judy Garland and Cyd Charisse, which should provide us with a generic cue—who migrate West to work in a restaurant. Certain Western conventions are nodded to initially: the girls are told aboard the train headed West that "You're bringing civilization. . . . You girls are bringing order to the West"; later, there is a comic brawl between these "Harvey Girls" and the local saloon girls. But the Western genre's fundamental traits (the individual male hero responding to the threat of savagery and physical violence within an ideologically unstable milieu) are not basic to the film. Once the characters and conflicts are established, the setting might as well be Paris or New York City or even Oz.

As I hope these examples indicate, the various Hollywood genres manipulate character and social setting quite differently in developing dramatic conflicts. We might consider a broad distinction between genres of *determinate space* and those of *indeterminate space,* between genres of an ideologically contested setting and an ideologically stable setting. In a genre of determinate space (Western, gangster, detective, et al.), we have a symbolic arena of action. It represents a cultural realm in which fundamental values are in a state of sustained conflict. In these genres, then, the contest itself and its necessary arena are "determinate"—a specific social conflict is violently enacted within a familiar locale according to a prescribed system of rules and behavioral codes.

The iconographic arena in determinate genres is entered by an individual or collective hero, at the outset, who acts upon it, and finally leaves. This entrance-exit motif recurs most in genres characterized by an individual hero: for example, the Westerner enters a frontier community, eliminates (or perhaps causes) a threat to its survival, and eventually rides "into the sunset"; the detective takes the case, investigates it, and returns to his office; the gangster, introduced to urban crime, rises to power, and finally is killed or jailed. In these genres, the individual hero incorporates a rigid, essentially static attitude in dealing with his very dynamic, contested world.

In contrast, genres of indeterminate space generally involve a doubled (and thus dynamic) hero in the guise of a romantic couple who inhabit a "civilized" setting, as in the musical, screwball comedy, and social melodrama. The physical and ideological "contest" which determines the arena of action in the Western, gangster, and detective genres is not an issue here. Instead, genres of indeterminate

Similarity and difference: the distinctive narrative contexts of the screwball comedy (It Happened One Night, above) and the gangster film (The Public Enemy, below) clearly overwhelm the apparent similarities between these two scenes. (Culver Pictures); (Culver Pictures)

space incorporate a civilized, ideologically stable milieu, which depends less upon a heavily coded place than on a highly conventionalized value system. Here conflicts derive not from a struggle over control of the environment, but rather from the struggle of the principal characters to bring their own views in line either with one another's or, more often, in line with that of the larger community.

Unlike genres of determinate space, these genres rely upon a progression from romantic antagonism to eventual embrace. The kiss or embrace signals the integration of the couple into the larger cultural community. In addition, these genres use iconographic conventions to establish a social setting—the proscenium or theater stage with its familiar performers in some musicals, for example, or the repressive small-town community and the family home in the melodrama. But because the generic conflicts arise from attitudinal (generally male-female) oppositions rather than from a physical conflict, the coding in these films tends to be less visual and more ideological and abstract. This may account for the sparse attention they have received from genre analysts, despite their widespread popularity.

Ultimately, genres of indeterminate, civilized space (musical, screwball comedy, social melodrama) and genres of determinate, contested space (Western, gangster, detective) might be distinguished according to their differing ritual functions. The former tend to celebrate the values of *social integration,* whereas the latter uphold the values of *social order.* The former tend to cast an attitudinally unstable couple or family unit into some representative microcosm of American society, so that their emotional and/or romantic "coupling" reflects their integration into a stable environment. The latter tend to cast an individual, violent, attitudinally static male into a familiar, predetermined milieu to examine the opposing forces vying for control. In making this distinction, though, we should not lose sight of these genres' shared social function. In addressing basic cultural conflicts and celebrating the values and attitudes whereby these conflicts might be resolved, all film genres represent the filmmakers' and audience's cooperative efforts to "tame" those beasts, both actual and imaginary, which threaten the stability of our everyday lives.

Plot structure: From conflict to resolution

As a popular film audience, our shared needs and expectations draw us into the movie theater. If we are drawn there by a genre film, we are familiar with the ritual. In its animation and resolution of basic cultural conflicts, the genre film celebrates our collective sensibilities, providing an array of ideological strategies for negotiating social conflicts. The conflicts themselves are significant (and dramatic) enough to ensure our repeated attendance. The films within a genre, representing variations on a cultural theme, will employ different means of reaching narrative resolution, but that closure is generally as familiar as the community and its characters. (Think of the general discomfort felt upon realizing, even quite early in seeing a genre film, that Cagney's heroic gangster would "get his" or that Tracy and Hepburn would cease their delightful hostilities and embrace in time for the closing credits.)

Actually, the most significant feature of any generic narrative may be its resolution—that is, its efforts to solve, even if only temporarily, the conflicts that have disturbed the community welfare. The Western, for example, despite its historical and geographical distance from most viewers, confronts real and immediate social conflicts: individual versus community, town versus wilderness, order versus anarchy, and so on. If there is anything escapist about these narratives, it is their repeated assertion that these conflicts can be solved, that seemingly timeless cultural oppositions can be resolved favorably for the larger community.

In a Hollywood Western, as in virtually any Hollywood genre film, plot development is effectively displaced by setting and character: once we recognize the familiar cultural arena and the players, we can be fairly certain how the game will be played and how it will end. Because the characters, conflicts, and resolution of the non-generic narrative are unfamiliar and unpredictable, we negotiate them less by previous filmic experiences than by previous "real-world" (personal and social) experiences. Clearly, both generic and non-generic narratives must rely to some degree upon real-world and also upon previous narrative-filmic experiences in order to make sense. In the genre film, however, the predictability of conflict and resolution tends to turn our attention away from the linear, cause-and-effect plot, redirecting it to the conflict itself and the opposed value systems it represents. Instead of a linear chain of events, which are organized by the changing perceptions of an individual protagonist, the genre film's plot traces the intensification of some cultural opposition which is eventually resolved in a predictable fashion.

Thus, we might describe the plot structure of a genre film in the following way:

establishment (via various narrative and iconographic cues) of the generic community with its inherent dramatic conflicts;

animation of those conflicts through the actions and attitudes of the genre's constellation of characters;

intensification of the conflict by means of conventional situations and dramatic confrontations until the conflict reaches crisis proportions;

resolution of the crisis in a fashion which eliminates the physical and/or ideological threat and thereby celebrates the (temporarily) well-ordered community.

In this plot structure, linear development is subordinate to and qualified by the *oppositional* narrative strategy. Opposing value systems are either mediated by an individual or a collective, which eliminates one of the opposing systems. Or else these oppositions are actually embodied by a doubled hero whose (usually romantic) coupling signals their synthesis. In either instance, resolution occurs, even if only temporarily, in a way that strokes the collective sensibilities of the mass audience. It is in this context that the genre film's function as cultural ritual is most evident.

In their formulaic narrative process, genre films celebrate the most fundamental ideological precepts—they examine and affirm "Americanism" with all its rampant conflicts, contradictions, and ambiguities. Not only do genre films establish a sense of continuity between our cultural past and present (or between present and future, as with science fiction), but they also attempt to eliminate the distinctions between them. As social ritual, genre films function to stop time, to portray our culture in a stable and invariable ideological position. This attitude is embodied in the generic hero—and in the Hollywood star system itself—and is ritualized in the resolution precipitated by the hero's actions. Whether it is a historical Western or a futuristic fantasy, the genre film celebrates certain inviolate cultural attributes.

Ultimately, the sustained success of any genre depends upon at least two factors: the thematic appeal and significance of the conflicts it repeatedly addresses and its flexibility in adjusting to the audience's and filmmakers' changing attitudes toward those conflicts. These can be seen, for example, in the Western hero's status as both rugged individualist and also as agent of a civilization that continually resists his individualism. The degree to which that opposition has evolved over the past seventy-five years has accommodated changes in our cultural sensibilities. Or consider science fiction, a literary and cinematic genre that realized widespread popularity in the late '40s and early '50s. This genre articulated the conflicts and anxieties that accompanied the development of atomic power and the prospect of interplanetary travel. Because science fiction deals with so specialized a cultural conflict—essentially with the limits and value of human knowledge and scientific experimentation—it is considerably less flexible, but no less topical, than the Western. Nevertheless, each genre has a static nucleus that manifests its thematic oppositions or recurring cultural conflicts. And each genre has, through the years, dynamically evolved as shown by the ways its individual films manipulate those oppositions. If we see genre as a problem-solving strategy, then, the static nucleus could be conceived as the problem and the variety of solutions (narrative resolutions) as its dynamic surface structure.

In this sense, a genre's basic cultural oppositions or inherent dramatic conflicts represent its most basic determining feature. Also the sustained popularity of any genre indicates the essentially unresolvable, irreconcilable nature of those oppositions. Resolution involves a point of dramatic closure in which a compromise or temporary solution to the conflict is projected into a sort of cultural and historical timelessness. The threatening external force in contested space is violently destroyed and eliminated as an ideological threat; in uncontested space the vital lover's spontaneity and lack of social inhibition are bridled by a domesticating counterpart in the name of romantic love. In each, philosophical or ideological conflicts are "translated" into emotional terms—either violent or sexual, or both—and are resolved accordingly. In the former, the emotive resolution is externalized, in the latter it is internalized. Still, the resolution does not function to *solve* the basic cultural conflict. The conflict is simply recast into an emotional context where it can be expeditiously, if not always logically, resolved.

As a rule, generic resolution operates by a process of *reduction:* the polar opposition is reduced, either through the elimination of one of the forces (in genres of determinate, contested space) or through the integration of the forces into a single unit (in genres of indeterminate, civilized space). The contest in determinate space generally is physically violent. Frequently, up until the resolution, there is more tension than action. The violent resolution usually helps the community, but only rarely does the hero assimilate its value system. In fact, his insistence that he maintain his individuality emerges as a significant thematic statement. As such, these films often involve a dual celebration: the hero's industrious isolationism offsets the genre's celebration of the ideal social order.

There is a certain logic and symmetry in the gangster's death, the Westerner's fading into the sunset, the detective's return to his office to await another case. Each of these standard epilogues implicitly accepts the contradictory values of its genre, all of which seem to center around the conflict between individualism and the common good. The built-in ambiguity of this dual celebration serves, at least partially, to minimize the *narrative rupture* resulting from the effort to resolve an unresolvable cultural conflict. This violation of narrative logic is itself fundamental to all of Hollywood's story formulas, in that the demand for a "happy ending" resists the complexity and deep-seated nature of the conflict.

Because genres of social order invariably allow the individual hero his formalized flight from social integration and from the compromising of his individuality, the narrative rupture is usually less pronounced than in genres of social integration. The cultural conflicts in genres of integration are revealed through the doubling of the principal characters—that is, through their opposed relationship, usually expressed as romantic antagonism. With the integration of their opposing attitudes into a cohesive unit (the married couple, the family), the conflicts are resolved and basic communal ideals are ritualized. But the cultural contradictions that inhibit integration throughout these films—between spontaneous individual expression and social propriety, for example—cannot be resolved without severely subverting the characters' credibility and motivation.

Are we to assume that the screwball couple's madcap social behavior and mutual antagonism will magically dissolve once they are wed? Or that the conflicts, which have separated the song-and-dance team throughout rehearsals, will somehow vanish after the climactic show? To avoid these questions and to minimize the sense of rupture, these genre films synthesize their oppositions through some formal celebration or social ritual: a Broadway show, a betrothal, a wedding, and so on. In this way, they don't actually resolve their conflicts; they reconstitute them by concluding the narrative at an emotive climax, at precisely the moment when the doubled principals acquiesce to each other's demands. The suggestion of living "happily ever after" tends to mask or gloss over the inevitable loss associated with each character's compromise. What is celebrated is the collective value of their integration into an idealized social unit.

In all genre films, there is a sense of loss. At the end of Shane, *the initiate-hero (Brandon De Wilde) must part with the hero (Alan Ladd).* (Wisconsin Center for Film and Theater Research)

This sense of loss accompanies the resolution of all genre films because of the contradictory, irreconcilable nature of their conflicts. Through violent reduction or romantic coupling, however, the loss is masked. It is, in effect, effectively redressed in the emotional climax. What is to become, we might very well ask ourselves, once the film ends, of the uninhibited music man after he weds the gold-hearted domesticator—and what's to become of her as well? What's to become of the savage frontier lawman once the social order he instills finally arrives? These are questions which, unless initiated by the films themselves, we know better than to ask. Genre films not only project an idealized cultural self-image, but they project it into a realm of historical timelessness. Typically, films produced later in a genre's development tend to challenge the tidy and seemingly naive resolutions of earlier genre films, and we will discuss this tendency in some detail when we examine generic evolution. What we should note here, though, and what is being masked by such a resolution is the fundamental appeal of both sides in a dramatic conflict. Whatever oppositions we examine in genre films—individual versus community, man versus woman, work versus play, order versus anarchy—these do not represent "positive" and "negative" cultural values. For one of the reasons for a genre's popularity is the sustained significance of the "problem" that it repeatedly addresses. Thus, generic conflict and resolution involve opposing systems of values and attitudes, *both of which* are deemed significant by contemporary American culture.

Narrative strategy and social function: Contradictions, happy endings, and the status quo

In surveying the setting, characterization, and plot structure of Hollywood film genres, we have made several general distinctions between genres of order and genres of integration. I have suggested that these two types of genres represent two dominant narrative strategies of genre filmmaking. Perhaps it would be useful to summarize these strategies.

Certain genres (Western, gangster, detective, et al.) center on an individual male protagonist, generally a redeemer figure, who is the focus of dramatic conflicts within a setting of contested space. As such, the hero mediates the cultural contradictions inherent within his milieu. Conflicts within these genres are externalized, translated into violence, and usually resolved through the elimination of some threat to the social order. The resolution in these films often is somewhat ambiguous. The hero, either through his departure or death at film's end, does not assimilate the values and lifestyle of the community but instead maintains his individuality. Genres that incorporate this narrative strategy I have termed *rites of order*.

Other genres (musical, screwball comedy, family melodrama, et al.) are set in "civilized" space and trace the integration of the central characters into the community. There is generally a doubled (romantic couple) or collective (usually a family) hero in these genres. Their personal and social conflicts are internalized, translated into emotional terms, with their interpersonal antagonism eventually yielding to the need for a well-ordered community. Integration invariably occurs through romantic love. After a period of initial hostility, the couple find themselves in a final embrace. The genres which incorporate this narrative strategy I have termed *rites of integration*.

There is considerable overlap between the rites, of course, in that all order genres address the prospect of social integration, and all integration genres are concerned with maintaining the existing social order. But this general distinction does provide a starting point for analysis. We have a set of assumptions to develop and refine while examining individual genres and their films. For the purposes of clarity and simplicity, the following chart may be useful.

CHARACTERISTICS OF GENRES OF ORDER AND GENRES OF INTEGRATION

	ORDER (Western, gangster, detective)	INTEGRATION (musical, screwball comedy, family melodrama)
hero	individual (male dominant)	couple/collective (female dominant)
setting	contested space (ideologically unstable)	civilized space (ideologically stable)
conflict	externalized—violent	internalized—emotional
resolution	elimination (death)	embrace (love)
thematics	mediation—redemption	integration—domestication
	macho code	maternal-familial code
	isolated self-reliance	community cooperation
	utopia-as-promise	utopia-as-reality

In examining both types of genres, one of our concerns must be the relationship between narrative strategy and social function. Although I have suggested that each genre represents a distinct problem-solving strategy that repeatedly addresses basic cultural contradictions, genres are not blindly supportive of the cultural status quo. The genre film's resolution may reinforce the ideology of the larger society, but the nature and articulation of the dramatic conflicts leading to that climax cannot be ignored. If genres develop and survive because they repeatedly flesh out and reexamine cultural conflicts, then we must consider the possibility that genres function as much to challenge and criticize as to reinforce the values that inform them.

As has often been said, Hollywood movies are considerably more effective in their capacity to raise questions than to answer them. This characteristic seems particularly true of genre films. And as such, the genre's fundamental impulse is to continually *renegotiate* the tenets of American ideology. And what is so fascinating and confounding about Hollywood genre films is their capacity to "play it both ways," to both criticize and reinforce the values, beliefs, and ideals of our culture within the same narrative context.

Consider Molly Haskell's description of the narrative resolution in certain melodramas of the 1930s and '40s: "The forced enthusiasm and neat evasions of so many happy endings have only increased the suspicion that darkness and despair follow marriage, a suspicion the 'woman's film' confirmed by carefully pretending otherwise"[5] (Haskell, 1974, p. 124). Implicit in Haskell's statement is the assumption that the audience knew better than to believe the pat "happy end." She assumes that the audience was sensitive, consciously or otherwise, to the narrative rupture involved in a melodrama's progression from conflict to resolution. One could just as easily argue the opposite, of course, that audiences actually believed and bought wholesale, consciously or otherwise, the "neat evasions of so many happy endings."

The fact is, however, that as genres develop their conflicts are stated ever more effectively, while their resolutions become ever more ambiguous and ironic. This would seem to support Haskell's position, and further to undercut the simplistic conception of the audience as utterly naive and of the Hollywood genre film as mere escapist entertainment. Let us consider, even if only briefly, the issue of a genre's increasingly sophisticated capacity for presenting its conflicts, a capacity which seems closely related to the process of generic evolution.

Generic evolution: Patterns of increasing self-consciousness

We have already noted that genre filmmakers are in a rather curious bind: they must continually vary and reinvent the generic formula. At the same time they must exploit those qualities that made the genre popular in the first place. As Robert Warshow puts it: "Variation is absolutely necessary to keep the type from becoming sterile; we do not want to see the same movie over and over again, only the same form"[6] (Warshow, 1962, p. 147). His point is well taken: the genre's "deeper" concern for certain basic cultural issues may remain intact, but to remain vital its films must keep up with the audience's changing conception of these issues and with its growing familiarity with the genre. But how does a genre evolve, and does its evolution follow any consistent or predictable pattern? If certain formal and thematic traits distinguish a genre throughout its development, what changes as the form evolves?

First, a genre's evolution involves both internal (formal) and external (cultural, thematic) factors. The subject matter of any film story is derived from certain "real-world" characters, conflicts, settings, and so on. But once the story is repeated and refined into a formula, its basis in experience gradually gives way to its own internal narrative logic. Thus, the earliest Westerns (many of which actually depicted then-current events) obviously were based on social and historical reality. But as the genre developed, it gradually took on its own reality. Even the most naive viewer seems to understand this. It comes as no surprise to learn that Western heroes didn't wear white hats and fringed buckskin, that gunfights on Main Street were an exceedingly rare occurrence, or that the towns and dress codes and other trappings of movie Westerns were far different from those of the authentic American West. In this sense, we recognize and accept the distinctive grammar—the system of storytelling conventions—that has evolved through the repeated telling of Western tales.

Simultaneously, however, we also realize that these real-world factors, basic to the genre's dramatic conflicts, are themselves changing. Consider how the changing image of Native Americans ("Injuns") has been influenced by our culture's changing view of Manifest Destiny, the settling of the West, and the treatment of peoples whose cultures were overwhelmed by the encroachment of civilization. Or consider how the atom bomb and space travel affected the development of the science fiction genre after World War II; consider the impact of organized crime on the gangster and detective genres in the 1950s. Perhaps the effects of these external social factors are best seen case by case. A genre's formal internal evolution, however, especially when considered in terms of our growing familiarity with it over time, does seem to follow a rather consistent pattern of schematic development.

In his chapter "Textuality and Generality" (*Language and Cinema*), Christian Metz considers the internal evolution of the Western. Metz suggests that, as early as 1946 with John Ford's *My Darling Clementine*, the "classic" Western had assumed "an accent of parody which was an integral part of the genre, and yet it remained a Western." He goes on to assert that the "superwesterns" of the 1950s "passed from parody to contestation," but that they "remained fully Westerns." He then observes that in many recent Westerns, "contestation gives way to 'deconstruction': the entire film is an explication of the [Western] code and its relation to history. One has passed from parody to critique, but the work is still a Western." Metz contends that with every "stage" of its evolutionary process, the Western sustains its essence, its generic identity. He concludes his discussion with a rather suggestive observation: "Such is the infinite text one calls a genre"[7] (Metz, 1974, pp. 148–161).

Metz views the Western genre not only as a system of individual films, but further as a composite text in itself. His point is that the Western represents a basic story, which is never completely "told," but is reexamined and reworked in a variety of ways. Within these variations, Metz discovers a pattern of historical development. His classic-parody-contestation-critique progression suggests that both filmmakers and audience grow increasingly self-conscious regarding the genre's formal qualities and its initial social function. Actually, Metz's view of the Western's formal evolution is quite similar to the views of various historians who have studied the historical development of styles and genres in other arts. Perhaps the most concise and influential study of this kind is Henri Focillon's *The Life of Forms in Art*, in which he develops a schema for the "life span" of cultural forms:

> Forms obey their own rules—rules that are inherent in the forms themselves, or better, in the regions of the mind where they are located and centered—and there is no reason why we should not undertake an investigation of how these great ensembles . . . behave throughout the phases which we call their life. The successive states through which they pass are more or less lengthy, more or less intense, according to the style itself: the experimental age, the classic age, the age of refinement, the baroque age.[8] (Focillon, 1942, p. 10)

Focillon's view is somewhat broader than Metz's. But he also observes that the continual reworking of a conventionalized form—whether it is an architectural style or a genre of painting—generates a growing awareness of the conventions themselves. Thus a form passes through an *experimental* stage, during which its conventions are isolated and established, a *classic* stage, in which the conventions reach their "equilibrium" and are mutually understood by artist and audience, an age of *refinement*, during which certain formal and stylistic details embellish the form, and finally a *baroque* (or "mannerist" or "self-reflexive") stage, when the form and its embellishments are accented to the point where they themselves become the "substance" or "content" of the work.

Using this strategy with film genres, we might begin with this observation: at the earliest stages of its life span, a genre tends to exploit the cinematic medium *as a medium*. If a genre is a society collectively speaking to itself, then any stylistic flourishes or formal self-consciousness will only impede the transmission of the message. At this stage, genre films transmit a certain idealized cultural self-image with as little "formal interference" as possible. Once a genre has passed through its experimental stage where its conventions have been established, it enters into its classical stage. We might consider this stage as one of *formal transparency*. Both the narrative formula and the film medium work together to transmit and reinforce that genre's social message—its ideology or problem-solving strategy—as directly as possible to the audience.

Leo Braudy describes the process of generic evolution: "Genre films essentially ask the audience, 'Do you still want to believe this?' Popularity is the audience answering, 'Yes.' Change in genre occurs when the audience says, 'That's too infantile a form of what we believe. Show us something more complicated' "[9] (Braudy, 1976, p. 179). This rather casual observation involves a number of insights, especially in its allusion to the "conversation" between filmmakers and audience and in its reference to audience "belief." The genre film reaffirms what the audience believes both on individual and on communal levels. Audience demand for variation does not indicate a change in belief, but rather that the belief should be reexamined, grow more complicated formally and thematically, and display, moreover, stylistic embellishment.

Thus, the end of a genre's classic stage can be viewed as that point at which the genre's straightforward message has "saturated" the audience. With its growing awareness of the formal and thematic structures, the genre evolves into what Focillon termed the age of refinement. As a genre's classic conventions are refined and eventually parodied and subverted, its transparency gradually gives way to *opacity*: we no longer look *through* the form (or perhaps "into the mirror") to glimpse an idealized self-image, rather we look *at* the *form itself* to examine and appreciate its structure and its cultural appeal.

A genre's progression from transparency to opacity—from straightforward storytelling to self-conscious formalism—involves its concerted effort to explain itself, to address and evaluate its very status as a popular form. A brief consideration of any Hollywood genre would support this view, particularly those with extended life spans like the musical or the Western. By the early 1950s, for example, both of these genres had begun to exhibit clear signs of formal self-consciousness. In such self-reflexive musicals as *The Barkleys of Broadway* (1949), *An American in Paris* (1951), *Singin' in the Rain* (1952), *The Band Wagon* (1953), and *It's Always Fair Weather* (1955), the narrative conflict confronts the nature and value of musical comedy as a form of popular entertainment. In accord with the genre's conventions, these conflicts are couched in a male-female opposition, but the boy-gets-

Parodies of established genres are a good indication of how we become familiar with a genre's conventions and appreciate seeing these conventions subverted. In a modern dance sequence from The Band Wagon, *Cyd Charisse and Fred Astaire parody the hardboiled detective genre.* (Hoblitzelle Theater Arts Collection)

girl resolution is now complicated by a tension between serious art and mere entertainment. These movies interweave motifs involving successful courtship and the success of The Show, and that success is threatened and resolved in a fashion which provides an "apology" for the musical as popular art.

In *The Barkleys of Broadway,* for instance, Ginger Rogers abandons musical comedy for "legitimate theater" but eventually returns both to the stage musical and to her former partner-spouse (Fred Astaire). Gene Kelly in *An American in Paris* must decide between a career as a painter, supported by spinster-dowager Nina Foch, and a "natural" life of dance and music with young Leslie Caron. In these and the other films, the generic conventions, which earlier were components of the genre's unspoken ideology, have now become the central thematic elements of the narrative. No longer does the genre simply celebrate the values of music, dance, and popular entertainment, it actually "critiques" and "deconstructs" them in the process[10] (Feuer, 1978).

The Western genre, which was entering its classic age in the late 1930s (*Stagecoach, Union Pacific, Dodge City, Destry Rides Again, Frontier Marshal,* all 1939), exhibits by the 1950s a similar formal and thematic self-scrutiny. Such films as *Red River* (1948), *I Shot Jesse James* (1949), *The Gunfighter* (1950), *Winchester 73* (1950), *High Noon* (1952), and *The Naked Spur* (1953) indicate that the genre had begun to question its own conventions, especially regarding the social role and psychological make-up of the hero. Consider, for example, the substantial changes in the screen persona of John Wayne or of Jimmy Stewart during this period. In such baroque Westerns as *Red River* and *The Searchers* (starring Wayne) and *Winchester 73, The Naked Spur, The Man from Laramie,* and *Two Rode Together* (Stewart), Wayne's stoic machismo and Stewart's "aw-shucks" naiveté are effectively inverted to reveal genuinely psychotic, antisocial figures.

Naturally, we do not expect a classic Westerner like Wayne's Ringo Kid in *Stagecoach* to exhibit the psychological complexity or the "antiheroic" traits of later Western figures. Our regard for a film like *Stagecoach* has to do with its clear, straightforward articulation of the Western myth. A later film like *Red River,* which incorporates a younger figure (Montgomery Clift) to offset and qualify the classic Westerner's heroic posture, serves to refine and to call into question the genre's basic values. These values are subverted, or perhaps even rejected altogether, in later films like *The Searchers, The Wild Bunch,* and even in a comic parody like *Butch Cassidy and the Sundance Kid.* In these films, the "code of the West" with its implicit conflicts and ideology provides the dramatic focus, but our regard for that code changes as do the actions and attitudes of the principal characters.

The Western and the musical seem to represent genres in which the evolutionary "cycle" seems more or less complete. However, not all genres complete that cycle or necessarily follow such a progression. For example, in the gangster genre, various external pressures (primarily the threat of government censorship and religious boycott) disrupted the genre's internal evolution. And in the war genre, the prosocial aspects of supporting a war effort directly ruled out any subversion or even the serious questioning of the hero's attitudes. War films that did question values were made after the war and generally are considered as a subgenre. There are also genres currently in midcycle, like the "disaster" or the "occult" genres popularized during the 1970s. The disaster genre, whose classic stage was launched with *The Poseidon Adventure* and *Airport,* has evolved so rapidly that a parody of the genre, *The Big Bus* (1976), appeared within only a few years of the form's standardization. Interestingly, the audience didn't seem to know what to make of *The Big Bus,* and the film died at the box office. Apparently the genre hadn't sufficiently saturated the audience to the point where a parody could be appreciated.

Thus, it would seem that, throughout a genre's evolution from transparent social reaffirmation to opaque self-reflexivity, there is a gradual shift in narrative emphasis from social value to formal aesthetic value. Because continued variation tends to sensitize us to a genre's social message, our interests, and those of the filmmakers, gradually expand from the message itself to its articulation, from the tale to the visual and narrative artistry of its telling. It is no coincidence, then, that so many directors, who worked with a genre later in its development, are considered *auteurs*. We tend to regard early genre filmmakers as storytellers or craftsmen and later ones as artists. Naturally there are exceptions—Ford's early Westerns, Busby Berkeley's '30s musicals, all of Hitchcock's thrillers—but these involve directors whose narrative artistry and understanding of the genre's thematic complexity were apparent throughout their careers.

Generally speaking, it seems that those features most often associated with narrative artistry—ambiguity, thematic complexity, irony, formal self-consciousness—rarely are evident in films produced earlier in a genre's development. They tend to work themselves into the formula itself as it evolves. We are dealing here with the inherent artistry of the formula itself as it grows and develops. A newborn genre's status as social ritual generally resists any ironic, ambiguous, or overly complex treatment of its narrative message. But as filmmakers and audiences grow more familiar with the message as it is varied and refined, the variations themselves begin to exhibit qualities associated with narrative art.

This does not mean that early genre films have no aesthetic value or later ones no social value. There is, rather, a shift in emphasis from one cultural function (social, ritualistic) to another (formal, aesthetic). And both are evident in all genre films. A genre's initial and sustained popularity may be due primarily to its social function, but a degree of aesthetic appeal is also apparent in even the earliest, or the most transparently, prosocial genre films. Each genre seems to manifest a distinct visual and compositional identity: the prospect of infinite space and limitless horizons in the Western, documentary urban realism in the gangster film, the "American Expressionism" of *film noir* and the hardboiled detective film, the musical's celebration of life through motion and song, and so on.

This aesthetic potential may have been tapped by filmmakers—writers, producers, performers, cameramen, editors, as well as directors—who quite simply made good movies. They manipulated any number of narrative and cinematic qualities that imbued their films with an artistry that may or may not have been common for the genre at that stage of its development. Whether considering artistically exceptional films early in a genre's evolution or the more self-reflexive films produced during its later stages, it is difficult not to appreciate the formal and ideological flexibility of Hollywood's genres. These story formulas have articulated and continually reexamined basic social issues, weaving a cultural tapestry whose initial design became ever more detailed and ornate, ever more beautiful.

Hollywood Film Genres

PART TWO

The Western   3

"This is the West, sir. When the legend becomes fact, print the legend."
—Newspaper editor in The Man Who Shot Liberty Valance

Western as genre

The Western is without question the richest and most enduring genre of Hollywood's repertoire. Its concise heroic story and elemental visual appeal render it the most flexible of narrative formulas, and its life span has been as long and varied as Hollywood's own. In fact, the Western genre and the American cinema evolved concurrently, generating the basic framework for Hollywood's studio production system. We might look to Edwin S. Porter's *The Great Train Robbery* in 1903 as the birth not only of the movie Western but of the commercial narrative film in America; and to Thomas Ince's mass production of William S. Hart horse operas during the teens as the prototype for the studio system.

The origins of the Western formula predated the cinema, of course. Its genealogy encompassed colonial folk music, Indian captivity tales, James Fenimore Cooper's *Leather-Stocking Tales,* nineteenth-century pulp romances, and a variety of other cultural forms. These earlier forms began to develop the story of the American West as popular mythology, sacrificing historical accu-

45

racy for the opportunity to examine the values, attitudes, and ideals associated with westward expansion and the taming and civilizing of the West. Not until its immortalization on film, however, did the Western genre certify its mythic credentials. The significance and impact of the Western as America's foundation ritual have been articulated most clearly and effectively in the cinema—the medium of twentieth-century technology and urbanization. And it was also in the cinema that the Western could reach a mass audience which actively participated in the gradual refinement and evolution of its narrative formula.

The early films

As America's first popular and industrial mass art form, the commercial cinema assumed a privileged but paradoxical function in its development of the Western myth. As a narrative mass medium, the cinema provided an ideal vehicle for disseminating the Western formula to the culture at large; as a commercial industry, it embodied those very socioeconomic and technological values which the Western anticipated in tracing the steady progression of American civilization. The height of the Western's popularity—from the late 1930s through the '50s—spanned an era when the American West and its traditional values were being threatened and displaced by the Modern Age. Twentieth-century technology and industry, the Depression with its Dust Bowl and flight to the cities, the ensuing World War and the birth of atomic power, the Cold War and the Korean conflict—these and other historical factors overwhelmed America's "Old West" and at the same time enhanced its mythic status. In constructing and gradually formalizing the actions and attitudes from the past on a wide screen, the Western genre created a mythical reality more significant and pervasive—and perhaps in some ways more "real"—than the historical West itself.

As cultural and historical documents, the earlier silent Westerns differ from the later Westerns. In fact, these earlier films have a unique and somewhat paradoxical position: Although they were made on the virtual threshold of the Modern Age, they also came at a time when westward expansion was winding down. Certain early cowboy heroes like "Bronco Billy" Anderson and William S. Hart did lay the groundwork for the heroic and stylized mythology of movie Westerns. But many other films, like *The Covered Wagon* (1923) and *The Iron Horse* (1924), were really historical dramas, depicting as accurately as possible the actuality of westward expansion. (In fact, *The Great Train Robbery* related events that had occurred only a few years previously and as such was something of a turn-of-the-century gangster film.) But eventually, the cumulative effects of Western storytelling in the face of contemporary civilization's steady encroachment served to subordinate the genre's historical function to its mythical one. In other words, efforts to document the historical West on film steadily gave way to the impulse to exploit the past as a means of examining the values and attitudes of contemporary America.

It's important to note in this context that during the Depression, as Hollywood moved into the sound era, the historical epics, which had dominated mainstream Western film production in the teens and '20s, faded from the screen, and the genre survived primarily in the form of low-budget "B" productions. These films rounded out the newly introduced double features—and also served to provide John Wayne, who made dozens of these "B" Westerns, with considerable acting experience. Occasional Westerns like *The Virginian* (1929), *Cimarron* (1930), and *The Plainsman* (1936) attracted the attention of mass audiences, but both the technical restrictions of early "talkies" and Hollywood's preoccupation during the '30s with contemporary urban themes effectively pushed the Western out of mainstream production.

The Western returned to widespread popularity in the late 1930s. The growing historical distance from the actual West along with developments in film technology—especially a quieter, more mobile camera and more sophisticated sound recording techniques—gave the genre new life. The tendency today is to laud John Ford's *Stagecoach* in 1939 for regenerating the Western movie formula, although Ford's film was only one of several popular mainstream Westerns produced in 1939 and 1940, among them *Jesse James, Dodge City, Destry Rides Again, Union Pacific, Frontier Marshal* (all 1939), *Sante Fe Trail, Virginia City, The Westerner, The Return of Frank James, Arizona,* and *When the Daltons Rode* (1940). The following war years proved to be a watershed period for the genre—and for Hollywood filmmaking in general—but by then the Western's basic structural design was well established and its gradual refinement already begun.

The landscape of the West

When we step back to get a broader picture, we notice that the Western depicts a world of precarious balance in which the forces of civilization and savagery are locked in a struggle for supremacy. As America's foundation ritual, the Western projects a formalized vision of the nation's infinite possibilities and limitless vistas, thus serving to "naturalize" the policies of westward expansion and Manifest Destiny.[1] It is interesting in this regard that we as a culture have found the story of the settlement of the "New World" beyond the Alleghenies and the Mississippi even more compelling than the development of the colonies or the Revolutionary War itself. Ironically, the single most evocative location for Western filmmaking and perhaps the genre's most familiar icon (after the image of John Wayne) is Arizona's Monument Valley, where awesome stone formations reach up to the gods but the desolate soil around them is scarcely suitable for the rural-agricultural bounty which provided America's socioeconomic foundation. The fact is, of course, that Hollywood's version of the Old West has as little to do with agriculture—although it has much to do with rural values—as it does with history. The landscape with its broad expanses and isolated communities was transformed on

The landscape of the West: a frame enlargement from the opening shot of **The Searchers,** *which not only frames Monument Valley but reinforces the audience's viewpoint from "inside" civilization, i.e., looking with the Woman out across the endless expanse of the American West.* (Private Collection)

celluloid into a familiar iconographic arena where civilized met savage in an interminable mythic contest.

The Western's essential conflict between civilization and savagery is expressed in a variety of oppositions: East versus West, garden versus desert, America versus Europe, social order versus anarchy, individual versus community, town versus wilderness, cowboy versus Indian, schoolmarm versus dancehall girl, and so on. Its historical period of reference is the years following the Civil War and reaching into the early twentieth century, when the western United States, that precivilized locale, was establishing codes of law and order as a basis for contemporary social conditions. The opening of virtually any Western "cues" us in to these oppositions: cowboys pausing on a hillside during a cattle drive to gaze at the isolated community in the distance (*My Darling Clementine*, 1946); a lone cowboy, who after riding into a pastoral valley, is accused by an anxious homesteader of gunslinging for land-hungry local ranchers (*Shane*, 1953); a rider on a mountainside watching railroad workers blast a tunnel above him and outlaws rob a stagecoach below (*Johnny Guitar*, 1954); the distant cry of a locomotive whistle and a shot of a black, serpentine machine winding toward us through the open plains as the steam from its engine fills the screen (*The Man Who Shot Liberty Valance*, 1962).

John Ford's *Stagecoach*

Even as early as Ford's 1939 film, *Stagecoach*, these oppositions are presented concisely and effectively. Ford's film marks the debut of Monument Valley in the Western genre, a fitting arena for the most engaging and thematically complex of all prewar Westerns.

The film opens with a shot of Monument Valley, framed typically beneath a sky which takes up most of the screen. Eventually we hear two riders approaching from across the desert and then see them coming toward us. As the riders near the camera, Ford cuts from this vast, panoramic scene to the exterior of a cavalry camp, and the horizon is suddenly cluttered with tents, flagstaffs, and soldiers. The riders gallop into the camp, dismount, and rush into the post. In the next shot, a group of uniformed men huddle around a telegraph machine. Just before the lines go dead, the telegraph emits a single coded word: "Geronimo."

This sequence not only sets the thematic and visual tone for Ford's film with economy of action and in striking visual terms, but also reflects the basic cultural and physical conflicts which traditionally have characterized the Western form. In Hollywood's version the West is a vast wilderness dotted with occasional oases— frontier towns, cavalry posts, isolated campsites, and so forth—which are linked with one another and with the civilized East by the railroad, the stagecoach, the telegraph: society's tentacles of progress. Each oasis is a virtual society in microcosm, plagued by conflicts both with the external, threatening wilderness and also with the anarchic or socially corrupt members of its own community. Ford's stagecoach, for example, is journeying to Lordsburg (what better name for an oasis of order in a vast wasteland?) through hostile Indian country. Its passengers must contend not only with Indian attacks but also with the conflicts which divide the group itself. The stagecoach carries a righteous sheriff, a cowardly driver, an alcoholic doctor, an embezzling bank executive, a whiskey drummer, a gold-hearted prostitute, a genteel gambler, an Eastern-bred lady, and the hero, an escaped convict bent upon avenging his brother's murder and, simultaneously, his own wrongful imprisonment.

In this film, as in the Western generally, the conflicts within the community reflect and intensify those between the community and its savage surroundings. The dramatic intensity in *Stagecoach* only marginally relates to the disposition of the hero, whose antisocial status (as a convict) is not basic to his character but results from society's lack of effective order and justice. Wayne portrays the Ringo Kid as a naive, moral man of the earth who takes upon himself the task of righting that social and moral imbalance. He is also a living manifestation of the Western's basic conflicts. Like the sheriff who bends the law to suit the situation, the banker who steals from his own bank, the kindly whore, or the timid moralizer who sells whiskey, Ringo must find his own way through an environment of contrary and ambiguous demands.

Ford's orchestration of the community's complex, contradictory values renders *Stagecoach* a truly distinctive film, setting it apart both dramatically and thematically from earlier Westerns. Within a simplistic cavalry-to-the-rescue and shoot-out-on-Main-Street formula, Ford's constellation of social outcasts represents a range of social issues from alcoholism to white-collar crime to individual self-reliance. Through these characters Ford fleshes out values and contradictions basic to contemporary human existence.

The appeal of the stagecoach's passengers derives from their ambiguous social status. Often they are on the periphery of the community and somehow at odds with its value system. Perhaps the most significant conflict in the Western is the community's demand for order through cooperation and compromise versus the physical environment's demand for rugged individualism coupled with a survival-of-the-fittest mentality. In *Stagecoach,* each of the three central figures—Ringo, Doc Boone (Thomas Mitchell), and Dallas (Claire Trevor)—is an outcast who has violated society's precepts in order to survive: Ringo is an accused murderer and escaped convict sworn to take the law into his own hands, while Doc Boone has turned to alcohol and Dallas to prostitution to survive on the frontier.

We are introduced to Dallas and Doc Boone as they are being driven out of town by the Ladies' Law and Order League, a group of puritanical, civic-minded women dedicated to upholding community standards. This scene is played for both comic and dramatic effect, but it does establish conformity and Victorian moralizing as elements of a well-ordered society. This initial view of the community's repressive and depersonalizing demands eventually is qualified by the film's resolution, however. Ringo and Dallas finally are allowed by the sheriff to flee to Ringo's ranch across the border. As the two ride away to begin a new life together, the camera lingers on Doc Boone, ever the philosopher, who muses, "Well, they're saved from the blessings of civilization." Beneath his veneer of cynicism, however, is an optimistic vision: the uncivilized outlaw-hero and a woman practicing society's oldest profession have been united and go off to seek the promise of the American West's new world.

The changing vision of the West

The gradual fading of this optimistic vision, more than anything else, characterizes the evolution of the Western genre. As the formula was refined through repetition, both the frontier community and its moralistic standard-bearers are depicted in increasingly complex, ambiguous, and unflattering terms. The Western hero, in his physical allegiance to the environment and his moral commitment to civilization, embodies this ambiguity. As such he tends to generate conflict through his very existence. He is a man of action and of few words, with an unspoken code of honor that commits him to the vulnerable Western community and at the same time motivates him to remain distinctly apart from it. As the genre develops, the Westerner's role as promoter of civilization seems to become almost coincidental. Eventually, his moral code emerges as an end in itself.

The stability of the Westerner's character—his "style," as it were—doesn't really evolve with the genre. Instead, it is gradually redefined by the community he protects. Both the hero and the community establish their values and world view through their relationship with the savage milieu, but as the community becomes more civilized and thus more institutionalized, capitalistic, and corrupt, it gradually loses touch with the natural world from which it sprang. Because the Westerner exists on the periphery of both the community and the wilderness, he never loses touch with either world. His mediating function between them becomes increasingly complex and demanding as the society becomes more insulated and self-serving.

Actually, the image of the classic Westerner who mediates the natural and cultural environments while remaining distinct from each does not emerge as a mainstream convention until the mid-'40s. In earlier films, the narrative conflicts were usually resolved with the suggestion that the Westerner might settle down within the community which his inclination toward violence and gunplay has enabled him to protect. The promise of marriage between Ringo and Dallas is indicative of this tendency, although their shared outlaw status and their eventual flight to Mexico undercut any simplistic reading of the film's prosocial resolution. A typical example of this tendency is William Wyler's 1940 film, *The Westerner*. In this film, the hero, Cole Hardin (Gary Cooper), mediates a violent confrontation between anarchic cattlemen and defenseless, idealistic homesteaders. These distinct communities are depicted in two narrative movements. The first shows Hardin's arrival and near lynching in a lawless cattle town run by the outrageous Judge Roy Bean (Walter Brennan), the self-appointed "law west of the Pecos." The second follows the hero's gradual assimilation into the community of homesteaders and his courtship of the farmer's daughter, Jane Ellen (Doris Davenport).

Bean's and Jane Ellen's worlds are locked in the familiar cattleman-homesteader struggle for control of the land, and Hardin is the only character who can function effectively in both worlds. Thus Wyler's film (from Jo Swerling's script) develops the classic configuration of the anarchic world of Male Savagery pitted against the civilized world of Woman and Home. The heroic Westerner, again, is poised between the two. Throughout the first half of the film, in which the competing ideologies are established, this configuration remains in perfect balance. Eventually, however, Hardin is won over by the woman-domesticator and turns against Bean, throwing off the film's narrative equilibrium. After Hardin prevails against Bean in a climactic gunfight, the Westerner is able to settle down with Jane Ellen in "the promised land."

The Westerner: *Gary Cooper portrays Cole Hardin, the classic mediator-hero whose rugged individualism allies him with Judge Roy Bean(Walter Brennan,behind Cooper), the self-styled "law west of the Pecos," but who eventually settles down with the farmer's daughter in "the promised land."* (Wisconsin Center for Film and Theater Research)

Nothing could be more damaging to the hero's image, of course. He has compromised his self-styled, renegade world view by acquiescing to civilization's emasculating and depersonalizing demands. The earlier silent Westerns and their later low-budget counterparts had understood the logic of sending the Westerner "into the sunset" after the requisite showdown, thereby sustaining the genre's prosocial function while reaffirming the hero's essential individuality. Perhaps it was John Ford's experience with silent Westerns that motivated him to temper the marital and communal values of *Stagecoach*'s resolution, or perhaps it was his intuitive understanding of what made the Western genre work. But certainly the ambiguous ending of Ford's film renders it decidedly more effective than most of the Westerns of its day. It was not actually until World War II and the ensuing postwar productions, though, that the Western hero and his particular role within the Western milieu would be radically reconsidered along the lines previously established in *Stagecoach*.

Stagecoach and *The Shootist*

By way of example, *Stagecoach* can be compared to a similar Western story told nearly forty years later: Don Siegel's *The Shootist* (1976). In both films, John Wayne portrays roughly the same sort of hero (Ringo Kid in the former and J. B. Books in the latter). Also, in both films, he is a legend in his own lifetime who enters a community, seeks out three of its most corrupt citizens, and eliminates them with characteristic dispatch. Beyond the superficial connections of character and plot, however, the two films are radically different. *Stagecoach* projects a generally positive view of the West's potential synthesis of nature and culture. This optimism is qualified somewhat by Ford's and screenwriter Dudley Nichols' sensitivity to the hero's ambivalent social commitment and to society's less civilized tendencies, but these reservations seem minimal when we examine *The Shootist*'s depiction of the hero and his milieu.

Siegel's film introduces its hero in one of the most self-reflexive sequences of any Hollywood movie. Under the voice-over description provided by the story's young narrator (Ron Howard), Books' violent "career" as a shootist is traced through flashbacks of the hero's gunfights, all of which are lifted from earlier John Wayne Westerns. This narrative device establishes Wayne/Books not as a historical entity, but rather as an amalgam of previous performances in Western movies:

The Shootist: *Don Siegel's 1976 Western cast John Wayne as J. B. Books, a mythic hero out of his element in turn-of-the-century Carson City, Nevada. Here, Books counsels young initiate-hero Gillum (Ron Howard) in the use of a handgun.* (Wisconsin Center for Film and Theater Research)

the genre has created its own field of reference. This introduction of the mythic hero is undercut by the film's setting, however. Carson City in 1901 is depicted in such realistic detail that Wayne's larger-than-life Westerner seems misplaced there. The community's paved streets, automobiles, telephone wires, and daily newspapers have more in common with our own environment than with a traditional community like Lordsburg with its dirt streets and rowdy saloons.

Wayne's portrayal of a mythic figure caught in real time—a familiar motif in many later Westerns—is intensified by the fact that he is dying of cancer; the very core of his physical and metaphorical being is rotting away. The community, now at an advanced stage of social development, has little need for his services, and he is allowed to remain in Carson City only after he assures the aging and ineffectual sheriff (Harry Morgan) that he does not have long to live.

Rather than die in bed with a dose of laudanum, Books arranges to shoot it out with the three local citizens who threaten community order (two of whom are portrayed, in another self-reflexive touch, by former TV Westerners Richard "Paladin" Boone and Hugh "Wyatt Earp" O'Brian). There is no sunset or Mexican ranch for our hero at the conclusion of this Western. Instead, Books is shot in the back by a bartender after killing the three villains, thus fulfilling his desire to die as violently (and functionally) as he has lived. The bartender in turn is killed by the narrator and surrogate hero, Gillum. And when Gillum throws aside his weapon and turns his back on Books, the hero who had outlived his time and place, he reaffirms the Westerner's demise.

French filmmaker Jean Renoir once suggested that "the marvelous thing about Westerns is that they're all the same movie. This gives a director unlimited freedom." The apparent contradiction in Renoir's statement is reflected in the contradictory relationship between *Stagecoach* and *The Shootist.* Siegel has taken essentially the same story of a heroic redeemer who enters a community and through his unique powers eliminates a threat to that community. However, his Western reexamines and undercuts Ford's earlier, essentially positive depiction of both the community and its redeemer. The subversive effect of *The Shootist* is heightened through the use of the narrator, an initiate-hero whose allegiance is torn between his community and the hero he has learned to worship.

Gillum is caught between the influence of his mother (Lauren Bacall) and the mythic redeemer-hero, who together represent the Western's basic contradictions and conflicts. As woman, mother, and domesticator, Bacall is both attracted and repulsed by hero Wayne/Books' violent, nomadic lifestyle. She and her son embody the promise of social order and the American Dream, and there is no place in their world for a dying gunfighter. The promise of marriage in *Stagecoach* is more the exception than the rule in its suggestion that the Westerner and the domesticator can be compatible. But it is Dallas' status as renegade outcast, not Ringo's potential for domestication, which renders their eventual union believable, and this is underscored by the film ending with the pair fleeing rather than embracing.

This narrative device of filtering the genre's conflicts through the perceptions of a young initiate-hero appears in many postwar Westerns. *Red River* (1948), *Shane* (1952), *The Searchers* (1956), *The Tin Star* (1957), *Rio Bravo* (1958), *The Magnificent*

Seven (1960), *Ride the High Country* (1962), *El Dorado* (1967), *Little Big Man* (1970), *The Cowboys* (1972), and various other Westerns employ this education-of-a-young-man motif, self-consciously reflecting upon the contradictory lifestyles of those inside and outside the community. The initiate-hero's choice of alternatives becomes progressively more difficult as the genre evolves and the community and the Westerner are shown in less romanticized terms.

Shane: The initiate-hero and the integration of opposites

This motif is used most effectively, perhaps, in *Shane*. The story is filtered through the consciousness of a young boy (Brandon De Wilde as Joey Starrett), and much of the film's clarity of vision and idealized simplicity derives from his naive perspective. The actions of the principal characters, the setting of a lush green valley, even the distant Rocky Mountains, attain a dreamlike quality under George Stevens' direction and Loyal Grigg's cinematography.

The film opens with Shane (Alan Ladd) riding into the pastoral valley where ranchers and homesteaders are feuding. (As in *The Westerner*, "open range" and fenced-in farmland manifest the genre's nature/culture opposition.) Shane is a man with a mysterious past who hangs up his guns to become a farm laborer for Joe Starrett (Van Heflin), the spokesman for the homesteaders in their conflict with the villanous Ryker brothers.

The film is a virtual ballet of oppositions, all perceived from Joey's viewpoint. These oppositions become a series of options for him—and us—that he must negotiate in order to attain social maturity. The following diagram summarizes these oppositions.

```
                            Marion
                              |
        Joe Starrett ---------+--------------- Shane
                              |
                              |
                                              familial conflicts
-------------------------------- JOEY -----------------------------------
                              ---               community conflicts

                            SHANE
     Joe Starrett --------------------- ------Wilson
     family ---------------------------|------Ryker brothers
     homesteaders---------------------|------ranchers
     domestication  -----------------|------male isolation
     (woman's world) ----------------|------(man's world)
     fences --------------------------|------open range
     crops, sheep---------------------|------cattle
     farm tools-----------------------|------guns
     social law ----------------------|------primitive law
     equality  ----------------------|------survival of the fittest
     future --------------------------|------past
```

Not only does this diagram indicate the elaborate *doubling* in the narrative, but it also points up the hero's mediation of both the rancher-homesteader conflict and the boy's confused notions of his ideal father figure. Although Starrett is the bravest and most capable of the homesteaders—and the only one respected and feared by the ranchers—he is basically a farmer of rural sensibilities and simple values. Starrett is clearly no match for Shane in either Joey's or his wife's (Jean Arthur) eyes, although the family proves strong enough to withstand the interloper's influence. By the end of the film, Marion's attraction to Shane complements her son's, although her family and her role as mother-domesticator remain her first concerns. In accord with her son's (and the genre's) sexual naiveté, the thought of Shane's and Marion's romantic entanglement is only a frustrating impossibility. Among Joey's parting cries to Shane as he rides away at the film's end is, "Mother wants you."

This sexual-familial conflict is, however, tangential to the film's central opposition between fenced land and open range. Nevertheless, it does reaffirm Shane's commitment to the values of home and family rather than those of power and cap-

The living legend and the initiate-hero: Raymond Chandler once wrote that Alan Ladd "is hard, bitter and occasionally charming, but he is after all a small boy's idea of a tough guy." George Stevens' Shane, seen primarily from initiate-hero Joey Starrett's (Brandon De Wilde) viewpoint, effectively reinforces Chandler's comment. (Penguin Photo)

ital. During the course of the film, Shane offers his services to the other farmers, but he is never really accepted because of his past and his stoic, detached manner. The cattlemen, who are generally seen drinking in the local saloon or else out harassing "sodbusters," show more respect for Shane than do the farmers, and attempt to recruit him at higher pay. Shane refuses, so the Rykers bring in Wilson (Jack Palance), a *doppelganger* from Shane's gunfighting past. Here, as in many genre films involving a violent, nomadic hero, the only real difference between the protagonist (Shane) and his antagonistic double (Wilson) has to do with their respective attitudes about social order and the value of human life.

The film ends with Shane knocking Starrett out with his pistol after a fierce fistfight. He knows he must face Wilson and the Rykers alone. Joey follows Shane to town to watch the confrontation in the deserted saloon. Shane prevails against the men but is wounded, and he rides off into the mountains as Joey's calls echo after him. Those mountains, which like Shane's mysterious, violent past had remained in the background throughout the film, emerge now as his Olympus, as the Westerner's mythic realm beyond the reality of dirt farms and ramshackle towns.

But while Shane's heroic stature is affirmed, there is still a shade of ambiguity which tempers that stature. Just before the gunfight in the darkened saloon, Shane suggests to Ryker that "his days are numbered." "What about you, gunfighter?" asks Ryker. "The difference is, I know it," replies Shane, who then turns to the black-clad Wilson. The two simply stare at one another before the exchange of ritual dialogue that will initiate the gunfight. As in an earlier scene when the two had met and silently circled each other, a mutual understanding and respect is implicit in the look they exchange in addition to the promise of a violent, uncompromising confrontation. After the gunfight Shane tells Joey that "There's no living with the killing," but it's clear enough from the relationship established between Shane and Wilson that there's no living without it either. Like J. B. Books and his victims in that Carson City saloon decades later, these men know their fate all too well. They purposefully end their days in a fashion that they could control and that we in the audience come to expect.

As these various examples indicate, the Westerner is motivated to further the cause of civilization by his own personal code of honor, which seems to be existentially derived. Often this code leads him to an act of vengeance. The vengeful hero is different from the classic Westerner in that his past—either his entire past or an isolated incident—is of immediate concern and provides him with a clear sense of mission. But he does share with the classic hero his characteristic function: he is an isolated, psychologically static man of personal integrity who acts because society is too weak to do so. And it is these actions that finally enforce social order but necessitate his departure from the community he has saved. In *Stagecoach, Winchester 73* (1950), *The Searchers* (1956), *One-Eyed Jacks* (1961), *Nevada Smith* (1966), and countless other revenge Westerns, the hero rids society of a menace, but in so doing, he reaffirms his own basic incompatibility with the community's values.

Occasionally the hero will accept a job as lawman to carry out his vengeance, as in *Dodge City* and *My Darling Clementine*, but once he has satisfied his personal drives, he leaves the community to fend for itself. In those films, it is assumed that the hero's elimination of the power-hungry town boss and his henchmen has purified the community and given it lasting social order. The destruction of the Clantons at the O.K. Corral by the Earp brothers and Doc Holliday in *My Darling Clementine* serves both to avenge the murder of James Earp and also to project an image of an orderly Tombstone into the indefinite future. As Wyatt Earp and his brother (Henry Fonda and Ward Bond) ride off across Monument Valley after their gunfight, the new schoolmarm from the East waves to them, framed in long-shot against the infinite expanse of desert and sky. With this image Ford captures and freezes forever—like the English poet John Keats' ageless figures on a Grecian urn—the Western's principal characters and their contradictory yet complementary ideals.

The changing hero: The "psychological" and "professional" Westerns

As an element of our national mythology, the Western represents American culture, explaining its present in terms of its past and virtually redefining the past to accommodate the present. The image of the Western community in Hollywood movies tends to reflect our own beliefs and preoccupations, and the Western's evolution as a genre results both from the continual reworking of its own rules of construction and expression and also from the changing beliefs and attitudes of contemporary American society.

As American audiences after World War II became saturated with the classic Western formula and also more hardbitten about sociopolitical realities, the image of the Western community changed accordingly, redefining the hero's motivation and his sense of mission. Hence the "psychological" Westerns of the late 1940s and the 1950s that traced the Westerner's neuroses (and eventual psychoses) stemming from his growing incompatibility with civilization as well as the cumulative weight of society's unreasonable expectations.

One of the more notable examples of this development is Fred Zinneman's *High Noon*, in which a local lawman (Gary Cooper) awaits the arrival of outlaws bent on avenging his having sent their leader to prison. The wait for the arrival of the outlaws provides the dramatic tension in the film, which is heightened by the fact that the townspeople ignore or evade Cooper's appeals for assistance. After he and his Quaker wife (Grace Kelly), a woman committed to nonviolence for religious reasons, finally confront and dispose of the outlaws, Cooper throws his badge into the dirt and leaves the community to fend for itself.

Howard Hawks' *Rio Bravo* (1958), supposedly a belated answer to Zinneman's "knee-jerk liberalism," describes a similar situation in an even more claustrophobic and helpless community. From Hawks' typically machismo perspective, however, the local lawman (John Wayne, with deputies Dean Martin, Walter Brennan, and Ricky Nelson) continually rejects offers of aid from the frightened citizenry, insisting, "This is no job for amateurs." Wayne and his cohorts prevail, and thus both the heroes and the community emerge with integrity intact. While *High Noon* and *Rio Bravo* each project substantially different views of the community and its redeemer-hero, both underscore the hero's incompatibility with that community. Ultimately, it is the hero's professional integrity and sense of responsibility to his job as lawman which induce him to act as an agent of social order.

The "professional" Western was, in fact, Hollywood's own answer to the psychological Western, much as Hawks' film had answered Zinneman's. In general, the psychological Western poses the question: how can the morally upright, socially autonomous Westerner continue to defend a repressive, institutionalized, cowardly, and thankless community without going crazy? The professional Western answers this question in one of two ways. The Westerner either works for pay and sells his special talents to the community that must evaluate his work on its own terms or else he becomes an outlaw.

The prospect of the classic, morally upright Westerner turning from his self-styled code of honor is closely related to the changing view of society in the Western. As the community's notion of law and order progressively squeezes out those rugged individualists who made such order possible, the Westerners turn to each other and to the outlaws they had previously opposed. At this point, the "honor among thieves" that the Westerner can find with other lawless types is preferable to buckling under to the community's emasculating demands.

Consequently, many recent Westerns incorporate a group that is led by an aging but still charismatic hero figure and whose demand of payment, either as professional killers or as outlaws, undercuts the classic Westerner's moral code. Thus the professional Westerns of the past two decades, most notably *Rio Bravo*, *The Magnificent Seven*, *The Professionals*, *El Dorado*, *The Wild Bunch*, *True Grit*, *Butch Cassidy and the Sundance Kid*, *The Cowboys*, *The Great Northfield Minnesota Raid*, *The Culpepper Cattle Company*, and *The Missouri Breaks*.

Gone in these films is the isolated, heroic cowboy with no visible means of support whose moral vision and spiritual values set him apart from—and essentially above—the community he defends. Now he is cynical, self-conscious, and even "incorporated"; these traits render him increasingly unheroic, more like one of us. Still, despite his gradual descent from heroic demigod (superior in many ways to nature as well as to other men) in early Westerns to a psychologically more complex and generally more sympathetic character, the Westerner does maintain distinct traces of his isolated sense of honor. He strikes a romantic pose even in the face of extinction.

Sam Peckinpah's *The Wild Bunch* (1969), for example, describes the exploits of an outlaw collective (William Holden, Ernest Borgnine, Warren Oates, Edmund O'Brien, Ben Johnson, et al.) in their sustained rampage through the American Southwest and in Mexico just before the outbreak of World War I. Whereas the outlaw collective violates with equal disregard the laws of God, man, and nature,

Perhaps the ultimate professional Western: Sam Peckinpah's The Wild Bunch (1968), a World War I—era saga of the fading West. Here, the Bunch (Ben Johnson, Warren Oates, William Holden, and Ernest Borgnine) embark on a climactic suicidal show-down with the Mexican Army. (Culver Pictures)

the real villain of the piece is progress. Big business, typified by the banks and the railroad, force the Bunch out of the United States and into a confrontation with a corrupt Mexican bandit army. When one of their own group is captured and tortured by the Mexican bandits (whose leader has given up his horse for an automobile and is doing business with German warmongers), the Bunch undertakes a final, suicidal act of heroism—something that is very much in America's "national interest." In one of the most spectacular showdowns ever filmed, the Wild Bunch and the bandit army destroy each other in a quick-cut, slow-motion dream of blood and death.

This paradoxical resolution is in much the same vein as those in *The Magnificent Seven* and *Butch Cassidy*. In both of these films, although outlaw collectives are forced by time and civilization to practice their trade outside the United States, they retain a certain allegiance to their heroic code with its basis in American ideology. And in all three films, the outlaw collective regenerates the sense of group mission—one similar to that which had been subdued by advancing civilization on the American frontier. This sense of mission still determines the behavior and attitude of the collective, and as such it almost becomes an end in itself: the heroic mediator's social function emerges as a self-indulgent, formalized ritual.

Sam Peckinpah has understood and articulated, perhaps better than any Western filmmaker since John Ford, the concept of the Westerner who has outlived his role and his milieu. Particularly in *Ride the High Country* (1962), *Major Dundee* (1964), *The Wild Bunch* (1969), and *The Ballad of Cable Hogue* (1970), Peckinpah evokes a strong sense of irony and nostalgia in his presentation of a cast of aging heroic misfits. His men are hopelessly—and even tragically—at odds with the inexorable flow of history. The most evocative of these films is *Ride the High Country*, made in the same year as Ford's *The Man Who Shot Liberty Valance*. (Both films express regret over the passing of the Old West and its values.) The film stars Randolph Scott and Joel McCrae, two familiar cowboys from countless '40s and '50s Westerns, who are now reduced to tending bar and sharpshooting in a Wild West show. The opening sequence in *Ride the High Country* immediately establishes the hero's displacement in the new West and shows what he must do to contend with it. McCrae (as Steven Judd) arrives in town having given up his bartending job to guard a mine shipment, happy to return to the type of work which had sustained him through his more productive years. The town itself is modern, with automobiles, policemen, and even a Wild West show, where Judd finds his former deputy, Gil Westrum (Randolph Scott), reduced to a sideshow attraction. This opening sequence not only pits the old West against the new, but it also sets up an opposition between McCrae/Judd and Scott/Westrum. The former has retained his idealistic desire to continue as an agent of social order; the latter manifests a pragmatic willingness to make a profit off his former lawman status. Judd recruits Westrum to help him with the mine shipment, although Westrum agrees only because he assumes he'll eventually grab it for himself. Judd's reactionary idealism and Westrum's self-serving adaptability provide the central conflict throughout the film. This split is intensified by the presence of an initiate-hero (Ron Starr as Heck Longtree) who must decide between the two opposing world views. The initiate ultimately rejects Westrum's scheme to rob the shipment, and Westrum himself finally elects to join Judd and Longtree in a climactic showdown with another band of outlaws. The flexible, practical Westrum and the initiate Longtree survive the gunfight, but Judd falls, mortally wounded.

The film's closing shot is an over-the-shoulder, point-of-view shot from ground level, where we gaze with the dying Judd at the "high country" in the distance. As in the closing sequence in *Shane* (although this film is much bleaker in its outlook), the Westerner's status is reaffirmed in mythic proportions. However, instead of riding into the mountains as Shane had done, into that timeless terrain beyond the reach of civilization, Judd must be satisfied with only a dying glimpse of them.

But not even Peckinpah's jaded vision can match that of Robert Altman's remarkable 1972 Western, *McCabe and Mrs. Miller*. In Altman's film, the reluctant hero miraculously prevails against three killers only to freeze to death as he lies wounded and drifting snow covers him. Actually, the plot in Altman's film is somewhat similar to that in *Shane*. A charismatic figure with a violent but shadowy past makes his presence felt in a community and finally confronts single-handedly those power-hungry forces seeking control of the town.

The two films have little in common otherwise. Whereas Shane rode into a lush, pastoral valley wearing fringed buckskins and a six-gun, McCabe (Warren Beatty) rides into the dismal, rain-drenched town of Presbyterian Church in a suit and a derby and carrying a concealed derringer. Rather than working the land, McCabe provides the mining community with its first whorehouse. In *McCabe,* it is not the land which must be protected, but rather the business which has become the life-blood of that particular community: McCabe's brothel. Marion Starrett's pure woman-domesticator is countered here by Constance Miller (Julie Christie), an experienced madam and prostitute (sex is simply a commodity of exchange), who expands McCabe's meager enterprise into the realm of big business.

The final showdown is precipitated when McCabe refuses to sell out his share of the "house" to an unseen corporation. As McCabe conducts an elaborate, cat-and-mouse gun battle through the streets with three hired killers sent by the corporation, the other townspeople are busy fighting a fire in the community's half-

An unlikely Westerner, John McCabe (Warren Beatty) welcomes an equally unlikely domesticator, Mrs. Miller (Julie Christie), to the community of Presbyterian Church, where she's arrived to help expand McCabe's local business interests. (Movie Star News)

built church. In an ironic counterpoint to the sunlit communal celebration on the church foundation in Ford's *My Darling Clementine* (1946), here the townsfolk work together to save a church which few of them would ever consider attending. In reality, the church in *McCabe* is just an empty shell, a facade as hollow as the values and the future of the community itself. McCabe's genuine act of heroism goes unnoticed as the townspeople work futilely to rescue a formal edifice without spiritual substance. Against his own better judgment, and against his beloved Mrs. Miller's protestations, McCabe finally joins those countless other Western heroes, reaffirming his own individual identity, protecting his own homestead and reinforcing the Western's essential theme that "a man's gotta do what he's gotta do."

Our idealized past: The Western

The Western, like the gangster and hardboiled detective genres, grudgingly recognized the inevitability of social progress as well as the individual sacrifice involved in society's progression. But despite the inexorable flow of civilization and history and its necessary transformation of the Western hero—or perhaps because of it—his heroic stature persists. The values associated with his individual character and posture are as important to us, the audience, as is the social order he provides. The violent resolution and departure of the Westerner at film's end, whether into the sunset or into the grave, not only ensure social order but also perpetuate the stoic self-reliance and willful violence embodied by the Westerner. Revisionist historians may insist that men like Wyatt Earp and Billy Bonney were hardly the heroic paragons that Hollywood movies have made them, but that is precisely the point of the genre film's mythic capacity. These films do not celebrate the past itself, but rather our contemporary idealized version of the past, which forms the foundation and serves as the model for our present attitudes and values.

John Ford and the evolution of the Western

Q: One feels that your sympathy in *Liberty Valance* is with John Wayne and the Old West.

Ford: Well, Wayne actually played the lead; Jimmy Stewart had most of the scenes, but Wayne was the central character, the motivation for the whole thing. I don't know—I liked them both—I think they were both good characters and I rather liked the story, that's all. . . .

Q: By the end of the picture, though, it seemed that Vera Miles was still in love with Wayne.

Ford: Well, we meant it that way.

Q: Your picture of the West has become increasingly sad over the years—like the difference in mood, for example, between *Wagon Master* and *Liberty Valance.*

Ford: Possibly—I don't know—I'm not a psychologist. Maybe I'm getting older.

—from an interview with Peter Bogdanovich[2]

We're all getting older, and with age we seem to become increasingly sensitive to the stuff that our dreams—and our myths—are made of. For myself, I began "getting older" somewhat prematurely; I grew up in the 1950s and '60s, cutting my generic teeth on the aberrant "anti-Westerns" of Anthony Mann and Budd Boetticher and Sam Peckinpah. And perhaps Ford's Westerns were the most subversive of all, because they seemed like traditional cowboy movies, and yet left one with a feeling of regret and nostalgia. One of my own epiphanal filmgoing moments occurred when I realized during the closing moments of *The Man Who Shot Liberty Valance* that tears were welling up in my eyes, and as a relatively naive tenderfoot I had no real idea why. After all, hadn't Jimmy Stewart, the town of Shinbone, and the American Dream prevailed? Hadn't the archvillain Lee Marvin been destroyed and the heroic John Wayne been laid to rest in peace? The answers to these questions, interestingly enough, do not come easily.

Joseph McBride and Michael Wilmington suggest in their comprehensive study of Ford that the film "shatters the purity of a myth even as it shows history accepting it."[3] *Liberty Valance*'s rich complexity, as evidenced by my own confused response to its contradictory impulses and ambiguous resolution, suggests that the Western genre had come a long way since the "horse operas" and "sagebrush melodramas" of a half-century earlier. Ford's career spanned that period, and more than any other filmmaker he influenced and understood the genre's gradual evolution. It had grown from naive, simplistic foundation ritual to a sophisticated formula in which American history and ideology—and the Western genre itself—could be reflected upon and examined in detail.

Ford's embellishment of the Western formula

John Ford directed Westerns from 1917 (*The Tornado*) to 1964 (*Cheyenne Autumn*). Of the hundred-plus Hollywood films Ford directed, roughly half were Westerns, and although his six Oscars were awarded for his "serious" films, it is increasingly obvious that Ford's Westerns represent the most significant portion of his cinematic legacy. Actually, after the introduction of sound, Ford had all but abandoned the genre because of budgetary and technical restrictions, but he returned with *Stagecoach* in 1939 and helped to regenerate the Hollywood Western's mass popularity. (According to legend, the initial response to Ford's *Stagecoach* proposal by studio heads at Fox was, "We don't make Westerns any more.") With *Stagecoach*, Ford fleshed out the formula's thematic tensions, visual spectacle, and inherent

**Director John Ford,
seated between
Jimmy Stewart and
John Wayne, on
the set of The Man
Who Shot Liberty
Valance.** (Hoblitzelle
Theatre Arts Collection)

mythic appeal as no previous Western filmmaker had—he even surpassed himself
and the countless silents he had produced. Ford's influence on the genre was so
substantial, in fact, that we might consider *Stagecoach* as having brought the latent
beauty and thematic complexity of the Western to the fore. And further, if it
weren't for Ford's Westerns, especially his more recent films, we might not be discussing the genre at all.

Andrew Sarris wrote in 1968 that "a Ford film, particularly a late Ford film, is
more than its story and characterizations; it is also the director's attitude toward

his milieu and its codes of conduct."[4] With this single sentence, Sarris outlines Ford's—and the genre's—evolution from the straightforward storytelling of a simple tale to a growing concern for the act of telling and the substance of that tale. With each successive Western after *Stagecoach*, Ford's attitude toward the classic Western formula became increasingly self-conscious, both stylistically and thematically. Gradually, he shifted his cinematic and narrative emphasis from the "subject matter" of the genre to its narrative form and cultural function. The question of influence is always difficult, even when considering so inventive a filmmaker working within so conventional a form. When we examine Ford's contributions to the genre, however, it seems fairly simple to determine that he was among the most (if not *the* most) influential of Western film directors. Further, the evolution of Ford's treatment of the genre is indicative of its overall historical development. In order to examine this development in some detail, we will compare and contrast four Ford Westerns produced in consecutive decades, all of which were widely popular when they were released and are now considered among Hollywood's greatest Westerns: *Stagecoach* (1939), *My Darling Clementine* (1946), *The Searchers* (1956), and *The Man Who Shot Liberty Valance* (1962).

Stagecoach as an advance in the genre

As I have already discussed, *Stagecoach* involves a straightforward narrative of classic Western concerns: the legendary, psychologically uncomplicated and stable hero (John Wayne as the Ringo Kid) helps protect the occupants of a stage from an Indian attack so that he can reach Lordsburg and avenge his brother's murder. After single-handedly ridding the town of the menacing Plummer brothers, Ringo leaves with Dallas to ride into the sunset and the promise of a new life beyond the limitless horizon.

Stagecoach, often criticized as being clichéd or conventional, actually represented a considerable advance in imagery and thematic complexity over previous and then-current Westerns—despite its essentially one-dimensional characters, its cavalry-to-the-rescue climax, and its "escape hatch" solution to Ringo's outlaw status. The film is visually unprecedented, both in its depiction of Monument Valley as the archetypal Western milieu and also in Ford's sensitive, controlled camerawork. Ford neatly balances the vast expanse of the valley against the enclosed, socially defined space of the stagecoach, the way stations, and other interior locations. He establishes a visual opposition that intensifies the hero's divided self (uncivilized renegade versus agent of social order) and the genre's essential nature/culture opposition.

Stagecoach also anticipates Ford's narrative and visual concern for community ritual, which became more pronounced in his later Westerns. As Ford well understood, these rituals—dances, weddings, funerals, and in this case, a childbirth—are virtually punctuation marks of the genre itself. They formally articulate and define the community and its collective values.

Ford establishes both his characters and his dominant themes by tracing the travelers' reactions to a variety of familiar events that emphasize many of society's values: the "democratic" balloting to decide whether to press on in the face of Indian attacks; a group meal in which seating arrangements and body language indicate the social status and attitudes of the participants; the unexpected birth of a baby to one of the travelers. The childbirth sequence is especially significant, complicating the journey's progress but also positing the savage wilderness as a potential utopia for future generations. It is during this crisis that Ringo's fellow renegades, Doc Boone and Dallas, verify their heroic credentials. They add a moral and humanistic dimension to the stagecoach's world in microcosm. The other passengers may represent more traditional roles of a civilized society, but these two transcend such a civilization characterized by its concern for social status and material wealth.

After Boone sobers up and successfully delivers the baby, Dallas cares for the mother and child through the night. As she shows the newborn child to the group, she and Ringo form a silent union (in a telling exchange of close-ups) that is realized in their later embrace. With this silent exchange, Ford isolates Ringo, Dallas, and the child as a veritable Holy Family of the frontier, and the motif is strengthened by the couple's final flight into the desert at film's end. It is thus the family, the nuclear social unit, that brings together Westerner and Woman and offers the promise of an ideal frontier community.

Clementine: A utopian Western

My Darling Clementine (1946), like *Stagecoach,* closes with a figurative embrace between Westerner and Woman, but in that later film the redeemer-hero rides off alone. There is only a vague suggestion that he will return to Clementine (Cathy Downs) and the community. In fact, *Clementine* is much less naive than *Stagecoach* in its recognition of the hero's basic inability to reconcile his individual and social roles. Still, it might well be considered more naive in its idealized portrayal of Wyatt Earp (Henry Fonda) as the stoic, self-reliant redeemer.

Ringo's character was essentially one-dimensional and static, but Ringo's outlaw status (although unjustified) gave an ambiguous edge to his prosocial, redemptive actions. *Clementine*'s hero and community, on the other hand, are depicted in the most positive light the Arizona sun could produce, and in that sense it is the more overtly mythic, classical Western of the two. The elements Ford had introduced in *Stagecoach*—sound, iconography (Monument Valley and John Wayne), and the orchestration of themes, values, and characters—solidify in *Clementine* into an unyielding and unqualified ritual form, celebrating the promise of the epic-heroic figure and the utopian community.

Like Ringo (and later Ethan Edwards in *The Searchers*), Earp is motivated by vengeance: after the Clantons kill his younger brother and steal his cattle, Earp accepts the job as Tombstone's marshal (which he had rejected earlier) and vows over his

"The new Marshall and his Lady Fair."
In My Darling Clementine, Wyatt Earp
(Henry Fonda) and Clementine Carter
(Cathy Downs) dance on the foundation
for the new church in Tombstone. (Museum
of Modern Art/Film Stills Archive)

brother's grave to avenge his death. As Earp says over his brother's grave early in the film, "Maybe when we leave this country, kids like you will be able to grow up and live safe." Although his primary motives involve blood lust, Earp's legal status renders him beyond reproach. Only one aspect of *Clementine* offsets Earp's spit-and-polish demeanor and provides an ambiguous edge to the narrative—the presence of Doc Holliday (Victor Mature) as Tombstone's resident saloon keeper and charismatic authority figure.

The device of using another central character who shares the hero's prosocial allegiance but not his motivation or world view appears frequently in Westerns. This "double" generally points up both the primitive and the cultivated characteristics of the hero and his milieu. Earp and Holliday emerge as oppositional figures on various levels: Earp is the archetypal Westerner, Holliday is a well-educated, Eastern-bred doctor; Earp is a stoic, laconic militarist who uses force only when necessary, Holliday is cultured and articulate but also prone to violent outbursts;

both run the town with self-assured authority, but Earp disdains Holliday's penchant for gunplay; Earp is a natural man who operates on instinct and savvy, Holliday is a cultivated man seeking refuge in the West from a failed romance and a demanding career.

Holliday is an interesting and somewhat unusual character within the Ford constellation. Like Doc Boone and later Dutton Peabody in *Liberty Valance*, he is cultured enough to quote Shakespeare but cannot live with himself or the savage environment without alcohol. Unlike the drunken philosophers in these films, however, his age and physical abilities are roughly on a par with the hero's, so he counters Earp on considerably more than just an attitudinal level.

The sharpest distinction between Earp and Holliday, of course, involves the film's namesake, Clementine Carter. Clementine has followed Holliday from Boston, virtually stepping over the dead gunfighters the temperamental doctor has left in his wake. Once she catches up with Holliday in Tombstone, Clementine must confront her own "primitive" double—the character of Chihuahua (Linda Darnell), a saloon girl of questionable breeding. Complementing the film's dominant law-and-order opposition, then, which pits the Earps and Holliday against the Clantons, are the foursome of Wyatt, Doc, Clementine, and Chihuahua, who form a fascinating network of interrelationships.

It is finally (and predictably) Clementine who tempers Earp's character. She gives a touch of humanity to his rigid attitude and takes the edge off his mythic stature. Apparently, as long as the Eastern figure is either a woman or an aging, philosophical alcoholic (this is invariably the case in Ford's Westerns), then he or she conceivably has something to contribute to the settling of the wilderness. Holliday's character is doomed from the start, however, and only time will tell whether a faster gunman or his diseased lungs will finish him. Through Earp and his mission, Holliday is able to die heroically in the climactic gunfight. Thus he joins Chihuahua, his female counterpart, who had died earlier under his own apparently misguided scalpel.

Like *Stagecoach, Clementine* was filmed on location in Monument Valley and on black-and-white film stock. The visual style in *Clementine* is considerably more lyrical and expressive than in the earlier film, however, especially in those daylight sequences where Ford frames the desert and monuments beyond the town in elaborate compositions. There is little sense of the horizon beyond the community in this film. This is partially because of the preponderance of night sequences, most of which focus either upon Doc's alcoholic rages or the Clantons' maniacal carrying-on. In the daylight sequences, we generally are only able to glimpse the horizon through manmade structures like fenceposts, boardwalks, and so on.

In the oft-cited church sequence, one of those rare moments when it seems as if the entire narrative is concentrated into a single image, Ford orchestrates an array of visual opposition. We see the contrast of earth and sky, of rugged terrain against horizon, of Monument Valley's vast panorama framed by the rafters and flagstaffs of the half-built church, of man and nature. In an eloquent ritual sequence, the townspeople hold a Sunday square dance, an interesting juxtaposition to the anarchic behavior of Tombstone's nighttime revelers. Earp approaches with Clementine, and the preacher orders the townspeople to stand aside "for the new marshal and his lady fair." As the two dance, framed against the sky, the genre's array of prosocial values and ideals coalesces into an extremely simple yet eternally evocative image.

Those ideals are affirmed as the Earps clean up Tombstone—just as Ringo had cleaned up Lordsburg—in a violent, climactic gun battle. But whereas the gunfight in *Stagecoach* occurs offscreen (Ford shows us Ringo from low-angle falling and firing his rifle, then the camera pulls in on the anxious Dallas), in *Clementine* it is an elaborate, murderous ballet. Ford contends that he choreographed the O.K. Corral sequence after the "real" Wyatt Earp's own description of the legendary battle; the conflict does seem like a military operation. Despite its ties with history, though—and there are few in this mythic tale—the gunfight is not staged in a naturalistic manner. Rather, it seems to be a dream of voices, gunshots, and dust.

The gunfight is initiated when a stagecoach passes the corral, raising clouds of dust. The six participants move in and out of the frame and the dust, firing at one another until only Wyatt and his brother Morgan (Ward Bond) remain standing. This ritualistic dance of death serves both to contrast and complement the earlier dance in the half-built church: social integration is viable only if community order is maintained. With that order ensured, Wyatt promises Clementine, who is now the new schoolmarm, that one day he will return. He and his brother then leave the community and ride westward across Monument Valley.

Ford's postwar Westerns

In the intervening decade between *My Darling Clementine* and *The Searchers*, the Western genre itself and Ford's attitudes toward it developed substantially. During this crucial period in the Western's generic evolution, from World War II through the early 1950s, Ford remained curiously distant from the mainstream "psychological" and "adult" Westerns. While other Hollywood filmmakers were turning the genre and its hero inside out with films like *Red River, The Gunfighter, Winchester 73, Rancho Notorious, High Noon, The Naked Spur,* and *Johnny Guitar,* Ford's Western filmmaking was distinctly out of step. During the late '40s he directed his "cavalry trilogy"—*Fort Apache* (1948), *She Wore a Yellow Ribbon* (1949), and *Rio Grande* (1950)—which traces the winning of the West from a militarist perspective, using rather straightforward cavalry-versus-Injuns oppositions. In 1948 Ford remade a 1920 silent film, *Marked Men*, under the title *Three Godfathers*; and in 1950 he directed his epic of westward expansion, *Wagon Master*, in which two young horse traders (Ben Johnson and Harry Carey, Jr.) guide a Mormon wagon train past hostile Indians and outlaw predators to establish a utopian pioneer community.

Interestingly, none of these films employs the classic configuration of the individual, self-reliant Westerner who mediates the natural and cultural forces of his

She Wore a Yellow Ribbon (1949) was the second of Ford's cavalry trilogy. These "military Westerns" kept Ford and his repertory company in the midst of Monument Valley, but on the periphery of the genre, as the Western formula underwent radical change after World War II. (Hoblitzelle Theatre Arts Collection)

milieu. In fact, there is no development of an individual hero. Although John Wayne stars in each of the cavalry films, his military status and direct commitment to the community severely compromise his more familiar role as isolated, self-styled redeemer. As a hybrid of Western and war genres, the cavalry films depict a male collective which functions as an individual unit within contested space. Its mission is to establish law and order, to spread Eastern American ideology throughout the West. Ford's "stock company"—principally Wayne, Ben Johnson, Victor McLaglen, Ward Bond, Harry Carey, Jr., and John Agar—composed this collective. Their male camaraderie and overt prosocial mission precluded any narrative concern for the individual hero or the delicate balance between civilization and savagery.

As superior officer of the military collective, Wayne's character is both the focal and the father figure within these films. The hard-bitten officers Wayne portrays show signs of age, but not too self-consciously—although Ford became increasingly demanding of Wayne in these roles and the actor's performances improved markedly. (Ford is reputed to have said of Wayne after seeing him in Hawks' *Red River*, "I never knew the big son-of-a-bitch could act.") Wayne does not appear in *Wagon Master*, although Johnson, Carey, Bond, and several other members of the Ford repertory company do. This film is an optimistic if somewhat saccharine tribute to America's pioneer spirit. Ford again develops a Western narrative without a central character or guiding sensibility, opting instead for a collective hero to share the film's mission.

After the cavalry trilogy, Ford took a five-year sabbatical from the Western genre in the early '50s and returned with a fascinating redefinition of it and its hero. In his triumphant 1956 tour de force *The Searchers*, Ford created the most complex, critical, and evocative portrait of the West and the Westerner that movie audiences had yet seen.

Ford's masterpiece: *The Searchers*

The Searchers is the story of an obsessive, nomadic hero (Wayne as Ethan Edwards) who arrives home after a three-year disappearance. Edwards had fought in the Civil War and then had vanished, apparently somewhere in Mexico. The day after he turns up, a band of renegade Indians massacre his family. We learn that Ethan's former sweetheart, Martha (Dorothy Jordan), now his brother's wife, had been sexually violated before she was killed, and that her two daughters were kidnapped by the Indians. The massacre sets Ethan and a young initiate-hero, Martin Pawley (Jeffrey Hunter), off on an epic, decade-long journey throughout the West (Monument Valley).

The object of their pursuit is the leader of the renegade Indian band, Scar (Henry Brandon), who has taken the sole living captive from the massacre as his squaw. Pawley, himself a one-eighth Cherokee who had been found in his infancy by Ethan and had been raised by the Edwards family during Ethan's prolonged absence, is intent upon returning his foster sister to civilization. Ethan's intentions are a good deal less altruistic. He is bent upon killing Scar to avenge his brother's wife's death, and he also plans to kill the captive squaw whom he considers unfit to return to the world of the White Man.

Throughout Ethan and Martin's search, the linear, chronological aspects of the complex narrative are subordinate to its oppositional structure, which centers on Ethan's character. The search itself does provide a temporal framework for the story, but the events depicted do not really fit into a cause-and-effect pattern. Instead, they progressively reveal and qualify the Westerner's contradictory, multifaceted personality. The entire film, in fact, might be read as a procession of characters with whom Ethan is doubled.

Upon his initial return, Ethan is set in opposition with his brother Aaron, a simple man of the earth who had remained in Texas and had wed Ethan's sweetheart, raised a family, and cultivated the wilderness in the name of civilization. This nomad-homesteader opposition is accentuated on the morning after Ethan's return when the Reverend-Captain Samuel Johnson Clayton (Ward Bond) thunders into the Edwards' household to enlist Aaron and Martin's aid in his pursuit of Scar's renegade band. Clayton is also a composite of contradictions, although he seems sufficiently comfortable with his dual institutional role of lawman and clergyman. His prosocial beliefs and functions offset Ethan's nomadic, antisocial nature both spiritually and socially. Even though they once were officers for the Confederacy, the men now sit on opposite sides of an ideological fence. Unlike Clayton, Ethan did not attend the Confederate surrender and he still relishes his status as rebel. "I figure a man's only good for one oath at a time," he tells Clayton. "I still got *my* saber. . . . Didn't turn it into no plowshare, neither." This attitude sets Ethan against both Aaron, the man who allowed himself to be domesticated by a woman and the land, and also Clayton, the warrior who now fights for both the laws of man and God.

Ethan's only law is his own, fashioned from his long-standing rapport with the wilderness. His character is shown throughout as being ignorant and unsympathetic to civilization and its ways, but his understanding of the desert expanse and his natural environment far surpasses that of any other white man in the film. He is in touch with his surroundings but out of touch with his people, and he clearly likes it that way.

Return of the renegade: frame enlargement from the opening sequence of **The Searchers,** *where prodigal Westerner Ethan Edwards* **(John Wayne)** *is welcomed by his brother's family to their Texas home.* (Private Collection)

Ethan's only connection with civilization is his feeling for Martha. For him, she transcends the distinction between the civilized and the savage. From the opening shot of the film when Martha glimpses Ethan approaching across the desert and welcomes him back into the familial fold, Ford subtly indicates that she is his reason for returning. After the massacre when Ethan comes back to the burnt-out homestead, she is the only family member to whom he calls out. Once he finds her body, Ethan's deepest fears and anxieties are animated and his obsessive search is set in motion.

The thematic core of *The Searchers* revolves around a series of male/female relationships involving sexual union, sexual taboo, and sexual violation: Ethan and Martha, Aaron and Martha, Scar and Martha, and by extension Scar and Martha's daughter Lucy (whom he rapes and kills after the massacre) and also daughter Debbie (whom he eventually takes for his squaw). Scar's sexual violation of Martha and her daughters, and Ethan's maniacal desire to avenge the deed by killing the Indian as well as his own niece, draw the two men into an intense and perverse rapport.

The relationship between Westerner and Woman had been a significant but generally subordinate motif in earlier films, but here it emerges as a dominant, motivating factor in the narrative. In a classical Western like *My Darling Clementine*, the hero's repression of his sexual and domestic inclinations was a positive character trait: as high priest of order in the West he was committed to an unspoken code of chastity and self-enforced solitude. In *The Searchers*, the hero's sexual repression—based in his guilt-ridden feelings about Martha and her daughters' violation—assumes psychotic proportions and finds release only when Ethan finally scalps Scar. That task completed, and his obsessions restored to their proper subliminal realm, Ethan turns his back on both the white and Indian cultures and wanders across the desert into oblivion.

While Scar and his renegade band appear to be a rather traditional threat to the civilized homesteaders, Ford's depiction of Indian culture and of the Scar-Ethan relationship appears to radically transform the Western's traditional portrayal of inhuman "Redskins." Unlike *Stagecoach*, where the Indians were simply natural hazards and had no individual or cultural identity, here they are the creators of an autonomous civilization which virtually mirrors the whites'. (In discussing *The Searchers*, Ford once stated: "The audience likes to see Indians get killed. They don't consider them as human beings—with a great culture of their own—quite different from our own. If you analyzed the thing carefully, however, you'd find that their religion is very similar to ours.")[5]

Because of this sympathetic portrayal of Indian culture, Scar and Ethan are cast in a curiously similar social status. Both are renegades from their own civilizations who violently avenge their respective families. Scar's two sons had been killed by whites years earlier, and his slaughter of Ethan's family is simply one in a series of retributions. Like Ethan, Scar knows the language and the cultural codes of his enemy, and like Ethan he has cultivated a hatred for that enemy so intense that it ultimately seems to transcend the original motivating desire for vengeance.

Scar and Ethan's relationship as brothers under the skin is enhanced by Ford's casting a blue-eyed (but well-tanned) Anglo, Henry Brandon, as Scar. Ford prided himself on casting of real Native Americans in his Westerns, but authenticity in this case was less vital than rhetorical and symbolic expression. Scar's physical characteristics distinguish him from his own people and accentuate his rapport with the Westerner. Their physical and motivational similarities are intensified when Ethan and Scar finally meet late in the film. In a bristling confrontation in Scar's camp, Ford mirrors not only their dialogue ("You speak good English"/"You speak good Comanche"), but he also mirrors our own perceptions of the two men. By filming the confrontation in a rare exchange of over-the-shoulder shots, he encourages the audience to assume Scar's as well as Ethan's viewpoint.

Ultimately, the similarities between Ethan and Scar, between protagonist and antagonist, underscore Ford's evolving conception of the conflicts and threats within the Western milieu. No longer does the Westerner have to deal with faceless "Injuns" who throw the defenseless community into chaos; now the threat involves that very same nomadic, self-reliant individuality which society cannot tolerate and which is shared by *both* the hero and the Indian. Ironically, this incompatibility between Ford's hero and society grows to a point where the hero's very presence generates disorder. The coincidence of Ethan's and later, Scar's unannounced arrivals into the precariously balanced community, coupled with their similar moral codes and renegade reputations, finally make it rather difficult to distinguish between Demon Indian and Redeemer Westerner.

Ethan's absolute, uncompromising, and obsessive character is continually juxtaposed with the initiate-hero, Martin Pawley. Martin embodies the opposites which Ethan cannot tolerate—he, like the captive Debbie, is both Family and Indian, both civilized and savage, both loved and hated. Martin accepts his dualities, however, and his capacity for reason and compromise repeatedly undercuts Ethan's manic quest for revenge. When Ethan tries to stir up Martin's blood lust by telling him that one of the scalps on Scar's lodgepole belongs to Martin's mother, Martin replies, "It don't make no difference." Martin learns the ways of the desert and the land from Ethan, but his ultimate goal is to return Debbie to her people and to settle a homestead with his childhood sweetheart, Laurie (Vera Miles). Martin is the one who finally kills Scar, not aggressively but in an act of self-defense, and this enables him to return to Laurie in Texas and to commit himself to rural and domestic values which Ethan had been unable (or unwilling) to do years earlier with Martha.

Significantly, though, once Martin honors that commitment, his role as initiate-hero evaporates, and he all but disappears from the narrative. The film's final moments focus not upon Martin's integration into the community but upon Ethan's inability to do so. Although finally able to embrace Debbie and return her to civilization, reaffirming his fundamental belief in Woman and Family, Ethan cannot commit his own life to those values. In the film's closing shot, Ethan stares through the doorway at the family's reunion celebration (and beyond it to the audience), then turns and slowly walks off across Monument Valley as the door closes and leaves the screen in darkness. This image reprises the film's opening shot, wherein Martha had opened a door to reveal Ethan approaching from the distance. This visual motif reaffirms our own perspective from inside the secure, if somewhat repressive, confines of society. It also demonstrates the hero's basic inability to pass through that doorway and enjoy civilized existence. Like the dead Indian whose eyes Ethan had shot out early in the search, Ethan is doomed to wander forever between the winds, endlessly traversing the mythic expanse of Monument Valley.

Ford's farewell to the Westerner

If we were to look to a small ranch outside the community of Shinbone some six years later, we might be able to hazard a guess about Ethan's fate after the close of *The Searchers*. Made between *Two Rode Together* (1961) and *How the West Was Won* (1963, in which Ford directed the Civil War episode), *The Man Who Shot Liberty Valance* is Ford's nostalgic and bittersweet farewell to the Westerner and his vanishing ideals.

The story is deceptively simple: Ransom Stoddard (Jimmy Stewart), an aging United States senator, has returned to the prosperous and progressive town of Shinbone where he had begun his career as a lawyer. Accompanied by his wife, Hallie (Vera Miles), Stoddard comes to town to attend the funeral of Tom Doniphon, a forgotten cowboy. The funeral must be financed by the county because Doniphon died without money, home, or even a handgun. At the inducement of an aggressive newspaper editor, Stoddard explains his presence and the significance of Doniphon through an extended flashback that takes up most of the film.

The flashback traces Stoddard's journey West fresh out of law school, his confrontation during the trip with a brutal, psychopathic outlaw (Lee Marvin as Liberty Valance), and his befriending of a charismatic but essentially aloof local rancher, Doniphon, played, of course, by John Wayne—here regenerating the epic Westerner. Stoddard promotes statehood for the community, while Valance is hired by ranchers "north of the Picket Wire" to prevent it, and the conflict between Stoddard and Valance intensifies until they meet in a traditional gunfight. Valance is killed, and Stoddard goes on to build a career as "the man who shot Liberty Valance."

We later learn (in a flashback within a flashback, a narrative device we hardly expect within the Western's usually straightforward story construction) that Doniphon, not Stoddard, was responsible for killing Valance. In this act of heroic self-destruction, Doniphon bequeaths to Stoddard the leadership of the community and, even more significantly, the hand of his "gal" Hallie.

After Stoddard completes the flashback story, the newspaper editor tears up his notes and throws them into the fire, delivering the film's—and Ford's—definitive self-critical statement: "This is the West, sir. When the legend becomes fact, print the legend." *Liberty Valance* is, in effect, Ford's effort to print both the fact and the

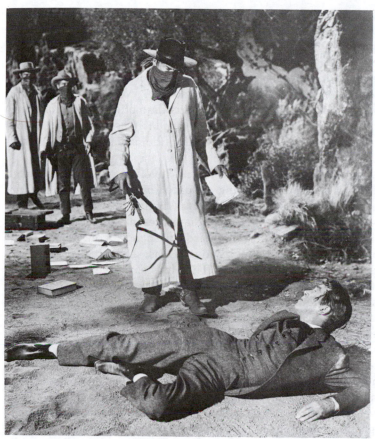

A lesson in "Western law": Eastern lawyer Ransom Stoddard (Jimmy Stewart) is rudely welcomed to the Western community of Shinbone by local outlaw Liberty Valance (Lee Marvin, behind the mask).
(Penguin Photos)

legend, both history and myth, and to suggest how the two interpenetrate one another. Ford is no longer primarily concerned with the vision of contemporary America drawn from stories about its past; instead, he concentrates on the very process whereby our present demands for a favorable vision distort and manipulate the past. Whereas *Stagecoach* and *My Darling Clementine* overtly celebrated the culture's idealized self-image, *Liberty Valance* deconstructs and critiques that image, finally acknowledging the necessary role of myth and legend in the development of history and civilization.

To examine the Western's amalgam of fact and fiction, Ford creates a world of formal artifice, a timeless theatrical realm in which the allegory is enacted. Abandoning the wide expanse of Monument Valley and the filmic "realism" of wide-screen color and location shooting, Ford shot *Liberty Valance* in black and white, and almost all of the flashback episode was performed on a sound stage. The opening and closing sequences of the film establish Shinbone roughly at the turn of the century, and are shot in exteriors under natural light. When Stoddard begins his flashback, however, Ford depicts the stagecoach amid the artificial trappings of a Western studio set under artificial studio lighting. In case we missed the point, a masked figure (who turns out to be Valance) comes from behind a *papier-mâché* boulder, dressed in a white, floor-length overcoat, and shouts, "Stand and deliver." He proceeds to rob the stage and terrorize its occupants, tearing apart Stoddard's law books after giving him a brutal lesson in "Western law."

With this initial flashback, Ford establishes conflict dramatically (Stoddard versus Valance) and thematically (Eastern versus Western law), as well as chronologically ("new" versus "old" Shinbone) and filmically (the actual Shinbone versus the stylized realm of the flashback).

Thus, Ford's distinction between fact and legend involves not only character, story, and thematics, but also the structuring of space (exterior versus studio, nature versus artifice) and time (present versus past). Whereas all Westerns address two time frames—the old West and the immediate present—*Liberty Valance* addresses three. Placing the *act of telling* (i.e., Stoddard's flashback "confession" to the reporter in turn-of-the-century Shinbone) between past and present reinforces Ford's concern with the *process* of mythmaking. The film's narrative framework, the stark stylization of the flashback story, and Ford's treatment of the principal figures all give the flashback a remarkable dreamlike quality. It is shown as the aging Stoddard might have imagined it. Stoddard himself looks much the same in the flashback as in the opening despite the quarter-century lapse—only his whitened hair indicates the advancing years. We never actually see Doniphon in the new Shinbone sequences, although his presence is felt even before the flashback when Stoddard opens the casket and orders the mortician to put Doniphon's boots and spurs on him. Doniphon, like Valance, has no business in the new Shinbone, with its telephones, paved sidewalks, and irrigation projects. Stoddard's "social man" has outlived the legendary Shinbone of his own imagination to survive in the modern world, but Doniphon and Valance, two self-consciously mythic figures, are consigned to the realm of memory and legend.

There are three mediating characters in *Liberty Valance*. First, the newspaper editor in the new Shinbone—vastly different from Dutton Peabody (Edmund O'Brien), the *Shinbone Star*'s founding editor (as witnessed in the flashback) and another of Ford's philosophical drunks—who functions much like Ford the filmmaker, mediating legend and fact, myth and history, past and present. Then there is Tom Doniphon, who mediates Valance's primitive savagery and Stoddard's naive idealism. Finally, we have Hallie, who like the editor—and the audience—must decide between Stoddard and Doniphon, between the promise of "a garden of real roses" and the cactus rose. Before Stoddard begins his flashback, Hallie rides off to Doniphon's deserted, burnt-out home to pick a cactus rose, and she eventually leaves it on his casket. The rose represents the torn allegiance felt by Hallie, Ford, and the audience between garden and desert, between nature and civilization.

Although Stoddard is the narrative focus and the guiding sensibility of the film—it is, after all, his story—the cactus rose is the film's emotional and thematic core, its symbol of a lost age when civilization and wilderness coexisted in a precarious but less compromising balance. (Tom often brought Hallie cactus roses when he came courting.) Ford does not mean, however, to condemn Hallie's choice of Stoddard any more than he means to indict the Western genre itself. Hallie's choice ultimately is as inevitable as ours: We were destined to follow a certain historical path in order to reach our present cultural condition, and we keep rewriting history to convince ourselves that we have taken the "right" path, that our destiny represents the fulfillment of promises made and kept.

As Stoddard's train winds back East to Washington in the film's closing sequence, he and Hallie agree to return eventually to Shinbone to live out their lives. What draws them back West, it seems, is a sense of loss and the ghost of Tom Doniphon—who was, as Ford said, "the central character, the motivation for the whole thing." Ringo, Wyatt Earp, and Ethan Edwards never lost sight of the horizon, and each was able to escape an enclosing, repressive society, avoiding what

Into the sunset: frame enlargement from the last shot of **The Searchers,** *an appropriate farewell for Wayne, Ford, and the genre itself.* (Private Collection)

Doc Boone had termed "the blessings of civilization." No such option was available to Tom Doniphon, however. His killing of Valance, which he himself describes as "cold-blooded murder," is finally an act of self-destruction. As surely as he eliminates Valance and saves Stoddard, he is committing himself to a life of isolated uselessness.

The ideal union of Westerner and Woman in the family, the one social institution revered by all of Ford's essentially antisocial heroes, has regressed from a reality (Ringo and Dallas) to a promise (Wyatt and Clementine) to an untenable situation (Ethan and Martha) to an outright impossibility (Tom and Hallie). With the steady enclosure of the genre's visual and thematic horizons, the hero's options are reduced to one single, inexorable reality: Doniphon does not ride off into the sunset or across Monument Valley, but into the Valley of Death.

With Tom Doniphon's death, Ford bids farewell to the Westerner and his heroic code. *The Man Who Shot Liberty Valance* is a fitting epitaph. It traces the death of that code and the basis for its mythic legacy. Some critics have noted the similarities in story and character between this film and *My Darling Clementine*, but the evolution of Ford's perspective and the genre's changing thematic emphases render the differences of those films more significant than their similarities. Time has turned Ford's—and the genre's—initial optimism into a mixture of cynicism and regret. Stoddard's glad-handing politician and Hallie's overwhelming nostalgia are the only elements remaining of the genre's faded utopian vision.

No filmmaker understood or articulated that vision with the style, sensitivity, and consistent quality of John Ford, and although the Western genre survives him it will be forever in his debt. Not only was Ford the best of Hollywood's Western storytellers, but he brought to that story a depth and complexity that place his Westerns among the most significant films of the American cinema.

The
Gangster Film

"The purpose of this film is to depict an environment, rather than glorify the criminal."

—Preface to The Public Enemy

"There's only one law: Do it first, do it yourself, and keep on doing it."

—Tony Camonte (Paul Muni) in Scarface

"Mother of Mercy, is this the end of Rico?"

—Dying words of Rico Bandello (Edward G. Robinson) in Little Caesar

The classic gangster films

The gangster genre has had a peculiar history. The narrative formula seemed to spring from nowhere in the early 1930s, when its conventions were isolated and refined in a series of immensely popular films. The three most successful were *Little Caesar* (produced by Warner Brothers and directed by Mervyn LeRoy in 1930), *The Public Enemy* (produced by Warner Brothers and

81

directed by William Wellman in 1931), and *Scarface* (produced by Howard Hughes and directed by Howard Hawks in 1932). Because of their overt celebration of the gangster-hero and their less-than-flattering portrayal of contemporary urban life, these films were as controversial as they were popular, and threats of censorship, boycott, and federal regulation forced the studios to restructure the gangster formula by the mid-'30s. Consequently, the gangster film enjoyed possibly the briefest classic period of any Hollywood genre. Its evolution was severely disrupted by external social forces, and its narrative formula was splintered into various derivative strains.

Although many of these strains have survived into the 1970s—the syndicate film, the caper film, the cop film, and so on—we are going to concentrate on those classic gangster films of the 1930s and their more immediate descendants. Urban criminals undoubtedly will remain a significant and marketable subject for feature filmmaking as long as our cities and the commercial cinema survive, but the prototype, that isolated, self-styled gangster best characterized by Cagney and Robinson, had all but disappeared from the screen by the early 1950s. Hollywood's postwar urban crime films will be discussed later; this chapter will concentrate on the gangster genre during its formative stages and as it evolved throughout the 1940s. We will focus upon Hollywood's development of the heroic, heavily stylized criminal sagas from the early 1930s through postwar throwbacks like John Huston's *Key Largo* (1948) and Raoul Walsh's *White Heat* (1949).

The gangster-hero and the urban milieu

Unlike the Westerner and the hardboiled detective, who were adapted to the screen from popular literary genres, the screen gangster was lifted directly from the current newspaper headlines. The accuracy of screen portrayals of figures like Al Capone, Bugsy Siegel, and Hymie Weiss rarely went deeper than the headlines. Hollywood exploited the notoriety and social significance of their real-world counterparts while it adjusted their character and environment to the peculiar demands of Hollywood narrativity. The romanticization of the gangster-hero and the stylization of his "underworld" milieu render the genre's connections with reality rather tenuous and complex. In fact, the '30s-based screen gangster and his dark, impressionistic world were all but dead by the late '40s. By then Hollywood's concern for organized crime and its preference for location shooting and urban realism had displaced the gangster biographies that dominated Depression-era crime films. As Hollywood's characterization of the criminal was taken out of the controlled studio environment and away from performers like Cagney, Robinson, and Bogart, the genre underwent a radical revision of its own mythology.

The mythology of the classic gangster film, like that of the Western, concerns the transformation of nature into culture under the auspices of modern civilization. The nature/culture opposition which plays so obvious and important a role in the Western is equally vital but considerably less obvious in the gangster

***The world of the gangster: what Warshow called "the dangerous and sad city of the imagination" is shown in this shot from the gang-war montage in Howard Hawks'
Scarface (1932).*** (Wisconsin Center for Film and Theater Research)

genre. Nature in the gangster film is conspicuous primarily in its absence—or rather in the ways it is repressed in the "social animal" who is the genre's focal character. The oncoming civilization which the Westerner had fled has now arrived with a vengeance, and the gangster has little choice but to accommodate his primitive and civilized impulses to that environment. There is no limitless horizon, no sunset in the distance for the urban renegade.

The gangster's milieu is the modern city, generally seen at night, with its enclosing walls of concrete and shadow, its rain-soaked streets, and its careening black automobiles. The gangster's setting, like that of the Westerner, is one of contested space where forces of social order and anarchy are locked in an epic and unending struggle. But whereas the Western depicts the initial and tremendous struggle to establish social order, the gangster film deals with an organized society's efforts to maintain that order. The urban environment is not merely an ideological frame of reference to be accepted or rejected by the hero as it is for the stoic, detached Westerner; instead, the city represents a complex, alienating, and overwhelming community that initially creates the gangster and eventually destroys him.

Robert Warshow, in his illuminating essay, "The Gangster as Tragic Hero," views the genre's milieu as a surreal extension of the gangster's own psyche. "The gangster is the man of the city," writes Warshow. "He must inhabit it in order to personify it: not the real city, but the dangerous and sad city of the imagination which is so much more important, which is the modern world." Not only is this city an extension of the gangster's imagination, but of the viewer's as well. In Warshow's terms, "The real city, one might say, produces only criminals; the imaginary city produces the gangster: he is what we want to be and are afraid we might become"[1] (Warshow, 1962, p. 131). Or in the words of Johnny Rocco (Edward G. Robinson) in *Key Largo:* "There are thousands of guys with guns—but there's only one Rocco." As both Warshow and Robinson/Rocco suggest, Hollywood places the urban criminal in the realm of American mythology. He is depicted with imaginative, stylized intensity and in heroic proportions that far remove him from the real-world criminal on which his character is based.

So although Rico ("Little Caesar") Bandello, Tommy ("Public Enemy") Powers, and Tony ("Scarface") Camonte were modeled after notorious men of that era—Rico and Tony supposedly after Al Capone, and Tommy Powers after Hymie Weiss—their screen portrayals bore little resemblance to the actual criminals. (In fact, many critics have argued that just the reverse is true, that "real" criminals tended to adjust their dress and demeanor so that they might resemble their depiction in the movies.)

In retrospect, it seems logical that Hollywood's characterization of the urban hero, whether as gangster or as cop, would undergo a substantial change during the 1930s. America's gradual shift from a primarily rural-agricultural to an urban-industrial nation, compounded by the Depression, Prohibition, and the other vagaries of city life, generated considerable cultural confusion and caused an extensive reexamination of our traditional value system. The urban lone wolf's brutality and antisocial attitudes in Hollywood films are simply components of an essentially positive cultural model—that of the personable and aggressive but somewhat misguided self-made American man. It's important to note in this regard that the depiction of Cagney as gangster in *The Public Enemy* is basically indistinguishable from that of Cagney as government agent in *G-Men* and other mid-'30s crime films. He may be advocating a different value system in each role, but his self-assured swagger, caustic disposition, and violent demeanor are basic to each.

There are notable precursors to the '30s gangster films. As early as D. W. Griffith's *Musketeers of Pig Alley* in 1912, urban-based crime provided an engaging dramatic subject. By the late 1920s, silent melodramas had begun to isolate certain narrative and stylistic devices which would work their way into the gangster films a few years later. Two of the more significant films of this period were *The Racket* (1927) and *Underworld* (1928). The latter film, directed by Josef von Sternberg for

Paramount, is a truly remarkable precursor of the gangster film which examines and dramatizes organized crime within a sordid, shadowy urban milieu. Like the silent Western epics of the 1920s, *Underworld* appears rather rudimentary because of its lack of sound effects and dialogue, as well as its dependence upon the conventions of silent melodrama.

Warner Brothers' conversion to sound movies in the late 1920s, coincidental with America's desperate social and economic climate, proved to be the catalyst in the evolution of the gangster film. Warners had generated the sound prototype for the musical (*The Jazz Singer*, 1927) and the next year provided the first sound gangster film (*The Lights of New York*, 1928). The studio dominated production in both genres for years. *The Lights of New York* is an eminently forgettable film except for one aspect: it demonstrated that sound effects and dialogue greatly heightened the impact of urban crime dramas. As later films would confirm, synchronous sound affected both the visual and editing strategies of gangster movies. The new audio effects (gunshots, screams, screeching tires, etc.) encouraged filmmakers to focus upon action and urban violence, and also to develop a fast-paced narrative and editing style. This style is most effective in those classic gangster films of the early 1930s, before the Production Code forced the genre into premature refinement.

The classic screen gangster represents the perverse alter ego of the ambitious, profit-minded American male. His urban environment, with its institutionalized alienation and class distinction, has denied him a legitimate route to power and success, so he uses the depersonalizing milieu and its technology—guns, cars, phones, etc.—to plunder its wealth. But somehow the massive, unthinking city, that concrete embodiment of civilization and urban order, is more powerful than either the self-reliant criminal or the generally inept police who pursue him. The ultimate conflict of the gangster film is not between the gangster and his environment nor is it between the gangster and the police; rather, it involves the contradictory impulses within the gangster himself. This internal conflict—between individual accomplishment and the common good, between man's self-serving and communal instincts, between his savagery and his rational morality—is mirrored in society, but the opposing impulses have reached a delicate and viable balance within the modern city. The gangster's efforts to realign that balance to suit his own particular needs are therefore destined to failure.

So the civilization which the Westerner held at bay now overwhelms the gangster-hero; the cowboy's distant fears have become the gangster's daily *angst*. The very buildings in which the gangster hides, the cars that he uses for murder and escape, the clothes, guns, phones, and other tools of his trade—all are emblems of a social order which eventually must destroy him. And these emblems create a system of iconographic components which assume a special significance in the narrative. Thus the gangster's urban milieu serves a dual function. On the one hand, it is a dark and often surreal arena of physical action and violence and serves as an expressive extension of the gangster's own sensibilities. But on the other, it represents the forces of progress and social destiny which the gangster cannot hope to conquer. The intangible forces of social order and civilization which have created the modern city certainly will crush a single anarchic malcontent.

The gangster prototypes: *Little Caesar* and *The Public Enemy*

The gangster's propensity for asserting his individual will through violent action and self-styled profiteering renders him an ideal screen persona. The fact that his assertiveness flaunts social order even heightens his individuality. He is surrounded by dull-witted underlings and pursued by inept police in a confused moral climate that allows him ample opportunity, in Warshow's words, "to assert himself as an individual, to draw himself out of the crowd"[2] (Warshow, 1962, p. 133).

One of the remarkable aspects of these early gangster films is their tendency to establish the hero's aggression and willful violence as a given, with little thought to the social conditions which nurture those impulses. For Rico Bandello in *Little Caesar*, for example, it seems only natural to graduate from robbing rural gas stations to big-time city crime. *Little Caesar* opens with Rico and his initiate-partner

Edward G. Robinson's portrayal of Rico "Little Caesar" Bandello established the type: ruthless, resourceful, ambitious, and ultimately self-destructive. (Museum of Modern Art/Film Stills Archive)

(Douglas Fairbanks, Jr., as Joe Massara) just having held up a gas station outside of Chicago. They hear about "Diamond Pete" Montana's criminal exploits in the city and decide to grab their own piece of the action. Rico and Massara arrive in the city, and Rico ruthlessly murders his way to mobster status, eventually displacing Montana as the city's gangster chieftain. Director LeRoy traces his precipitous rise to wealth and power in a fast-paced, episodic narrative style with occasional peaks of violent action. There is little time for reflection—on the part of the characters or the audience.

The only character capable of self-examination is Joe Massara, who eventually decides to desert Rico and go straight. Massara's change of heart is motivated, predictably enough, by the love of a good woman—a rare commodity in the gangster genre where women invariably are depicted as sexual ornaments, mere emblems of the gangster's socioeconomic status. Massara and his lover-domesticator become a professional song-and-dance team (jumping from one Warner Brothers formula to another), and agree to turn state's evidence against Joe's former mentor. Rico learns of their betrayal, and his inability to execute Massara adds an interesting twist to the gangster's otherwise murderous mentality. Ironically, his plan for vengeance leads to his own death. Rico's dying epithet—"Mother of Mercy, is this the end of Rico?"—reflects our own disbelief that this heroic, willful, urban demigod ever could be destroyed.

The number of gangster films generated by *Little Caesar*'s popular success indicates that Rico Bandello's end was just the beginning of the screen persona he helped to establish. Rico's irrational brutality, his disdain for law and order, and his enterprising business mentality are presented as inherent elements of his criminal nature. Later gangster films would attempt, even if only half-heartedly, to provide some motivational basis for that criminality.

At one point in *The Public Enemy*, for example, in an exchange between Tommy Powers and his girlfriend (Jimmy Cagney and Jean Harlow), the girl tells him: "You *are* different, Tommy, and it's a matter of basic character. . . . You don't give, you take. Oh, Tommy, I could love you to death." While this reaffirms the hero's criminality (and indicates it is sufficiently appealing to win the affection of Jean Harlow), the film does attempt to account for Powers' violent and antisocial behavior. *The Public Enemy* opens with documentary-style footage of inner-city tenements and the Depression poor who inhabit them. Once we are introduced to the principal characters—as children, significantly—and to their interpersonal and ideological conflicts, this documentary style is abandoned for a more impressionistic, visually expressive technique. Tommy is first depicted as a young boy stealing a girl's skates and is beaten by his insensitive father when his older brother decides to snitch on him.

In the first of many powerful visual sequences in the film, we see Tommy in a low-angle shot being led away from the camera down a shadowed hallway by his father, who takes him into a room and beats him with a strap. The actual beating takes place off-camera but is set up in such a way that the viewer's imagination makes the scene worse than it would be if actually filmed. The horror is accentuated, of course, by the use of off-screen sound—Tommy's cries and the sounds of the strap striking him. Wellman establishes the fundamental brutality of Tommy Powers and his community with this scene and at the same time generates sympathy for the main character. He also suggests that Tommy's criminality may be traced back into his childhood. The fact that his brother matures into a dull but well-meaning war hero and streetcar conductor prevents us from interpreting Tommy's antisocial behavior as a function of his environment, but we are never told the reasons for the brothers' contradictory values and attitudes.

The Public Enemy employs a fast-moving, elliptical, episodic story line that pinpoints the gangster-hero at various high points in his ill-fated career. One of the interesting distinctions between Tommy Powers and his counterparts in *Little Caesar* and *Scarface*, however, is that here the gangster's criminality is not a path to power and wealth. It is essentially an end in itself. Cagney's character, Tommy, is brutal, reckless, and unwavering in his perverse devotion to anarchy, to his gang, and to his family—especially his mother (Beryl Mercer) and his sidekick, Matt Doyle (Edward Woods). Wellman traces Tommy and Matt's progression from petty street hoods to saloon toughs to well-skilled criminals with one binding thread: the cohesion of the gangster-family.

Powers' commitment to Matt and his criminal lifestyle is juxtaposed with his devotion to his widowed mother, and these dualities frame the film's climax and resolution. Matt eventually falls in love, reaffirming the values we associate with Tommy's mother, but he is killed in an ambush meant for Tommy who vows revenge. He challenges the rival gang responsible for Matt's death, and we know this is virtually an act of suicide. With the camera viewpoint outside the rival gang's lair, Powers enters alone, exchanges gunfire off-screen, and then stumbles back into the street (and back on camera), muttering, "I ain't so tough," and falling into the gutter.

Later from his hospital bed, Tommy shows signs of remorse and reform, but clearly it's too late for him. The film's closing sequence takes place in the Powers' home, where Tommy's mother and brother anxiously await his return after learning he's been kidnapped from the hospital by the rival gang. The film closes with one of the most striking images in any gangster film: We hear a knock at the door and see Mom looking up from the bed she is preparing for her son's convalescence. Then Wellman cuts to a low-angle shot from inside the front door. The door opens and the gangster-hero, swaddled in bloodstained sheets, stares blankly beyond the camera and stands rigid for a moment before he topples directly toward the viewer. Tommy's tragic demise emerges as an indictment not only of the urban criminal, but also of the urban society that created and destroyed him. Thus *The Public Enemy* represents a considerable achievement for its director, who effectively exploited the audience's ambiguous regard for the sympathetic yet murderous public enemy.

If the gangster is to be considered a tragic figure, as he is by Warshow and others, then what is his "tragic flaw"? Fundamentally, it is his inability to channel his considerable individual energies in a viable direction. Society is partially re-

Tommy Powers (James Cagney) looks on helplessly as his partner (Edward Woods) is assassinated by rival gangsters in The Public Enemy (1931). (Wisconsin Center for Film and Theater Research)

sponsible, of course, in that it denies individual expression and provides minimal options to the struggling, aggressive male from an inner-city, working-class background. The only options to a life of crime—or so these films would seem to assert—are the police force, the priesthood, or the city transit company. The audience is attracted to the gangster, in fact, because he is a dynamic, self-reliant individual applying himself in the only profitable and engaging occupation available. For a brief time, at least, the gangster is on top of his own pathetically limited world.

Because of his fierce drive to express his individuality and to achieve personal success, the gangster-hero is often at odds not only with society and its institutions (the judiciary, the police force, the banks) but with other criminal organizations as well. The classic Hollywood gangster may be devoted to an immediate gang-family, as is Tommy Powers, but he is certainly not a scion of organized crime. Anarchy runs deep within his character, and he resents conforming to any organization, regardless of its ideological persuasion. The gangster's self-sufficiency makes him a middle-man, like the Westerner—it pits him against both police and rival gangs. Unlike the heroes of Monument Valley, however, the gangster is not totally sympathetic. His role is ambiguous only from his own amoral, utterly pragmatic perspective; we in the audience realize that the hero's misdirected efforts ensure only temporary success and doom him to eventual failure and death.

Like the obligatory gunfight which resolves the Western's conflicts, the death of the movie gangster is an essential generic formality. As Colin McArthur has observed, "That the gangster must ultimately lie dead in the streets became perhaps the most rigid convention to the genre"[3] (McArthur, 1972, p. 55). On a superficial narrative level, the gangster's death serves to enhance the genre's celebration of social order and sense of community morality. We must acknowledge, however, that this endorsement of social order is qualified throughout the story by the importance of the gangster's willful self-assertion. It also is tempered by the fact that his very death is the consummate reaffirmation of his own identity.

Stephen Karpf addresses these ambiguities in his analysis of the classic gangster films, suggesting that, "Even with Rico's death it cannot in fact be said that the film taught a moral lesson. Rico was in many respects an admirable person. He bettered himself in the only way he understood. There was never [any] indication that the more socially acceptable characters and their way of life were preferable to Rico and the road he had chosen. The point is made even more graphically in *The Public Enemy* when individuals on the right side of the law are shown to be either boring or hypocritical. Rico's death is in a great measure gratuitous, a kind of sacrifice to an external code, enforced from outside the construct of the film"[4] (Karpf, 1973, pp. 59–60).

While Karpf seems to be building a case for LeRoy, Wellman, and other directors bowing to the pressures of industry censorship, we should keep in mind that the Production Code as such was not enforced until approximately three years after the release of these films. If there is any operative "code" in these movies, it is Hollywood's implicit code of social order, which governed the resolution in virtually all of its classic genre films. This gangster's death may honor an artificial, gratuitous code, but no more so than the romantic embrace which resolves the musical comedy, or the gunfight which resolves the Western. In fact, these classic gangster sagas maintain a narrative balance between the hero's individuality and the need for social order as effectively as any of Hollywood's countless genre films, despite their overtly prosocial "message" and predictable execution of the hero at film's end.

The consummate gangster saga: Howard Hawks' *Scarface*

If any of the early gangster films seemed intent upon upsetting that balance, it was Howard Hawks' brilliant but disturbing *Scarface*, whose characterization of the gangster and his milieu created a nightmarish vision of urban malaise that could not be offset by the hero's eventual death in the gutter. Paul Muni's portrayal of the maniacal, tragicomic "Scarface" Camonte, accentuated by Hawks' direction and narrative pacing, depicts with sustained wit and intensity one gangster-hero's precipitous rise and fall. Hawks establishes the film's surreal landscape and its code of irrational brutality in the very opening sequence. A mob leader is executed while attending a lavish party in his honor, and the assassination generates a gang war for control of the city. The war enables the aggressive Camonte to rise through the ranks and eventually displace his own criminal mentor as the city's chief gangster. Unlike the savvy thugs portrayed by Cagney and Robinson in earlier films, Muni's "Scarface" is not clearly superior in courage and intelligence to his rivals or his own henchmen. In fact, his rise to power seems somewhat arbitrary, due primarily to the fact that Camonte was among the first gangsters in the city to procure a machine gun, that new innovation in the technology of urban warfare.

Perhaps what so disturbed audiences about *Scarface* was Muni's characterization of the less-than-heroic gangster-hero. Rico and Powers' obvious superiority to their colleagues and their environment—i.e., their participation in the myth of the self-made American man—served to temper their criminality. But Tony Camonte's primitive brutality, simple-minded naiveté, and sexual confusion made him a figure with little charisma and with virtually no redeeming qualities. Most of the film centers upon Tony's devotion to his mother and his insane overprotection of his sister (Ann Dvorak). Eventually, Tony's sister and his partner (George Raft

The most intense and disturbing portrayal of the American gangster was Paul Muni's Tony Camonte in Scarface *(1932). Here, Camonte (right) defies local police as his sidekick, Little Boy (George Raft), looks on.* (Wisconsin Center for Film and Theater Research)

as "Little Boy," a role which established Raft's persona as a subdued, coin-flipping hoodlum) fall in love, and Tony responds with rage. He murders Little Boy when he discovers that the couple are sharing an apartment, and learns too late that they were actually married.

Little Boy's death precipitates Camonte's fall from criminal grace. Not only has Tony eliminated his own spiritual guide and chief strategist, but brought his obsessive desire for his sister out into the open. Appropriately, Tony and his sister die together in a barrage of police gunfire. They are both resigned to their inevitable demise by this point—in fact, Tony has devolved by film's end into a virtual human ape. After his sister is shot and killed, Tony runs wildly into the street in a final suicidal expression of his individual identity, thus providing the requisite death-in-the-gutter finale.

The gangster and the audience

Tony's moral/mortal retribution in the final moments of the film doesn't begin to offset the disturbing intensity and antisocial nature of his character. Outraged citizens, special interest groups (especially the Catholic Church), and even the federal government felt that this film was worthy of censorship. Unlike Rico's dying appeal to the "Mother of Mercy" and Powers' remorse from his hospital bed, Camonte expresses no regret either for his criminal career or his impending death. There is no indication at the end of the film that he has seen the error of his ways.

Like the earlier gangster biographies, *Scarface* incorporated a written prologue that stated its prosocial intentions. *Little Caesar* had opened with a biblical reference: "He who lives by the sword shall perish by the sword"; *The Public Enemy* insisted that its aim was "to depict an environment, rather than glorify the criminal." *Scarface* opens with the assertion that the film is an "indictment" of the social conditions that produce criminal types, and it asks the viewer, "What are you going to do about it?" This prosocial posturing was lost on the audience, though, as was the sequence that was subsequently inserted because the producers felt the film was still too overtly anarchic for the public's sensibilities.

In this added sequence, a group of well-meaning bureaucrats decry the evils of crime and injustice. One of the establishment figures actually speaks directly into the camera about the evils of crime and social disorder. In a similar sequence later in the film, a dogmatic outspoken cop offers this response to a colleague who suggests that Camonte is a "colorful character":

> What color is a crawling louse? Say, listen, that's the attitude of too many morons in this country. They think these big hoodlums are some sort of demigods. What do they do about a guy like Camonte? Sentimentalize him. Romance. Make jokes about him. They had some excuse for glorifying our old Western badmen. They met in the middle of the street at high noon, waited for each other to draw. But these things sneak up and shoot someone in the back and then run away.

These scenes are so out of character with the rest of the film that they now seem almost comical, and in a sense they further legitimatize Camonte's antisocial disposition. Moreover, the failure of this and other disclaimers to undercut the gangster-hero's appeal is a good indication of the rhetorical power of Hollywood's narrative codes: camerawork, editing, dialogue, characterization, and even the star system work together to engage our sympathy for the criminal. So from a technical (as well as a thematic) standpoint, the gangster-hero functions as an *organizing sensibility* in these films, serving to offset the other characters' naive moralizing and to control our perception of his corrupt, Kafkaesque milieu.

Beyond the fact that we will rally behind the gangster's perverted dedication to the American ideals of rugged individualism, capitalism, and upward mobility, we also sympathize with the trace of humanism that invariably leads to his downfall. In each of the films we've been discussing, the gangster's demise is not caused by his criminality nor by the efforts of the police; instead, his death results from his own inability to sustain his code of anarchic ruthlessness. Adherence to Tony Camonte's dictum—"Do it first, do it yourself, and keep on doing it" (which might just as easily be Dale Carnegie's)—enables the gangster to progress smoothly through his life of crime. Only when he violates this code of brutal self-reliance does he fall.

His violation invariably is generated by a commitment to the gang-family. Camonte in *Scarface* is maniacally protective of his sister and kills his partner for robbing her of her virtue; Rico in *Little Caesar* cannot bring himself to kill his former partner who is about to turn state's evidence; Tommy Powers in *The Public Enemy* is killed trying to avenge the murder of his childhood friend and partner against impossible odds. In each instance the willful individualist compromises his virtuous selfishness and unwittingly seals his own fate. Thus the gangster finally is victimized by his own inability to escape the influence of mother, home, and culture. After all, even the most hard-bitten hoodlum loves his mother; even the most animalistic criminal is in some ways human.

The gangster's humanity is perverted by social forces which have confused his moral perspective, however, giving "human nature" itself a rather ambiguous twist within the gangster's peculiar ideology. Each of the classic gangsters displays a deep devotion to family that is projected onto their sidekicks (Joe Massara in *Little Caesar*, Matt Doyle in *The Public Enemy*, and Little Boy in *Scarface*). The sidekicks are presented at the outset of the films as initiate-heroes but, like their counterparts in many Westerns, they eventually reject the gangster-hero for the more traditional values of marriage, home, and family. Rejection by his junior partner leads directly to the hero's death in these films, indicating that his gangster-family cannot displace society's traditional family structure.

The gangster's confused sexuality is underscored not only by his devotion to— and often his jealousy of—his partner, but also by the way he treats women. Whereas the gangster inevitably is devoted to his mother, he treats all other women as mere emblems of his criminal lifestyle. They are like the clothes, automobiles, jewelry, and other ornaments of his profession. Any efforts by a woman

Awaiting the final shootout: with everyone except his sister either dead or having deserted him, Scarface Camonte is about to "get his." But critics and authorities wondered whether his death at the film's end sufficiently offset the romanticized portrayal of the gangster-hero. (Wisconsin Center for Film and Theater Research)

to domesticate him are spurned, a convention which is graphically displayed in *The Public Enemy*, when one of Tommy's girlfriends (Mae Clarke) nags him at the breakfast table and is rewarded with a grapefruit in the face.

The gangster's latent humanism, then, extends only as far as his own gangster-family and ultimately serves an ironic, paradoxical narrative function: It enhances the gangster's heroic appeal, but it also ensures his destruction. Most significantly, it subverts the apparent moral and social messages that these classic gangster films superficially project. The notion that "crime doesn't pay" is continually qualified by the suggestion that the criminal, regardless of social class, education, or opportunity, can control his own destiny in an otherwise alienating, depersonalizing environment. Destiny may kill him, but the intensity of the hero's commitment to his fate indicates that power and individuality are more important than a long life.

The popularity of these early films did little to sway the variety of governmental, educational, religious, and other special interest groups who felt that they were providing unwholesome role models for impressionable viewers. In fact, the volume of their outcry was roughly proportional to the popularity of the films in question. By the time *Scarface* was released in 1932, it was evident that the Hollywood studios and the previously ineffectual MPPDA (Motion Picture Producers and Distributors of America) somehow would have to accommodate the growing public concern over the effects of gangster films on the society at large. The studios' collective decision to abide by their own Motion Picture Production Code, largely ignored since it had been established in 1930, seemed by 1934 to be the only way to avoid either massive boycotts or, worse still, federal intervention and censorship.

END

The production code and the death of the classic gangster

1. No picture shall be produced which will lower the moral standards of those who see it. Hence the sympathy of the audience shall never be thrown to the side of crime, wrongdoing, evil, or sin.

2. Correct standards of life, subject only to the requirements of drama and entertainment, shall be presented.

3. Law, natural or human, shall not be ridiculed, nor shall sympathy be created for its violation.

—"General Principles" of the MPPDA's Production Code[5]

These moral guidelines for Hollywood filmmaking were published in 1930, the same year as *Little Caesar* and before its many offspring were produced. It seems that most filmmakers ignored the General Principles and the Production Code. Or perhaps more appropriately, they simply took them for granted; Hollywood didn't have to publish a manifesto to assert that its genre films were mass-cultural morality tales. But even the prosocial messages—for example, that "crime doesn't pay"—could be undercut or severely qualified via narrative strategy and the style of cinematic presentation.

As Part One of this book suggests, the ambiguity of the gangster film's or of any other Hollywood genre's value system is virtually built into its narrative formula. In the early years, this ambiguity was realized and exploited only by the more talented and sensitive filmmakers, but it is ultimately this ambiguity and its accompanying narrative complexity that rendered the formula flexible enough to work its way into the fabric of American culture. Despite the film industry's avowed efforts to support the status quo (as much from economic necessity as from moral commitment), filmmakers and audiences were cooperating in refining genres that examined the more contradictory tenets of American ideology. Hollywood studio heads may have consistently placated educators, religious leaders, government officials, and other civic watchdogs with cosmetic "self-regulation" of movie content.

But the popular film narratives that were reworked and refined into genres were not so simplistic in their treatment of social reality.

Patterns of industry censorship

The film industry's earliest efforts to stem the tide of public concern over objectionable subject matter led to the National Board of Censorship in 1908. This board proved to be an adequate industry-based means of regulation until the feature film emerged as the standard movie fare in the mid-teens. As the conventions of the Hollywood narrative were developed, particularly the conflict-to-resolution plot structure that enabled filmmakers to treat "immoral" codes of behavior condemned at film's end, our culture's moral guardians loudly objected. When state censorship was threatened, the studios countered in 1922 by forming the Motion Picture Producers and Distributors of America (MPPDA, which in 1945 became the Motion Picture Association of America, the MPAA). This organization was designed to reaffirm and strengthen the industry's policy of self-regulation.

The MPPDA was run by former Postmaster General Will H. Hays—and was termed the "Hays Office"; by 1924, it devised a "Formula" that governed the adaptation of novels and stageplays for the screen. This regulatory gesture had little impact on the industry, so in 1927 the Office came up with a slightly stronger list of "Don'ts and Be Carefuls"[6] (Steinberg, 1978, pp. 450–460). Like the earlier Formula, this list was composed of suggestions on the treatment of those areas of content deemed potentially objectionable: profanity, nudity, drug abuse, perversion, prostitution, interracial marriage and procreation, scenes of childbirth, sex hygiene, ridicule of religion or the clergy, and the "willful offense to any nation, race, or creed." (The range of moral issues in this brief list alone indicates the complexity of the nation's values and attitudes, although these contradictions clearly were ignored by the Association.) All of the above were off-limits to filmmakers "irrespective of the manner in which they are treated," whereas the subjects of crime, theft, firearms, brutality, rape, seduction, and law enforcement fell under a separate heading—"special care."

It was not until the "talkies" and the concurrent Jazz Age morality that the need to bolster the "be carefuls" became apparent to industry heads. In 1930 Martin Quigley and the Reverend Daniel Lord were commissioned to draft a more comprehensive and detailed code. Quigley, publisher of the *Motion Picture Herald*, and Lord, a Jesuit priest who had served as moral adviser on earlier productions, wrote the MPPDA's Production Code which, for a quarter of a century, set down the law for Hollywood movies.

The Code opens with a preamble in which its authors state the range and influence of the Hollywood cinema: "Though regarding motion pictures primarily as entertainment without any explicit purpose of teaching or propaganda, [motion picture producers] know that the motion picture within its own field of entertainment may be directly responsible for spiritual and moral progress, for higher types of social life, and for much correct thinking"[7] (Steinberg, 1978, p. 460). In a later portion of the document, "Reasons Supporting Preamble of Code," Quigley and Lord are even more direct in their correlation of the industry's Production Code with the country's moral code. Theatrical motion pictures, they assert, are both "entertainment" and "art," and as such carry certain "moral obligations."

Regarding film as entertainment, they write:

> Mankind has always recognized the importance of entertainment and its value in rebuilding the bodies and souls of human beings. But it has always recognized that entertainment can be of a character either HELPFUL or HARMFUL to the human race. . . . Hence the *Moral importance* of entertainment is something which has been universally recognized. . . . A man may be judged by his standard of entertainment as easily as by the standard of his work.

And regarding film as art:

> Though a new art, possibly a combination art, [the cinema] has the same object as the other arts, the presentation of human thought, emotion, and experience, in terms of an appeal to the soul through the senses. . . . Art can be morally good, lifting men to higher levels. This has been done through good music, great painting, authentic fiction, poetry, drama. Art can be morally evil in its effects. This is the case clearly enough with unclean art, indecent books, suggestive drama. The effect on the lives of men and women is obvious.

After outlining the various criteria which render commercial cinema the most widespread and influential of all forms of mass-cultural communication, Quigley and Lord offer the following summation: "In general, the mobility, popularity, accessibility, emotional appeal, vividness, straightforward presentation of fact in the film make for more intimate contact with a larger audience and for greater emotional appeal. Hence the larger moral responsibility of the motion pictures"[8] (Steinberg, 1978, pp. 464–467).

Unlike the previous "Formula" and the "Don'ts and Be Carefuls," the 1930 Production Code was initially designed as more than simply a litany of vague suggestions for filmmakers. The Code seems to have been used essentially as a public relations device but was not closely enforced during the early 1930s. This is evident not only in the gangster genre but also in other areas: in the titillating, suggestive Mae West comedies, in von Sternberg's direction of the sensuous (and often adulterous) Marlene Dietrich, and in the casual amorality of the upper-crust comedies such as Lubitsch's *Trouble in Paradise* and Cukor's *Dinner at Eight*. Even the musicals of the period reflected Hollywood's more liberal—or what Quigley and Lord would have considered more decadent—moral attitudes. *Gold Diggers of 1933*, for example, dealt with prostitution and hustling ("gold digging"), and even included a production number in which women were shot in nude silhouette.

Recasting the gangster

Hollywood's evolving sexual mores generated less public consternation than did its portrayals of criminals and their violent, antisocial lifestyles, however. The growing popularity of gangster films between 1930 and 1933 put increasing pressure on Hollywood and the MPPDA to enforce its Production Code. The most effective pressure came from the Catholic Church, whose Legion of Decency, formed in 1934, threatened Catholics with eternal damnation for viewing any movies that it "condemned." The Hollywood studios, anxious about losing the Catholic audience, decided to put some teeth into the existing Hays Code, and initiated the Production Code Administration (PCA) under Joseph Breen.

Not only did the PCA judge all films released, it also fined those studios which did not abide by its decisions. So the Hays Office became the Hays-Breen Office,

Recasting the gangster: rather than portray a gangster-hero whose criminality was a given element in his character, many post-1934 films centered upon impressionable youths forced to decide between criminality and going straight. In William Wyler's Dead End (1937), Joel McCrea's character is poised between law and order and the local hood (Humphrey Bogart). (Hoblitzelle Theatre Arts Collection)

and the gangster genre, along with a few others, underwent a substantial overhaul. As stipulated within the Production Code,

> The treatment of crimes against the law must not:
>
> 1. Teach methods of crime.
> 2. Inspire potential criminals with a desire for imitation.
> 3. Make criminals seem heroic or justified[9] (Steinberg, 1978, p. 469).

LeRoy, Wellman, Hawks, and the various other filmmakers involved in the gangster genre's classic (1930–1933) period certainly could have argued that their films were within the moral framework of the Production Code, especially since they honored its implicit demands of moral retribution. But the gangster-hero's position within the genre's narrative structure—i.e., as hero, as the organizing sensibility through whom we perceive the urban milieu—generated considerable sympathy for his behavior and attitude. These filmmakers were capable of stylizing the gangster's milieu to reflect his psyche (through lighting, composition, set design, camerawork, editing), thus casting the urban environment and its social institutions in a generally unfavorable light.

Once they displaced the gangster figure from the center of the narrative—either by doubling him with a more effective prosocial figure, by instilling in him some "redeeming" qualities, or simply by reducing him to a supporting role—both the urban crime story and its style of presentation changed considerably. When the gangster was no longer "organizing" his world and its events, Hollywood's portrayal of urban crime became less vividly impressionistic, less intense, and less ambiguous—although not necessarily less brutal or violent. When the gangster was no longer the hero of the urban crime film he became, quite simply, a hardened criminal.

Genre variations in the late 1930s

After 1933, the genre went into a period of diffusion and decline which extended throughout the decade, and only occasionally was it able to recapture the visual style, characterization, and narrative complexity of the classic gangster sagas. During the latter half of the decade, the genre was dominated by two watered-down variations: the gangster-as-cop variation (*G-Men, Bullets or Ballots, Public Enemy's Wife, Racket Busters*, etc.), in which Cagney, Robinson, and other former screen gangsters were recast as lawmen who were virtually carbon copies of the criminal characters; and the Cain-and-Abel variation (*Manhattan Melodrama, Dead End, Angels with Dirty Faces*, etc.), which counterbalanced the gangster with an equally strong (or perhaps stronger) prosocial figure. This latter variation was anticipated by *The Public Enemy*, in which Cagney's swaggering hoodlum was counterpointed by his straight-arrow brother. Cagney's thug utterly overwhelms his sibling, however. Thus the prosocial character functions in that film primarily as a foil for the gangster-hero. In the Cain-and-Abel variation, this opposition is more balanced, in that a more significant character was written (and generally a more prominent star was cast) as an "answer" to the gangster's criminal posture.

Manhattan Melodrama (1934) is among the earliest and most interesting of this gangster variation. It was directed by W. S. van Dyke for Metro-Goldwyn-Mayer and starred William Powell and Clark Gable as the "doubles." The film opens with a priest saving two boys (one of whom is played by Mickey Rooney) whose parents are killed in a steamship fire. The boys are raised by an immigrant Jew, and eventually become well known: Blackie (Gable) as a professional gambler and womanizer with underworld connections; Jim Wade (Powell) as the District Attorney who ultimately prosecutes Blackie and later, as governor, refuses to stay his execution in the electric chair. The doubling of the principal characters is enhanced by the story's love interest (Myrna Loy as Eleanor), whose initial infatuation with Blackie dissolves once she meets the conservative, dependable Jim Wade. "It's the latest style to be callous about home and family," she tells Blackie when she leaves him. Eleanor wants these traditional values and finds them in her relationship with Wade.

The film's closing sequences, certainly among the more bizarre in '30s crime films, show the final confrontation between the two "brothers." Jim Wade, now the governor, is anguishing over whether to commute Blackie's death sentence. His doubts are resolved by the grinning, wise-cracking Blackie, who tells him, "It's okay, Jim, I'm just no good." (A reprise of the film's title theme, "The Bad in Every Man," is played over this exchange of dialogue.) As the pair walk Blackie's "last mile" to the chair, the condemned criminal's reasoning becomes even more lucid: "As far as I'm concerned, you're the best friend I ever had. But above all, you're the governor." Through all this, Gable's captivating charm and irrepressible grin counter the heavy-handed dialogue, reinforcing its illogic and providing an almost surreal tone to the scene. In a brief epilogue following the execution, Jim Wade resigns as governor because of his association-brotherhood with Blackie and walks off into the unknown with Eleanor. In retrospect, Jim's fate is not altogether preferable to Blackie's, whose stylish demise underscores his individual appeal and finally makes him the more sympathetic character of the two.

This death-with-dignity motif is given an even more outrageous twist in *Angels with Dirty Faces* (Michael Curtiz, 1938), where Cagney's familiar gangster is doubled with Pat O'Brien, who is typecast as an inner-city priest. Both products of the same dingy, working-class environment, Cagney and O'Brien select opposing lifestyles that lead them both to death row, where O'Brien as prison chaplain convinces the condemned Cagney to pretend he is a coward to keep the local slum kids from idolizing him. The ever-heroic Cagney agrees to the deception and dies screaming and whining—something that would be totally out of character for both the star and his role were it not for the fact that we in the audience know the truth. Beyond the ambiguous dimension this lends to Cagney's character, there are other contradictions involved: for example, although the slum kids on the screen (actors in a movie) believe in Cagney's cowardice, the audience (real slum kids among the

In **Angels with Dirty Faces (***1938***), Cagney's gangster serves as a negative role model for the now-familiar Dead End Kids.** (Robert Downing Collection)

people in it) view his death as a final, heroic gesture. Once again, some fancy narrative footwork has masked the celebration of rugged, stoic individualism behind a thin veneer of prosocial posturing.

A less ambiguous and therefore less interesting variation of the gangster genre in the late 1930s was the gangster-as-cop formula, in which the hero retained his brutal, cynical style but was cast as an agent of social order. Such films featured a tough, self-reliant cop who operates by his own rules to fight crime, thus sustaining much of the heroic appeal of his gangster predecessor. In *G-Men* (1935), Cagney plays an attorney (Brick Davis) raised by a businessman with gangster ties. When an associate is killed by criminals, Brick rejects a career as a "shyster" to join the FBI. William Kighley's direction of this film, especially those segments describing the training programs and crime-fighting procedures of "the Bureau," employs a detached, documentary style. This naturalistic portrayal apparently was designed both to enhance the crime-fighters' rather than the criminals' appeal and to lobby for the use of firearms by FBI agents.

Throughout the film, Cagney/Brick is at odds with the criminal element as well as his own superior officers. The eventual showdown with the mobsters responsible for his friend's death is precipitated by the hero's own cocky, aggressive style of police work. Ultimately, this variation on the gangster formula proved noticeably lacking in dramatic conflict: an ambitious cop doing his job, no matter how single-mindedly, is much less engaging and complex than an ambitious gangster attacking society.

Related to the gangster-cop films was the middle-man variation, in which the hero is aligned with neither the prosocial nor the criminal forces, although he develops close ties with each. This kind of film generally involves an initiate-criminal's decision—motivated by the love of a good woman and/or the sudden recognition of the error of his ways—to go straight, thereby placing himself between the forces of crime and social order. Such a variation takes the supporting character from the classic gangster films (the subordinate partner of the gangster who eventually rejects crime for the values of hearth and home) and recasts him as the central character.

Perhaps Raoul Walsh's *The Roaring Twenties* (1939) is the most interesting example of this variation. The opening of the film is a seeming throwback to the classic gangster biographies of the early '30s, with Cagney portraying racketeer Eddie Bartlett (supposedly modeled after Larry Fay). Eventually, however, the film lapses into the middle-man motif, when Bartlett falls for a good woman (Priscilla Lane as Jean), whose refusal to marry him precipitates his fall from power. By the film's end Cagney has quit the rackets but cannot escape his criminal past, although he does redeem himself in a final selfless act: to save Jean's husband he executes a ruthless former henchman (played by Humphrey Bogart) who had taken over his chieftain role, and is then gunned down on the steps of a church, pursued by hostile gangsters and police alike. As Eddie lies dead, his former moll (Gladys George) evokes the fate of the classic gangster with the film's closing line: "He used to be a big shot."

This middle-man variation enabled filmmakers to celebrate the mediating hero's individual virtues and also to liberate him from a certain death. In the more effective films of this type—like *Johnny Apollo* (Henry Hathaway, 1940), *Dark City* (William Dieterle, 1950), and *Underworld USA* (Sam Fuller, 1961)—the protagonist's vacillation between a life of crime and an awakened social consciousness offsets the prescribed resolution of death and moral retribution. The hero may miraculously beat the rap and get the girl, as does Charlton Heston in *Dark City;* or he may be unable to completely sever his underworld ties. Cliff Robertson in *Underworld USA* embarks upon a criminal career that recalls Cagney's in *The Roaring Twenties*, and both films end similarly with the dying hero staggering down a crowded street. A freeze-frame close-up of Robertson's clenched fist, the final image in Fuller's remarkable film, is yet another graphic emblem of the gangster-hero's refusal, even in death, to succumb to the social forces that have created and destroyed him.

The bandit films of the early 1940s

After the 1930s, the "syndicate" variation of the urban gangster film displaced the more naive and romantic original: the classic lone wolf was evolving into an "organization man." Whereas this style of film presented a more accurate view of urban crime, its characters were scarcely as engaging as their classic counterparts. So by the early 1940s, the genre's narrative logic had evolved to a stage that precluded the success of the isolated gangster within his urban arena. This problem generated yet another variation of the gangster film—the "rural gangster" or "bandit" films. *The Petrified Forest* (1936) and Fritz Lang's *You Only Live Once* (1937) had anticipated this variation. These films cast the gangster-hero into a rural environment, thereby setting up oppositions between gangster and police and also between urban and rural values. In addition, the late-'30s regeneration of the Western genre seems to have contributed to this variation, especially in those films that center upon the Western outlaw.

In Henry King's *Jesse James* (1939), for instance, Jesse and Frank James (Tyrone Power and Henry Fonda) are virtuous country boys whose mother (Jane Darwell) is killed and their land stolen in a conspiracy of big business interests (i.e., the railroad, the banks, and local lawmen). After the film's opening title sequence, we read a preface that sees "The Iron Horse" as an "ogre" that violates the virginal landscape, thus placing both the West and its socializing forces in a context that seems more appropriate to the gangster genre than to the Western. After Jesse has been killed by a disloyal gang member, the local townspeople gather around his grave to celebrate the memory of a renegade hero who had opposed the interests of unenlightened capitalism. It's difficult to avoid associating this deification of Power's Western gangster with the classic gangsters from earlier films who also died fighting society's dehumanizing, fascistic impulses.

The contemporary rural bandit-hero, a virtual hybrid of the city gangster and the Western outlaw, emerged full-blown in 1941 with Raoul Walsh's *High Sierra*. This film takes Humphrey Bogart out of his supporting-role status and follows his character, Roy Earle, through the Sierra Nevada Mountains in his flight from the cops. In the process, Bogart establishes a star-crossed romance with Ida Lupino, learning too late the error of his ways and the transcendent value of human love.

The more effective films of this gangster variation—principally *High Sierra*, Nicholas Ray's *They Drive by Night*, Arthur Penn's *Bonnie and Clyde*, and Robert Altman's *Thieves Like Us*—created heroes of tragic proportions who reevaluated their past misdeeds but realized the inevitability of their fate. Such an ambivalent portrait of the hero and his changing values is a great deal more complex morally and socially than that of the late-'30s bandit precursors. In those films, the criminal was either utterly depraved (Bogart's Duke Mantee in *The Petrified Forest*) or completely sympathetic (Henry Fonda in *You Only Live Once*). The hero's transition in the more effective films from hardened, cynical gangster to humane, sensitive lover taxes the genre's demands of moral retribution. The tragic irony of the hero's certain death is intensified by his new capacity for romantic love, a radical reorientation of the gangster's perverse, misdirected sexuality. Critics of the gangster genre have long noted the hero's generally aberrant and repressed psychosexual identity. There were suggestions of Rico's homosexuality in *Little Caesar* and of an incestuous rapport between Tony and his sister in *Scarface*. The gangster's preoccupation with firearms, his inhuman brutality, and his mistreatment of any

The legendary Bonnie Parker and Clyde Barrow were given heavy treatment in the rural-bandit variation of the gangster genre—their story has been retold in some half-dozen Hollywood movies. Perhaps the most successful film about them was Arthur Penn's 1967 version, Bonnie and Clyde. (Pictured here, Faye Dunaway, Michael J. Pollard, and Warren Beatty.) (Private Collection)

woman outside his immediate family accentuated his apparent sexual confusion. Rural bandit films, however, seem to indicate that flight from urban decadence heals the gangster's antisocial and "unnatural" impulses, even if it cannot cure the more serious problems that will lead him, inevitably, to his death.

Key Largo and White Heat: The gangster's epitaph

There were city-bred gangsters, though, whose flight into the country met with less romantic ends. Certainly the most significant of these are Johnny Rocco (Edward G. Robinson in Key Largo, 1948) and Cody Jarrett (James Cagney in White Heat, 1949), whose characters seemed to be nostalgic reincarnations of Rico Bandello and Tommy Powers. In these later films, the gangster figures had to share the limelight with another screen persona popularized during the 1940s, the detective. Bogart's Sam Spade provided the prototype in John Huston's The Maltese Falcon, a film that struck an ideal balance in the characterization of the urban redeemer-hero who operates by his own instincts and moral code, divorced from both the city's criminal element and its ineffectual and usually corrupt prosocial agencies. This detective formula is significant not only because it represents a variation of the gangster/urban crime formula that dominated postwar filmmaking, but also because it provided a narrative context in which the classic gangster could effectively come back to the screen, even if for only a brief glimpse, in the late 1940s.

The classic gangster's intense but ill-fated return was most notable in another pair of films directed by John Huston and Raoul Walsh. These are Huston's *Key Largo*, which traces the return of a war hero (Bogart) to the States, where he falls in love with the widow (Lauren Bacall) of a dead war buddy and defends her from a fleeing gangster (Robinson); and Walsh's *White Heat*, in which an undercover detective (Edmund O'Brien) infiltrates a notorious bandit gang and brings their leader (Cagney) to justice. Ultimately, the detective story in each of these films merely provides a framework for briefly resurrecting the screen gangster, who would be returned to the grave at film's end. Although the detective figure prevails in each film, thus honoring the contract of moral retribution, neither gangster dies in the gutter: Bogie finishes off Robinson on a runaway fishing boat in the Atlantic Ocean, whereas Cagney is blown into oblivion when his exchange of gunfire with O'Brien ignites the huge gas tank on which Cagney is standing. Cagney/Jarrett's apocalyptic demise seems especially fitting for Hollywood's screen gangster, as his seething villainy rises in a towering mushroom cloud in the film's closing image.

The classic gangster's last hurrah: Edward G. Robinson as Johnny Rocco in **Key Largo** *(1948); James Cagney as Cody Jarrett in* **White Heat** *(1949).* (Wisconsin Center for Film and Theater Research); (Culver Pictures)

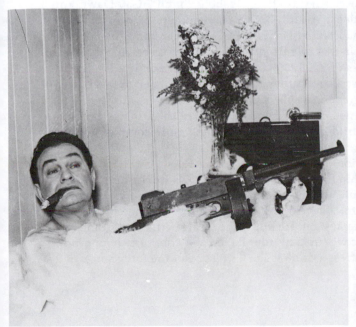 

Although Robinson/Rocco's death in *Key Largo* is somewhat less dramatic, the actor's portrayal of the aging anarchist who the criminal world has all but forgotten is evocative and disturbing. Robinson's Johnny Rocco is a mobster who has been deported as an "unfriendly alien" and terrorizes a remote Florida resort while he waits for the chance to pull off a grandiose "job" that will return him to kingpin status. His opposition with war hero/lover/detective Frank McLoud (Bogart) presents a fascinating example of how stars and genres themselves evolve and intermingle. *Key Largo* is a hybrid of the '30s gangster film (dominated by Robinson) and the '40s detective film (dominated by Bogart), and one of its more interesting aspects is the way Huston orchestrates their interaction. Bogart and Robinson alternately dominate the narrative until their final confrontation. In various stages of the film, we recall other film situations: Robinson's role in *Little Caesar*, the Robinson-Bogart pairing in late-'30s gangster films where Bogart invariably played henchman to Robinson's star persona (*Bullets or Ballots, Kid Galahad, The Roaring Twenties, Brother Orchid*), Bogart's graduation to leading-man roles in the early 1940s (*High Sierra, The Maltese Falcon, Casablanca*), and his successful pairing with Bacall in the mid-'40s (*To Have and Have Not, The Big Sleep, Dark Passage*).

Key Largo's narrative is framed by a romantic melodrama featuring Bogart and Bacall. The core of the film, however, is Robinson's characterization of Rocco and his reunion with Bogart's McLoud—a reunion that sees their previous film roles reversed. When Bogart/McLoud arrives at the island resort in the opening sequence, Robinson/Rocco is hiding out, off-screen, and the plot at this point concerns itself with the Bogart-Bacall relationship (their box-office clout had been enhanced by their marriage a year earlier). Once the couple is firmly established, Robinson/Rocco emerges from an upstairs suite and immediately assumes control of the film.

Robinson's performance as the aging, decadent gangster is impeccable, as is Claire Trevor's portrayal of Rocco's hard-bitten, alcoholic "moll," Gay Dawn, for which the actress won an Academy Award. Bogart plays something of a reluctant hero in this conflict, a man exhausted by his wartime heroics, and thus he remains a peripheral figure. Ironically, in this role Bogart reverses the screen role that first drew attention to him in *Petrified Forest* (1936). In it he played Duke Mantee, a brutal outlaw whose gang terrorizes a small group of people, including two lovers, in a remote locale. Now, in *Key Largo*, Bogart plays the victimized lover who is himself terrorized—and in what becomes typical of the "minor" roles in many gangster films after the mid-'30s, the intruding gangster is by far the more complex and interesting figure.

Throughout the middle section of *Key Largo*, Robinson/Rocco is the focal character and controlling force within the narrative. Huston allows Robinson considerable range in his characterization, and the actor retains just enough sadistic brutality to prevent the audience from developing a sentimental attachment to him. Rocco verbally abuses everyone in sight. He dupes the local sheriff into killing two rebellious citizens in order to cover up a murder he himself committed; he promises his pathetic, despoiled mistress a drink if she'll sing one of the torch songs that once made her the toast of the underworld, and then refuses her the drink once she has humiliated herself.

Perhaps the most effective and illuminating scene is the shaving sequence, where Rocco (framed in low-angle medium-close-up) reminisces about his lost power and prestige while one of his lackeys dutifully shaves him. Robinson articulates the gangster persona and his fall from grace in striking terms, pontificating on the pragmatics of street crime and reaffirming his own privileged role within the criminal constellation. "There are thousands of guys with guns," he brags, "but only one Rocco."

The narrative conflicts are resolved when a squall hits the resort, upsetting the gangster's operation and forcing Rocco's gang to flee the Keys in a fishing boat. Bogart/McLoud is forced to pilot the boat and kills all the henchmen while Robinson/Rocco remains below, setting the scene for a climactic confrontation. Whereas the hero's execution of the inhuman criminal is very much in keeping with Bogart's virile detective-redeemer role, the shootout is a distinct inversion of the Robinson-Bogart pairings in earlier gangster films. *Key Largo*'s showdown situates Bogart/McLoud topside, looming above a hatchway until Robinson/Rocco emerges from below. Huston films the sequence in an enchange of point-of-view shots so that we view the hero from below framed by the hatchway and then view the villain-victim from above, entrapped within the bowels of the boat and pleading for his life. The Bogart character is well aware of Hollywood's code of retribu-

Humphrey Bogart, having graduated from gangster-henchman to hard-boiled hero by the 1940s, confronts Robinson's over-the-hill gangster in Key Largo. (Culver Pictures)

tion, of course—having been victimized by it himself in countless crime sagas—and he pumps bullets into Robinson with obvious relish.

Strong stuff, indeed. But not even *Key Largo*'s brutal finale can prepare us for the psychotic brutality of *White Heat*, which appeared the following year. An effective subversion of the rural bandit variation with its love-conquers-all-but-death plot, *White Heat* traces the perverted life and loves of gangster Cody Jarrett (Cagney), who kills cops and his own gang members with equal disregard and whose heart belongs only to Mother. From the film's opening title shot of a locomotive pulsing toward the camera out of a dark tunnel, until the final apocalyptic explosion which destroys the hero ("I made it, Ma, top o' the world"), Raoul Walsh's narrative is a morass of Freudian imagery and psycho-sexual undercurrents. In fact, the film is as much a sexual psycho-drama as it is a gangster saga, because of Cagney/Jarrett's classic Oedipal relationship with his gangster-mother (Margaret Wycherly). She is the apparent focus of his recurrent seizures, and after she is killed by his jealous, cuckolding wife (Virginia Mayo) and his former initiate-partner, Jarrett experiences a transference of his relationship with her to a detective masquerading as a gangster (Edmund O'Brien).

The overt, unromanticized brutality and emotional shock tactics of *White Heat* are striking even to contemporary audiences. With unrelenting intensity Cagney/Jarrett's violent outbursts are directed indiscriminately at anyone who challenges or crosses him. The film opens with the outlaw gang robbing a train in rugged mountain terrain. When one of the engineers overhears Cody's name, Cody shoots him, and later assigns one of his men to kill a gang member who was accidently burned during the robbery and cannot travel with the fleeing gangsters.

In an ironic foreshadowing of Cody's own plight, the gang member had been struck by escaping steam and had grabbed his face, screaming in agony, much as Cody himself would do during his later seizures. The jet of scalding steam, then, is a visual manifestation of Cody's mental condition—the "white heat" of the film's title—that intensifies until the inevitable explosion at film's end. Not only does Cody's pathological state provide a rationale for his aberrant behavior, it also exonerates society from any responsibility for his criminality. We learn that his outlaw father had been confined in a mental institution and had died of similar seizures. As the narrative develops, it becomes increasingly obvious that Cody is willing to gamble with death because he assumes the same fate that had destroyed his father awaits him.

Cody's sole redeeming quality, like that of Cagney's Tommy Powers in *The Public Enemy*, is his love for his mother, but in *White Heat* even this quality is perverted. It is Ma Jarrett herself who schooled her son in criminality and gang leadership, and Cody's devotion to her borders on the psychopathic. After the initial train robbery and the return to his mountain hideout, Cody has an attack in front of the gang, and it is Ma who takes him into a bedroom and sits him on her lap, soothing his pain and encouraging him to be even more ruthless. Only Cagney could pull off a scene like this one—cringing with mental anguish while sitting on his mother's lap—and throughout the film the actor's caustic demeanor and subtle

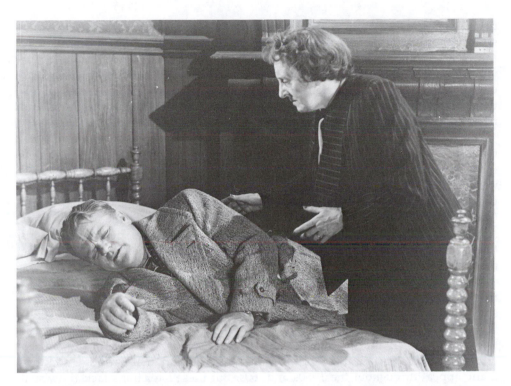

Mental heat and mother love: the most serious threats to Cody Jarrett's gangster status in White Heat *are his recurring mental seizures and his skewed Oedipal fixation for "Ma" (Margaret Wycherly).* (Culver Pictures)

vulnerability render even the inhuman Cody Jarrett somewhat sympathetic. The film is filled with actions and dialogue that virtually no one but Cagney could deliver with any credibility: He assures the pathetic, whining Mayo, "You'd look good in a shower curtain"; punches a lackey who had left a radio on and tells him, "If that radio's dead, it's gonna have company"; he locks a double-crossing gang member in a car trunk and then gives him "a little air" by shooting the trunk full of holes; he walks alone at night after his mother's death and later tells O'Brien, "It was a good feeling, walking out there—just me and Ma."

Although O'Brien's undercover detective, who initially befriends and eventually betrays the gangster-hero, clearly is intended to counterbalance Cagney/Jarrett's antisocial posture, Walsh's characterization of him tips the scale toward the criminal forces. In fact, *White Heat* recalls the classic gangster films where the police and their crime-fighting procedures were scientific and methodical to the point of comic banality. In one sequence three undercover agents are following Ma Jarrett in separate autos. This exchange of dialogue occurs as they establish radio identities: "We'll use the ABC method. I'm B." "I'm C." "I'm A." Walsh plays the scene straight, cutting from one car to another with the same dull precision exhibited by the agents. When Ma spots the autos, however, the camera assumes her subjective viewpoint. The cutting pace increases, and the narrative recovers its visual and emotional intensity. Throughout Walsh portrays the prosocial forces as objectively, as straightforwardly, as "stylelessly" as possible, reserving his technical and narrative flourishes for the gang.

The ultimate flourish, of course, is the film's climactic inferno. O'Brien informs the local police of the intended payroll heist at a chemical plant. When the gang is intercepted, the members disperse throughout the plant's maze of pipelines, steel walkways, and chemical storage containers. One by one, they are killed or surrender in their flight through this surreal garden of modern technology. Finally only Cody is still at large, and with night about to fall, he climbs to the top of a huge storage tank. During an exchange of gunfire with his pursuers, he lapses into his final seizure, and one of his own bullets sets off a tremendous blast, illuminating the night sky and bidding the antihero an appropriate farewell.

The deaths of Robinson/Rocco in *Key Largo* and Cagney/Jarrett in *White Heat* mark the figurative demise of the classic gangster-hero, that irrational, aggressive social animal who had been born and bred on Hollywood lots and who had so effectively conveyed the darker side of America's city life. The coincidental relaxation of censorship and the audience's increasing sophistication about organized crime worked to sustain much of the gangster genre's original narrative and thematic appeal throughout the 1950s and '60s. But these later films lack the visual and emotional appeal as well as the dynamic individual performances of the classic gangster films. In retrospect, the gangster genre is one of the few Hollywood formulas that did not grow old gracefully, that did not become richer and more complex with age. This may have been at least partially due to the genre's "unnatural" evolution after the Production Code redirected its development.

Unlike the vast majority of the prosocial urban crime films that they spawned, the classic gangster sagas display an intuitive, spontaneous, and highly expressive vision of the American Dream gone berserk. The gangster and his bleak urban milieu brutally exposed the contradictory values, the confused sensibilities, and the existential *angst* of contemporary American life. During the 1930s, however, Hollywood was only beginning to examine these issues. The years during and following the war, with the concurrent rise of *film noir* and the hardboiled detective film, proved to be a fertile period for extending both Hollywood and the audience's general concern for the quality of America's urban-industrial lifestyle.

The Hardboiled-Detective Film

5

Film noir, Citizen Kane, and the rise of American Expressionism

Whoever went to the movies with any regularity during 1946 was caught in the midst of Hollywood's profound postwar affection for morbid drama. From January through December deep shadows, clutching hands, exploding revolvers, sadistic villains and heroines tormented with deeply rooted diseases of the mind flashed across the screen in a panting display of psychoneuroses, unsublimated sex and murder most foul.

—D. Marsham, Life magazine (August 25, 1947)

The emergence of *film noir*

Throughout the 1940s, a stylistic and thematic trend was developing in Hollywood which by the end of the decade determined the look and the feel of the industry's most popular and significant productions. *Film noir*, as the style was dubbed by French critics, so dominated late '40s and early '50s films— principally those shot in black and white and involving the issue of urban

111

order—that it came to identify both the narrative-cinematic style of those films and also the historical period during which they were produced.

Generally speaking, *film noir* ("black film") refers to two interrelated aspects: visually, these films were darker and compositionally more abstract than most Hollywood films; thematically, they were considerably more pessimistic and brutal in their presentation of contemporary American life than even the gangster films of the early 1930s had been.

This trend was evident as early as 1941 in films like *Citizen Kane, The Maltese Falcon,* and *High Sierra,* but not until the postwar era did it develop to maturity. As Marsham suggests in his review of Robert Siodmak's *The Killers,* 1946 seems to have been a significant year in the development of *film noir.* It marked an onslaught of films as dark in theme as they were in visual style: *The Big Sleep, Notorious, The Stranger, Gilda, The Blue Dahlia, The Postman Always Rings Twice, Lady in the Lake, Cornered, So Dark the Night, The Razor's Edge, The Strange Love of Martha Ivers,* and others. Even optimistic, culturally reinforcing romances such as Frank Capra's *It's a Wonderful Life* and William Wyler's *The Best Years of Our Lives* derive much of their dramatic impact from the countercurrent of anxiety and alienation which lurks just beneath the surface—and which is apparent in their ironic titles.

In retrospect, the mid-'40s emerges as a period of remarkable growth for Hollywood filmmaking. This period is all the more astonishing when we consider the ensuing events—the HUAC hearings, the Paramount case, the growth of television, and so on—which restricted and redirected that growth. Hollywood's formal and cultural concerns would change radically by the mid-1950s, but not until Hollywood filmmakers had refined *film noir* and created what may well be the "expressionist cinema" par excellence.

The clearest manifestation of American Expressionism—and I believe the films of this period collectively merit that term—is found in the successful marriage of the *film noir* style and the widely popular hardboiled detective story. These two factors—one stylistic and the other generic—are closely interrelated but are not equivalent. The majority of '40s and '50s detective films reflect the *noir* style visually and thematically, but so do films of other genres: melodramas (*Mildred Pierce, The Strange Love of Martha Ivers*); Westerns (*I Shot Jesse James, The Gunfighter, High Noon*); gangster films (*They Drive by Night, Key Largo, White Heat*); and Hitchcock's psychological thrillers (especially *Notorious* and *Strangers on a Train*). Non-genre films like *The Lost Weekend* and *Sunset Boulevard* (both directed by Billy Wilder) and even Olivier's *Hamlet* exhibit distinct *noir* influences, so it is evident that the style developed great range and flexibility in postwar filmmaking.

Film noir was itself a system of visual and thematic conventions which were not associated with any specific genre or story formula, but rather with a distinctive cinematic style and a particular historical period. The conventions of the *noir* style were based on a variety of technical, narrative, and ideological developments which took place throughout the 1930s and early '40s. The gangster and urban crime films of the Depression era, along with the widely popular horror films, certainly anticipated the darker vision of *noir* films a decade later. The style of German Expressionism, refined at the Ufa studios during the 1920s, undoubtedly influenced Hollywood's later development of *film noir*, due especially to the number of German filmmakers who, whether for political or economic reasons, left that country for America before and during World War II. Directors like Ernst Lubitsch, F. W. Murnau, Fritz Lang, Billy Wilder, Douglas Sirk, and E. A. Dupont, along with countless technicians, scriptwriters, and performers, participated in Hollywood's own expressionist period.

Coincidentally, German expatriate film theorist Siegfried Kracauer (whose critical history of Ufa in the 1920s, *From Caligari to Hitler*, traced the cycle of German Expressionism) later suggested that the essence of cinema lies in its paradoxical capacity to "cling to the surface" of objects and events and thereby to "reveal" their true nature[1] (Kracauer, 1960, p. x). This viewpoint seems to have been shared by many of the German expatriate filmmakers who complemented Hollywood's traditional obsession with plot and dialogue with a heightened concern for set design, composition, lighting, and camerawork. This narrative technique made not only a film's characters but also its individual world, its *mise-en-scène*, to speak for itself.

A number of technological advancements during the 1920s and '30s also contributed to Hollywood's *noir* style. The evolution of "faster" Panchromatic film stock and camera lenses allowed for greater light sensitivity, so filmmakers had considerably more flexibility in their manipulation of lighting and depth of field (i.e., how much of the visual field is lit and in sharp focus). This development generated increased concern for visual contrast (the relationship between light and dark) and the frequent use of *chiaroscuro* lighting, in which only a portion of the screen is lit and the remainder is in total or semi-darkness. When these lighting techniques were used to depict crime, intrigue, and mental anxiety, especially within a heavily shadowed urban milieu, they gradually assumed narrative and thematic connotations of their own. The generally flat lighting and facile optimism that seemed to dominate 1930s Hollywood cinema gradually gave way to a bleaker vision of the world, which was more psychologically "realistic" and yet more visually abstract.

Film noir and the American Dream

One of the more significant aspects of this changing visual portrayal of the world, of course, is that it reflected the progressively darkening cultural attitudes during and after the war. Hollywood's *noir* films documented the growing disillusionment with certain traditional American values in the face of complex and often contradictory social, political, scientific, and economic developments. On the one hand, big business and widespread urban growth offered Americans increased socioeconomic opportunity but on the other, it left them with a feeling of deepening alienation. Changing views of sexuality and marriage were generated by the millions of men overseas and by the millions of women pressed into the work force. The postwar "return to normalcy" never really materialized—the GIs' triumphant homecoming only seemed to complicate matters and to bring out issues of urban anonymity and sexual confusion. Two fashionable intellectual and literary trends of the period were existentialism and Freudian psychology, both formally articulating the individual, familial, and mass-cultural concerns which were troubling postwar America.

These concerns tinged Hollywood's traditional macho-redeemer hero and domesticating heroine with a certain ambiguity and brought two other character types into the midst of the Hollywood constellation: the brutally violent, sexually confused psychopath and the aptly named *femme noire*, that sultry seductress who preys upon the hero and whose motives and allegiance generally are in doubt until the film's closing moments.

The sexual psychopath had made his debut in horror films and in the classic gangster films, but not even Paul Muni's Scarface could compare with Robert Ryan's murderous anti-Semite in *Crossfire* (1947) or Lee Marvin's scalding hoodlum in *The Big Heat* (1953). Or consider Jimmy Cagney's Cody Jarrett in *White Heat,* who is considerably more menacing and brutal than was his Tommy Powers some two decades earlier. The more overtly psychopathic types in *noir* films generally appeared in supporting roles and eventually were disposed of by the male leads, who were slightly more stable but equally threatened and insecure agents of the social order.

Les femmes noires, conversely, often had leading roles and functioned to manipulate—to double-cross or occasionally to domesticate—the male lead. Many Hollywood actresses, in fact, reached star status in the '40s with their portrayals of either good-bad sirens (Veronica Lake, Lauren Bacall, Gloria Grahame), betraying temptresses (Rita Hayworth, Ava Gardner), or outright black widows (Joan Crawford and Barbara Stanwyck, the last two having achieved stardom in the '30s playing straight roles).

The postwar concentration on individual alienation and sexual confusion was intensified by certain international issues, primarily the Cold War and the Bomb, carrying with them the threat of nuclear holocaust. In an essay on Hollywood sirens, Michael Wood writes: "The symbolism is enough to frighten off any but the most intrepid Freudians: the bomb dropped on Bikini was called Gilda and had a picture of Rita Hayworth painted on it. The phallic agent of destruction underwent a sex change, and the delight and terror of our new power were channeled into an old and familiar story: our fear and love of women"[2] (Wood, 1975, p. 51). In essence, the technicians at Bikini were simply extending the process of Hollywood filmmaking and American mythmaking by "channeling" cultural (or even global) concerns into a variety of "old and familiar" stories. Alluring women, petty criminals, fascistic police, even interplanetary invaders—all of these postwar stereotypes expressed our preoccupations with issues of international ideology (communism being the ultimate state of alienation and dehumanization) and atomic-age technology (with global suicide now possible through nuclear destruction).

Certain components of the *noir* style (sexual insecurity, destructive brutality,

and a degree of moral complacency) flowed together as a sort of thematic subcurrent in the earlier *noir* narratives. Occasionally they would seep to the surface
through some minor character or in an oblique, darkened visual style which consistently undercut the homespun American values being espoused in the plot. Can
Frank Capra convince us that it is, indeed, such a "wonderful life" after painting so
bleak a picture of it? Will Mildred Pierce find happiness returning to the pathetic
husband she earlier had demolished and apparently forgotten? Don't we remember—and relate to—Spencer Tracy's "father of the bride" primarily because of his
bizarre nightmare about the upcoming wedding and the dimension it adds to his
character? It is ultimately this dream sequence that so clearly distinguishes Vincente Minnelli's *Father of the Bride* from domestic comedy-dramas of other periods
and other styles. *Noir* ingredients abound in it: impressionistic lighting, an environment rendered surreal through set design and camerawork, the general feeling of the character's inadequacy and alienation—all of the horror stemming from
the impending wedding of Tracy's daughter (Elizabeth Taylor).

But this film represented *film noir*'s brighter side. By 1950 the style had technically and thematically overrun Hollywood's output of black-and-white urban-
based films (including "urban Westerns" like *High Noon*). The American urban
environment was no longer merely a context for examining sociocultural problems; it now emerged as a highly expressionistic visual arena for filmmakers
whose concerns were aesthetic as well as sociological.

Consider a representative sampling of Hollywood's productions in 1950: *The
Asphalt Jungle, Where the Sidewalk Ends, Steel Helmet, Sunset Boulevard, The Gunfighter,
Lawless, Union Station, Dark City, Winchester 73, The Furies, All About Eve, No Way
Out, Panic in the Streets, Night and the City, Breaking Point, Kiss Tomorrow Goodbye,
Caged,* and on and on in an endless procession of dark visions and disturbed
dreams. These films may have been motivated by many issues—urban decadence,
a subliminal "answer" to HUAC, a delayed response to the forced optimism of the
Depression and the war—but the cinematic style of presentation consistently
overshadowed social concern in *noir* films. As the style became increasingly familiar to both filmmakers and audiences, the tenets of American Expressionism became evident: style determines substance, mood overwhelms plot, narrativity (the
process of storytelling) emerges as narrative, emphasis is shifted from the *what* to
the *how,* form becomes inseparable from content.

Paul Schrader suggests that "*film noir* attacked and interpreted its sociological
conditions, and, by the close of the *noir* period, created a new artistic world which
went beyond a simple sociological reflection, a nightmarish world of American
mannerism which was by far more a creation than a reflection. Because *film noir*
was first of all a style, because it worked out its conflicts visually rather than thematically, because it was aware of its own identity, it was able to create artistic solutions to sociological problems"[3] (Schrader, 1972, p. 13). Implicit in Schrader's
thought is the notion that Hollywood filmmaking itself had been undergoing a
formal evolution. The thematically naive, formally transparent linear narratives of

the early sound era were steadily giving way to more complex, convoluted, and formally self-conscious films. Hollywood movies became visually and thematically more stylized, more opaque.

This process of evolutionary development seems to be an almost natural feature in the history of any form—whether that of a single genre or of Hollywood cinema as a whole. As a form is varied and refined, it is bound to become more stylized, more conscious of its own rules of construction and expression. We cannot designate the precise point at which Hollywood moved into this stage of formal refinement, its expressionist period, because the shift in social and aesthetic priorities was gradual and uneven. Schrader does point to John Huston's 1941 film, *The Maltese Falcon*, as the birth of *film noir*, and suggests that "most every dramatic Hollywood film from 1941 to 1953 contains some *noir* elements" (Schrader, 1972, p. 13). Schrader's time frame and his indication of the pervasiveness of *noir* techniques seem accurate enough, but I tend to disagree with his assigning so much importance to *The Maltese Falcon*. Huston's film did introduce the hardboiled-detective story and its persona (Bogart as Sam Spade) to the screen, as it did the archetypal *femme noire* (Mary Astor as Brigid O'Shaugnessy), but the *noir* characterization and private-eye framework are not supported stylistically. Despite its cynical tone, *The Maltese Falcon* employs a relatively uncomplicated linear narrative and conventional well-lit visual arena. It does little more than anticipate the visual and narrative-thematic extremes of films produced only a few years later. A much more significant work in the evolution of the *noir* tendencies is Orson Welles' 1941 opus, *Citizen Kane*.

Noir techniques in *Citizen Kane*

Welles' contribution to American Expressionism is substantial, extending well beyond the influential *Kane*. In fact, Welles later directed, scripted, and performed in films which mark its peak (*Lady from Shanghai*, 1948) and its *dénouement* (*Touch of Evil*, 1958). These two later films refine the *noir* techniques and themes which distinguish them from the prosocial '30s films. It was *Kane*, though, that provided viewers and filmmakers with the narrative prototype for 1940s Expressionism. We might begin our discussion of this film by noting how well *Kane* accommodates Schrader's seven "recurring techniques" which characterize *film noir*:

1. the majority of scenes are lit for night,

2. as in German Expressionism, oblique and vertical lines are preferred to horizontal,

3. the actors and setting are often given equal lighting emphasis,

4. compositional tension is preferred to physical action,

5. there is an almost Freudian attachment to water (and also to mirrors, windows, and other reflective surfaces),

6. there is a love of romantic narration, and

7. the complex chronological order reinforces the feelings of hopelessness and lost time.

Only a very few films incorporated all of these techniques, of course, and *Citizen Kane* was one of them.

Even a casual recollection of *Kane* should call to mind its wealth of *noir* stylistics, realized primarily through set design, lighting, and camera placement. Except for the pseudodocumentary "News on the March" early in the film, Welles gives us a dark, claustrophobic environment (especially through deep-focus, low-angle interior shots), which seems oppressive to its inhabitants as well as to viewers of the film. Many of the most memorable sequences—Kane's death, Thompson receiving his "Rosebud" assignment in the projection room, Kane firing Jed Leland—are shot in such a way that not only the principal characters' faces but also large portions of the set are obscured. Because Welles uses low-angle, slightly tilted shots the world he conveys through his camera is one of slashing diagonals and oblique shadows, of hidden truths and skewed visions. This strategy is intensified by the fact that the story is filtered through the personal impressions of the reporter

Perhaps the most evocative visual sequence in Citizen Kane *is the projection-room sequence (shown here in frame enlargement), in which Thompson is given his "Rosebud" assignment.* (Private Collection)

Thompson and the various individuals he interviews. We never see Thompson's face during the film, which enhances our identification with his journalistic enterprise—to "get the story"—and also necessitates his investigation and interviews being shot in semi-darkness or from a predominantly subjective point of view.

If ever there were a film which denied the form-content distinction (and most truly great films do) it was *Citizen Kane.* Welles' story and his technique, his narrative and style of storytelling, consistently cooperate in addressing complex thematic issues: the tension between subjective and objective impressions of reality; the limitations of any historical process, whether on film or in human memory, to reveal the truth; and ultimately the inability of anyone (including the filmmaker-narrator) to ever really "know" another human being.

As various critics have suggested, one of the more fascinating formal dimensions of *Kane* is that its union of form and content is used to investigate the nature of human and cinematic perception. Consider the opening moments of the film, when we are shown Xanadu ("No Trespassing") and Kane's death. The "News on the March" documentary and Thompson's assignment to solve the "Rosebud" riddle follow immediately after. These sequences establish Kane's character and indicate the inadequacy of an objective historical accounting to reveal anything but the most superficial aspects of a man's life—hence the "Rosebud" assignment. But these opening sequences also convey the *filmmaker's* related investigation of the film medium's range of expression and its necessary relationship to knowledge, memory, imagination, and finally, to human history itself.

The impressionistic introduction of Xanadu in *Kane*'s opening shots initiates our surreal journey into the gothic mansion (the single light source from Kane's bedroom maintains its exact location within the frame in each successive shot) and ultimately into the psyche of Kane himself. A reverse-angle shot of the window takes us inside Kane's room. The camera then cuts to an extreme close-up which locates us inside the glass ball Kane is holding. Inside the ball is a miniature cottage and an eternal snowfall suspended in clear liquid.

Welles then cuts to another extreme close-up—Kane's lips mouthing his dying epithet—although the "snow" from inside the glass ball now fills the entire visual field. We realize, of course, that it's not snowing in Kane's room but in his memory, and this realization emphasizes the importance of illusory reality over the logic of objective visible reality. With Kane's dying word, the camera follows the glass ball as it rolls from his hand across the bed and shatters on the floor. Another tight close-up focuses on the broken glass, and in its distorted, wide-angle reflection we see the nurse enter the room. (As Pauline Kael and others have pointed out, there apparently was no one in the room to hear Kane whisper "Rosebud" just before he died. Far from undermining the film's credibility, this actually reinforces the primacy of the film's internal narrative logic and also of the camera-viewer's privileged perspective.)

Kane's death scene is immediately followed by one of the most jarring audio and visual cuts in cinematic history—we are literally torn from this somber,

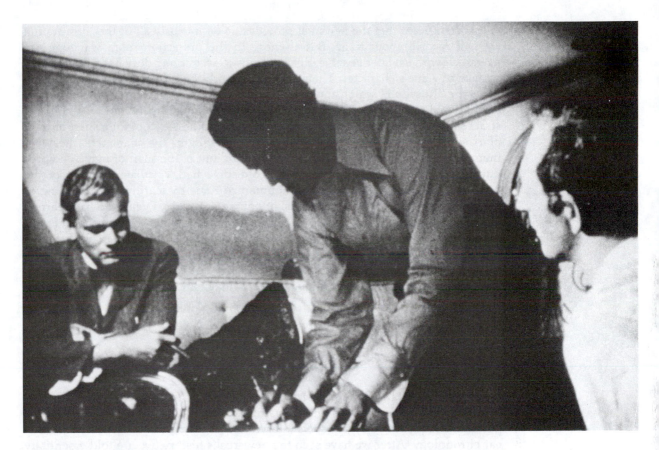

The lighting in this sequence carries a sense of foreboding: a frame enlargement of the young Kane leaning into darkness as he signs his idealistic "Declaration of Principles." (Private Collection)

other-worldly experience by the "News on the March" report of Kane's death and his personal history. The cinematic strategy of this sequence is diametrically opposed to that of the impressionistic opening. Now we are presented with "history," an objective, superficial documentation of Kane's life. No longer does a probing camera move freely with an apparent will of its own into the darkest reaches of Kane's environment and his mind; instead it is restricted physically and films Kane from a proper journalistic "distance." No longer is the *mise-en-scène* an expressive extension of Kane's psyche; instead. we are in the familiar, well-lit "real world." No longer are we privileged observers with access to a dying man's innermost thoughts; instead, we must view Kane as the rest of the world does. No longer do the filmmakers *create* a distinct separate reality; they simply *record* the immediate surface reality of sociohistorical events.

It is significant that the newsreel provides us with nearly all of the information we will receive about Kane. But as those in the projection room watching the newsreel (with us) later observe, this journalistic accounting does not penetrate the surface of Kane's character. Their frustration with the information they have initiates the "Rosebud" search and thus provides the film with something resembling a traditional plot and character motivation even though it is the most visually abstract sequence in the film. The room is in total darkness except for a shaft of light pouring in from the projection booth which back-lights the characters, throwing them into eerie silhouette as they move into and out of the shaft of light. The producer of the documentary laments the cold, detached, calculated quality of the newsreel, suggesting that Thompson humanize Kane by learning the meaning of his dying word. Thompson's quest is, of course, hopeless. Even if he had learned the apparent meaning of "Rosebud" (as we do at the film's end) and it had provided a human interest story, the solution to the riddle would scarcely have affected his own conclusion that a single word can never sum up a man's life. Welles' conclusion, like Thompson's, seems to be that all perception, whether human or filmic, is observation qualified by imagination; it is documentation informed by interpretation.

Citizen Kane as a detective film

In its narrative strategy and plot structure, *Citizen Kane* is a detective film: Thompson's investigation motivates the reconstruction of Kane's history. Because of the particular sequence of Thompson's interviews, we learn about Kane's life in a linear chronology. After we have seen the newsreel's history, we are told essentially the same story in the same linear progression by the various figures interviewed by Thompson. This enforced narrative line is made to appear arbitrary—for example, Susan's initial interview is postponed because she's drunk—but the effect is of a chronological reconstruction. Even the significant time lapses in Kane's biography are handled *within* the flashbacks rather than between them, so each flashback has a narrative coherence unto itself.

Thus *Kane*, like many other *noir* classics (most notably *Double Indemnity, Mildred Pierce, The Killers, Out of the Past, Letter from an Unknown Woman,* and *Sunset Boulevard*), employs a circular dual-time structure. The cinema-present investigation is set in motion by an enigma—generally a crime but in this instance, a single word—initiating the reconstruction of events in cinema past. The end result of this narrative strategy is not simply to explain or demystify the enigma, but also to set a tone of fatalism which will underscore the inexorable destiny of the principal characters. No one, especially the detective-observer who eventually reconstructs the past, can affect that destiny.

The detective-observer is clearly a surrogate for the viewer and functions as an organizing sensibility both visually and conceptually. This situation is complicated in *Kane* by two significant factors. First, we in the audience have privileged information that no one inside the narrative is privy to: Thompson does not see Kane's death, the broken globe, the burning sled. (Actually, Thompson physically "sees" nothing in the flashbacks whereas we in the audience do, which gives us an even stronger position as collective observer-investigator.) Second, because each of the flashbacks, including the newsreel, employs a different narrator, Thompson's viewpoint is diffused. The issue of point of view becomes more complex as the investigation progresses and as the subjective recollections accumulate. Thatcher, Bernstein, Leland, Susan, Raymond, even the newsreel commentator, have all interpreted Kane's life somewhat differently, and as each interpretation is piled on top of the preceding one, the "facts" of Kane's life as presented in the newsreel are further confused.

During Raymond's flashback, which recalls Susan's flight from Xanadu and the aging Kane's rage, Welles presents us with our final image of the decadent Ameri-

With his face again hidden in darkness, Kane is confronted by his wife (Ruth Warrick) and a political rival (Ray Collins) in his "love nest" with mistress Dorothy Comingore. As this low-angle shot indicates, camera position can enhance the effect of noir lighting. (Museum of Modern Art/Film Stills Archive)

can demigod. Kane has torn apart Susan's deserted bedroom and is now pacing zombielike through the shadowy hallways of his mansion. He passes between two gigantic mirrors and his image is reflected into infinity. This shot visually reinforces the film's central theme: Charles Foster Kane, and the American Dream he had come to represent, cannot be reduced to a single coherent image but instead must be interpreted subjectively by those who have known him. As the various viewpoints coalesce to depict the "real"—and ultimately unknowable—Kane, we gradually realize that the emptiness at the core of the man, a spoiled, willful tyrant obsessed with his loss of innocence and the inhuman isolation of wealth and power, represents our own uneasiness with the American Dream.

The birth of Expressionism and the death of Hollywood

Such cultural misgivings—and herein lies the basis for American Expressionism—were articulated more clearly in terms of narrative style and characterization than in terms of plot. Although most *noir* films incorporate Hollywood's requisite "happy ending" to take care of superficial plot conflicts, the bleak, fatalistic depiction of the American urban milieu qualified—if it did not totally deny—that resolution. Throughout the 1940s, Hollywood's problem-solving function was shifting away from its predominantly sociological impulse and giving more attention to cinematic artistry. Social problems would continue to motivate and provide a narrative context for *noir* films during this decade, of course, but the solutions to these problems became increasingly artificial, formalized, stylized to the point where, as Schrader suggests, narrative resolution was as significant aesthetically as it was sociologically.

The reasons for these shifting priorities are numerous. They involved the evolution of film technology and narrative technique, complicated by a variety of industrial, ideological, and socioeconomic pressures. By the early 1950s television already had begun to co-opt Hollywood's mass audience—moviegoing was no longer the cultural ritual it had been for the past quarter-century, and this new development also encouraged filmmakers to reconsider the medium's social and aesthetic functions. The effects of this development were evident in Hollywood's rites of order, in those urban crime and Western films whose cultural concerns were to rationalize and celebrate social order. Furthermore, the genres involving social integration which came into prominence during the 1950s, especially family melodrama and science fiction, took their narrative and thematic appeal from a heavily stylized rendition of their milieu and characters.

Thus, three seemingly unrelated issues—*noir* techniques, a collective cultural *angst*, and the cinema's reconstituted and dwindling mass audience—coalesced after the war into a period of self-consciousness and self-criticism. This unprecedented formalism and aestheticism generally escaped American viewers because it evolved so naturally from Hollywood's formally transparent and prosocial narrative tradition. But consider how filmmakers from other cultures recognized and exploited the formal and aesthetic properties of American Expressionism—as in the French New Wave's obsession with the hardboiled detective, or the New German cinema's infatuation with '50s family melodramas. The ultimate irony is that the American mass audience, whose participation in the development of the Hollywood film industry had generated the world's foremost national cinema, began leaving the theaters just when their economic and spiritual investment promised its greatest returns. Thus, those *noir* films of the late 1940s and early 1950s have attained dual historical status: they represent the height of Hollywood's narrative sophistication and visual expression, but they also signal an era of formalism and self-indulgence, a confused social conscience, and a vanishing audience. In short, the American expressionist cinema foreshadowed the death of the Hollywood studio system and of America's national cinema.

The hardboiled-detective genre

Down these mean streets a man must go who is not himself mean, who is neither tarnished nor afraid. The detective in this kind of story must be such a man. He is the hero; he is everything. He must be a complete man and a common man and yet an unusual man. He must be, to use a rather weathered phrase, a man of honor—by instinct, by inevitability, without thought of it, and certainly without saying it. He must be the best man in his world and a good enough man for any world.

—Raymond Chandler, "The Simple Art of Murder"[4]

In the early 1940s, the evolving gangster/urban crime formula and the burgeoning *film noir* style coalesced with other cultural factors to generate the most significant product of American expressionist cinema: the hardboiled-detective film. Distinct both from the classic gangster film, which focused on the criminal and his underworld milieu, and from the urban crime film, which traced the peace-keeping efforts of law-and-order agencies, the hardboiled-detective film assumed the viewpoint of the isolated, self-reliant "private eye." Like the classic Westerner, the hardboiled detective is a cultural middle-man. His individual talents and streetwise savvy enable him to survive within a sordid, crime-infested city, but his moral sensibilities and deep-rooted idealism align him with the forces of social order and the promise of a utopian urban community.

By the time the hardboiled detective appeared on the screen in John Huston's *The Maltese Falcon* (1941), its narrative formula already had been established on the radio and in popular magazines and pulp novels. Huston's film, which he both scripted and directed, lifts a great deal of its dialogue and most of its story line from Dashiell Hammett's 1929 novel, *The Maltese Falcon.* There had been earlier attempts to adapt *The Maltese Falcon* to the screen—in Roy del Ruth's 1931 *The Maltese Falcon* and William Dieterle's 1936 *Satan Was a Lady*—but neither met with much success. The detective duo of Nick and Nora Charles in the Thin Man series did provide '30s audiences with a glimpse of the formula, in that these films interjected a tone of black humor and social commentary into the classical detective tradition.

The Thin Man series, from Hammett's novel of the same title, was initiated in 1934 and it launched William Powell and Myrna Loy on a six-film, twelve-year jaunt as one of Hollywood's more popular couples of the era. (Actually, the "Thin Man" himself was a murder victim in the initial story, but the description became associated with Powell's detective character.) The hardboiled dimension of Hammett's initial conception, however, was neutralized by W. S. van Dyke's straightforward direction of the first four in the series and by his willingness to let the witty Powell-Loy repartee dominate the films. Although the last of the Powell-Loy films was made in 1946 at the height of the hardboiled-detective genre's popularity, this now-conventional detective couple was scarcely affected by *noir* stylistics.

The development of the detective formula is closely related to certain developments in American literature—in fact, the birth of detective fiction (Edgar Allan Poe's "The Murders in the Rue Morgue" and "The Purloined Letter" in the 1840s) also marks the birth of the short story. Poe's detective-protagonist, Dupin, was the prototype for the classical detective: highly cultured, aristocratic, eccentric, scientific, and capable of complex deductive reasoning. Like his offspring—most notably Arthur Conan Doyle's Sherlock Holmes and Agatha Christie's Hercule Poirot—his primary motivation was a personal delight in puzzle-solving, and his cases involved the assigning of individual guilt to anyone who upset what was, in the final analysis, an orderly and benevolent universe. The classical detective's cases generally were related to the reader by an observant but intellectually inferior sidekick or acquaintance who managed to keep the reader one step behind the detective. Perhaps the most significant aspect of the classical detective formula is the "solution" itself. "Crime" in these stories is usually an isolated act of moral and social aberration. The detective's solution identifies the criminal and thereby recovers the social equilibrium which had been temporarily disturbed by the criminal's misdeeds. In effect, crime in the classical detective film is an individual responsibility, not a social one, and its solution is simply a flexing of the cerebral muscles, which serves to reestablish and thus reaffirm the social and moral status quo.

On the screen, too, the differences are apparent between the hardboiled detective and his "classical" predecessor—principally we can see this in the Sherlock Holmes series, as well as those films featuring Charlie Chan, Mr. Moto, the Thin Man, and others. The classical detective (not to be confused with the classic stage of the films in which he appeared) had a cultivated wit and used scientific methods of deduction—especially as characterized by Basil Rathbone's Holmes, Warner Oland's Chan (Oland was replaced in 1938 by Sidney Toler), and Peter Lorre's

Moto. The classical detective was evidently part of a generally well-ordered society whose occasional problems could be solved with deductive reasoning. In contrast, the hardboiled detective, like the *noir* style which provided the visual and psychological tone of his films, displayed a world view considerably less optimistic in its vision of modern society. His vision reflected the alienation, anxiety, and moral confusion of wartime and postwar America.

The hardboiled writers of the 1920s and '30s paved the way for these films. Their detective fiction subverted the classical tradition in a number of significant ways. The earliest practitioners of the hardboiled formula were Carroll John Daly and Dashiell Hammett (Hammett initially published under the name of Peter Collinson), who wrote stories for the popular pulp magazines. Among these was *Black Mask*, which had been founded in 1920 by H. L. Mencken and George Jean Nathan, and which by the mid-'20s was publishing hardboiled-detective stories almost exclusively. Daly's Race Williams and Hammett's "Continental Op," like Raymond Chandler's Philip Marlowe a decade later, certainly were far removed from their classical counterparts. They operated more by instinct than by intellect; they submerged themselves inside a sordid, malevolent urban milieu and generally resorted to violence in order to survive. Whatever solutions they presented to crimes were at best tentative and incomplete, revealing only a single thread in the complex fabric of contemporary social corruption.

One of the basic tenets of the earliest hardboiled writing was that it recognized criminality as an ugly activity involving brutal, unthinking types. Raymond Chandler once observed, "Hammett gave murder back to the people who commit it for reasons and with tools at hand. . . . He dropped murder back into the alley"[5] (Chandler, 1944, p. 58). Crime for these writers was not a mere plot device which led to a complex battle of wits between upper-crust society types; it was a pervasive social farce which permeated the urban environment and virtually all of its inhabitants. Interestingly enough, Chandler himself went on to take his Philip Marlowe novels to the suburbs and the mansions of the seemingly well-to-do. In these novels, however, as opposed to those of the classical detective writers, the upper crust were as morally corrupt as the inhabitants of Hammett's alleys.

Chandler's image of Los Angeles, told from Marlowe's witty, cynical first-person viewpoint, is that of a paradise thoroughly perverted by the community's shared lust for wealth and power. Marlowe and the other hardboiled detectives attempted to isolate themselves from their decadent milieu, as did their classical counterparts. The hardboiled detective's isolation, however, is not a function of intellect and breeding, but instead represents his outright rejection of a society whose values and attitudes he cannot accept or even understand. A self-styled existialist, he has refined his own personal, pragmatic code based on traditional, outmoded values like rugged individualism and fair play. If the classic Westerner had donned a wrinkled trenchcoat and passed through a time warp, he might strike a similar pose.

Because hardboiled-detective fiction relies so heavily upon a basic conflict between the hero's value system and that of his corrupt social environment, it seems to be most effective when it emphasizes the detective's perspective. Either the detective relates his own story via first-person narration, or else an omniscient narrator who shares the hero's outlook tells the story. Although the detective formula was ideal for pulp literature and radio, where it flourished in the 1930s, it presented a rather difficult problem for those who wanted to adapt the medium to a movie screen (where the narrator's "voice" is the camera rather than an individual participant in the narrative). By the 1940s, however, Hollywood's increased sophistication in both technical and narrative capabilities, along with the mass audience's deepening moral and sociopolitical anxiety, enabled the hardboiled detective to emerge as a dominant film hero.

The hardboiled prototype: Huston's *The Maltese Falcon*

I would like to focus on three key films which heralded the birth and development of the hardboiled-detective genre in American movies: Huston's *The Maltese Falcon* (1941), Billy Wilder's *Double Indemnity* (1944), and Edward Dmytryk's *Murder, My Sweet* (produced in 1944, released in 1945). These were three of Hollywood's finest wartime productions, and they involve adaptations of works by the leading hardboiled American writers: Dashiell Hammett (*The Maltese Falcon*), James M. Cain (*Double Indemnity*), and Raymond Chandler (whose *Farewell, My Lovely* underwent a title change for its first film version). Chandler, in fact, was perhaps the single most significant writer—both as a novelist and screenwriter—to participate in the genre's evolution. He provided either script or story for *Murder, My Sweet; Double Indemnity; Lady in the Lake; The Blue Dahlia; The Falcon Takes Over; The Big Sleep; Strangers on a Train;* and more recently *Marlowe; Farewell, My Lovely;* and *The Long Goodbye.* As Chandler wrote to another mystery writer in 1948:

> I did not invent the hard boiled murder story and I have never made any secret of my opinion that Hammett deserves most or all of the credit. Everybody imitates in the beginning. . . . Since Hammett has not written for publication since 1932 I have been picked out by some people as a leading representative of the school. This is very likely due to the fact that *The Maltese Falcon* did not start the high budget mystery picture trend, although it ought to have. *Double Indemnity* and *Murder, My Sweet* did, and I was associated with both of them.[6] (Gardiner and Walker, 1977, p. 52)

Actually, *The Maltese Falcon* did establish the basic plot line and constellation of characters for Hollywood's "hardboiled" formula, while the two later films introduced distinctive *noir* stylistics into the formula to provide a narrative and visual strategy which complemented the basic structure. As effective as Hammett's story and characterization are in *The Maltese Falcon* story, director Huston's linear plotting and transparent narrative-visual style lack the expressive qualities of the later *noir*-influenced detective films. Consider, though, the cast of characters in Huston's

The Maltese Falcon, *John Huston's influential 1941 private-eye film, set the narrative standards for the hardboiled formula. Here, the principals (***Humphrey Bogart** as Sam Spade, along with Peter Lorre, Mary Astor, and Sidney Greenstreet*) examine the film's namesake.* (Hoblitzelle Theatre Arts Collection)

adaptation of Hammett's novel: Humphrey Bogart as Sam Spade, the prototype for Hollywood's urban private eye; Mary Astor as Brigid O'Shaughnessy, the seductive and treacherous *femme noire;* Lee Patrick as Effie Perrine, the attractive and dedicated secretary with whom the detective maintains an honorable, almost familial, rapport; Sidney Greenstreet as Kasper Gutman, the well-bred, amoral heavy; Peter Lorre as Joel Cairo, the squeamish, effeminate, double-dealing crook; Elisha Cooke, Jr., as Wilmer, Gutman's witless but obedient "gunsel"; and Ward Bond and Barton MacLaine as local police detectives who maintain a difficult but vital relationship with the detective-hero. They hound him incessantly while he does most of their work for them.

These characters—and in many cases the actors who played them—compose the essential constellation within the genre. Sam Spade, of course, is the narrative and perceptual center of the film, the organizing sensibility who observes, influences, and ultimately defines the seamy urban world he inhabits. In *The Maltese*

Falcon, that world is characterized more through Spade's words, actions, and attitude than by Huston's lighting, camerawork, or *mise-en-scène*. There *is* a degree of visual stylization here which anticipates later hardboiled-detective films: exterior sequences generally occur at night, interiors are crowded and often shot from below eye level to suggest a feeling of oppressive enclosure, the light source occasionally is situated within the frame to heighten the contrast and create a darker, more threatening atmosphere than that of earlier detective and urban crime films. *Falcon* was of great cinematic interest, but Huston had not yet developed the eye for expressive lighting and camerawork that would distinguish such later works as *The Treasure of the Sierra Madre, Key Largo* (both 1948), *The Asphalt Jungle* (1950), and his delightful parody of *noir* intrigue, *Beat the Devil* (1954).

These later Huston films represent the ultimate accomplishment of Hollywood's expressionist period: a wedding of bleak visual style with a cynical thematic perspective. Whereas *The Maltese Falcon* lacks that level of visual sophistication, its plot and characters do project the dark thematic vision which would later typify the genre. The plot involves a single episode in an ongoing search for the "Falcon," a jewel-encrusted statuette which had been painted black and had thereby eluded its pursuers for centuries. The coveted Falcon, like the American Dream of instant wealth and the power that it represents, finally is discovered to be a counterfeit. Unlike Spade, whose hardboiled exterior hides a vulnerable moralist and a man of uncompromising integrity, the Falcon and those who covet it are caught up in a perpetual drama of duplicity, greed, and false appearance. Spade, of course, is the thematic "answer" to this world of avarice and superficial elegance, but he has become this way only by isolating himself from the outside world. Physically, he inhabits a seedy, spartan office which seems to be his only habitat; occupationally, he is engaged in a pursuit of truth as opposed to financial reward; emotionally, he maintains a lifestyle which resists prolonged human interaction or commitment (except to his secretary, with whom he has developed a wonderful platonic rapport); morally, he is dependent on an outdated value system which continually places him at the mercy of manipulative women and cynical, greedy villains.

In a certain sense, the detective's very occupation—and by extension his isolated, moralistic world view—implies that he must be at the mercy of external social forces. Like the Westerner, the hardboiled detective is not only a man apart, but he is a *social mediator:* his capacity for violence and streetwise savvy ally him with the outlaw element, although his values and attitude commit him to the promise of a well-ordered community. The detective is too familiar with legitimate society to trust its values and motives—in fact, the detective-hero in these films usually has left the force or the D.A.'s office because of institutional restrictions or corruption.

Thus his role is that of a cultural go-between, of an individual willing to bridge the ideological chasm between the civilized and the criminal for whoever can pay his "twenty-five bucks a day and expenses." The classic Westerner's historical context gives the promise of civilization an essentially positive, optimistic tone. For the detective, conversely, the ideal of social order is denied by the urban reality around him. This ideal represents not simply a promise, but a broken promise. The detective isolates himself from both the civilized and the savage because, in his contemporary urban milieu, he cannot distinguish between them. The civilized and the savage now inhabit the same world and speak the same language in characters like Kasper Gutman and Brigid O'Shaughnessy.

Sam Spade lives from one case to the next and constructs his own value system in the process of his work. If society is corrupt, as Spade's investigations would seem to indicate, then we must look within ourselves for guidance and meaning. In *The Maltese Falcon*, Spade's primary motive for becoming involved in the search for the coveted Falcon is the death of his partner, Miles Archer, a man Spade couldn't stand and whose name he removed from the office door immediately after the killing. Spade eventually discovers that Brigid, who had initiated the investigation, was in fact Archer's murderer.

Brigid is the archetypal hardboiled heroine: beautiful, apparently helpless and victimized, drawing the detective into the intrigue and then exploiting his particular talents—and his naive romanticism—in her perverse quest for wealth and power. Spade, after he has become Brigid's lover, realizes that he is simply another of her victims, and none of her entreaties is effective at the end of the film. Spade turns her over to the police along with Gutman and his coterie of villains. With stoic detachment, Spade informs his lover that it is "bad business" to let the murderer of one's partner go unpunished, and, more importantly, that he refuses "to play the sucker for anyone." Bogart's portrayal of a man torn between love and duty reinforces the detective-hero's ongoing but futile search for truth and genuine human contact. "Sure I love you, but that's beside the point," Spade tells Brigid before sending her away. "I'll have some rotten nights after I've sent you over, but that will pass."

Typical of much hardboiled-detective fiction, Gutman's overt villainy and Brigid's sexual manipulation provide separate but interrelated plot developments which merge at the film's climax. The witty, aristocratic, self-indulgent Gutman poses a tangible and engaging threat to Spade, although Brigid emerges at the film's end as the more menacing villain. In playing the role of victim so effectively, Brigid had victimized Spade, Gutman, Cairo, and the various other men searching for the Falcon. Her own pursuit of the Falcon, which had precipitated a series of murders and other misdeeds, is considerably more difficult to comprehend than is the behavior of Gutman, Cairo, or even Spade himself. We are familiar with brutal, unethical men pursuing wealth and power, but here we are confronted with the image of an avaricious, utterly self-serving woman, and the effect is fascinating and disturbing.

The resolution in *The Maltese Falcon* finally identifies those responsible for Archer's death, but the "real" Falcon is still very much at large. In the detective's inability to "solve" anything more than a single isolated incident in an endless quest for power and material wealth, the character's narrative function becomes clear. Like the Westerner, the detective-hero activates the cultural conflicts inherent within his social milieu. His actions may resolve some immediate social conflict, but the community itself remains basically unchanged. The hero's inability either to effect real change or to find solace in the ideal of romantic love reaffirms his isolation and his commitment to apparently outmoded values. Once the case is closed, the detective recedes into the oblivion of his seedy office, a contemporary version of the Westerner's sunset. The difference between the office and the prairie beyond—between the enclosed and infinitely open, between the vertical and the horizontal—exemplifies the differences between the two heroes and their cultural contexts. The Westerner's horizon is virtually limitless, and he can keep the advance of civilization at his back; the detective's horizon is all but invisible through the smog and darkness beyond his drawn venetian blinds. The "natural" world is alien to him, and all the detective can do is follow his instincts for survival and allow time to run its inevitable course.

The *noir* influence: *Murder, My Sweet* and *Double Indemnity*

What *The Maltese Falcon* contributed to Hollywood's hardboiled-detective formula in characterization, plot, and theme, *Murder, My Sweet* reinforced through narrative and visual technique. This 1944 adaptation of Chandler's *Farewell, My Lovely,*

Edward Dmytryk's Murder, My Sweet *marked the first successful marriage of film noir stylistics and the hardboiled-detective story. Here, Philip Marlowe (Dick Powell) is manhandled by client Moose Malloy (Mike Mazurki).* (Culver Pictures)

directed by Edward Dmytryk (perhaps the most underrated stylist of Hollywood's expressionist period), depicts the urban milieu as a bleak cityscape in which shadows are as expressive as the characters they envelop. The plot, a typical morass of duplicity and false appearances, is related in flashback by Chandler's stock detective-hero, Philip Marlowe. Dick Powell, cast against his usual musical and romantic lead roles, played Marlowe; there would be later Marlowe incarnations by Bogart, Robert Montgomery, James Garner, Elliot Gould, and Robert Mitchum, among others. The flashback framework in Dmytryk's film is a brilliant stroke, allowing the detective's voice-over, first-person narration to advance the action and at the same time provide an ironic counterpoint to the visuals. Furthermore, the dual time structure, in which the detective (in the present) describes the events of the past, enhances the mood of futility and fatalism. This is a world of victims, entrapped by social circumstances or by their own greed and lust in an ongoing tale of violence and deceit.

Murder, My Sweet opens with Marlowe being grilled by police about a murder in which he is implicated. The sole light source—or so Dmytryk's lighting leads us to believe—is a desk lamp in the center of the frame, casting the set in semi-darkness and obliterating the features of the interrogating cops. Marlowe begins his flashback verbally, relating his initial involvement with the case. As the camera pulls in slowly on the light's reflection on the desk top, the scene dissolves to Marlowe's darkened office, where the detective-hero sits alone. The camera is situated over Marlowe's shoulder (an essential convention in the genre, encouraging viewer identification with the detective's vision), and as the lights of the city flash on and off, Marlowe's reflection appears, vanishes, and reappears in the window glass. Then suddenly, another face appears reflected in the glass—that of Moose Malloy (played by the gigantic, menacing Mike Mazurki), whose disembodied visage is suspended above the lights and shadowed silhouettes of Los Angeles. With these initial images, Dmytryk literally *realizes* the detective's isolation and attitude while seeming merely to introduce the film's narrative.

In this sequence and throughout *Murder, My Sweet*, Dmytryk's camerawork, lighting, and *mise-en-scène* function to draw the viewer ever deeper into Marlowe's bleak netherworld. After the initial flashback sequence, Marlowe and Malloy walk to a sleazy downtown bar looking for a woman who had befriended Malloy before the prison term he has just completed. As we learn later, that woman is now the wealthy Mrs. Grayle (Claire Trevor), who had seduced and betrayed Malloy years before and now will attempt to do the same to Marlowe. In one of the film's most evocative visual passages, the two men climb a narrow, dimly lit stairway which seems to swallow them up with each step. Dmytryk had the walls and ceiling of this set slanted inward to distort the visual perspective and emphasize the hero's metaphoric journey into the urban maelstrom.

The intensity of this journey is visualized even more dramatically in the film's bizarre dream sequences. Marlowe is knocked out repeatedly in the course of his investigation, and Dmytryk treats the hero's loss of consciousness with techniques such as blurring of focus, fading to black, and so on. The most effective sequence of this type occurs when Marlowe is trapped inside a dark, seemingly deserted house and given an injection. Marlowe's drug-induced visions and his subsequent efforts to regain consciousness are shown from his subjective viewpoint, and effectively convey his mental and physical isolation within a nightmare world.

His viewpoint is countered throughout by the lavish, expensive world of the film's *femme noire*, Mrs. Grayle, who combines the Gutman and Brigid O'Shaughnessy roles from *The Maltese Falcon*. By the time Marlowe meets her, Mrs. Grayle has graduated from exploiting small-time hoods like Malloy and is into big-time corruption. She spins a seductive web which ensnares her emasculated husband, pathetic playboys, jewel thieves, and even Marlowe himself. Like Spade in the earlier film, Marlowe accepts money from manipulative clients who assume that he can be bought, although his own moral code eventually prevails. Unlike Spade, however, the detective-hero in *Murder, My Sweet* is not left alone in the end. Mrs. Grayle's "good" stepdaughter, Ann Grayle (Anne Shirley), is essentially opposed to the *femme noire*: she is unselfish, kind, devoted to her father despite his weakness and thus to the values of hearth and home, and she is genuinely concerned for the detective's well-being.

Once Marlowe completes the flashback story and the police are convinced of his innocence, he is allowed to leave the police station with Ann. His eyes are bandaged when he leaves the station (due to a burst of gunfire too near his face during a climactic shootout), and he initially is unaware of Ann's presence. The bandaged eyes serve a dual narrative function: they visually reaffirm the social and moral "blindness" associated with the hero's naive romanticism, and they also provide a pretext for bringing Marlowe and Ann together.

Their closing embrace presents us with a narrative epilogue quite different from that of *The Maltese Falcon*. In *Murder, My Sweet* the detective realizes some solace, some kind of reprieve from a world otherwise devoid of human contact and concern. However, we realize that the reprieve is only temporary; regardless of the hero's physical debility or emotional attachment at the conclusion of a case, when we meet him again he will be on his own, ready to immerse himself once again in what Chandler once termed "a world gone wrong."

In retrospect, the script and characterization in *Murder, My Sweet* are not quite on a par with those of *The Maltese Falcon*. Dmytryk's direction and camerawork, nevertheless, do anticipate the wedding of story and style which would distinguish later hardboiled-detective films like *The Big Sleep, The Killers, The Third Man, The Big Heat,* and *Touch of Evil.* Another 1944 production vital to the development of the genre is *Double Indemnity,* directed by Billy Wilder and co-scripted (from a novel by James M. Cain) by Wilder and Chandler. Theirs was a stormy collaboration. (Chandler: "Working with Billy Wilder on *Double Indemnity* was an agonizing experience and has probably shortened my life, but I learned from it about as much about screenwriting as I am capable of learning, which is not very much." Wilder: "He [Chandler] gave me more aggravation than any other writer I ever worked with.")[7] (Henley, 1978). Despite their squabbles, the two writers created one of the decade's most dramatic screenplays and three of its strongest characters: Phyllis

Hardboiled hero and the femme noire: two different incarnations of Marlowe—Powell in Murder, My Sweet and Bogart in The Big Sleep—enjoy an intimate moment with women whose motives and allegiance are very much in doubt. Murder, My Sweet (Wisconsin Center for Film and Theatre Research); The Big Sleep (Culver Pictures)

Dietrichson (Barbara Stanwyck), Walter Neff (Fred MacMurray), and Barton Keyes (Edward G. Robinson).

James M. Cain's original story and narrative style certainly would qualify as "hardboiled," even though a detective is not the central character. The story focuses upon a personable but essentially weak and amoral insurance agent (Neff) who is convinced by a seductive suburban siren (Phyllis) to murder her boorish bourgeois husband and bilk the insurance company on a double-indemnity, accidental-death clause. All of this is observed from a distance by Barton Keyes, a close friend of Neff's and chief claims investigator for the insurance company. The story is related from Neff's perspective and not from Keyes', although the authors' narrative strategy does transform the film into a detective story. Cain's original story, which followed Neff through his relationship with Phyllis, had a simple linear plot, but the screenwriters decided to use the flashback time frame that Dmytryk and his screenwriter, John Paxton, had used in *Murder, My Sweet.* This narrative device again provided a context for voice-over narration, only this time the implicit theme of fatalism is given a new and significant slant: The narrator, Neff, identifies himself at the very outset of the film, even before the flashback begins, as the victim of Phyllis' ploys and as her husband's killer.

Double Indemnity opens with a car careening through dark, rain-soaked city streets and eventually stopping in front of an office building. A lone figure staggers out and makes his way into the building and enters an office. It is Walter Neff, who sits at a desk, turns on the lamp (the only visible light source in the frame), and begins speaking into a dictaphone as blood begins to saturate his coat. Neff is addressing Keyes, and tells him: "I killed Dietrichson. . . . I killed him for the money—and for a woman. [Pause to inhale on a cigarette, his face barely visible in the shadows.] I didn't get the money, and I didn't get the woman. It all started. . . ."

With that Wilder cuts to Neff's first meeting with Phyllis, and the cinema-past plot line is set into motion. Not only does this opening sequence engage our curiosity and sympathy for Neff, but it also encourages us to cast ourselves, along with the as-yet unidentified "Keyes," in the role of investigator-observer. This perspective is enhanced by the fact that Neff seems so detached from his cinema-past self. As we learn through his narrative, Neff's involvement with Phyllis has enabled him to enter the world of moral and social evil. He now recounts his experience with the objective, fatalistic air of a dying man who finally has realized the error of his ways and is able to investigate his own tragic fall.

In a *Time* magazine review of *Double Indemnity,* James Agee wrote that the film "is to a fair extent soaked and shot through with money and the coolly intricate amorality of money; you can even supply the idea, without being contradicted by the film, that among these somewhat representative Americans money and sex and a readiness to murder are as inseparably interdependent as the Holy Trinity"[8] (Agee, 1958, p. 119). In Neff's inability to distinguish between his lust for Phyllis and his lust for easy wealth and intrigue, he is drawn into a chain of events—instigated by Phyllis—which had begun long before they met. (She already had murdered her husband's first wife; she now intends to use Neff to kill her husband and later use her stepdaughter's boyfriend to dispose of Neff.) From the moment when Neff first glimpses Phyllis at the top of a stairway wearing only a towel and gold anklet, he begins a ride that takes them both, in his own prophetic words, "to the end of the line."

Their courtship begins predictably enough, with the two exchanging sexual banter. Later there is a torrid affair and eventually a murder plot is hatched between them. Phyllis' alluring sensuality leads the unwitting Neff into the conspiracy, but once the murder has been committed, their sexual relationship steadily disintegrates and with it the perverse attraction they initially had for one another. In what is perhaps the darkest and most intense sequence in any '40s film, Neff and Phyllis consummate their physical relationship in a brilliantly understated dance of death, which culminates in a symbolic embrace. The traditional values of romantic love, monogamy, and procreative sexual fulfillment have been turned inside out: love has turned to greed and lust, the bond of marriage has been shattered, and the climactic "sex act" is performed with a gun. In almost total darkness (for most of the sequence we can see only portions of their faces), Phyllis shoots Neff from several feet away but is unable to fire again, confessing, "I never loved you . . . until a minute ago, when I couldn't fire that second shot." For the first time in her black-widow career, Phyllis has felt something for her victim ("I never thought that could happen to me"), but now it is too late, as it was for Neff the minute he first saw her. With Neff's parting words to Phyllis—"I'm sorry, baby, I'm not buying"—the confusion of sexual and material lust is reaffirmed, and as they embrace, he fires twice.

This deadly coupling returns us to the film's opening moments. Neff's descent into the heart of darkness is complete, but he stops to record it for Keyes—and for us—before fleeing.

Neff has come to understand his own weakness, and as narrator he is virtually doubled with his former cinema-past self. He has arrived at the truth; he understands Phyllis' capacity for evil and his own as well, but unlike the hardboiled-detective-hero he has learned this only through self-destructive human experience. Walter Neff is, finally, one of us. He has gone to his office not to await another case and to hold the evil temporarily at bay like Marlowe, but to acknowledge that it has enveloped and destroyed him. It's worth noting here that Wilder initially ended the film with Walter's execution in the gas chamber, but he later opted for the film's existing conclusion depicting a confrontation between Keyes and the dying Walter Neff in the office.

Robinson's portrayal of the betrayed but still devoted colleague and father figure makes this ending pay off. Keyes is a nine-to-five detective, a claims investigator privy to volumes of statistics but finally getting his information from the "little man" in his gut. His paternal rapport with Neff silences his inner suspicions and enables Neff to dupe the company, although Neff's final confession absolves the killer of his betrayal. As Keyes lights one last cigarette for his dying friend, Neff mutters the now-familiar salutation: "I love you too, Keyes." This gesture of love between two men, whose relationship throughout the film served to counterpoint

Walter's perverse obsession with Phyllis, provides the single trace of hope in an otherwise dark and nihilistic world, but this trace dies with Walter.

The genre's postwar development

In adapting *Double Indemnity* to the screen and adding the flashback framework, Chandler was able to test one of his own fundamental hypotheses about quality detective fiction: "The best mystery story is one you would read even if the last chapter were torn out"[9] (Gardiner and Walker, 1977, p. 130). Chandler and Wilder didn't exactly tear out the last chapter—instead they put it at the beginning. The fact that they let the audience in on the solution underscores the fact that detective fiction of this type is engaging primarily because of the world it depicts and the world view of its principal characters. The "problem" confronted in this and other *noir* films is the necessary alienation, misdirected ambition, and sexual confusion of contemporary urban life. The answer it proposes, in essence, is a stoic detachment which enables one to survive and maintain one's self-respect. Sam Spade and Philip Marlowe survive with their instinctive savvy and sensitivity; Walter Neff is absolved when he realizes his guilt. In all these cases, the message is clear: the only solution to the crime of modern existence is personal integrity and self-sufficiency, which are, in the last analysis, their own reward. What these and later hardboiled-detective films celebrate is not the value of law and order or the power of deductive reasoning, but rather the individual style of the isolated hero. This is a man who can deal with the chaos of urban society and still walk away with a shrug.

The industry's predictable response to the success of *Murder, My Sweet* and *Double Indemnity* was an onslaught of *noir* mysteries, many of which hit the screen in 1946. Included in the group were *The Lady in the Lake, The Killers, The Blue Dahlia, Cornered, The Dark Corner, The Dark Mirror, Dark Alibi, So Dark the Night, Gilda, Fallen Angel, Notorious,* and *The Big Sleep.* This latter film was directed by Howard Hawks and scripted by Leigh Brackett, Jules Furthman, and William Faulkner and cast Bogart as Philip Marlowe and Lauren Bacall as the *femme noire.*

Bogart and Bacall were a natural matchup for *The Big Sleep,* as they were for *Dark Passage* in 1947 and *Key Largo* in 1948. Bacall's screen debut in 1944 (at age 19) in Hawks' *To Have and Have Not* and her instant connection with Bogart—both on and off screen—had distinguished that otherwise mediocre film. By 1946, their impending marriage and tangible on-screen rapport, along with Bogart's established "hardboiled" persona, heavily contributed to the success of *The Big Sleep.* The Bogart-Bacall chemistry was not lost on director Hawks, who was by this time well versed in the conventions of screwball comedy (*Twentieth Century,* 1934; *Bringing Up Baby,* 1938; *His Girl Friday,* 1940). Hawks managed to alternate—depending upon whether Bogart/Marlowe was on screen alone or sharing a scene with Bacall/Vivian—between visually and dramatically intense sequences of action and violence and sequences between Bogart and Bacall of comic banter and bold sexual innuendo.

The film opens as Marlowe arrives at the Sternwood mansion in response to a request from the family patriarch. The old man, seated in his hothouse surrounded by orchids, assigns Marlowe to dispose discreetly of his daughter Carmen's gambling debts. Marlowe serves as Sternwood's emissary to the outside world—which is not simply the criminal milieu but the world at large. Marlowe agrees to take the case, and upon leaving the Sternwood mansion he meets Vivian, Carmen's older sister. Their initial verbal parrying shows off the film's shifting priorities as well as Hawks' capacity to redirect his stylistic and dramatic emphases. Unlike *The Maltese Falcon*, in which Brigid feigns helplessness to secure Spade's commitment, or *Double Indemnity*, in which Phyllis' control over the weak-willed Walter is never in doubt, in *The Big Sleep* Marlowe and Vivian are portrayed as equals. Their jousting ostensibly concerns sister Carmen and Marlowe's assignment, but its real significance lies in the sexual subcurrent which culminates later in a remarkable discussion of horse racing and in Vivian's assertion that "it all depends on who's in the saddle."

The Vivian-Marlowe relationship, like the Ann-Marlowe relationship in *Murder, My Sweet*, poses an interesting complication of the hardboiled-detective formula. Not only does it distract our attention from the detection process, it also interjects a tone of optimism into an essentially nihilistic and *angst*-ridden environment. Hawks maintains a delicate balance between Marlowe's existential isolation (as detective) and the promise of human contact and fulfillment (as lover-spouse), through two narrative devices: at certain opportune moments, he emphasizes Vivian's relationship with gangster Eddie Mars, thereby keeping her commitment to Marlowe continually in doubt, and he qualifies the optimism of romantic love with allusions to pornography (Geiger and Mars' "book" racket), to Carmen's promiscuity and drug addiction, and to Geiger and Carroll's homosexual relationship. We actually wonder near the end of the film whether Vivian will help Marlowe to escape from and execute Mars' henchmen. Because we are unsure of her commitment to him until late in the film, their genuine—and unconventional—relationship dominates neither the film nor our image of the detective-hero; the romance emerges as a rare oasis in a wasteland of anxiety and alienation.

Other filmmakers were not so careful about maintaining a balance between romance and mystery, and their films suffered as a result. In *The Blue Dahlia* (1946) and *Dark Passage* (1947), for instance, the relationship between the detective-hero and the mysterious woman (Alan Ladd and Veronica Lake in the former, Bogart and Bacall in the latter) blossoms into a romance which finally displaces the initial hardboiled-mystery plot and atmosphere. This narrative displacement is especially disappointing in *Dark Passage*, which might have been one of the most distinctive and engaging detective films of the period.

The opening sequences in *Dark Passage*, tracing the prison escape and ensuing flight of the hero, are shot from the protagonist's first-person perspective. This subjective point-of-view strategy is sustained through the hero's coincidental meeting with and befriending of the heroine (Bacall) and culminates in a bizarre rendezvous with an unlicensed plastic surgeon who miraculously transforms the escaped convict into Humphrey Bogart. The transition from this camera-eye technique to a more conventional narrative style is bridged with a surreal dream sequence much like that in *Murder, My Sweet,* which is initiated by the surgeon's anesthetic. Just before the surgeon administers the drug, he leans into the camera-subject and asks, "Ever see a botched plastic job?" The horrific dream which ensues takes us into the mind of the protagonist, but once the dream ends, we finally can "see" the hero and are thereafter disengaged from the first-person camera technique.

Once the protagonist receives his new identity, he begins his search for those who wrongfully sent him to prison and also cultivates his relationship with Bacall. Just when it seems that the evidence implicating him in a number of murders is too damaging to refute, he and Bacall escape with her riches to South America. As Bogart and Bacall dance serenely on a moonlit shore in the film's closing sequence and we realize that the murders will never be solved, expectations generated by the detective plot dissolve. This incredible romantic resolution is especially disturbing in light of the film's dynamic opening and its consistent manipulation of the detective-hero's viewpoint.

Director Delmer Daves was not the first Hollywood director to attempt this camera-as-character strategy to enhance the viewer's identification with the detective. Robert Montgomery's 1946 adaptation of Chandler's *The Lady in the Lake* is certainly the most notable example. After an opening sequence in which actor-director Montgomery (who plays Philip Marlowe) directly addresses the camera to establish the flashback-narrative context, the remainder of the film is shot entirely from Montgomery/Marlowe's physical perspective. The detective-hero speaking directly into the camera lens itself violates the implicit codes of Hollywood filmmaking, rupturing the filmic world's enclosed autonomy. But this initial rupture doesn't begin to prepare us for the sustained first-person camera technique.

While this technique clearly is designed to draw the viewer into the closest possible identification with the detective-hero and his attitude, its ultimate effect is essentially the opposite. Instead of strengthening our empathy for the hero, it serves to further distance us from him, repeatedly reminding us that his perceptions are radically different from ours. The detective-hero is still our avenue of narrative access and his is the organizing sensibility, but as Montgomery's dizzying experiment indicates, narrative filmmaking is most effective when we weigh our own perceptions against those of the hero. It is not enough for us to observe the detective's milieu through his eyes; we must also watch the detective observing his own milieu.

As the more effective hardboiled-detective films demonstrate, viewer identification can be realized adequately through conventional point-of-view and shot/reverse-shot strategies. Generally, a master shot establishes the spatial context and the central character's position within it, and is followed by a close-up or medium-close-up of that character, and then a reverse-angle shot of what the character (now the camera-as-character) actually "sees." Thus a filmmaker initially might establish an omniscient viewpoint to open a sequence and move in and out of the central character's perspective as the sequence demands. The various narrative devices—particularly the flashback framework and also the manipulation of lighting and camerawork to represent the detective's isolated view—more than compensate for the cinema's inability to replicate detective literature's subjective, first-person narrator.

Actually, by the late 1940s the possibility of drawing the viewer into a direct relationship with the detective-hero became increasingly remote as the genre and its central character were subtly altered. Following a historical pattern similar to that of the sound Western, the hardboiled-detective genre began with an essentially naive protagonist of epic-heroic stature, but he lost his invincibility during the postwar years. The early hardboiled-detective film, like the classical Western with its mediator-hero, was naive in its assumption that a hero could hold his corrupt world at bay and survive through his adherence to a self-styled value system. And just as the Westerner eventually began to buckle under the physical, moral, and historical expectations we had placed on his character, so too did the stoic, upright detective. The Westerner, as it happened, could handle the strain and adapt to changes in the audience and the industry, whereas the hardboiled detective could not. By the late 1940s the Spade-Marlowe prototype already had become something of an anachronism.

Perhaps the Western community's historical and physical distance from contemporary audiences enabled its filmmakers to assume an increasingly negative view of the hero and of American urbanization. Another factor which contributed to the genre's postwar success was the industry's technological development. The more frequent use of Technicolor and the innovation of widescreen formats during the early 1950s heightened the Western's visual appeal but were basically incompatible with the hardboiled-detective genre and its *noir* stylistics. Furthermore, the sociohistorical immediacy of the "hardboiled" community, milieu, and plot conventions could not be adjusted to the Cold War anxieties over urban order and still maintain its distinctive narrative framework. In an era of HUAC and blacklisting, when it was considered "un-American" to subvert or even to challenge the ideological status quo, the hardboiled private eye and his decadent milieu faded from American movie screens. The Western effectively confronted topical issues during the Cold War, usually by adjusting the character and role of the Westerner: Wayne as the psychotic capitalist-rancher in *Red River* (1948), Gregory Peck as the conscience-plagued killer in *The Gunfighter* (1950), Jimmy Stewart as the crazed, womanized bounty hunter in *The Naked Spur* (1953), Joan Crawford as the gun-toting saloon owner whose "guilt by association" with local outlaws nearly gets her lynched in *Johnny Guitar* (1954). These and scores of other Cold War Westerns called into question, albeit indirectly, such basic American values as capitalism, democracy, rugged individualism, isolationism, marriage, romantic love, and the nuclear family—and they were able to do so within the genre's traditional narrative framework.

When compared with the remarkably flexible Western formula, the detective genre seems particularly limited. As filmmakers reworked the private eye's essentially antisocial lifestyle to accommodate the political climate—often with a change in occupation to police detective or insurance investigator—he lost his moral and attitudinal edge. The "twenty-five bucks a day and expenses" which had sustained the self-employed detective simply could not be replaced by a weekly paycheck and a commitment to some "legitimate" agency of social order. Unlike the Westerner, who was never quite one of us, the private eye could not be given a prosocial role without radically compromising his and the genre's distinctive thematic appeal.

The genre was also technically inflexible. The emphasis on "street realism" and location shooting in postwar filmmaking meant that the romantic detective in his office retreat would be replaced by a hard-nosed cop on the beat in such "police documentaries" as *The House on 92nd Street* (1945), *The Naked City* (1948), *Call Northside 777* (1948), and *Where the Sidewalk Ends* (1950). Removing the private eye from the controlled environment of the Hollywood studio and placing him in the "real" world—besides giving him a real occupation—further emasculated the detective genre.

Two of the films which come closest to surviving the genre's alteration are Robert Siodmak's *The Killers* (1946) and Rudolph Mate's *D.O.A.* (1949). The former ostensibly is based on a Hemingway short story in which a gas station attendant learns that two hoodlums are in town to murder him, and he inexplicably waits in his room for the killers to arrive. Hemingway's story merely provides the narrative point of departure in Siodmak's film, however; the remainder of the film follows the efforts of an insurance investigator (Edmund O'Brien as Riordan) to identify the killers. The investigation, in which a host of minor characters provide information in a dozen flashbacks, gradually reveals the character of the dead man, Swede (Burt Lancaster in his screen debut). Swede, it seems, was a washed-up prize fighter turned small-time hood, whose troubles were caused not by his commitment to a life of crime but rather to *femme noire* Kitty Collins (Ava Gardner). Swede laments just before he is killed that he "did something wrong, once." This dying epithet (shades of "Rosebud") seems to involve a huge payroll robbery that was covered by Riordan's company, but we eventually realize through Riordan's sleuthing that Swede's tragic error was a more archetypal and fundamental one: he had been seduced and betrayed by the sultry black widow, Kitty.

Riordan's obsession with the case, which his boss insists is a waste of company time, brings him into Swede's world, where eventually he meets Kitty. Riordan avoids her efforts to use him, recovers the payroll, and in the words of his boss, brings "next year's premiums down one tenth of a cent." While Riordan's personal fascination with the case emphasizes his commitment to some higher moral code, his ultimate allegiance to the insurance company and thus to the socioeconomic status quo sets him distinctly apart from the hardboiled, unaffiliated detective. Swede's existential plight, however, and Riordan's growing identification with the dead man tend to offset this resolution. The film's prosocial implications are

"I did something wrong, once." *It turns out that what Swede (Burt Lancaster in his screen debut) did wrong was not falling in with gangsters, but falling for the wrong woman (Ava Gardner, right).* (Culver Pictures)

qualified even more severely by Siodmak's visual stylization: the initial killing is shot in varying degrees of darkness (we never even see Swede's face until later in the flashbacks), and the investigation process itself takes Riordan deep into Swede's dark past.

Darkness in *The Killers* is an artificial, studio-produced effect, though, and considerably different from the bleak atmosphere of Rudolph Mate's location-*noir* thriller, *D.O.A.* This incredible film may be Hollywood's ultimate articulation of urban *angst* and Cold War paranoia. In the film's opening sequence, Edmund O'Brien, again portraying an insurance agent/investigator, stumbles into a police station to describe a murder—his own. He was spending a few days in the Big City (San Francisco) to escape his small-town agency and his domesticating secretary-fiancée, when he was poisoned for no apparent reason with a lethal dose of a mysterious, radium-derived drug which was slipped into his drink. The following day, O'Brien, realizing that his physical discomfort was too severe to ascribe to a hangover, went to a hospital emergency room and learned there that he had only a few days to live.

Mate's dynamic, energetic camera follows him as he runs in panicked desperation through the streets of San Francisco. With his imminent death a foregone conclusion, the condemned man conducts his final investigation, the results of which he relates to the local police with his dying breath. The investigation takes us through the city's back streets, its cheap dives, and abandoned warehouses, all captured in realistic detail. The film's flashback structure and the hero's existential plight are reminiscent of earlier *noir* detective films, but Mate's documentary techniques, especially his use of natural, available light in the exterior location work, enhances the theme of urban isolation. This style works well in *D.O.A.*, but it does mark a significant departure from earlier urban detective films with their visual intensity and dramatic preoccupations.

The police-detective variation

The hardboiled detective also survived in the guise of the displaced cop. Examples of this hybrid—an amalgam of the detective and gangster-as-cop formulas—can be traced back into the 1940s in Preminger's *Laura* (1944) and Dmytryk's *Crossfire* (1947) and culminate in Welles' brilliant *Touch of Evil* (1958). In these films, the cop's disillusionment and individual isolation arise out of the very ideals that had motivated Spade and Marlowe to opt for private practice rather than institutional police work. Like their "hardboiled" counterparts, these cops are committed to the utopian ideal of urban order, but their agencies have been corrupted either by ineptitude or avarice—if not both, as in Fritz Lang's *The Big Heat* (1953)—and thus idealism has turned into cynicism. The cop functions by his own self-styled moral code, but his ultimate allegiance to the force undercuts his initial isolation as well as his mediating function. In the '40s variations, however, allegiance to the force often seems to be a gratuitous plot device, and consequently the hero's narrative function and attitude seem closely aligned with those of the hardboiled detective. Most '50s variations involve a cop-crusader out to "clean up the force," legitimizing his own prosocial function and individual idealism within a traditional agency.

In Fritz Lang's *The Big Heat*, for example, police detective Dave Bannion (Glenn Ford) quits his job when the gangster-politico who controls the force's commanding officers kills Bannion's wife with a bomb meant for him. Lang's graphic depiction of Bannion's psychopathic desire for personal and social retribution effectively makes the point that urban order can be achieved only at the price of human life and mental stability. Bannion's character is mirrored throughout by Lee Marvin's mindless, maniacal hood, Vince Stone, who both reflects and opposes Bannion's attitudes and behavior.

The hero eventually cleans up the force and returns the urban community to a state of equilibrium, but not until we have been shown that urban order is merely temporary and gratuitous. Like so many '50s crime films, especially those steeped like this one in *noir* stylistics, the prosocial resolution is distinctly at odds with the narrative. Corruption is seen not as a function of individual criminality but of the urban socioeconomic system itself. Bannion confronts this corruption only after his wife is dead; once he has resigned from his job, he has virtually nothing left to lose. His eventual return to the force after he has sent the gangster chieftain to prison resolves the superficial plot complications, but it cannot offset the film's deeper and more lasting impressions: the bleak urban wasteland "out there" beyond the secure, well-lit police station, the scalding coffee Marvin throws in the face of a betraying siren (Gloria Grahame), the death and/or mutilation of every significant female character in the film, and so on.

This familiar tension between the initial statement of the narrative "problem" and its eventual resolution represents a recurring dilemma for the genre analyst. That is, assuming that the basis for a genre's appeal is its formal articulation of some basic cultural contradiction, and assuming that as the genre develops it

In Fritz Lang's manic detective thriller The Big Heat, *Dave Bannion (Glenn Ford, pictured here with Lee Marvin) strikes out on his own to clean up the corruption both on the police force and in the streets.* (Penguin Photos)

learns to articulate that contradiction more directly, then it necessarily follows that its "solution" to the problem will become increasingly forced, stylized, artificial. Lang, like many of his contemporaries in Hollywood, became a master of the requisite happy ending, and resolved immediate social conflicts with a forced optimism that only emphasized the contradictory nature of the values involved in his films. The last line of dialogue in *The Big Heat*, for instance—in which a grinning, reinstated Bannion, about to leave the station on another case, turns and says, "By the way, don't forget the coffee"—would seem to be Lang's knowing wink about the forced optimism of the prosocial outcome to an audience still numb from the coffee-flinging incident earlier in the film.

Certain filmmakers, though, did not transform the genre film's happy ending into an ironic thematic counterpoint. Many of Hollywood's finest directors, like John Ford and Orson Welles, used the resolution as a way of lamenting the price which society must pay when it confronts its own contradictory value system. In Ford's later Westerns, just as in Welles' 1958 film, *Touch of Evil*, the ending deals with the death of the traditional hero, whose rugged self-reliance and violent demeanor finally are at odds with the community he had served to promote and protect.

Touch of Evil traces the efforts of special investigator Mike Vargas (Charlton Heston) to clean up the narcotics traffic and also the corrupt police force in a sleazy Mexican-American border town. As the film's complex narrative unwinds, however, this surface plot gradually dissolves to reveal the film's primary concerns: the nature and process of police justice and the exploration of a new type of hero, the technocratic supercop. Heston's macho hero is juxtaposed with Hank Quinlan (played by Welles, who also directed and scripted the film), a seedy, obese, intimidating cop with a remarkable track record for solving difficult cases. The reason for his success, Vargas discovers, is Quinlan's talent for planting bogus evidence and using third-degree tactics to extract confessions. Welles' portrayal of the aging, corrupt cop finally victimized by one of his own schemes is so effective that Quinlan emerges as the film's most sympathetic character. During the course of the action, Vargas uncovers the truth about Quinlan's police procedures, even winning Quinlan's long-time friend and partner (Joseph Calleia as Sergeant Pete Menzes) to his cause. As this occurs, Quinlan self-destructs before our eyes. He works with and then murders one of the dope-runners Vargas has been investigating and desperately tries to frame Vargas for this crime and so divert attention from his own misdeeds. His end is foretold by the fading madam of a Mexican brothel (Marlene Dietrich) whom he turned to for solace. When he asks her to read his fortune, she gently tells him, "You haven't got any. Your future is all used up."

Meanwhile, in order to record Quinlan's confession, Vargas convinces Menzes to help him carry an electronic eavesdropping device. But even though he is drunk, Quinlan detects Vargas' scheme and is able to gain momentary control over his nemesis. It is at this point that Quinlan shoots Menzes; then, just as he is about to execute Vargas, the dying Menzes shoots his old partner in the back. As Quinlan

Hardboiled baroque: Orson Welles not only played detective Hank Quinlan in Touch of Evil *(1958), but he directed the film and adapted the screenplay as well. In this shot, Welles' framing, lighting, and characterization coalesce into an image of a world as stylized as it is corrupt.* (Culver Pictures)

floats face down in the garbage-strewn Rio Grande at film's end, the various characters gather on the bank to mourn his death. We are now informed that the suspect Quinlan has tried to frame has confessed to the very murder which had initiated the Vargas-Quinlan confrontation. When one of the mourners suggests, "Well, Hank [Quinlan] was one hell of a detective," Dietrich replies caustically, "And a lousy cop."

As this informal eulogy suggests, Welles created in the character of Hank Quinlan the necessary culmination of the hardboiled-detective figure. Here the detective's self-styled relativism has hardened into moral absolutism, his sense of integrity and fair play has given way to the demand for self-preservation, and perhaps most significantly, his spiritual isolation and self-indulgence have affected his physical form—he has grown old and disgustingly fat.

Welles' (and cameraman Russell Metty's) cinematic vision of this dark, surreal, urban environment also emphasizes the institutional decay that has infected it. Although the film was shot on location in Venice, California, the lighting and use of distorting wide-angle lenses create a baroque, disorienting, and threatening atmosphere. The visual distortion is offset by Welles' penchant for long takes—most notably in the film's opening sequence and later when Quinlan plants the evidence in the suspect's apartment—these give a sense of spatial integrity to the milieu which at the same time the camera lens distorts. Thus the filmic world is both real and artificial, both familiar and abstract, much like the hardboiled hero himself. In humanizing the previously romanticized hero—even to the point of his advancing age and death—while situating him in a distorted urban milieu, Welles effectively articulates both the social immediacy and the mythic abstraction inherent within the genre. Such qualities are concentrated in a central character whose death signals the passing of the traditional hardboiled detective and his world. *Touch of Evil* stands as one of the genuine masterpieces of detective fiction and of Hollywood expressionist cinema.

Quinlan's death notwithstanding, the hardboiled detective did survive the 1950s—although he was more prevalent in popular literature than in the cinema. Spade and Marlowe gradually made way for a less heroic, more brutal private eye, best typified by Mike Hammer in the widely popular Mickey Spillane novels (*I, the Jury, Kiss Me Deadly*, etc.). Spillane's talent for exploiting mindless cruelty and sexual titillation drew literally millions of readers into Hammer's world—a much wider market than for the Hammett and Chandler books.

Despite Spillane's success, however, only Robert Aldrich's 1955 film, *Kiss Me Deadly*, brought Hammer to the screen with any real flavor. Ralph Meeker portrays Hammer, a character whom Aldrich himself described (in an interview with François Truffaut) as "an antidemocrat, a fascist"[10] (Sadoul, 1972, p. 178). No longer an isolated moralist, Hammer's detective assumes a more assertive, overtly ideological role in his self-assigned mission to rid society of corruption. Unlike his romantic predecessors, at odds with both the criminal elements and the insensitive prosocial forces, Hammer is a hard-bitten pragmatist whose values are based firmly in the paranoid absolutism of Cold War America. Hammer's pragmatism also leads him to take divorce cases—the "real-life" bread and butter of private detectives—which his generic forefathers had steadfastly disdained. In *Kiss Me Deadly*, Hammer lives in an art-deco pad (decorated with checkerboard linoleum, tacky statuettes, and pop paintings), drives a sportscar, hunts down smuggled radioactive materials, and pursues his secretary, with whom he has more than a platonic rapport. Professionally, her primary function is to lure decadent married men into bed so that her boss can strong-arm them. Hammer finally gets the girl and the materials, only to be destroyed in the film's final moments by an apparent atomic holocaust. (Aldrich: "I made the ending ambiguous to avoid police interference"[10] [Sadoul, 1972, p. 178].)

Hammer is ultimately no further removed from his heroic predecessors than, say, Jimmy Stewart's maniacal Westerner is from his own classic predecessors in

'50s films such as *The Naked Spur* and *The Man from Laramie*. But while the self-reflexive "psychological Westerns" were popular throughout the 1950s, Aldrich's "psychological detective film" stands virtually alone. Hammer's obvious commitment to '50s Americanism and the ideological status quo—what Aldrich termed his "fascism"—actually places him closer to the disillusioned cops of that era than to the hardboiled detectives of the previous decade. The new hero fulfills the detective's traditional mediating function by having sole access to both the prosocial and anarchic forces, but his allegiance to the prosocial is never in doubt. Hammer's detective is at bottom a self-appointed cop who disdains police procedure and legal loopholes and metes out justice on his own terms without fear of bureaucratic or judicial interference. The ironic effect of *Kiss Me Deadly* is that Hammer's very refusal to question the value system he blindly supports encourages the viewer to take the opposite stance. The man is all action and no *angst*, a pathetic extension of the hardboiled hero into an era of moral and political absolutism. Ultimately, the only difference between Hammer and the cops he continually derides is that he doesn't have to follow the rules.

Regeneration in the New Hollywood

The classic hardboiled-detective formula and its romantic knight-errant hero disappeared from the screen after the 1940s and lay dormant until the New Hollywood of the 1960s and '70s unearthed them. The revival seems to have begun in 1966–67 with a handful of interesting but generally uninspired private-eye sagas: Jack Smight's *Harper* (1966) and Blake Edwards' *Tony Rome* and John Boorman's muddled but occasionally brilliant *Point Blank* (both 1967), to name a few. Philip Marlowe himself returned to the screen in *Marlowe* (1969), based on Chandler's *The Little Sister*. *Marlowe* is consistently true to the "hardboiled" formula and style, even within its '60s-hip milieu and bright Technicolor photography. Much of the film's modest success is due to James Garner's relaxed, understated portrayal of the hero and also to Los Angeles' continuing reputation as the center of urban American decadence. (Garner's success with his "Maverick" television role is an apt indication of the resemblance between the Westerner and his contemporary hardboiled counterpart.)

This return to the hardboiled-detective formula reached a peak in the 1970s with such films as Robert Altman's *The Long Goodbye*, Arthur Penn's *Night Moves*, and Roman Polanski's *Chinatown*. Actually, these films represent the cream of a fairly substantial crop of detective films (including *Farewell, My Lovely; The Big Sleep; The Late Show;* and *The Big Fix*), as well as a number of parodies (*Gumshoe, Pulp, Shamus, The Cheap Detective*), and also some interesting variations on the private-eye formula (*The Conversation, Three Days of the Condor, Marathon Man, Klute*). The displaced cop or police detective enjoyed a new vitality during this period due to the resurgence of the private-eye genre, most notably in *Bullitt, Madigan,* and *Dirty Harry*.

Television was also well into the hardboiled formula during the 1970s, producing such hardboiled series as *City of Angels, Harry O,* and *The Rockford Files,* in addition to a number of sanitized, softboiled detectives (*Mannix, Barnaby Jones, Cannon,* et al.) and streetwise cops (*Baretta, Kojak, Starsky and Hutch,* et al.). Ironically, television's heaviest contribution to the formula was during the '50s and early '60s, when Hollywood's hardboiled output was virtually nil. Consider some of the more popular series of the '50s: *Martin Kane, Private Eye, Ellery Queen, The Third Man, Peter Gunn, Richard Diamond, Private Detective, Mr. Lucky, 77 Sunset Strip,* and *Man with a Camera.* The private eye in these series was a watered-down version of his cinematic ancestor, and the cinema's *noir* stylistics were difficult to achieve on the television screen. "Shooting for the box" demanded a style of flat, low-contrast

Chinatown *was the best of the 1970s crop of detective thrillers, flashing back to '30s Los Angeles but seen through the eyes of a distinctly contemporary hero (Jack Nicholson as Jake Gittes). Here, director Roman Polanski (at left with his back to the camera) assumes the bit part of a gangster trying to temper Gittes' professional enthusiasm.* (Culver Pictures)

lighting and unobtrusive camerawork during those black-and-white years. But even in this diluted format, it was evident that the detective-hero was waiting in the wings, eager for a change in cultural climate that once again would require him to seek out the conflicts and contradictions within his environment.

The weather certainly changed in the 1960s, and cynicism, alienation, and frustrated romanticism reappeared, along with a nostalgic longing for the supposed simplicity of pre-'60s America. The detective's world was a more complex place now than it had been: instead of a "just" world war, there was Vietnam; instead of women waiting at home for their guys, there was the Women's Movement; urban blight had intensified to spawn ghettos and race riots; and development of the bomb was responsible for estimations of "overkill" and "nuclear parity."

These and other cultural realities indicated a substantial revaluation of American ideology, and the detective-hero necessarily reflected the change in values. As did his '40s prototype, the screen detective of the 1970s accepted social corruption as a given and tried to remain isolated from it, still the naive idealist beneath the cynical surface. But the new detective of the '70s inhabited a milieu he was unable to understand or to control—even in a period film like *Chinatown* where that milieu is depicted as late-'30s Los Angeles. No longer a hero-protector, the detective in more recent films is himself the ultimate victim. His inability to control his milieu and his destiny may result in his death, as in *Night Moves*, or in a final act of uncharacteristic anger, as when Marlowe cold-bloodedly assassinates his own double-crossing client at the end of *The Long Goodbye*.

Perhaps the clearest image of the contemporary hardboiled detective's ineffectuality appears in the closing moments of *Chinatown*. In the course of Polanski's film (scripted by Robert Towne), L.A.'s Chinatown emerges as the metaphoric center of urban duplicity and corruption. The detective (Jack Nicholson as Jake Gittes) had once worked the Chinatown beat for the D.A.'s office but had resigned under mysterious circumstances. The film's plot eventually leads Gittes back to Chinatown, where his client-lover (Faye Dunaway as the *femme noire*) finally is killed and the villain (John Huston, director of *The Maltese Falcon*) gains control over the community. As Gittes walks away from the dead woman's car and from the apparently unassailable villain, his partner delivers the film's closing line, a fitting epitaph for the hardboiled-detective genre itself: "Forget it, Jake, it's Chinatown."

The
Screwball Comedy

6

"Show me a good piggybacker and I'll show you a real human. I never met a rich man yet who could give piggybacks."

—Peter Warne (*Clark Gable*) *in* It Happened One Night

In 1934, Hollywood produced two of the most critically and commercially successful romantic comedies in its history: *Twentieth Century* (directed by Howard Hawks, scripted by Ben Hecht and Charles MacArthur) and *It Happened One Night* (directed by Frank Capra, scripted by Robert Riskin). The films, released within a few months of each other, marked the culmination of a type of screen comedy popularized during the early sound era—fast-paced, witty comedies of manners exploiting the foibles of America's leisure class, best exemplified by Ernst Lubitsch's *Trouble in Paradise* and *Design for Living* and in George Cukor's *Dinner at Eight*. In the tradition of those upper-crust romantic comedies, *Twentieth Century* and *It Happened One Night* reassured Depression audiences that the filthy rich were, after all, just folks like you and me, and that although money didn't necessarily buy happiness, it certainly generated some interesting social and sexual complications.

Whereas these two films extended the filmic comedy of manners, however, Capra's *It Happened One Night* introduced a dimension that would effectively reconstitute Hollywood's romantic comedy tradition. Into the frantic, decadent world of the idle rich, Capra injected a sense of homespun populism and middle-class ideology. This narrative and thematic variation was refined throughout the 1930s in a great many socially-conscious battles of the

150

sexes, most notably in *My Man Godfrey*, *Mr. Deeds Goes to Town* (1936), *The Awful Truth*, *Easy Living*, *Nothing Sacred* (1937), *Bringing Up Baby*, *You Can't Take It with You*, *Holiday* (1938), *Bachelor Mother*, *In Name Only*, *Mr. Smith Goes to Washington* (1939), *His Girl Friday*, *My Favorite Wife*, *The Great McGinty*, *Christmas in July*, *Philadelphia Story* (1940), *The Lady Eve*, *Meet John Doe*, *Here Comes Mr. Jordan*, and *The Bride Came C.O.D.* (1941).

By restructuring the fast-paced upper-crust romance, the screwball comedy dominated Depression-era screen comedy and provided that period's most significant and engaging social commentary. As historian Georges Sadoul has pointed out, "*It Happened One Night* established a new style whose theme became stereotyped in hundreds of romantic comedies of the thirties"[1] (Sadoul, 1972, p. 160). It is not surprising that Capra's film was reworked and refined into a distinct formula. The movie broke box-office records nationwide and gathered Academy Awards for its director, screenwriter, leading actor, leading actress, and for best picture of 1934. It is also not surprising that the screwball comedy genre generated by Capra's film has received such scant critical attention, because it lacks easily identifiable elements of setting and iconography. As Sadoul suggests, the screwball comedy is distinguished essentially by its style and theme. The genre derives its identity from a style of behavior (reflected in certain camerawork and editing techniques) and from narrative patterns that treat sexual confrontation and courtship through the socioeconomic conflicts of Depression America.

This generic trend was anticipated by the early-'30s romantic comedies, primarily in their narrative pacing and their concern for class distinctions and attitudes. Hawks' *Twentieth Century*, for instance, traces the efforts of a Broadway producer (John Barrymore) to convince his ex-wife (Carole Lombard), who earlier had left him and the Broadway stage for Hollywood stardom, to return to the legitimate theater. Most of the action occurs aboard a train (the Twentieth Century Limited). Both the claustrophobic atmosphere of the compartments and the constant motion provide an ideal context for Barrymore and Lombard's incessant jousting as well as an apt metaphor for contemporary American life.

Hawks manages the film's breakneck pace and the exchanges of witty, sarcastic dialogue with precise timing. In the early 1930s, Hollywood still was adapting to sound, and the type of romantic interplay used in screwball comedy effectively balanced word and action. As the Barrymore-Lombard confrontation intensifies throughout the film, they find themselves in progressively more restricting circumstances, culminating in Barrymore's outrageous "death scene" in a narrow aisle amid his goggling fellow passengers. Although we in the audience identify both with Barrymore's efforts to recover his starlet-wife and also with her marvelous resistance, our primary sympathies lie with the passengers who are both bemused and befuddled by this comic rendition of "how the other half lives." The milieu of these upper-crust comedies is one whose values are worlds away from those of Hollywood's mass audience. It was not until *It Happened One Night* that the ideological distance between these disparate worlds was bridged effectively.

The prototype: *It Happened One Night*

Capra's film, at first glance, has a good deal in common with Hawks' *Twentieth Century*. Both trace the cross-country odyssey of an antagonistic couple whose battle of wits eventually dissolves into mutual affection. Both are directed in a style that gives equal play to verbal and visual comedy and propels the plot along rapidly. What distinguishes *It Happened One Night* from the other upper-crust comedies of manners of that period, though, is that Capra and Riskin clearly base the couple's antagonism in their socioeconomic differences (i.e., social class, income, attitudes toward work, leisure, money, and so forth). The working out of their antagonism, therefore, emerges as the central thematic issue in the narrative. In other words, the film suggests that if the working-class stiff and the spoiled heiress can overcome their ideological disparity and finally embrace, then we should not lose faith in the traditional American ideal of a classless utopian society—or at the very least, of a society in which real human contact between the classes could occur.

Plot and theme in the screwball comedy are essentially a function of character, with the lovers set in opposition along both sexual and socioeconomic lines. In *It Happened One Night,* she (Claudette Colbert as Ellie Andrews) is the runaway daughter of an industrial tycoon, fleeing to marry an obnoxious playboy; he (Clark Gable as Peter Warne) is a maverick newspaper reporter whose cynical veneer masks his commitment to traditional American values. The two meet coincidentally and form an uneasy alliance, embarking on a comic odyssey from Miami to New York City: She needs his streetwise savvy and ready cash to avoid discovery by her father's detectives. He needs the exclusive story of her flight to bolster his flagging career.

Despite the difference in social class, it becomes increasingly obvious that they share the same ideals of individual self-assertion, direct and honest human interaction, and a healthy disregard for depersonalizing social restrictions. Beneath Peter's tough, macho exterior is a sensitive moralist waiting for the "right woman" to domesticate him. He respects women, marriage, hard work, and an honest dollar; he resents Ellie's easy, irresponsible affluence and all it represents. As the film progresses through a gamut of social settings and comic situations, Peter's cynical demeanor and Ellie's haughty insensitivity gradually break down, resulting in their predictable embrace and promise of marriage at film's end.

It is a tribute to the particular talents of Gable and Colbert, not to mention director Capra and screenwriter Riskin, that *It Happened One Night* works so well. Peter and Ellie's mutual attraction and eventual coupling come from shared values and attitudes that run deeper than their backgrounds. Thus their stormy courtship is credible and engaging. Our initial introduction to these characters cues us to their similarity—each is flaunting some traditional authority figure. Ellie reacts to her domineering father's veto of her wedding plans by leaping from his yacht; Peter is fired in an exchange of insults with his editor over the telephone. While these acts of willful individualism ally the principals, their differing social class

It Happened One Night: *differences in social class enhanced the romantic antagonism between heiress Ellie Andrews (Claudette Colbert) and reporter Peter Warne (Clark Gable). These differences were manifested in the "Walls of Jericho," which, hung between their beds during their cross-country odyssey, eventually came tumbling down.* (Penguin Photos)

separates them. Ellie is rejecting her father to marry an even more superficial and insensitive aristocrat (King Westley, played by Jameson Thomas). She is, in a sense, simply swimming from one yacht to another. Peter, on the other hand, has a good deal more to lose in standing up to his boss, especially from the viewpoint of a Depression audience. Significantly, Peter is fired while he is in a phone booth at a bar where he has been commiserating with other victims of the Depression, all of whom overhear his phone call and applaud his standing up for the rights of the working man.

But Peter's confrontation with his editor is simply another in a long line of similar collisions. Ellie's rejection of her father represents a somewhat more severe break, although her choice of such a boorish fiancé initially hides the severity of that break. As her relationship with Peter puts Ellie in closer touch with her feelings and values, however, she realizes that her playboy fiancé actually had little to do with her running away. Ellie's rebellion against her father's stifling propriety and insensitivity has already prepared her for rejecting the playboy as well. It is Peter, of course, who brings out Ellie's deeper sensibilities, and in the process he learns that human goodness is not a function of social class. Their mutual education is complete when, midway through the film, the two exchange lessons in acts of genuine Americana: he teaches her the pleasures of riding piggyback, she teaches him the value of a shapely calf in hitchhiking.

Once Peter and Ellie have gotten past their differences and recognize their "deeper" mutual attraction, the narrative concerns are redefined. Both Peter's desire for the exclusive story and Ellie's for her fiancé must be undone so that the couple can commit themselves to one another. This act is finally accomplished, interestingly enough, through the intervention of Ellie's father. Mr. Andrews (Walter Connolly), in fact, is an important character in the screwball comedy: he is the patriarch-aristocrat who somehow has lost sight of the very qualities (self-reliance, assertiveness, an enlightened sense of the real meaning of material possessions) that enabled him to attain wealth and prestige. Peter and Ellie's flight reeducates her father, and it is finally through his encouragement that Ellie vetoes marriage to Westley and elopes with Peter.

Peter's own father figure, his editor, also is transformed during the film from an insensitive ogre to a sympathetic paternal advisor, who upon realizing that Peter has fallen in love, has only the reporter's best interests at heart. The fact that Peter has fallen for a woman who might provide Page One copy for the newspaper is perhaps one reason for his change of heart, although Peter's romantic idealism prohibits any exploitation of his lover's notoriety. Ultimately, both father figures in the film change from depersonalizing tyrants into benevolent patriarchs who rediscover through the lovers those traditional American values so easily forgotten within a chaotic urban-industrial climate.

The two are countered throughout by the playboy fiancé who "learns" nothing in the course of the film and remains mired in the same elitist, upper-class value system that Peter had helped the others to renegotiate. The character of Westley represents the second-generation rich who, unlike the senior Andrews, did not "earn" their position on the social register but received it through birthright. His inherited wealth, in this film and in others like *My Man Godfrey*, *Easy Living*, and *Holiday*, is continually at odds with the inheritance of certain basic values (marriage, home, family, productivity, self-reliance, personal integrity) that transcend birthright and social class.

It is ultimately the film's "marriage" of the aristocracy and the working middle class that provides its strongest thematic statement. The prospect of marriage had provided a narrative and thematic undercurrent throughout the film. But it is not until the closing sequence that Ellie, who has hesitated until the last possible moment, follows her father's advice and bolts from a lavish wedding to elope with Peter. Only then is the ideal of marriage celebrated in proper perspective. The film's two false marriages—the impending marriage of Ellie and Westley and the pretended marriage between Ellie and Peter during their travels to conceal her true identity—prepare us for the "real" marriage at the end.

The pretense of Ellie and Peter's marriage en route from Miami to New York was affirmed by the metaphoric "Walls of Jericho," a blanket Peter hung between the couple's beds representing both his sense of propriety and also the personal, sexual, and ideological distances between the two young people. In the film's closing sequence the walls come tumbling down—off-screen, of course—signifying the union of the screwball couple as well as of their respective value systems. Thus their personal union serves to celebrate integration into the community at large, into a social environment where cultural conflicts and contradictions have been magically reconciled.

Few screwball comedies were able to reproduce the effect of *It Happened One Night*, although scores of them attempted to. Without an artificial plot device to overcome narrative illogic and to resolve the sociosexual conflicts, the screwball comedy requires a precise handling of its opposed couple and their values if it is finally to unite them without appearing either cynical or naive. Because the more effective Depression comedies reconciled sexual and ideological differences involving fundamental contradictions in our culture, resolving the plot often demanded a rather severe narrative rupture. Capra's film for the most part avoids any break in narrative logic or character development in moving from conflict to resolution. However, it does require that Ellie and her father substantially change their attitudes and values. Ellie's transformation is motivated by her contact with Peter and with "middle America" during their comic-epic odyssey; her father's reevaluation seems more a product of osmosis. But whatever inconsistency we may find in him is offset by the fact that he finally gets what he wanted from the start: someone other than King Westley for a son-in-law.

The screwball genre's dilemma: Reconciling class differences

Most of the screwball comedies that followed—and even some of the very best of the genre—tended to reconcile their conflicts either through an unmotivated change in character or through some artificial plot device. This was true even of the more successful offspring of Capra's influential comedy—films like *My Man Godfrey, Mr. Deeds Goes to Town, Easy Living,* and *Nothing Sacred*. These used similar dramatic devices to establish their central conflicts but could not find successfully logical resolutions to them. The four films refined the essential ingredients of *It Happened One Night*, reaffirming its promise of sexual-marital communion within a classless utopian environment. Each incorporates a principal couple from differing backgrounds whose initial antagonism gradually turns into romantic love. Each uses conflicts based not only in sexual and class distinctions, but in generational ones as well, setting a powerful, crusty but ultimately benevolent father figure against his spoiled, self-indulgent heirs. The only children in screwball comedy, notably, are the lovers themselves, and their eventual growth into social and sexual maturity is complemented by the education of their figurative parents. This recur-

A scavenger hunt provides diversion for high-society types in My Man Godfrey, turning up "forgotten man" Godfrey (William Powell), who is actually a Boston blue blood out to see how the other half lives. (Culver Pictures)

ring narrative tactic enhances the genre's prosocial posture, not only in bridging the "generation gap," but also in reaffirming the heritage of our forefathers and the necessity of a socioeconomic seniority system.

As in Capra's earlier film, the conflicts begin when the couple meet because of mistaken or altered identity. "Godfrey" (William Powell) is a Boston blue blood living as a hobo who becomes a butler for the family of an eccentric woman (Carole Lombard). Mr. Deeds (Gary Cooper) is a small-town tuba player, greeting-card poet, and volunteer fireman who inherits a fortune and goes to New York, where he falls in love with a "lady in distress" (Jean Arthur), who is actually a newspaper reporter bent upon exploiting him. Mary Smith (Jean Arthur) in *Easy Living* is a struggling secretary who is mistaken for the mistress of an industrial tycoon by his son (Ray Milland), when the old man inadvertently "gives" the secretary a mink coat. In *Nothing Sacred*, a small-town girl (Carole Lombard) is convinced by a drunken doctor that she is suffering from a rare disease and is later transformed into a national *cause célèbre* by a conniving New York reporter (Frederic March).

These later screwball comedies intensified sexual conflicts by extending certain socioeconomic distinctions and by giving them added narrative emphasis, particularly the work/leisure and the rural/urban oppositions. The screwball comedy has a rather odd rapport with the gangster genre in this regard; both flourished in the 1930s and dealt with the erosion of traditional, essentially rural-based values with the gradual urbanization and industrialization of American life. Inevitably, regardless of the basis of the couple's sexual conflicts, things are resolved when one or both of them realizes how financial and material values are less important than the traditional, spiritual, and egalitarian values that contemporary city life threatens to render obsolete.

The genre's rural/urban opposition, usually treated in terms of small-town versus metropolitan attitudes, provided fruitful narrative conflict, because it carried both thematic significance and an endless source of comic situations. The small town/big city conflict is peripherally at issue in *It Happened One Night*. Peter's populist savvy and self-reliance give him a certain rapport with "the folks" they meet beyond the city's depersonalizing confines, but he is basically a city slicker—a smooth-talking, streetwise hustler capable of dealing with any situation gracefully. In later screwball comedies, particularly Capra's Deeds-Smith-Doe trilogy, the role of the city slicker assumes increasingly negative connotations. Either the hero's or heroine's traditional values and attitudes are attributed directly to a rural background and small-town sensibilities. In fact, as the screwball comedy genre evolved, the rural/urban opposition was paralleled with the working class/leisure class opposition. In *Mr. Deeds Goes to Town*, for example, the rural/urban conflict complemented the basic socioeconomic distinctions. Longfellow Deeds' inheritance quite naturally leads him from the modest confines of Mandrake Falls to a mansion in New York City and the chaotic lifestyle his vast wealth necessarily provides.

Godfrey, Mr. Deeds, and other homespun aristocrats

Ellie's altered identity in *It Happened One Night* enables her to step temporarily into the realm of the middle class, but in *Mr. Deeds*, the small-town middle-American hero undergoes an identity change which casts him into the realm of the idle rich. *Nothing Sacred* and *Easy Living* employ similar narrative strategies. The central character—in each case a working woman—is mistakenly thrust into an upper-class urban milieu. *My Man Godfrey* recalls *It Happened One Night* in that it brings a populist hero into the home of an amusing but utterly decadent, bourgeois family. *My Man Godfrey* establishes its oppositions in the opening sequence, when a group of obnoxious, formally-attired aristocrats on a scavenger hunt descend on Powell/Godfrey and a group of hobos lamenting their impoverished state. They settle on Godfrey, who openly derides them for their insensitive snobbery but is drawn into the hunt by a madcap debutante (Lombard). Godfrey's sustained criticism of the idle rich takes a curious turn when we eventually learn that he is in fact the renegade heir to a wealthy family but has taken to the streets to forget an unpleasant love affair.

Godfrey's having seen "both sides of the tracks" endows him with considerable—almost magical—powers: He pawns a valuable necklace (which Lombard's sister had planted in his room and then accused him of stealing) and invests the money. He makes enough money to save his employer's family from bankruptcy and to build a posh nightclub, "The Dump," to provide employment for his old comrades from the hobo camp. Godfrey's enlightened capitalism is a function both of his breeding and of his having rubbed elbows with the downtrodden. Still, the end results of his living two lives are not really all that positive. His investment cleverness does pave the way (in gold) for the predictable Powell-Lombard clinch at the film's end. Yet we don't get the impression that anyone has actually learned anything. Godfrey initially had decried the social and economic inequities of Depression America, but his later actions—rescuing the unappealing Bullock family from poverty, putting his hobo friends to work in a club patronized by the upper class, and finally marrying the shrill, irresponsible Irene Bullock—all seem at odds with those ideals he had previously espoused.

Thus *My Man Godfrey*, after addressing certain problems and contradictions within the American capitalist system, eventually turns to that very system to resolve those problems. The narrative rupture of this resolution is not atypical of Depression-era romantic comedies. They find fault with the existing social system only in order to establish dramatic conflicts and then resolve those conflicts by reaffirming that system and its values.

In *Mr. Deeds Goes to Town*, this rupture is delayed until the highly emotional closing sequence. Through the course of the film, Cooper/Deeds becomes so disenchanted with the trappings of wealth that he decides to give his twenty million to the Depression poor, only to have jealous relatives and shyster lawyers challenge his sanity. The film ends with Deeds' sanity hearing, where an elderly judge listens dispassionately to the opposing sides and then declares Deeds to be "the sanest man who ever walked into this court." Deeds, his beloved reporter, Babe Bennett (Jean Arthur), and the poor folks who had packed the courtroom then celebrate the victory of the little people—and the system—over the forces of unenlightened capitalism.

The dramatic and emotional intensity of this finale serves, above all, to conceal the narrative's fundamental illogic. What made Deeds' character humorous throughout the film was not simply his duck-out-of-water situation, but the fact that indeed the existing capitalist system had no place or patience for a genuinely benevolent, humane millionaire. The unavoidable truth is that within the range of "normalcy" as ascribed by contemporary society, the screwball Deeds simply cannot function, and a newspaper reporter like Bennett will exploit his weird behavior. This keeps us amused with Deeds until the trial, just as Babe Bennett's readers are amused, but then we are denied the truth of the situation by Capra's idealistic, utopian resolution.

Capra relies heavily on dramatic technique during the courtroom sequence to make this narrative reversal work. by steadily playing up Deeds' role in the proceedings (he initially refuses to defend himself but eventually triumphs with his country wit and Christian-democratic values), by increasing the narrative pace of the sequence with shorter camera takes and more movement within the frame, by countering Deeds' down-home wisdom with the stereotypical idiocy of the lawyers and psychiatrists who testify against him, and by an effective use of reaction shots of Babe and of the sympathetic audience in the gallery. We identify with those "folks" in the gallery, of course, and as their emotional reaction to Deeds intensifies so does our own. Eventually, our emotional commitment to the quixotic "little guy" overcomes a more reasoned response.

Another element that injects a degree of credibility into the outcome of Deeds' hearing is the figure of the presiding judge. Again we have the timely intervention of an enlightened father figure, a representative of the status quo who is reeducated by the uninhibited hero in the fundamentals of American democracy. Mr. Andrews' encouragement of Ellie's union with Peter, Mr. Bullock's unwitting assistance of Godfrey, the judge's acquittal of Deeds—each of these represents a reconciliation of generational as well as socioeconomic and sexual differences.

Antagonism and the embrace: Narrative logic and narrative rupture

We should be careful, however, not to overstate the genre's prosocial thematics. One of the more engaging attributes of the genre film is its capacity to play both ends against the middle, to celebrate the contradictions within our culture while seeming to do away with them. In examining generic rites of order, we noted the basic ambiguity inherent within the hero's character and attitude: he is an agent of a social order whose values he himself cannot assimilate. Whether it's the Westerner riding into the sunset, the private eye returning to his office, or the gangster lying dead in the gutter, the hero's individuality is uncompromised. In the screwball comedy—and indeed in all rites of integration—there is a similar ambiguity, although it is realized through different narrative means. On the one hand, the couple's final embrace signifies their integration into the community, but on the other, their "screwball" behavior and disdain for propriety undercut the possibility that they will become conventional citizens once they marry. The role of the assertive, witty, self-reliant woman; the injection of traditional middle-class values (monogamy, democracy, equal opportunity, rugged individualism, etc.) into a decadent urban milieu; and the screwball couple's uninhibited "pursuit of happiness"—these three elements offset and ultimately balance the prosocial implications of marital promise.

Regardless of their screwball antics, the final embrace of two representatives from disparate socioeconomic backgrounds certainly carried prosocial implications in the early days of this genre. In the later 1930s and into the '40s, however, America's preoccupation with the Depression and urban issues diminished and the overt ideological concerns of the screwball comedy formula receded. Of the three directors who dominated the genre in the 1930s—Frank Capra (*It Happened One Night, Mr. Deeds Goes to Town, You Can't Take It with You, Mr. Smith Goes to Washington*); George Cukor (*Dinner at Eight, Sylvia Scarlet, Holiday, Philadelphia Story*); and Howard Hawks (*Twentieth Century, Bringing Up Baby, His Girl Friday*)—only Capra continued to foreground the problem of socioeconomic disparity (*Meet John Doe, It's a Wonderful Life, State of the Union*). It's somewhat ironic that Capra, who along with screenwriter Robert Riskin virtually invented the 1930s screwball comedy, did not evolve with the genre. While Capra's '40s films, especially *It's a Wonderful Life,* are richly rewarding studies in individual authorship and in Hollywood narrativity, they are out of touch with the mainstream comedies of that period, in their espousal of populist utopian ideals that wartime and postwar audiences found increasingly untenable.

Reeducating the patriarch: in Frank Capra's You Can't Take It with You, *Anthony Kirby, Jr. (Jimmy Stewart) and Sr. (Edward Arnold) work their way through not only the age-old generation gap, but a gap in social and economic values as well.* (Private Collection)

Cukor, Hawks, Preston Sturges, George Stevens, and other directors of screwball comedies in the late '30s and '40s, however, went pretty much in the opposite direction from Capra. These filmmakers relied upon socioeconomic differences as a basis for the couple's initial antagonism, and traced the gradual dissolution of their disparities as they were overwhelmed by mutual attraction and screwball antics. The difference is important: whereas these latter directors let the lovers resolve enormous social conflicts, Capra became increasingly obsessed with the conflicts themselves to the point where settling them became impossible (the only resolution for the hero in both *Meet John Doe* and *It's a Wonderful Life* is suicide).

Despite his tendency to weigh down his comedy with heavy-handed thematics, Capra's contribution to the film romances of the Depression cannot be overestimated. Even those comedies by other filmmakers that focused on the wealthy (*The Awful Truth, Holiday, Philadelphia Story,* et al.) followed Capra's tactic of injecting middle-class ideology into the eventual embrace. Cukor's *Holiday* (1938), for instance, treats the disruption of a staid, aristocratic household by a wealthy but indecorous suitor (Cary Grant as Johnny Case). He finally breaks off his engagement to the snobbish, insensitive Julia Seton (Doris Nolan) so that he can marry her sister (Katharine Hepburn as Linda). The action takes place almost entirely within the Seton mansion, shifting between the daughters' former playroom and the rest of the house. The playroom (Linda's favorite place) is the only purely functional, reasonably furnished room in the otherwise lavish, overstuffed environment. The more Linda is repressed by her upper-crust milieu, the more she longs for her playroom and the childhood innocence and freedom it represents.

Linda initially associates her sister's fiancé, Johnny/Grant, with the world "outside" the playroom. His Harvard education and stock-market wizardry have enabled him to retire at thirty, and therefore he is considered a prize catch for her debutante sister. Johnny's improper witticisms and madcap behavior, however, particularly as expressed in his double-back flip-flop, distress his fiancée and endear him to Linda, just as Peter's piggyback ride broke through Ellie Andrews' crust of social decorum. But we eventually learn that Johnny's background is working class, and that he could attend college only after laboring in a steel mill, a laundry, and on a garbage truck. Once again, a middle-class background and its value system work their magic, legitimating Johnny's screwball antics and providing Linda with something more substantial than her social class to believe in. Whereas Julia and her father consider Johnny's behavior and attitudes "revolutionary," Linda realizes that they are Johnny's only defense against the depersonalizing constraints of wealth and propriety.

Predictably, Grant's and Hepburn's characters finally recognize their compatible values and attitudes. Johnny informs his fiancée, "We've got to make our own lives. . . . I love feeling free inside even better than I love you." Clearly relieved, Julia recedes into the dull but secure realm over which her father presides. She wants nothing to do with "feeling free inside." She thereby leaves the screwball couple to their own devices and an uncertain (although well-financed) future. The significance of Linda's self-realization and liberation from the Seton dominion is underscored by her brother Ned (Lew Ayres), who sympathizes with Linda but cannot let go of the comfortable affluence offered by the family aristocracy. The price Ned pays for his comfort, however, is his own peace of mind and sense of worth—only alcohol can insulate him from the pathetic, hollow existence of the idle rich. Johnny and Linda are the only characters within the Seton milieu capable of personal growth, and they come to understand themselves through their commitment to each other. Johnny's broken engagement to Julia and Linda's liberation from her family unite the couple in a utopian embrace. A working-class background joins a sense of enlightened capitalism here in the promise of a better—and infinitely more enjoyable—world.

If we in the audience assign any credibility to *Holiday*'s idealistic resolution it is only because of the Grant-Hepburn pairing (which would recur in *Bringing Up Baby* that same year and *Philadelphia Story* some two years later) and also from director Cukor's adept handling of their romantic coupling. Like Capra, Hawks, and later Preston Sturges (*Christmas in July*, 1940; *The Lady Eve*, 1941; *Sullivan's Travels*, 1942; and *Palm Beach Story*, 1942), Cukor understood that the appeal of the screwball couple was only incidentally related to their eventual embrace. The ongoing, dynamic "battle of the sexes" between a man and woman of relatively equal wit, grace, and sexual magnetism who sustain a delicately balanced rapport of mutual attraction and antagonism is really what holds the audience's attention. It's worth nothing that the final embrace in *Holiday*, as in many screwball comedies, is treated off-handedly, like an afterthought. In fact, a number of these films—*My Man Godfrey*, *Bringing Up Baby*, *His Girl Friday*, and many of the Tracy-Hepburn films—resolve the sexual battle/betrothal without a kiss. Altogether different from the romantic melodramas of the period with their tight clinches and close-ups, the screwball comedies show the lovers in motion, usually from some distance (two-shots—two characters in a frame—and medium shots prevail). Their relationship is expressed in style and attitude rather than in kisses and declarations of love.

The divorce-remarriage variation

The issue of sexual contact is rarely among the immediate concerns of the screwball couple, although it may provide a context for sight gags and verbal puns—as in the timid scholar's endless search for a missing bone in *Bringing Up Baby* ("Where's my intercostal clavicle?" "Your *what?*" "My intercostal clavicle—my bone. It's rare. It's precious."). Any sexual union in these films is antecedent to an emotional and attitudinal union; the lovers must get their heads and hearts together before their bodies. In a variation of the genre where the screwball couple is already married, the plot generally concerns their divorce and/or remarriage. As the Depression waned and as the genre's thematic concerns shifted from class issues to more overtly sexual and marital issues, this variation became increasingly

The second time around: Philadelphia Story (1940), which featured Jimmy Stewart as the lovestruck reporter covering the remarriage of Cary Grant's ex-wife, brought the screwball comedy beyond courtship and into the throes of marriage and divorce.
(Hoblitzelle Theater Arts Collection)

popular. It was refined throughout the '30s and peaked with films like *The Awful Truth* (1937), *His Girl Friday* (1940), *Philadelphia Story* (1940), and in several of the Tracy-Hepburn films, particularly *Woman of the Year* (1942) and *Adam's Rib* (1949).

The narrative strategy of these films is to situate the screwball couple's embrace not at the film's end, but well before its opening. The couple is already socially integrated—they've already married—and the films trace their efforts, both individually and together, to maintain some kind of identity within that most traditional of all social institutions. There may be incidental ideological or occupational conflicts, but the real tension derives from a difficult marital union that simply will not disentangle. The central characters in this remarriage variation often are more anarchic and outrageous than those screwball couples in the courtship stage. Their battling is enhanced by their marriage; as a married couple, the principals have long since honed their antagonism to a razor-sharp edge. And further, this antagonism results, not from socioeconomic disparity or differing backgrounds, but from the fact that these two people know each other all too well.

163

Like most other Hollywood genres, the screwball comedy developed its own repertory of distinctive, clearly typed characters, including Cary Grant, Katharine Hepburn, Spencer Tracy, Jean Arthur, Jimmy Stewart, Carole Lombard, and others. Just as a growing familiarity with John Wayne tended, along with his advancing age, to affect the Western's evolution, so did our changing impressions of these comedic personalities affect the development of the screwball comedy.

It's worth noting that films very much in the tradition of *It Happened One Night* were still being produced in the early 1940s. One of the box-office hits of the 1940–1941 season, for example, was William Keighley's *The Bride Came C.O.D.* The film is a virtual reproduction of Capra's 1934 prototype, depicting a crusty aristocrat (Edward Arnold) who opposes his daughter's betrothal to an obnoxious playboy (Jack Carson). This opposition initiates her flight/"kidnapping" by a streetwise working stiff whom she eventually marries with her father's blessings. The lovers are portrayed, oddly enough, by James Cagney and Bette Davis, both of whom were cast against type. Like Peter Warne, Cagney's Steve Collins must cast his lot with a shrill, self-centered debutante in order to save his job (in this case, the mortgage on his airplane is about to be foreclosed). In the process of educating her in traditional middle-American ethics, his own cynical, antagonistic posture is overcome by the power of romantic love. Their chaotic odyssey takes them from Los Angeles to the desert by plane and eventually, after Davis causes the plane to crash, they cross the desert by foot, finding refuge in a ghost town—an interesting variation on the rural/urban opposition.

The aristocratic father figure in this film is somewhat more sympathetic than we might expect, and Jack Carson is less so—he is a tuxedoed, gold-bricking orchestra leader. From the very outset, the patriarch's rejection of Carson as a potential son-in-law seems eminently reasonable, even if somewhat primitively expressed ("I don't mind a fortune-hunter in the family, but I won't stand for a piano player"). Despite his status as a Texas oil tycoon, Davis' father clearly has his middlebrow, middle-American sensibilities intact, so much so that he and Cagney operate in a sort of unspoken collusion throughout. As Davis suffers loudly through their ordeal in the desert, for instance, Cagney's sarcastic attitude recalls her father's: "You must have faced crises like this at the Stork Club, when the waiter brought you the wrong wine."

Davis eventually comes around to Cagney's—and her father's—viewpoint, finally admitting that her previous lifestyle had been "silly, useless, impulsive." Cagney warms to her as well, and their union is secured when Davis' fur coat, which had initially been an emblem for her social elitism, is finally used to cover the two of them—thus "blanketing" their socioeconomic and interpersonal differences. But as often as the couple pays lip service to these differences, the setting through most of the film—Cagney's plane, the desert, the ghost town—removes them from real-life social circumstances and situations. Consequently, *The Bride Came C.O.D.* must rely heavily on the Cagney-Davis repartee (which never really does strike the right balance) and upon a more fundamental battle of the sexes than had most earlier screwball comedies. In this sense, the film seems more like the divorce-remarriage comedies of its own era.

The couple's antagonism in these films was based on their dynamic, witty sexual confrontation. This strategy typifies the Tracy-Hepburn comedies of the late '40s and early '50s, particularly *Adam's Rib* and *Pat and Mike*, which based the couple's sexual jousting in a courtroom and a tennis court, respectively. These were among the few romantic comedies of the period that sustained the ideological tensions and dynamic sexual interplay of earlier screwball comedies. The masterpiece of this type, however, was Howard Hawks' *His Girl Friday*.

Screwball comedy shaded black: *His Girl Friday* and *Meet John Doe*

Hawks' 1940 classic was a remake of Lewis Milestone's 1931 film, *The Front Page*, which was itself adapted from a play by Ben Hecht and Charles MacArthur. The principal characters are an ace crime reporter intent on marrying and leaving his newspaper and his conniving editor who stops at nothing to prevent his departure. In the original screen version (as well as in Billy Wilder's 1974 remake with Jack Lemmon and Walter Matthau), both characters are men. The 1931 film works well, but Hawks' version is one of those rare cases where the remake outshines the original, principally due to Hawks' decision to recast the mutinous crime reporter as a woman (Rosalind Russell as Hildy Johnson) playing against an ex-editor who is also her ex-husband (Cary Grant as Walter Burns). Recasting the editor-reporter duo as a divorced couple and accenting their antagonism with frantic narrative pacing and rapid-fire, overlapping dialogue, Hawks created one of the premiere achievements of screwball comedy, a film whose comic and emotional edge clearly distinguishes it from others of this genre.

In the opening sequence of Hawks' film, the battle lines are clearly drawn. Hildy breezes into the office of her former boss and husband, informing him that she intends to marry a dull but devoted insurance salesman from Albany (Ralph Bellamy) and enjoy the hearth, home, and secure relationship that Walter could never provide. Walter intends to get Hildy back on the job and into his life, although we're never sure whether his primary interest in Hildy is as wife or as reporter. He is an insufferable but somehow endearing chauvinist, the consummate conniver who treats everyone—from his ex-wife to a convicted murderer to the city mayor—with equal disrespect. He blames Hildy and the institution of marriage for their split: "It would've worked out if you'd been satisfied with just being editor and reporter," he tells her during their initial confrontation, "but not you—you had to marry me and ruin everything."

Despite Hildy's avowed desire to leave the city, the paper, and Walter, it is apparent that she cannot live without them. The pathetic alternative lifestyle she threatens to choose—a life of domestic bliss in Albany with an insurance salesman and his mother—cannot be taken any more seriously by the audience than by Walter, whatever her protestations to the contrary. But beyond that, Hildy clearly enjoys competing with men on their own turf and their own terms, and she consistently outdoes her rival reporters. Although Hildy insists her reporting career is behind her and that she must catch a train that afternoon for Albany, Walter convinces her to do one last story to prevent the execution of a demented cop-killer. While Walter and the male reporters are interested in the execution for its value in newspaper sales, Hildy's interest in the condemned Earl Williams is humane and genuine, and her superior reporting is a function of her femininity as well as her intellect. One of the few poignant moments of this otherwise dark comedy occurs when she discovers her male colleagues browbeating Williams' hysterical girl-friend. Hildy stands in the doorway to the pressroom and says simply, "Gentlemen of the press. . . ." Nowhere in the film is her professional integrity and sexual identity more strongly reinforced, not even in her tearful surrender to Walter at film's end.

It is this surrender, of course, the moment when antagonism miraculously yields to the forces of love, that resolves their sustained confrontation. But "resolves" hardly seems to be the right word, since this particular marital battle is destined to continue indefinitely. The film ends without a prolonged clinch or a kiss. The two embrace momentarily (in a medium–two-shot, under the only music played throughout the film) and then start out the door on another assignment and another honeymoon—with Hildy carrying the suitcase. Hildy's resignation to "the way things are" is underscored by the fact that it was Walter's conniving, not her reporting, that had won Earl Williams a reprieve from the hangman, which indicates to the audience that cynical pragmatism is a more effective social force than genuine human commitment. Whereas Peter Warne's naive idealism had proved contagious and redemptive in *It Happened One Night*, in *His Girl Friday* Hildy's values and ideals consistently are overwhelmed by the sociopolitical realities of her marital and occupational roles. But because Hildy is the central character and organizing sensibility within this chaotic, amoral milieu, we clearly are more engaged by her beliefs than are the cynical, self-concerned characters around her. So while the film's resolution may not overtly reaffirm Hildy's values or unite the lovers in a utopian embrace, it does offer a point of equilibrium, a delicate balance between Hildy's humanistic idealism and Walter's self-indulgent pragmatism.

Thus this subversive comedy takes a broad swipe at heroic throwbacks like Capra's Longfellow Deeds or Jefferson Smith. Hawks suggests that the little guy has little hope of surviving—let alone changing—the grim realities of contemporary social existence. In contrast, Capra refused to abandon his populist ideals, thrusting John Doe himself into the breach in 1941 with *Meet John Doe*. Doe (Gary Cooper) is a down-and-out baseball pitcher who is transformed—by a newspaper woman, in fact—into a national political figure, a spokesman for "all the John Does of the world." Doe eventually despairs when he realizes that he is merely a pawn in a vast political-industrial power grab, but is prevented from suicide at film's end when the now-enlightened newswoman (Barbara Stanwyck) convinces him that a living Christ-figure can be more productive—and more American—than a crucified one.

Capra certainly isn't playing for laughs with this bleak resolution. The "em-

Populist as demagogue: By the early 1940s, even Capra's sentimental humor was wearing thin. In Meet John Doe, reporter Ann Mitchell (Barbara Stanwyck) convinces a pair of hobos (Walter Brennan and Gary Cooper) to help with a publicity stunt which catapults them into national political prominence. (Wisconsin Center for Film and Theater Research)

brace" in the closing sequence has Doe/Cooper standing in a snowstorm holding the unconscious Stanwyck in his arms. She had passed out after leaving a sickbed to forestall his suicide. The homespun Capra hero had, much like the American public, become hard-bitten about the inequities and ambiguities of contemporary American life—to the point where Capra's "serious" treatment of these issues in *Meet John Doe* seems more melodramatic than comic. As dark as the comedy had been in *His Girl Friday*, Hawks did encourage us to laugh at ourselves, our values, our social environment. He encouraged us to laugh at the screwball comedy formula itself, at the unlikely prospect of a sympathetic hero attempting to change the world, even to change his or her "better half." Hawks went on to direct some rather lightweight but zany comedies like *I Was a Male War Bride* (1949) and *Monkey Business* (1952), which did less to develop the screwball formula's thematics than to anticipate television's burgeoning "situation comedy."

Undercutting the genre: The films of Preston Sturges

If there is any single Hollywood filmmaker whose work extended the formula into its mannerist stage, it was writer-director Preston Sturges. In the span of five years, Sturges created eight of Paramount's—and the screwball genre's—most successful and self-reflexive films: *The Great McGinty, Christmas in July* (1940), *The Lady Eve* (1941), *Sullivan's Travels, The Palm Beach Story* (1942), *The Miracle at Morgan's Creek, Hail the Conquering Hero, The Great Moment* (1944). Sturges had served his apprenticeship in Hollywood as a screenwriter, and earlier had scripted one of the screwball formula's most popular Depression-era films, *Easy Living* (Mitchell Leisen, 1937). When he graduated to writer-director, Sturges made it quite clear that he had every intention of turning the screwball comedy formula inside out. In *The Great McGinty*, a hobo (Brian Donlevy as Dan McGinty) earns a few dollars by voting forty times for a local political boss (Akim Tamiroff). The hero then gradually bluffs his way through the state machinery and winds up in the governor's mansion. McGinty's nagging wife (Muriel Angelus) convinces him to go straight, however, and when he does, his personal and occupational facade collapses. In the film's closing sequence, Donlevy and Tamiroff are together again, running a saloon in some South American banana republic. The reuniting of the two con men is Sturges' final perversion of the formula's climactic embrace and its typically utopian resolution.

In this and in his later wartime comedies, Sturges exploits the basic narrative conventions of the screwball genre: the dynamic battle of the sexes, cases of mistaken identity and blind luck which miraculously bring the hero to prominence, the small-town hick's struggle to negotiate life in the big city, the comic-satiric depiction of the ruling class, and so on. Sturges' manipulation of the genre's conventions consistently and pleasantly throws the formula askew. His heroes couldn't be further removed from Capra's—rather than self-reliant, they are confused and easily duped; rather than idealistic, they are openly cynical, seeking not the perfect mate or a utopian community but only an "easy living" of irresponsible affluence. Sturges' archetypal small-town folk hero is the stumbling, stammering Eddie Bracken, a character actor endearing for his pathetic rather than his heroic qualities. In both *The Miracle at Morgan's Creek* and *Hail the Conquering Hero*, Bracken has greatness thrust upon him in situations which play up both his own ineptitude and society's irrational mania for hero worship.

The Miracle at Morgan's Creek involves a small-town girl (Betty Hutton) who gets drunk at a service party and is wedded and bedded by a soldier who goes overseas the following day but whose name she cannot recall. She ropes Bracken into marriage without letting him know she's pregnant, and both of them achieve national celebrity status when she delivers sextuplets. *Hail the Conquering Hero* also parodies the genre's rags-to-riches/bum-to-celebrity strategies but this time from Bracken's viewpoint. Here our reluctant hero is discharged from the Marines for chronic hay fever, only to be "pitched" as a genuine war hero to his hometown by a group of

Undercutting Capracorn: in Sullivan's Travels, *Joel McCrea portrays a comedy direc-tor intent upon making "serious" social films, a role clearly modeled after Capra's own career; in* Hail the Conquering Hero *(below), Eddie Bracken's bumbling asth-matic can't prevent service buddies from palming him off on hometown folks as a war hero.*

Marines playing a practical joke. Bracken eventually runs for mayor of the town, and though he later admits his duplicity, he is finally forgiven by the community. Capra's populist conception of the essential wisdom and innate goodness of "the folks" is turned upside down in Sturges' comedies, which satirize an array of America's cultural foibles: its undying commitment to the Horatio Alger myth of instant success, its celebration of the small-town folk hero, its sexual prudery, its blind adherence to social conventions, and most of all, its collective irrationality. The general public provides easy targets for hucksters, politicians, advertisers, reporters—and even for filmmakers, as in *Sullivan's Travels*.

Perhaps Sturges' best film, *Sullivan's Travels* seems to have been made with Frank Capra in mind. A self-important comedy director (Joel McCrea as John L. Sullivan) wants to make highbrow social-problem films, so he sets out disguised as an American everyman to discover the meaning of life on city streets and country roads. A succession of comic mishaps separate Sullivan from his elaborate entourage. Eventually he is involved in a fracas and winds up on a chain gang. In a typical example of Sturges' wit, however, our hero finds The Truth in this most unlikely environment. Sullivan's fellow prisoners are able to lose themselves for a time, despite their unspeakable living conditions, laughing at a Mickey Mouse cartoon. Through them, Sullivan rediscovers the transcendent value of comedy and of human laughter. He later is able to reveal his true identity and return to Hollywood. There he weds a madcap blonde he had met on the road (Veronica Lake in a solid comic performance) and decides to continue directing film comedies. Ironically, Sturges himself also continued making screwball satires, but after two years his career suddenly disintegrated. Like Capra, Sturges had been able to parlay his popular and commercial success into an independent production venture (and an initial partnership with Howard Hughes), and like Capra he gradually lost touch with his once-massive audience.

Postwar developments: The genre winds down

It is interesting in retrospect that neither Capra's unselfconscious celebration of American life in his postwar movies (*It's a Wonderful Life, State of the Union*) nor Sturges' later self-reflexive parodies (*Mad Wednesday, Unfaithfully Yours, The Beautiful Blonde from Bashful Bend*) were very successful. It would seem that the public wanted only watered-down versions of the screwball formula. The genre's gradual reformulation is best indicated, perhaps, by the end of the Spencer Tracy/Katharine Hepburn partnership (their 1953 confrontation in *Pat and Mike*, by the way, is resolved with only a handshake), and the concurrent rise of Doris Day and Rock Hudson as Hollywood's foremost romantic couple. Although Day and Hudson's more engaging films (*Pillow Talk*, 1958; *Send Me No Flowers*, 1964) provide an interesting view of America's sociosexual mores during the insecure prosperity of the

'50s, they scarcely display the formal dynamics and thematic complexity of their predecessors.

In the later stages of the screwball genre's evolution (the model for television's "situation comedy"), the attitudes and behavior of the principals are often motivated by some external social or marital-familial complication which is beyond their control. We have, for example, the army's bureaucratic blunder resulting in sex-role reversal in *I Was a Male War Bride* (1949), the chimpanzee's creation of the youth serum "B-4" in *Monkey Business* (1952), even the kindly homicides committed by the hero's spinster aunts in *Arsenic and Old Lace* (1944). Each of these films depicts a romance that is threatened when some mishap transforms an essentially rational central figure—Cary Grant in all three movies—into a virtual lunatic. The resolution untangles the complications and thereby allows the couple to reunite, indicating a return to social and interpersonal equilibrium.

The classic screwball comedies, however, made the madcap behavior inherent to the characters themselves regardless of their social circumstances. The last thing we would associate with the narrative-generic resolution in those films is a return to "normal" behavior. Our familiarity with the couple's peculiar behavior and attitudes is such that we do not expect a pat, prosocial resolution. Thus their eventual embrace represents not simply a point of closure and social integration; it is ultimately imbued with a certain open-endedness. The previously sustained intensity of frantic action and uninhibited behavior prevents our assuming that any social institution, even marriage, will "tame" the screwball couple.

In the screwball comedy's celebration of the vital spontaneity and freedom of certain forms of individual human expression, the woman generally behaves with the same impropriety and disdain for social decorum as her male counterpart. The conventional portrayal of the heroine as either a sultry "siren" or else a domesticating, socially restrained homebody is completely turned around here. The screwball heroine is, as Molly Haskell has observed, a woman who defies all conventions except for the sexual ones, and perhaps it is ultimately her role that gives the genre its distinctive appeal[2] (Haskell, 1974, p. 93). Many movies stress the contradictions that plague the American male, particularly his choices between love and duty, between familial and occupational commitments, between personal and social identities. In the screwball comedy, this ambivalence usually is extended to the woman's realm, qualifying her "natural" role as mother-domesticator and adding an anarchic (or at least nontraditional) dimension to the screwball couple's courtship/marriage.

From the class-conscious Depression romances through the wartime parodies and the postwar situation comedies, the screwball genre creates the picture of a utopian community in which sexual and ideological conflicts are magically resolved. Significantly, both the courtship and remarriage formulations suggest that the utopian ideal is only possible within the existing social framework. Whether it's espousing enlightened capitalism or enlightened marital-sexual relationships, the screwball comedy ultimately supports the status quo. In the best screwball

Tracy and Hepburn: By the late 1940s, the genre was depending less on screwball characters than on comic situations for laughs. Among the few notable exceptions were such Tracy-Hepburn pairings as Adam's Rib (1949). (Robert Downing Collection)

comedies, this prosocial impulse is well disguised or even directly subverted, and therefore the audience can dismiss the resolution/embrace as casually as do the embattled lovers themselves. The filmmakers who created the quality comedies knew that what is appealing in their films is not the naive promise of romantic love or of some utopian dream, but rather, the conflict itself. In screwball comedy, the ongoing battle of the sexes has an arena, a collection of quality players, a system of narrative-thematic rules, and perhaps most importantly, a sense of humor. And we in the audience can examine from a secure but familiar distance the complex, ambiguous, seriocomic nature of America's courtship and marriage rituals.

Frank Capra and Robert Riskin: "The Capriskin Touch"

"Maybe there really wasn't an America, maybe it was only Frank Capra."

—Writer-actor-director John Cassavetes in American Visions[3]
(Black, 1977, p. 75)

The collaborators

Frank Capra understood, perhaps better than any other Hollywood director of his time, the necessary relationship between romantic comedy and social conventions—and between Hollywood movies and American ideology. From the earliest stages of his career as a gag writer for producer Hal Roach and as writer-director on some of Harry Langdon's best silent comedies, Capra refined his comic style that pitted the "little guy" against the faceless, inhuman forces of "the system." Perhaps Capra's own career provided the blueprint: he was himself an immigrant hustler who, as legend has it, bluffed his way into filmmaking. With personal experience informing his sentimental optimism, Capra's homespun heroes repeatedly overcame society's depersonalizing influence. His films were filled with self-sufficient individualists, good neighbors, and benevolent institutions.

The consistency of Capra's vision throughout his career, and especially during the Depression, was due largely to the relatively high degree of control he had over the filmmaking process. Not only did his *It Happened One Night* change the face of Hollywood romantic comedy, it also ensured the economic stability of Columbia studios during the Depression. Subsequently, studio boss Harry Cohn allowed Capra considerable authority in the preparation, scripting, and postproduction, as well as the actual shooting, of his films. Cohn's gamble clearly paid off. Along with Howard Hawks' films (principally those with Cary Grant), Capra's romantic comedies—*It Happened One Night, Mr. Deeds Goes to Town* (1936), *Lost Horizon* (1937), *You Can't Take It with You* (1938), and *Mr. Smith Goes to Washington* (1939)—brought Columbia from "Poverty Row" status to that of a major studio during the 1930s. Columbia slumped when Capra left in 1939, although his personal success continued with *Meet John Doe*, which he himself produced in 1940. For this film, he briefly reunited with screenwriter Robert Riskin, who had done all of Capra's scripts except for *Mr. Smith Goes to Washington. Doe* was Capra and Riskin's last collaborative effort as writer and director; they each went separately into independent production afterward.

Along with Ford, Hawks, Leo McCarey, and a very few other '30s directors, Capra represents the ultimate commercial filmmaker of the classical tradition. He was a thorough craftsman well-versed in the technology and capabilities of the film medium; he was thematically and stylistically consistent, successful with both critics and the public; and most importantly, he was able to create a tightly constructed, internally coherent film narrative with intellectual as well as emotional appeal. Throughout his career, Capra jealously guarded his role in the filmmaking process. He was known to hold up production for recasting and script changes; he insisted upon authority over the "final cut" (i.e., the fully edited version); he was a driving force in the establishment of the Directors' Guild and acted as its first president. In John Ford's introduction to Capra's autobiography, *The Name Above the Title*, there is an apt description of Capra's self-assigned role on the studio lot. Ford says that Capra describes "what it's really like on the motion picture set, that democratic little monarchy where a hard-nosed director of the 'one picture-one director' school reigns as king, congress, and court of highest appeal." Ford goes on to assert that "Capra has not only achieved a place of distinction in that select company of really fine film directors. . . . He heads the list as the greatest motion picture director in the world"[4] (Capra, 1971, p. x).

Lavish praise, indeed, and written a full three decades after Capra's "kingdom, congress, and court" was long gone—after suffering a steady decline from its 1930s peak. For a director who had established a career on an ability to anticipate and exploit the sensibilities of the mass audience, Capra's postwar films—*It's a Wonderful Life* (1946), *State of the Union* (1948), *Riding High* (1950), *Here Comes the Groom* (1951), *Hole in the Head* (1959), and *Pocketful of Miracles* (1961)—seem to have been severely out of touch with that same audience. While other Hollywood filmmakers were articulating the collective *angst* and brooding nihilism of postwar America, Capra continued to champion the cause of common sense and the inherent goodness of the average citizen. These themes still had some clout with movie audiences, although not the way they had during the Depression years. While all but two of Capra's postwar works (*Riding High* and *Pocketful of Miracles*) were among the most popular films of the years in which the)y were released, Capra found it increasingly difficult to finance his projects. When he did get financing, he tended to lapse into sentimental remakes of earlier successes. In fact, the Frank Capra who churned out some fourteen features in the decade preceding the war managed only six films since then, and several of those were remakes. (See table at the end of this chapter.)

Capra's fall from popular and critical grace seems to have begun when he split with Robert Riskin after *Meet John Doe*. The same is true for Riskin, interestingly, in reverse. Aside from his scripts for Capra, Riskin had only one moderate success, *The Whole Town's Talking*, directed by John Ford in 1935. Aside from his work with Riskin, Capra had only one genuine box-office hit, *Mr. Smith Goes to Washington*

(1939), a film clearly derived from the earlier Capra-Riskin collaboration on *Deeds* several years before. Capra himself believes that he did his best work with scripts other than Riskin's. He has referred to *It's a Wonderful Life* as "my favorite film" (as well he should) and to *State of the Union* as "my best directing job" (arguable), but these are essentially the only real high points in his uneven postwar career[5] (Capra, 1977, p. 12). Capra had asked Riskin to join him, William Wyler, and George Stevens when they organized Liberty Films in 1946, but Riskin was off on an unsuccessful venture of his own as an independent writer-director. As it turned out, each continued to make films for some time, but neither attained anything near the success they had had realized while working together.[6]

It is ultimately that period from 1934 to 1941, from *It Happened One Night* through *Meet John Doe*, that provides the basis for what we now term a "Capra film." His earlier work, both with and without Riskin, mark his apprenticeship as a Hollywood filmmaker: Whatever significance a film like *American Madness* (1932) has now is due primarily to the fact that it anticipated later successes. And the post-*Doe* films seem to have done well for a variety of reasons other than Capra's own "touch": *Arsenic and Old Lace* (which Capra shot in 1941 in only four weeks but didn't release until 1944 when he was overseas) was a faithful adaptation of Joseph Kesselring's hit Broadway play, and *State of the Union* (1948) was the fifth in a "series" of Tracy-Hepburn pairings. The only postwar film in which Capra does demonstrate his touch is his semi-autobiographical variation of the Deeds-Smith-Doe trilogy, *It's a Wonderful Life* (1946).

But whatever the cinematic and commercial shortcomings of Capra's postwar work, it certainly was superior to Riskin's. Riskin's scripts simply didn't work for any other director but Capra—even John Ford, whose direction of *The Whole Town's Talking* (1935) seems curiously off-balance and uneven. Judging from the work they did both with and without each other, it's difficult to avoid the simple fact that Capra and Riskin were ideally suited to the other's talents. Riskin's tightly constructed plots, with their outrageous sociosexual complications, endearing minor characters, and homespun heroes, were effectively balanced by Capra's unobtrusive (and essentially dialogue-oriented) camerawork and by his deft handling of both the comic and the sentimental without becoming maudlin.

As the working relationship between Capra and Riskin should indicate, referring to this movie as a "Capra film" or that one as a "Ford film" implies quite a bit more than the mere presence of the director on the shooting set. Designating the director as *auteur* acknowledges his *administrative* as well as his *creative* role in the actual filmmaking process. Few critics would contend that the director is the sole author of a movie, although the director's function as *the* controlling force during production renders him the only person involved who has even the potential for film authorship.

The "Capriskin" symbiosis provides a rather clear-cut example of Hollywood's collaborative production system and also of the complex workings of genre production. In fact, their Depression-era films have come to assume a somewhat paradoxical status in the history of the screwball comedy: On the one hand, their early-to-mid-30s films played a significant role in initiating and sustaining Hollywood's socially sensitive romantic comedies; on the other hand, their late-30s films (along with *Doe* in 1941) represent a variation that is actually a subgenre unto itself. Despite Capra's primary influence on mainstream screwball comedy, the Deeds-Smith-Doe trilogy took him in a very different direction—and away from the genre's ideological contact with the American mass audience.

The films: 1934–1941

With *It Happened One Night*, Capra officially graduated to genuine "star director" status. His dynamic direction of Riskin's script, itself adapted from Samuel Hopkins' short story "Night Bus," brought to fruition the promise of earlier Capra-Riskin collaborations such as *Platinum Blonde* (1931), *American Madness* (1932), and *Lady for a Day* (1933). After *It Happened One Night*'s legendary sweep of the Academy Awards, Capra (along with Leo McCarey) went on to dominate American screen comedy until the war. Of his next five films (*Deeds*, 1936; *Lost Horizon*, 1937; *You Can't Take It with You*, 1938; *Smith*, 1939; and *Doe*, 1941), all but *Smith* were scripted by Riskin, who adapted all his screenplays from other works: *It Happened One Night* from "Night Bus," *Deeds* from Clarence Budington Kellington's "Opera Hat," *Lost Horizon* from James Hilton's *Shangri-La*, *You Can't Take It with You* from the Kaufman-Hart Broadway play, and *Doe* from Robert Presnell and Richard Connell's "The Life and Death of John Doe." The single non-Riskin screenplay (for *Smith*) was written by journeyman Sidney Buchman from a story by Lewis R. Foster, though its structural and thematic proximity to the *Deeds* script would seem to merit Riskin at least indirect credit.

It Happened One Night marked the virtual birth of the screwball formula—i.e., that filmic comedy of manners in which the romantic couple's antagonism and anarchic demeanor are contingent upon their sociocultural disparity. But despite this film's tremendous success and its effect upon subsequent Depression comedies, it is actually an aberration in Capra's *oeuvre*. It is Capra's only genuine *romantic* comedy of this period, the only film in which the couple's courtship-embrace is of primary narrative concern. In Capra's other films, and especially those from 1936 until the war, his dominant interest is not the couple, but rather the ideological and material differences separating them. As such, *It Happened One Night* has a dual, paradoxical significance. Its success encouraged other filmmakers to develop romantic comedies in which ideological disparities motivate the lovers' antagonism, whereas Capra's own later films turned the strategy back on itself, using the lovers' mutual attraction to investigate the values and beliefs that separate them.

This may sound like a rather subtle distinction, but it is vitally important to our emotional and intellectual negotiation of these films. Each Capra film after *It Happened One Night* is progressively less a romance (although no less "romantic" in its portrayal of the hero and in its naive optimism), and each film is also less a com-

Longfellow Deeds (Gary Cooper) provided the prototype for Capra's "little guy" hero: an honest, loyal, self-reliant man of few words and of rural sensibilities, able to rise to any occasion that city life and its myriad "slickers" might generate. (Penguin Photos)

edy. While all of these films involve a courtship, each successive resolution-embrace is more artificial, more incidental to the plot. This is obvious even in characterization: The hero is portrayed not as a willful candidate for domestication, but rather as a throwback to the self-styled American whose traditional values initially disrupt and eventually redeem Big City decadence. The woman is less a genuine "love interest" than an audience surrogate whose initial cynicism and blind professionalism lead her to betray the bumpkin-hero, but who is eventually won over, along with the audience, to his peculiar world view.

Consider the comic performers in the Deeds-Smith-Doe trilogy: Gary Cooper (*Deeds, Doe*) and Jimmy Stewart (*Smith*), playing opposite Jean Arthur (*Deeds, Smith*) and Barbara Stanwyck (*Doe*). Quite different from the Gable-Colbert pairing in *It Happened One Night*. Both Cooper, the stoic, deliberate man of action, and Stewart, the drawling country boy whose honesty was beyond question, portray the American hero as a man of integrity and grass-roots wisdom. Each embodies the gangly loner who is slow to speak but dependable in a crisis—and it's no surprise that both Cooper and Stewart did some of their best work in Westerns. Jean Arthur and Barbara Stanwyck, conversely, represent Hollywood's version of the urban career woman: tough, articulate, professional, manipulative, more at home in a tweed suit than an evening gown. Capra's reputation for effective casting is well deserved—the Cooper-Arthur pairing in *Deeds*, Stewart-Arthur in *Smith*, and Cooper-Stanwyck in *Doe* provide us with just enough suggestion of romance to sustain our emotional empathy and interest, but never so much that our attention is distracted from the films' sociopolitical concerns.

The closest to a genuine screwball romance in Capra's post-1934 films is *You Can't Take It with You*, with Jimmy Stewart and Jean Arthur. In this contemporary comic rendition of *Romeo and Juliet*, the family quarrels that separate the lovers involve skyscrapers and urban planning. Stewart's father (Edward Arnold in his standard caricature of the big business aristocrat) wants to purchase a dilapidated wood frame house from Arthur's grandfather (Lionel Barrymore) and replace it with a high-rise office building. Barrymore refuses to sell; Stewart falls out with his father; Arthur goes into hiding. Things finally are resolved when the aristocrat is won over by the eccentric, poor-but-happy patriarch and his houseful of screwballs. Although the conciliation does lead to the embrace-betrothal of Stewart and Arthur, Capra's concerns basically lie with the ideological wedding of their respective families and their conflicting value systems.

You Can't Take It with You was Capra's first film after his only notable failure of this period, *Lost Horizon*, a ponderous and overblown vision of Shangri-La. The commercial and critical failure of *Lost Horizon* taught Capra the value of presenting utopia as an ideal always a little beyond man's reach, but an ideal that is presented in very real terms. With *You Can't Take It with You*, Capra brought his utopian vision back to familiar ground. Situated in the midst of a decadent metropolis, Barrymore's utopian family-community of inventors, dropouts, and other assorted anarchists sustains a delicate equilibrium which is in constant danger of being disturbed by the unenlightened outside world. Once inside Barrymore's domain, however, even the most hardened urbanite shows signs of recovering the lost innocence and idealism of traditional America—as evidenced by the insensitive capitalist's final decision to take up the harmonica and forgo the skyscraper he'd planned. Barrymore's closing speech against money, unchecked urban progress, income tax, and all "isms" except Americanism broadcasts Capra's thematic preoccupations. The utopian dream is inherent within the existing social order, he seems to be saying, if one simply knows how and where to look.

In Capra's next two films, *Smith* and *Doe*, he self-consciously returns to the basic *Deeds* formula, although his talents as a film director and his sociopolitical concerns had developed markedly in the intervening years between *Deeds* (1936) and *Smith* (1939). *Smith* may well be the most effective of the Deeds-Smith-Doe trilogy, as it finds a narrative and formal middle ground between *Deeds* and *Doe*, as well as an ideological one. Compared with *Deeds*, *Smith* has a tighter, more internally consistent narrative, more credible character motivation and development, and a more reasonable view of the inherent conflicts of national politics. With the later *Doe*, the narrative machinery became too predictable, the characters were somewhat overstated and caricatured, and the thematic distinction between enlightened and unenlightened capitalism was blurred. Capra clearly was concerned in *Doe* with steeling his 1941 audience for war, but his cries for self-reliance and blind cooperation had hardened into an ideological manifesto, and his hero is dangerously close to the fascist-capitalist demons he attempts to exorcise. As Andrew Sarris has suggested, "With *Meet John Doe*, Frank Capra crossed the thin line between populist sentimentality and populist demogoguery. Capra's political films . . . had always implied a belief in the tyranny of the majority, but John Doe embodied in Gary Cooper a barefoot fascist, suspicious of all ideas and all doctrines, but believing in the innate conformism of the common man"[7] (Sarris, 1968, p. 87).

The Deeds-Smith-Doe trilogy

At the core of the Deeds-Smith-Doe formula is the ordinary man in extraordinary circumstances. In each of the trilogy films, a down-home hybrid of Jesus Christ and Abe Lincoln is drawn by some freak accident into sociopolitical prominence.

Deeds is comforted during a difficult moment in his sanity hearing by Babe Bennett (Jean Arthur). In the end, he is miraculously declared "the sanest man who ever walked into this court." (Wisconsin Center for Film and Theater Research)

The big city is rife with shysters, slickers, and power-crazed bosses who are bent on exploiting both the hero and his new-found celebrity status. The heroine in these films is essentially a foil for the hero's sentimental rural-agrarian folk wisdom. Initially she is cynical about the hero but eventually comes around. In *Deeds* and *Doe* the heroine is a newspaperwoman who uses her mass medium to capitalize on the hero's eccentricities; in *Smith* she is the hero's congressional secretary whose familiarity with Washington's political machinery makes her dismiss the hero as a naive, ineffectual hick. In each film, the hero's unabashed and unrelenting appeals to the heroine's—and to our—deep-seated traditional values win her over, so that her primary function at film's end is not so much to embrace as to applaud the hero.

If we agree that fascism involves the merging of state and big business functions and the consequent dehumanization of the individual, then it's fair to say that each film in Capra's trilogy is increasingly anti-fascist. But we should also note that many of the individual components of fascism—manipulation of the mass media, demands for conformity with a national ideology, overt appeals to patriotism and isolationism—are fundamental to the films' success with American audiences. This is countered to some degree, particularly in *Deeds*, by the hero's personal integrity and the value assigned to the individual's inalienable freedom of choice.

Gary Cooper's Longfellow Deeds is a small-town businessman, volunteer fireman, and tuba player whose life undergoes a rather drastic change when an unknown relative dies and wills Deeds a fortune. Deeds' wealth draws him to New York, where he is victimized by city slickers and duped by newspaperwoman Babe Bennett (Jean Arthur), who strings him along because he is good copy, pretending to be Deeds' "lady in distress." After an education in urban decadence and corrupt business practices, Deeds decides to give his money to the poor. As previously stated, efforts to prevent Deeds' philanthropy finally lead to a sanity hearing, where he proceeds to demolish every bit of evidence brought against him with a combination of anti-intellectual folk wisdom and anti-capitalist sentiment. Capra's deft use of reaction shots and narrative pacing build the sequence to an emotional peak, climaxing when Deeds punches the shyster-prosecutor and is proclaimed sane by the presiding judge. Deeds embraces Babe Bennett, who had confessed her duplicity and also her love for the hero while on the witness stand, and at the film's end, the two face the promise of an ideal marriage within an enlightened community.

Mr. Smith (1939) owes many structural and thematic debts to *Deeds*. In *Smith*, a naive and idealistic Boy Scout troop leader from a rural community (Jimmy Stewart as Jefferson Smith) is miraculously elected to succeed a United States senator who has died in office. Upon his arrival in Washington, his cynical secretary (Jean Arthur) indicates that his election was rigged by political bosses who assume he will be easily manipulated. Smith opposes them, of course, taking on his own party and the immensely popular but corrupt senior senator from his state (Claude Rains). In a twenty-three-hour filibuster before the Senate, Smith attempts to convince his colleagues and a gallery filled with "the people" (all those other "Smiths" of the world) of the political abuses threatening to destroy the system. As in *Deeds*, a familiar social ritual—here a Senate debate rather than a judicial hearing—provides a forum for the film's climactic confrontation. Once again Capra plays the stereotypical characters and populist thematics off against the reactions of the audience in the gallery—and the audience in the theater as well. Unlike *Deeds*, though, the conclusion of this film is somewhat ambiguous. Rains' senator eventually succumbs to Smith's sustained verbal assault, confessing, "I'm not fit to be a senator," but the corrupt machinery behind him remains, at least for the moment, intact.

The difference between *Deeds* and *Smith* is ultimately more a matter of quality than of substance. The two films tell much the same story; the latter film simply tells it better. *Smith* is superior to *Deeds* in almost every way: the direction, camerawork, and editing are more controlled and effective yet less obtrusive, the script is better paced and the characters more credibly developed, the performances are less caricatured, and the social problem is less easily resolved. The narrative and technical balance in *Smith* is not evident in *Meet John Doe*, however. As Stephen Handzo has suggested, "If *Mr. Smith* is archetypal Capra, *Meet John Doe* (1941) is Capracorn Kabuki, with the earlier film's formal richness solidifying into formula and ritual"[8] (Handzo, 1972, p. 12).

Even contemporary observers noted the hardening of the *Mr. Smith* prototype into a familiar narrative pattern. *New York Times* critic Bosley Crowther, for example, made this observation in a 1941 review of *Meet John Doe*: "Actually, this is not our first introduction to John Doe. Mr. Capra has already presented him under the names of Longfellow Deeds and Jefferson Smith, the fellows, you remember, who went to town and to Washington, respectively. He is the honest and forthright fellow—confused, inconsistent, but always sincere—who believes in the basic goodness of people and has the courage to fight hard for principles"[9] (Crowther, 1941, p. 12).

Crowther considered *Doe* to be the best of the Capra trilogy, asserting that "this is by far the hardest-hitting and most trenchant picture on the theme of democracy that the Messrs. Capra and Riskin have yet made—and a glowing tribute to the anonymous citizen, too." But the citizens of America didn't buy the tribute in the numbers that they had bought *Deeds* and *Smith*. In fact, the lukewarm reaction at the box office signaled the beginning of the end of Capra's widespread popularity and of his status as an American ideologue.

Meet John Doe, despite its roots in the social-conscious screwball tradition of the '30s and in the romantic comedy generally, is by no means a comedy nor is it a screwball romance. Once again Capra tells us his familiar tale: a conniving woman reporter (Barbara Stanwyck) dupes a naive but honest small-town hick (Gary Cooper) into public prominence but later regrets her duplicity as the good ol' boy wins her heart. Capra and Riskin use the romantic angle merely as a vehicle for sociopolitical conflicts, however, and the couple's romance fades into the background as the narrative develops.

The pretext for John Doe's rise to prominence is not the sudden death of a rich

Vox populi: *during Jefferson Smith's marathon filibuster in Mr. Smith Goes to Washington, he receives vocal encouragement from Jean Arthur and the other "folks" in the Senate gallery.* (Wisconsin Center for Film and Theater Research)

relative or a state senator, but rather the impending loss of Ann Mitchell's newspaper job due to the Depression. In a fit of fury after being given notice, she composes a letter under the name John Doe, in which she laments the social and spiritual decay of the American way of life and threatens to commit suicide on the following Christmas Eve. Public reaction to the letter saves Mitchell's job, but also requires that she produce its author. Enter Long John Willoughby, a vagabond country boy and sore-armed ex-pitcher who has been riding the rails with another social outcast, "The Colonel" (Walter Brennan). The Colonel is an interesting addition to the otherwise familiar constellation of characters, as he provides a mouthpiece for the typically tight-lipped hero. Mitchell convinces Willoughby to assume the identity of the mythical Doe, and although her own intentions are innocent enough, a fascistic industrialist (Edward Arnold as D. A. Norton) who controls her paper begins to manipulate Doe's increasing public visibility. Norton, whose "enterprises" are supported by media networks and his own police force, initiates nationwide John Doe clubs and rallies. His intention is to create a third political party and thereby control not just the city but America itself. The Colonel repeatedly warns Long John that his fame and fortune will come to no good, and at one point delivers a startling—at least by Hollywood's standards—diatribe against unenlightened capitalism:

> All right, you're walking along without a nickel in your jeans. You're free as the wind. Nobody bothers you. Hundreds of people pass you by in every line of business—shoes, hats, automobiles, radios, furniture, everything. They're all nice lovable people and they let you alone, right?
>
> Then you get ahold of some dough and what happens? All those nice sweet lovable people become heelots! A lot of heels! They begin creeping up on you, trying to sell you something. They got long claws, and they get a strangle hold on you, and you squirm and you duck and you holler, and you try to push them away, but you haven't got a chance. They got you.
>
> The first thing you know, you own things. A car, for instance. Now your whole life is messed up with a lot more stuff. You get license fees and number plates and gas and oil and taxes and insurance and identification cards and letters and bills and flat tires and traffic tickets and motorcycle cops and courtrooms and lawyers and fines and a million other things. And what happens? You're not the free and happy guy you used to be. You got to have money to pay for all those things. So you go after what the other fellow's got. And there you are—you're a heelot yourself.

The Colonel's speech, which is delivered directly at the camera-viewer, effectively prepares us for Long John's eventual identity crisis. Long John himself does not see that crisis coming, and by the time he must face it, The Colonel has left him and returned to the freedom of the road. Once Doe/Willoughby realizes that he's been exploited and, even more importantly, that socioeconomic imperatives do create a community of "heelots" with little regard for such traditional values as love, honesty, and integrity, he decides to go through with his—or rather Ann Mitchell's—promised suicide. The issue now becomes how to convince the hero *not* to kill himself. After fleshing out the conflicts and contradictions inherent within our society so effectively, it's little wonder that Capra had difficulties finding his way out of the narrative. In each of his films Capra had grown more adept at articulating those conflicts, and in this film he developed a problem that simply could not be resolved.

Capra actually had begun production on *Meet John Doe* before the shooting script for the film had been completed, and he and Riskin worked out several different endings during production. In an unprecedented demonstration of his own populist leanings, Capra initially released the film to various first-run theaters with different endings. Perhaps the John Does of America would select the resolution which best suited their sensibilities. Apparently none of the endings did. Capra then recalled his cast and crew to shoot a final scene that was added to the initial release print. This resolution—in which the hero is convinced by Ann Mitchell

Between two worlds: If there is a mediating figure in Capra's trilogy it's invariably the woman who is caught between her big-city job and her growing devotion to the homespun hero. Here, in Meet John Doe, Barbara Stanwyck's reporter balances—thematically and visually—the consummate "heelot" (Edward Arnold as D. B. Norton) and the consummate folk hero, Long John Willoughby (Gary Cooper). (Wisconsin Center for Film and Theater Research)

and others not to jump from a building but rather to devote his life to "the people"—fails on virtually all counts. The social ambiguities and inequities of the narrative remain, Norton is still very much in power, and Long John hasn't begun to make any sense of his own role in the scheme of things—but then only a miracle could have resolved the dilemmas facing John Doe/Willoughby's divided self.

Not that Capra was above resorting to miracles. In his postwar populist manifesto, *It's a Wonderful Life* (1946), another suicidal everyman-hero (Jimmy Stewart as George Bailey) is convinced of life's essential goodness by his guardian angel. In turning to divine intervention to resolve the conflicts of this film, Capra acknowledges in no uncertain terms that the contradictions of the American community he so lovingly explored are timeless and irreconcilable. Capra's films paint a remarkably consistent and sensitive portrait of American life throughout its urban-industrial growing pains and up until the dawn of the atomic age. Despite his belief in the goodness of the common people and their values, that portrait is not wholly optimistic due to Capra's increasingly complex view of social problems and his difficulty—both narrative and ideological—in solving those problems.

Whether we agree with Handzo and other critics that Capra's films progressively "became more pessimistic" or whether we assume that his vision became more sophisticated and complex and thus more ambiguous, we cannot help but marvel at that vision. Capra's films survive remarkably well, and some, like *It's a Wonderful Life* and the trilogy films, are destined to stand among the most significant cultural documents ever produced by Hollywood. It's also remarkable how neatly Capra's career coincides with Hollywood's own. His decline in popularity after the war reflects the gradual eclipse of Hollywood's "classic" era. As such, Capra's films are among the last genuinely transparent, straightforward celebrations of American life that Hollywood produced.

FRANK CAPRA AND ROBERT RISKIN FILMOGRAPHY
1930–1950

Year	CAPRA	RISKIN
1930	Ladies of Leisure	
	Rain or Shine	
1931	Dirigible	Illicit
	Miracle Woman -------------------	Miracle Woman
	Platinum Blonde ------------------	Platinum Blonde
1932	Forbidden	
	American Madness ----------------	American Madness
1933	The Bitter Tea of General Yen	
	Lady for a Day ------------------	Lady for a Day
1934	It Happened One Night ------------	It Happened One Night
	Broadway Bill -------------------	Broadway Bill
1935		The Whole Town's Talking
1936	Mr. Deeds Goes to Town -----------	Mr. Deeds Goes to Town
1937	Lost Horizon --------------------	Lost Horizon
1938	You Can't Take It with You --------	You Can't Take It with You
1939	Mr. Smith Goes to Washington	The Real Glory
1941	Meet John Doe -------------------	Meet John Doe
1944	Arsenic and Old Lace	The Thin Man Goes Home
1946	It's a Wonderful Life	Magic Town
1948	State of the Union	
1950	Riding High --------------------	Riding High*

* *Riding High* was a remake of Capra/Riskin's 1934 film, *Broadway Bill*; Capra's 1961 film, *Pocketful of Miracles*, was a remake of his earlier collaboration with Riskin, *Lady for a Day* (1933).

The Musical 7

Where there's music there's love.

—Written on a wall sampler in a diner in For Me and My Gal

"We begin with nothing but a dream—but in the end we'll have a show."

—Jack Buchanan in The Band Wagon

The movie musical is among our culture's most widely loved yet least understood or appreciated popular forms. This unprecedented—and peculiarly American—genre emerged during the late 1920s and early '30s from its roots in vaudeville, music hall, and theater, and reached a remarkable level of artistic and cultural expression by the 1940s. What we now term "musical comedy" actually developed concurrently, and with considerable cross-fertilization, in popular theater and the commercial cinema. Most of the genre's initial impetus came from New York City's heavy musical and theatrical orientation. As the form developed, however, Broadway could not compete with Hollywood's enormous budgets and salaries, both of which were functions of the movies' mass distribution system and its eager national audience. Thus musicals became standard fare for neighborhood theaters as well as those on the Great White Way. And perhaps even more significantly, the musical comedy made its home in film because this medium could capture the wondrous magic of Fred Astaire and company in such a way that it can be rediscovered indefinitely, as long as the celluloid and the human heart still endure.

186

The year 1927 is perhaps the most significant in the early growth of the musical. On stage, it marked the debut of *Show Boat,* considered the first musical *play*—as opposed to the musical "revue" (an uninterrupted series of musical numbers) or to those pseudocomedies which interspersed unrelated musical numbers and comedy routines. This was also the year that marked the debut of the "talkie" in American film, Warner Brothers' *The Jazz Singer,* which also happened to be Hollywood's first musical. *The Jazz Singer* is really not much of a movie—musical, talkie, or otherwise—but it anticipated a number of significant aspects of the movie musical. The genre's vital relationship with the star system began here (Al Jolson played the lead), as did the potential for audience engagement through the performers' directly addressing the camera/audience. And as the film's title implies, the genre developed a vital relationship with such lowbrow musical forms as jazz and swing. The success of *The Jazz Singer* was surpassed the following year when Jolson and Warners teamed up again for *The Singing Fool,* an only slightly more sophisticated version of their 1927 hit.

If Hollywood filmmakers entertained any doubts concerning the future of the film musical, those doubts vanished in 1929 with MGM's *Broadway Melody.* This

"You ain't heard nothin' yet": *Al Jolson's now-famous line in* **The Jazz Singer** *referred to the birth of the "talkie" in Hollywood, but it might just as well have referred to the birth of the movie musical.* (Museum of Modern Art/Film Stills Archive)

first "100% All Talking, 100% All Singing" musical broke box-office records (in those theaters already equipped for sound) and won the Academy Award for Best Picture for 1928–29. (From 1927 to 1933, the awards were considered along seasonal—August 1 to July 31—rather than calendar years.) The film's success seems to derive from a number of factors, principally its interweaving of the musical numbers with a "backstage" subplot. Using the theme of America's success ethic, *Broadway Melody* traces the efforts of two sisters to graduate from vaudeville to the "big time" in New York. The girls become part of a backstage community in the process, so that their preparation for the climactic show serves as a pretext both for rehearsal-production numbers and also for romantic entanglements. The backstage romance, which became a familiar narrative device in '30s musicals, provides a formal and emotional framework for the performers, acting as a sort of barometer for the show's success. The film's title suggests its debt to New York stage musicals, but the evolution of the backstage Cinderella success story is equally a product of Hollywood filmmaking.

Broadway Melody also marked Arthur Freed's debut—he composed the score and wrote the lyrics for the film. Freed stayed with MGM and eventually produced that studio's most successful and sophisticated musicals, among them *Meet Me in St. Louis* (1944), *Yolanda and the Thief* (1945), *The Pirate* (1948), *Easter Parade* (1948), *On the Town* (1949), *An American in Paris* (1951), *Singin' in the Rain* (1952), and *The Band Wagon* (1953). As MGM's postwar achievements indicate, producer Freed (along with directors Vincente Minnelli, Stanley Donen, Gene Kelly, and others) understood the complex relationship between a film musical's production numbers and the story which provides their narrative framework. Some critics have dismissed the musical's subplots as mere padding for the production numbers, but in so doing they have missed the point of the genre's formal and emotional appeal. All genre films—and all Hollywood movies, to differing degrees—involve the promise of utopia. From the basic tension between everyday reality and its imaginary reflection on the screen, to the more complicated narrative tension between a film's "realistic" conflicts and its "idealistic" resolution, movies project utopian visions of a potentially well-ordered community. In the musical, the same reality-to-utopia strategy is also evident in the plot. The musical's gradual narrative progression toward a successful show and the principal performers' embrace project a utopian resolution, but this resolution is anticipated whenever the performers break into song and dance.

Thus within the backstage musical—or within any musical that culminates in an elaborate production number—the tensions between object and illusion, between social reality and utopia, are worked out on at least two distinct levels of action. The first is through the overall plot structure, when the various complications resolve themselves in the production of a flawless show. The second is at numerous points within the narrative itself when the characters transcend their interpersonal conflicts and express themselves in music and movement. Even in those "integrated" musicals in which lyrics and dance are directly related to the conflicts of the story, this utopian motif is sustained because of each musical number's individual autonomy and also because the numbers are building up to the climactic musical production that will magically resolve those conflicts. Thus the musical genre's basic oppositions derive from a narrative distinction between the dramatic *story,* in which static, one-dimensional characters act out familiar social conflicts and are oblivious to the camera/audience, and the *musical production numbers,* in which those same characters acknowledge their status as dynamic entertainers and perform directly to the camera/audience. This formal opposition reinforces the genre's social concerns, which center around American courtship rites and the very concept of entertainment.[1] (Altman and Feuer, *loq.*)

The musical comes of age: *42nd Street* and *Gold Diggers of 1933*

These motifs became conventions in the literally hundreds of early-'30s musicals which were spawned by *Broadway Melody*'s enormous success. By 1933, the Hollywood musical began showing signs of maturity, principally with *42nd Street* and *Gold Diggers of 1933.* Both were produced by Warner Brothers and featured the lavish choreography of Busby Berkeley, a transplanted Broadway musical director whose work dominated the genre throughout the decade. The elaborate production numbers in *42nd Street* and *Gold Diggers of 1933* were framed by backstage romances between Dick Powell and Ruby Keeler, and each film traced the efforts of struggling chorus girls to "make it." As directed by Lloyd Bacon, *42nd Street* treats the formula conventionally, with the struggling starlet winning both a starring role and the male lead's heart just in time for the musical finale.

Berkeley's musical direction and unusual camerawork during the musical sequences are the distinguishing elements in this film. His most significant innovation was to liberate the camera from a static position in front of the stage. Berkeley used a single moving camera (occasionally complemented by another camera overhead), which actually participated in the musical numbers. The fluid, dynamic camera became standard in later musicals and was perhaps the single most significant formal development in Hollywood '30s musicals. It gave the production sequences a uniquely cinematic dimension that could not be duplicated on a theater stage.

The gritty, cynical backstage story of *Gold Diggers of 1933,* enhanced by Mervyn LeRoy's capable direction, places the film in a class by itself among the usually more lighthearted Depression musicals. The film opens with an outrageous production number featuring starlets garbed in huge coins singing, "We're in the Money." We realize this is a rehearsal number when it is interrupted by the police, who close down the theater and the show for lack of funds. This ironic prelude leads into a story involving the efforts of a group of "gold-digging" chorus girls (among them Keeler, Joan Blondell, and Ginger Rogers) to find work. Beneath the film's whimsical tone lurks an array of socioeconomic issues, which range from

42nd Street: *this behind-the-scenes look into the production of a stage musical and romancing of its producer (Warner Baxter, center) solidified the formula for the backstage musical. (Can you spot Ruby Keeler and Ginger Rogers in the chorus lines?)* (Robert Downing Collection)

unemployment to prostitution. These issues provide a thematic subcurrent that counters the musical's "escapist" rhetoric and generate a context for considerable social comment. This culminates in the performance of a distinctly anti-utopian number, "Remember My Forgotten Man." Paradoxically, the downbeat, blues-ballet finale also marks the girls' return to the stage and to the ranks of the employed. The film's ending therefore resolves the immediate conflicts regarding the characters' jobs and musical expression, although the social milieu into which they are integrated is itself painfully disordered.

These two Warner Brothers-Busby Berkeley collaborations set off a series of "realistic" backstage musicals, including several more *Gold Diggers* films, although few had the bite of the 1933 original. Just as Warners' early-'30s gangster films were tempered by the revitalized Production Code in 1934, so were Warners' musicals. Sex and violence were toned down in the studios' amoral success sagas to the point where both the gangster and musical genres' social thematics were substantially reformulated. Actually, the Code forced Warners into step with Paramount, MGM, and RKO, which were already doing lighter, more fantasy-oriented treatments of courtship and entertainment in Depression America.

190

MGM dominated the genre throughout the 1940s, beginning with *The Wizard of Oz* and *Babes in Arms* in 1939. But the mid-to-late-'30s belonged to RKO with its Fred Astaire-Ginger Rogers films, particularly *Top Hat* (1935), *Follow the Fleet* (1935), *Swing Time* (1936), and *Shall We Dance?* (1937). While these films lacked the brilliant staging and dynamic camerawork of Berkeley's films for Warners, the complementary talents and personalities of Astaire and Rogers gave the RKO musicals a distinctive—and much copied—quality. Astaire's vital and uninhibited music man perfectly balanced Rogers' wise-cracking, talented but domestically inclined counterpart, and the couple's musical courtship ritual became a convention in Hollywood's late-'30s musical comedies.

While Astaire and Rogers' characters and courtship could be copied, the stars themselves could not. No performer in the history of the musical has been able to match Astaire's collective talents as singer, dancer, actor, and star persona. The last quality is the most important, since the musical tends to be bound to the star system more closely than any other genre. The status of actors as icons, embodying a set of particular values, attitudes, and actions, is important to any cinematic formula. But Bogart's detective, Cagney's and Robinson's gangsters, Grant and Hepburn's screwball couple, and even Wayne's heroic Westerner could not assume the intrinsic significance of the musical's star performers, particularly Astaire, Rogers, Gene Kelly, and Judy Garland, each of whom could both dance and sing. The principal reason for the enhanced significance of their personalities has to do, of course, with the range of dramatic and performance demands that are placed upon the musical star. Just as the genre operates by means of a balance between story and music and between reality and illusion, so must its central characters balance and interrelate their dramatic personalities with their talents as musical performers.

Fred Astaire and the rise of the integrated musical

The influence of Fred Astaire on the Hollywood musical cannot possibly be overestimated. In fact, I am inclined to argue that Astaire was almost solely responsible for the genre reaching its classical stage in the late '30s and the 1940s. The world of any musical film is not so much an actual place as it is the aural and visual rendition of an *attitude*—and Fred Astaire embodied that attitude. He made us believe that the world is a wondrous and romantic realm imbued with musical rhythm and grace, with endless pretexts for personal expression through motion and music. Although this attitude is evident in every musical film from *The Jazz Singer* on, not until the mid-'30s did the story and performance become truly *integrated*. In Astaire's RKO films, and later in MGM's quality musicals—all of which feature Astaire and/or Gene Kelly—the musical's characteristic attitude was not merely a posture assumed by the performers when on stage. Rather it emerged as a pervasive world view that affected the entire community and all its inhabitants. The genre gradually evolved, as Michael Wood has observed, into "the musical

Ginger Rogers and Fred Astaire, performing the title number from Swing Time (1936). They were the first romantic couple to integrate courtship and musical performance into a coherent narrative experience. (Robert Downing Collection)

that says what it has to say in music, as distinct from a movie that has music in it"[2] (Wood, 1975, p. 152).

In fact, when Arthur Freed brought Vincente Minnelli, who became MGM's premiere musical director, to Hollywood in 1940, Minnelli had a low opinion of film musicals, because of their failure to integrate the world of the story with that of the performances. In Minnelli's words: "The field seemed wide open. There weren't any musical talents before or behind the cameras which impressed me . . . except one. The Fred Astaire dance numbers were the only bright spots in musicals of the late 1930s, though I found the stories inane." Minnelli claims he was not impressed with the "spectacular effects" in Berkeley's Warner Brothers musicals. "His devices were ingenious, but they bore little relation to the story or to the 'reality' of the piece," suggests Minnelli. "Like most musicals of the period, his were crudely made backstage stories. The songs weren't integral to the plot"[3] (Minnelli, 1974, p. 117).

Minnelli, ever the master of the backhanded compliment, may be overstating the issue. The integration of the movie musical's dramatic and performative "realities" was anticipated in many of the earlier musicals, as in *Gold Diggers of 1933* when Dick Powell serenades the chorus girls through their open apartment windows. But this sequence is considerably less integral than most of Astaire's late-'30s work. In *Broadway Melody of 1940*, for instance, the backstage milieu is not reserved for the romantic subplot, nor are the musical numbers assigned to a rehearsal or traditional stagebound context. Astaire's "I've Got My Eyes on You" is performed onstage in an empty theater as his love interest and future partner (Eleanor Powell) eavesdrops. The music man's dual role (lover and performer) is thus linked with the film's dual narrative strategies (courtship romance and musical show). But it was not until later musicals like *Easter Parade*, which opens with Astaire dancing "down the avenue" singing his greetings to passersby, that Astaire's dual roles became indistinguishable from one another.

The integrated, life-is-music strategy did liberate the musical to a large degree from the confining backstage format, but the principal characters were still cast as performers and the narrative still built to a climactic musical finale. There are moments in some of the post-1940 musicals, though, which recall the earlier tendency of pulling musical numbers virtually out of nowhere. The "Trolley Song" sequence in *Meet Me in St. Louis* (1944) and the "Be a Clown" finale in *The Pirate* (1948), for example, demonstrate that even the integrated musical never lost sight of the primary importance of the "show," whether it was presented as an onstage production or as the "natural" expression of a musically inclined community.

Although these two sequences might seem somewhat arbitrarily motivated, they are very much in tune with the attitudes of their performers (Garland in the former, Garland and Kelly in the latter). They also are in tune with what John Belton has called the musical genre's "atmosphere of illusion"[4] (Belton, 1977, p. 36). This atmosphere came not only from the attitudes and talents of the performers, but also from stage and set design, musical composition, art direction, and the overall strategy of the director. This strategy differed in many ways from that employed in the backstage musicals. In the latter, the performance and story were clearly distinguished from one another and necessitated a change in the characters' attitudes as they moved between the two contexts. Stanley Donen, boy wonder of MGM's peak years (most notably with his direction of *On the Town*, *Singin' in the Rain*, and *It's Always Fair Weather*, all co-directed with Gene Kelly), has described the difference between the backstage and the backstage musical this way:

> The whole drift of the Busby Berkeley kind of musical was towards "realism." Everything happened on the stage and you were supposed to suspend your imagination just long enough to believe it was happening on the stage.... You always saw where the music came from. Nobody ever took off into the surrealism of the musical the way [Ernst] Lubitsch or Astaire or [René] Clair did. What *we* did was not geared toward realism but towards the unreal.... An opera has its own reality but it isn't what you'd call day-to-day reality, and the same with the musical.[5] (Donen, 1977, p. 28)

Internal logic and the atmosphere of illusion

As Donen suggests, the Hollywood musical's peculiar reality derives not from the viewer's real-world experiences or even from the enforced realism of the Warners-style backstage setting. It emanates from the romantic, illusory nature of American popular music and courtship rituals and from the attitudes of those who participate in them. To a certain limited extent, *all* musicals are integrated, in that they incorporate dramatic story and musical performance into a coherent narrative context. But rather than create a realistic—or at least plausible—world whose inhabitants find reasonable motives for breaking into song (rehearsals, shows, etc.), the music itself seems to determine the attitudes, values, and demeanor of the principal characters in these later films. As the musical genre evolved it sacrificed *plausibility* for *internal narrative logic,* steadily strengthening its basis in fantasy and artifice and steadily expanding its range of narrative, visual, and musical expression.

For example, the opening sequence in *It's Always Fair Weather* (1955) presents a collage of V–E Day celebrations and a musical tribute to returning GIs. A portion of the collage flashes back to battlefield action, but the film's "atmosphere of illusion" is established immediately as we notice that the shells are exploding *in tempo* with the music. After this implausible phenomenon has set the scene, we are prepared when, moments later, three drunken GIs (Gene Kelly, Dan Dailey, and Michael Kidd) pirouette gracefully through MGM's backlot rendition of New York City. Rather than disguise the genre's fantastic illogic, as had earlier backstage musicals, this and other films exploited and heightened it. There are even frequent self-conscious allusions to the genre's strategy of surreal artifice. In *Yolanda and the Thief,* con man Fred Astaire acts as his own set designer and lighting director in staging a "scene" to convince a naive heiress that he's her guardian angel; in *Singin' in the Rain,* Gene Kelly takes Debbie Reynolds onto a vacant movie sound stage, manipulating its lights and wind machine—its technology of artifice—to "set the stage" for a love song; in *The Band Wagon,* a stage director's outrageous effects (onstage explosions, moving stairways, etc.) finally force the performers to flee the stage; in *An American in Paris,* Gene Kelly acts as musical director, encouraging what seems like half the population of Paris to participate in the "I Got Rhythm" number.

Also certain films quite early in the genre's development clearly exploited the musical's potential for fantasy. Ernst Lubitsch's *The Love Parade* (1929), for instance, which starred Maurice Chevalier and introduced Jeannette MacDonald to the screen, traces the efforts of a bored aristocrat to come to terms with his wife, the Queen of Sylvania. Like other Paramount musicals of this period, the film displays a fluid visual style, takes place in an exotic, fairy-tale realm, and exhibits a distinctly European flavor and wit. As such, it was quite different from its backstage counterparts. The influence of these fantasy musicals survived through the 1930s primarily in MGM's musical "operettas" with Jeannette MacDonald and Nelson Eddy (*Naughty Marietta,* 1935; *Rose Marie,* 1936; *The Girl of the Golden West,* 1938;

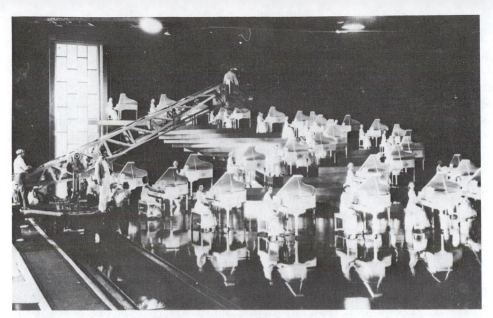

Reality and illusion are relative—and often misleading—concepts in the world of the movie musical. Above, Busby Berkeley directs a musical number from Gold Diggers of 1935; *below, Stanley Donen directs a number from* On the Town. *Paradoxically, the backstage plot in the Berkeley film renders it more "realistic" than the utopian fantasy of* On the Town, *although the later film was shot on location in New York City.* Gold Diggers of 1935 (Hoblitzelle Theatre Arts Collection); On the Town (Culver Pictures)

New Moon, 1940; et al.), most of which struck a fine balance between music and drama. The highbrow status of the music in these films, however, as well as their debt to traditional operatic forms, distinguished the musical operettas from the mainstream musicals of the period that relied upon popular music, dance, and a healthy disregard for the grim realities of Depression America.

Donen has suggested, "If you can put your finger on a really broad, general difference between the Lubitsch and Clair musicals and something like *Seven Brides* [*for Seven Brothers*] or *Singin' in the Rain*, it is energy, which has to do mainly with a) America and b) dancing"[6] (Donen, 1977, p. 27). These operettas seem less cinematic than their '30s counterparts, in that they suffer from stilted performances and generally static camerawork, and are therefore less engaging than the backstage musicals and the Astaire-Rogers romances of the same period. Ultimately, the later integrated, self-reflexive musicals—particularly MGM's *Yolanda and the Thief* and *The Pirate*—seem to take certain qualities from both the operettas and the backstage films. From the latter, they took the dancing and dynamic filmmaking techniques but left the "realistic" narrative context; from the operettas they took the integrated musical romance and fantastic logic but left the European manners, the static camerawork, and the primacy of song over dance.

Unlike the other genres we have already considered, the musical did not evolve toward the use of realistic social conflicts or more psychologically plausible characters—unless we consider the realism and the plausibility of the *music itself*. The balance between story and music was sustained despite the growing sophistication of filmmakers and audience. One need only sit through a few films that lost sight of that balance—the lavish, talent-filled *Ziegfeld Follies*, for example—to understand the importance of story, character, and attitude in providing a narrative framework for the production numbers. The story also involves the audience in the musical experience more directly than could any non-narrative musical revue. In the backstage musical, certain basic editing and camera techniques (shot/reverse shot, point-of-view, etc.) encourage the movie audience to identify not only with the central characters (the lovers/performers), but also with the imaginary theater audience for whom the characters perform. Even more effective are the community sing-along numbers in integrated musicals, like the "I Got Rhythm" and "Trolley Song" sequences already mentioned. These associate the movie audience not simply with an audience in some imaginary theater, but rather with those "folks" inhabiting a wondrous locale where everyone makes music.

The musical as courtship rite

The musical, therefore, draws performer and viewer into a close rapport that is enhanced by the performers' "offstage" conflicts involving courtship, love, and marriage. The genre's most familiar romantic conflict—and in the musical, romantic relationships invariably are conflicted—involves a dynamic, spontaneous hero (generally a man, but occasionally a woman, as in *Living in a Big Way* and *Gentlemen Prefer Blondes*) who compromises his uninhibited vitality when he falls in love with a talented, domestically oriented counterpart. The basis of the music man's appeal is his unique style: He embodies energy, grace, and rhythm, and these gifts somehow enable him to resist social propriety. He is talented and egotistical, uninhibited and tactless, an accomplished performer and a self-serving child.

The music man initiates his partner musically and sexually. In fact, *Babes in Arms*, *Easter Parade*, and *The Barkleys of Broadway* contain references to the hero as a "Svengali" because he teaches the female lead to perform. In instructing his musical partner in song and dance, the music man also introduces her to a generally liberated attitude toward life itself. He often goes to considerable lengths to instruct when the woman is an unwilling student. In *The Pirate*, for example, traveling performer Serafin (Gene Kelly) actually hypnotizes a beautiful stranger (Judy Garland) in order to coerce her to perform because social decorum and an impending marriage have stifled her capacity for musical and sexual expression. In *Swing Time*, an anarchic Fred Astaire condescends to take dance lessons in a stuffy, institutionalized studio in order to meet Ginger Rogers and liberate her from the inhibiting atmosphere.

While the music man may be an expert at expressing his musical disposition, however, his social and sexual inclinations must be refined by his female counterpart. In compliance with Hollywood's implicit requirement that a "good" woman also be a domesticator, the heroine eventually applies the reins of social propriety to the man. Both Gene Kelly (in *For Me and My Gal*) and Fred Astaire (in *Easter Parade*) play Svengali to Judy Garland for quite some time before each finally kisses her and delivers the same line: "Why didn't you tell me I was in love with you?" So wrapped up is the music man in his own expressive character that the sexual—and by extension marital—implications of the couple's partnership escape him. Their relationship is always social and sexual as well as musical, of course, anticipating the climactic musical embrace at the end. With that final eruption of song and dance, the narrative integrates the performers/lovers into a single unit of musical and romantic energy.

In the show-finale musicals, the ideal couple generally works its way out of a complex romantic tangle involving wealthy and attractive minor characters who have tried to distract the principals from their musical-utopian ideal. Typically, the ideal couple is not together at the opening of the film, each is involved with another partner. Because the woman-domesticator governs the musical's social thematics, the male lead's "other woman" usually is a more significant character to the narrative than the female lead's "other man." The music man most often is distracted by some Hollywood siren—an alluring, morally questionable type who appeals to his more primitive qualities. She may be a hustling chorus girl (Gale Robbins in *The Barkleys of Broadway*, Ann Miller in *Easter Parade*) or a wealthy patron in search of a gigolo (Nina Foch in *An American in Paris*), but whatever situation she is in, by contrast she amplifies the heroine's virtues.

In the backstage musicals, the romantic entanglements provide greater narrative tension than the success-story theme. Of course, the star system itself defused any doubts we might have had regarding the performers' dreams of "making it"—that is, the very talents that landed the actors their parts in Hollywood musicals certainly will enable them to succeed in the films' backstage subplots. Is there any doubt that Mickey Rooney and Judy Garland will hit the big time in *Babes in Arms* and *Babes on Broadway*, or that Garland will succeed as Astaire's partner in *Easter Parade*? Even in *Broadway Melody of 1940*, in which Astaire's protégé and partner (George Murphy) inadvertently lands a major part intended for Astaire, it is obvious, as Astaire teaches Murphy the part and how to woo the leading lady, that Astaire ultimately will get both the part and the girl.

Both the impending show and the couple's courtship naturally propel the narrative toward its musical resolution. As Michael Wood observes, "The music marks the progression toward getting the show on the road, and finally celebrates the show itself as the end of all the quarrels that were threatening its very existence"[7] (Wood, 1975, p. 154). The show integrates and mediates the conflicting attitudes and lifestyles of the characters, thereby celebrating their natural (musical) and cultural (marital) union in the act of performance. In the backstage and show-oriented musicals, this development is obvious, since the narrative culminates in a formalized musical celebration. Many later integrated musicals also used this strategy. The story was resolved by some community event or socially sanctioned festivity—weddings, parades, state fairs, banquets, and the like—which brings the couple together and provides a pretext for musical expression. In the weddings which resolve *Yolanda and the Thief* and *Funny Face*, in the trial which resolves *The Pirate*, in the parades which resolve *Easter Parade* and *The Music Man*, in the fairs which resolve *Meet Me in St. Louis* and *State Fair*, familiar cultural rituals are set to music and transform the community into an idealized utopian realm.

One of the more distinctive examples of this community ritual-as-show motif is the climactic Art Students' Ball in *An American in Paris* (1951). The ball is the high point of the season for Parisian aesthetes. It also provides a narrative context for Gene Kelly and Leslie Caron's surrealistic dream-ballet. In this brilliant twenty-minute musical finale, the conflicts that separated the lovers magically dissolve in a lush, dynamic homage to French painting and culture, set to George Gershwin's musical score. The musical finale, where not only man and woman but even the elite and popular arts can coexist, represents one of the genre's—and Hollywood's—greatest cinematic achievements. Interestingly, this climax is not so far removed from those of the *Gold Diggers* and *Broadway Melody* series of the '30s that also culminated in up to twenty minutes of uninterrupted performance. But these earlier backstage films had considerably less narrative tension and complexity because of the degree to which the stage-bound show itself determined the characters and conflicts.

In the musical's conventional geography, the modern metropolis is at once the promised land and proving ground for amateur performers. It is also the proverbial den of iniquity that "Mom" warned Mickey Rooney about in *Babes on Broad-*

way. The American success ethic generally is associated with New York City, al-though occasionally, another large, exotic city will do—like Paris in *For Me and My Gal,* when Judy Garland musically queries, "How ya gonna keep 'em down on the farm, after they've seen Par-ee?" New York City's nasty reputation is a significant element in *Meet Me in St. Louis*—as Tootie Smith (Margaret O'Brien) declares, she "would rather be poor than go to New York." In fact, the primary dramatic con-flict in this film centers upon Tootie's father's promotion and transfer to New York. Again the paradox: the family patriarch's business success threatens to up-root his family from the homespun security of their turn-of-the-century Midwest-ern community. Studio heads at MGM balked at this story line, but producer Arthur Freed convinced them that the New York/St. Louis opposition provided an engaging dramatic conflict. Consider Hugh Fordin's description of a preproduction story conference:

> Collectively and individually, Thau, Mannix, Katz, Cohn, L. K. Sidney, the knights around the conference table, voiced their negative opinions. There is no plot, no action, no conflict. Freed jumped right into the battle. "There is no con-flict? These people are fighting for their happiness! Where is the villain? Well, the villain is New York!! What more do you want?"[8] (Fordin, 1975, p. 73)

Tootie's family remains in St. Louis and celebrates with everyone else at the World's Fair finale. The joy they all feel prompts sister Rose's assertion that "we don't have to take a train or stay in a hotel to see it. It's right here in our own home town."

In perceiving "happiness" in traditional, familial, rural-based values rather than in the romance and professional success available in the big city, *Meet Me in St. Louis* is typical of a distinct musical subgenre dating back to *Hallelujah* (1929) and extending through such films as *The Wizard of Oz* (1939), *The Harvey Girls* (1945), *Summer Holiday* (1946), *Seven Brides for Seven Brothers* (1954), *Oklahoma!* (1955), *The Music Man* (1962), and *State Fair* (1963). Charles F. Altman appropriately terms these "folk musicals," referring both to their celebration of traditional values and their use of derivative folk dance and music[9] (Altman, *Semiotexte,* forthcoming). Arthur Freed shares Altman's opinion, having submitted the following request to do *The Harvey Girls* as a musical rather than a dramatic film: "I have been particu-larly attracted to do this with music, as I believe only music can perpetuate in a dignified manner the romance and American folk quality of this wonderful project"[10] (Fordin, 1975, p. 153).

While Hollywood's folk musicals differ from the show musicals in that sexual courtship is subordinate to familial and community concerns, both forms integrate spontaneous, dynamic musical expression into a potentially repressive social com-munity. The woman-domesticator is high priestess of this ritual, dictating the limits of social propriety while learning to express herself in song and move-ment. Ultimately, the union of the musical couple is significant beyond its resol-ution of the immediate love story. The genre's array of formal and cultural contradictions—object/image, reality/illusion, story/performance, work/play, stasis/movement, repression/expression, community/individual, and particularly man/woman—are resolved forever through the climactic show, which projects their ideal merger into the infinite expanse of mythic time.

Sexual courtship in the musical invariably is shown as conflict. Generally we are given little reason beyond the show itself to believe that the conflicts, which complicated the couple's relationship throughout the film, will magically dissolve once the performance is over. Anyway, it is precisely because of the irreconcilable nature of these conflicts that the genre's narrative strategies have developed. The musical finale and its celebration of romantic love ultimately prevent us from speculating beyond the film's closing moments. Consider an exception: In one of Vincente Minnelli's first MGM musicals, *Yolanda and the Thief* (1945), a brief epilogue follows the climactic wedding celebration. The heroine's (Lucille Bremer) guardian angel shows Bremer's new husband (reformed con artist Astaire) a photo of the couple some five years hence with their children at their sides. Astaire knits his brow, turns to find the angel has vanished, and with a shrug reaches to embrace his new bride and a life of domesticity.

The effect of this epilogue—of ending the film emphasizing social rather than musical integration, or the music man's compromise—projects an image of the idealized couple into real time. In this way, it subverts the happily-ever-after strategy of the wedding-show. Interestingly enough, Minnelli learned rather quickly that the audience preferred him to stress the musical over the social-marital union. His next musical romance, *The Pirate* (1948), ended with a very different type of epilogue. *The Pirate*'s sustained sexual battle (between Gene Kelly and Judy Garland) and its mistaken-identity subplot are resolved in a climactic public trial that evolves into a musical celebration and romantic embrace. This would seem to be the film's finale, but Minnelli cuts from the trial to a tight close-up of Kelly announcing to the camera/audience: "The best is yet to come." With that, the screen erupts into Garland and Kelly's energetic "Be a Clown" number, and a title card next to the stage informs us that the two have formed a traveling musical troupe. Like the epilogue in *Yolanda and the Thief,* this sequence projects the couple's union beyond the realm of the story. Unlike that earlier epilogue, however, this functions to extend the ritualistic show-celebration itself into the indefinite future, stressing the couple's performative rather than marital union.

The musical film's resolution reinforces the ideal of individual, spontaneous expression in the character of the music man, who "gets the girl" with his style and charm. The finale strategy subverts any speculation as to whether the sexual-marital-performative union will diminish the spontaneity of either character once their performance ends. Significantly, we rarely see the completion of the musical's show-finale. Whether it is the Broadway show that will run forever, the musical troupe that will never stop touring, or the utopian community that will never stop singing and dancing, the climactic show is ultimately what the musical is all about, from the character/performers' perspective as well as our own. In its consummate expression of individual joy and community integration, the musical

Alternative epilogues: the post-wedding sequences in Yolanda and the Thief *(above) and* The Pirate *(below), both directed by Vincente Minnelli, indicate the importance of culminating the narrative on a musical note.* Yolanda and the Thief (Hoblitzelle Theatre Arts Collection); The Pirate (Private Collection)

show not only resolves the cultural conflicts and contradictions of its narrative formula, but it also proves to be that formula's sole reason for existence.

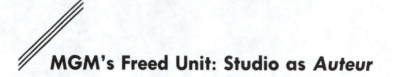

MGM's Freed Unit: Studio as *Auteur*

Today, when film cultists point to my contributions in the progress of the movie musical, I plead not guilty. The true revolutionary was Arthur [Freed]. He, more than any one man, made it possible. He gave creative people extraordinary freedom.

—Vincente Minnelli, "The Freed Unit"[11]

My evaluation of Arthur Freed as a producer is this: His greatest talent was to know talent, to recognize talent and to surround himself with it. . . . He knew style—he didn't do it, but he had an eye for it. He had to decide what to do—he put his stamp on it—like the president of the country.

—Irving Berlin[12]

There was no such thing as a "unit" except in [Arthur Freed's] head. And it is precisely because of that that, in my opinion, there really was such a thing as a "Freed unit."

—Stanley Donen[13]

Perhaps more than any other form of cinema, the Hollywood musical relies upon the film industry's collaborative production system. A successful musical necessarily requires the combined talents of various individuals—performers, composer, lyricist, set designer, art director, musical director, choreographer, as well as director, scriptwriter, cinematographer, and editor. It is no surprise, then, that the two film directors most often lauded as musical *auteurs*, Busby Berkeley and Vincente Minnelli, were adept in a number of production roles: Berkeley as choreographer, producer, and musical director; Minnelli as art director, costume designer, and stage producer. Paradoxically, the complex production demands of the Hollywood musical both intensify and diffuse the director's individual responsibilities, in that he must rely upon so many other craftsmen for the creation of a coherent narrative that effectively integrates their various contributions.

As I suggested in the previous overview, the musical genre reached its creative and popular zenith after World War II in a period dominated by MGM's remarkable output. Among MGM's most notable musicals are:

1944	*Meet Me in St. Louis*
1945	*Yolanda and the Thief*
1946	*Ziegfeld Follies, The Harvey Girls*
1947	*It Happened in Brooklyn, Till the Clouds Roll By*
1948	*Easter Parade, The Pirate, Summer Holiday*
1949	*On the Town, Take Me Out to the Ball Game, The Barkleys of Broadway*
1950	*Annie Get Your Gun, Summer Stock*
1951	*Show Boat, An American in Paris, Royal Wedding*
1952	*Singin' in the Rain, The Belle of New York*
1953	*The Band Wagon, Kiss Me Kate, Lili*
1954	*Brigadoon, Seven Brides for Seven Brothers*
1955	*It's Always Fair Weather, Kismet*

This output includes Broadway stage adaptations (*Show Boat, Annie Get Your Gun*) and vaudeville revues (*Ziegfeld Follies*), but considerably more significant are those genuine *Hollywood* musicals produced during the so-called Golden Age. At once more cinematic and narratively complex than the adaptations, MGM's integrated show musicals demonstrate a consistent balance of story and performance, style and substance, word and music, dance and song. They are in a class by themselves among Hollywood's musical films.

The premiere director during MGM's peak years was unquestionably Vincente Minnelli. His sense of visual expression and capacity to incorporate highbrow forms (particularly ballet and classical music) into what was then considered a middlebrow medium distinguished his works when they were first created and have sustained their popularity over the years. But looking back over Minnelli's musicals—principally *Meet Me in St. Louis, Yolanda and the Thief, The Pirate, An American in Paris,* and *The Band Wagon*—one realizes that his individual contribution to MGM's Golden Age may be somewhat overrated. Many qualities often attributed to him are also evident—and equally well developed—in postwar musicals directed by Minnelli's colleagues at MGM, especially Donen, Kelly, Charles Walters, and even on occasion Busby Berkeley in his post-1940 films for MGM (like *For Me and My Gal* and *Take Me Out to the Ball Game*).

Because of its collaborative creative process, its symbiosis of art and industry, the creation of a movie musical may be considered a function of its producer as well as its director. This seems particularly true in the case of Arthur Freed, who produced the vast majority of MGM's most popular and critically acclaimed musicals. (See his list of credits at the end of this chapter.)

Unlike most musical producers, Freed's training was not as a businessman or an entrepreneur. He began as a composer and lyricist, developing throughout his career an increasingly sensitive and sophisticated conception of the genre's range of expression. The repeated success of Freed's productions indicates that his musical and cinematic sensibilities were complemented by his administrative, executive, and financial savvy. Perhaps better than any other Hollywood filmmaker, Freed exemplifies the contradictory accomplishments of the medium as both industry and art form.

Freed's creative contributions and his organizational-administrative talents have already been examined admirably by Hugh Fordin in his study of MGM's musicals, *The World of Entertainment*, and by Minnelli in his autobiography, *I Remember It Well*. I would like to complement these studies by examining some of MGM's Freed-produced musicals, and to discuss the formal, narrative, and thematic qualities that distinguish his films as the musical genre's crowning achievement. We will consider films directed by different individuals (Minnelli, Donen-Kelly, Charles Walters), featuring different performers (Astaire, Rogers, Kelly, Garland, Oscar Levant, Frank Sinatra, Dan Dailey, et al.), and using different narrative strategies (backstage, fantasy, integrated romance). Indeed, if any single element unifies these films, it is producer Arthur Freed and the unique vision he lent them. Although various Freed unit productions will be cited in the following analysis of MGM's Golden Age, we will concentrate on these productions:

The Pirate	(Vincente Minnelli, 1948, with Gene Kelly and Judy Garland)
Easter Parade	(Charles Walters, 1948, with Astaire and Garland)
The Barkleys of Broadway	(Walters, 1949, with Astaire and Rogers)
On the Town	(Gene Kelly and Stanley Donen co-directed, 1949/1950, with Kelly, Sinatra, Ann Miller, et al.)
An American in Paris	(Minnelli, 1951, with Kelly and Leslie Caron)
Singin' in the Rain	(Donen-Kelly, 1952, with Kelly and Debbie Reynolds)
The Band Wagon	(Minnelli, 1953, with Astaire and Cyd Charisse)

Integrated romance and the promise of utopia

By the mid-1940s, the integration of musical show-making and American courtship, which began with the Astaire-Kelly RKO productions of the late 1930's and the musical operettas of that period, had solidified into the musical genre's guiding narrative strategy. During the 1940s, though, when MGM grew to dominate the musical genre while the inimitable Astaire-Rogers team underwent a decade-long separation, some rather significant developments took place within the musical's basic narrative structure. No longer did the stage-bound theatrical show dictate the attitudes, behavior, and romantic inclinations of the central characters. The characters' courtship itself determined their capacity for show-making. No longer did the lovers' shared status as performers isolate them from the rest of their world because of their unique abilities. No longer did the musical numbers function primarily as an "escape" from the social reality and sexual conflicts of the story. The rupture between the musical's story and its show—and between dramatic character and musical performer—was gradually giving way to a coherent, integrated narrative. The climactic show-finale still ruled, but its narrative pretext was no longer simply "putting on a show" for a hypothetical theater audience. By now the musical served not only to showcase entertainers, but also to celebrate courtship, romantic love, and the promise of utopia.

Even the backstage musicals of MGM's Golden Age (*Easter Parade*, *The Barkleys of Broadway*, and *The Band Wagon*) are considerably more integrated musically and more complex narratively than those produced before and during the war years. *Easter Parade* and *The Barkleys* each involves professional performers (Astaire and Garland in the former and a reunited Astaire and Rogers in the latter) and a backstage subplot, but their differences from their backstage predecessors are established immediately. The first complete musical number in each is not a rehearsal or an onstage performance, but an integrated musical expression of the characters' disposition in a "real-life" situation: Fred singing Happy Easter to passersby "on the avenue" and then dancing with a bass drum; Fred and Ginger spatting and then

Together again: Fred and Ginger ended a decade-long separation with **The Barkleys of Broadway,** *something of a divorce-remarriage musical and a throwback to their backstage romances at RKO during the 1930s.* (Hoblitzelle Theatre Arts Collection)

making up in their apartment with the "You'd Be Hard to Replace" number. Also in the opening credit sequence from *The Barkleys*, we are introduced to the performers, who have already married and made it into the big time. During the credits we watch Fred and Ginger completing a successful performance, and we realize that the conventional climactic show and the accompanying embrace have taken place. In a way reminiscent of the divorce-remarriage variation of the screwball comedy, what previously had been the genre's point of resolution (the show/embrace) now serves as its point of departure.

Both *Easter Parade* and *The Barkleys* cast Astaire in his familiar role of the professional entertainer who initiates a woman partner to the physical and spiritual values of musical expression. In *Easter Parade*, the initiate-heroine (Garland) is a waitress from Michigan whom Fred takes on after his former partner leaves him for individual star billing. In *The Barkleys*, the male-female relationship is more complex. Ginger leaves Fred and musical comedy for the "legitimate" stage but discovers that she is not a dramatic actress. Eventually, the ever-industrious Fred salvages her performance by pretending to be her director and rehearsing her over the phone. When Ginger promises "no more plays" at the end of the film, Fred replies: "Then we'll have nothing but fun set to music!" With that, the two begin a dance around their apartment that dissolves into the film's onstage "Manhattan Downbeat" finale. Thus Fred's natural instincts prevail, musical comedy emerges as superior to stage drama, and the musical show itself is reaffirmed as an expression of the musical couple's romantic embrace.

Easter Parade also projects a utopian vision in which love-making and show-making are interrelated. Astaire's musical initiation of Garland, like his reintroducing Ginger to show-making in *The Barkleys*, renders him a sort of high priest of the genre—his role is to convince each partner, and ultimately the audience, that life can be "fun set to music." Both *Easter Parade* and *The Barkleys* are substantial departures from earlier backstage musicals, although their principal characters do find themselves in a privileged onstage context at film's end. These late-'40s films may anticipate the integrated musical romances of the 1950s (*On the Town, An American in Paris, Singin' in the Rain*, et al.), but they also demonstrate that the backstage conventions were not dispensed with overnight.

Even in a fantasy musical like *The Pirate*, which uses an exotic, other-worldly locale (a Caribbean island), director Minnelli opts for a thinly integrated stage-bound finale with the closing "Be a Clown" number. Early in the film, the heroine (Garland) insists to her overly protective aunt: "I know there's a practical world and a dream world—and I shan't mix them up." Minnelli's strategy is precisely the opposite. The real and the imaginary in this film are so "mixed up" they are indistinguishable from one another. Minnelli's narrative agent is Gene Kelly (as Serafin, the leader of a musical troupe that performs worldwide) whose repeated overtures to Garland's subliminal musical/sexual psyche gradually cause her dreams to overwhelm and define her "practical world." Kelly hypnotizes Garland—with a spinning mirror, appropriately—and she is transformed from a virginal recluse to a dynamic, aggressive performer. Before long even Garland's daydreams are projected through musical/sexual performance: her awakened imagination projects the overtly erotic saber-dance ballet.

Even more significant, though, is the film's closing "Be a Clown" sequence. Ultimately, this stage-bound epilogue honors the musical's show-finale convention rather artificially, much like the "Manhattan Downbeat" number that closes *The Barkleys*. In each film, the final number has a dual narrative purpose. It functions as an epilogue to the romantic story, occurring after the lovers' integration-embrace and being performed on a theater stage that exists somewhere "outside" the world of that love story. Yet, these numbers are anything but epilogues. They represent a *falling action* in terms of story, but a *high point* in a genre whose dominant narrative strategy is putting on a show.

Because roughly half of *The Barkleys'* production numbers occur onstage, and because a dissolve (in which one sequence visually overlaps with another) connects the embrace in the lovers' apartment with the "Manhattan Downbeat" finale, the narrative rupture is not severe. The narrative strategy in *The Pirate*, however, tends to emphasize the rupture at the end of the film. Although Kelly portrays a professional performer, the majority of the production numbers are well integrated into the love story both spatially and attitudinally. They express emotions that are established within the love story, and do so within its physical world. Thus we are scarcely prepared for the abrupt change in strategy which takes us from the climactic trial to the closing "Be a Clown" number.

The Pirate's romantic conflict is resolved when the villainous Walter Slezak (as Don Pedro, a local aristrocrat), who had been engaged to Garland and had accused Kelly of being a notorious pirate, is himself revealed to be the real pirate in Kelly's trial. The trial sequence ends with a long shot of the community celebrating the Kelly-Garland embrace and setting upon Slezak/Pedro. Kelly then informs the camera/viewer (in a jarring tight close-up) that "the best is yet to come," reaffirming the musical genre's primary show-making function and introducing Kelly and Garland's dynamic closing duet. This sequence is distinctly out of touch with the story since we have no idea where or when the stage-bound finale is actually taking place.

The evolution of the music man: Fred Astaire and Gene Kelly

Actually, that non-integrated epilogue is an unusual element in the entire Kelly oeuvre. Kelly's musicals integrated both story and performance more effectively than did Astaire's, for reasons that have as much to do with their different musical personalities as with the genre's evolving narrative sophistication. Compared to Astaire's suave, detached professional performer whose musical talents enabled him to escape reality's social and sexual conflicts, Kelly's music man was more clearly "one of us." He portrays a more natural than a cultivated figure, and his musical expression represents an effort to redefine and resolve social complications rather than to transcend them. The "Niña" number in *The Pirate*, for example, in which Kelly acrobatically serenades and sexually disarms the female population of the community, not only establishes Kelly's musical persona but also projects his life-is-music attitude. This strategy became a familiar one in Kelly's later musicals, and in most of his "trademark" performances, he quite literally takes that attitude to the streets: the "I Got Rhythm" number in *An American in Paris*, the title song from *Singin' in the Rain*, the roller-skating "I Like Myself" number in *It's Always Fair Weather*. In each of these sequences, Kelly interweaves social and musical realms more effectively than Astaire had ever done—or apparently had ever wanted to do.

Astaire always seemed confident that he could create his own self-contained musical reality virtually at will, whereas Kelly seems to be saying that escaping reality through music is not enough—one must refashion the existing world into a fantastic realm where dancing and singing are as natural as walking and talking. Leo Braudy describes the two musical personalities:

> The figure of Fred Astaire implies that dance is the perfect form, the articulation of motion that allows the self the most freedom at the same time that it includes the most energy. The figure of Gene Kelly implies that the true end of dance is to destroy excess and attack the pretensions of all forms in order to achieve some new synthesis. . . . Astaire may mock social forms for their rigidity, but Kelly tries to explode them. Astaire purifies the relations between individual energy and stylized form, whereas Kelly tries to find a new form that will give his energy more play. Astaire dances onstage or in a room, expanding but still maintaining the idea of enclosure and theater; Kelly dances on streets, on the roofs of cars, on tables, in general bringing the power of dance to bear on a world that would ordinarily seem to exclude it.[14] (Braudy, 1972, pp. 147, 148–149)

I get the feeling while watching Astaire's films that I would have to *be* Fred Astaire in order to realize the utopia that his figure promises, while Gene Kelly seems to suggest that as soon as we understand what he is trying musically to express, the gap between social reality and utopian fantasy can be bridged. None of us can ever be Fred Astaire, of course, and so he elicits more awe and wonder than empathy. Kelly's musical everyman, conversely, is more sympathetic and engaging, although he does not seem as illusory or fantastic as Astaire. This distinction applies to the romantic subplots as well: Astaire's musicals tend to involve naive romantic conflicts whose eventual outcome is obvious from the credits—it is simply a matter of Ginger or Judy (or whoever) performing up to his accomplished level. The sexual conflicts in Kelly's musicals invariably are more complex and more closely related to his paradoxical character. His own efforts to synthesize his social and musical identities are directly related to his romantic interests. Because Astaire's special talents spirit him—and his partner, finally—away from mundane reality, his persona seems confident in any situation. In Kelly's desire to adjust social reality to his own musical disposition, however, he often emerges as his own worst enemy in both social and sexual relationships. Even in Kelly's first film, MGM's

For Me and My Gal (1942), his relationships with his fellow vaudevillians, with his draft board, and especially with his on-again, off-again partner Judy Garland are confused and stormy. The artificial performance-embrace at the end doesn't even begin to integrate Kelly's social and musical selves.

The war years were Kelly's period of apprenticeship, just as the early Depression years had been Astaire's. By the late 1940s, Kelly's star was ascending and Astaire's was beginning to wane. The distinctions between their musical personalities, of course, are a function of age and history as well as personality. The progression from Astaire to Kelly as MGM's dominant musical persona is remarkably consistent with developments in other genres. Kelly's talented, insecure music man/misfit shares a certain rapport with the psychological Westerner and the disillusioned cop, who took the place of their heroic, unselfconscious predecessors. Even Astaire's well-established persona was affected by these subtle changes during the postwar years.

The Band Wagon, for example, is a backstage throwback which was designed for Astaire and directed by Minnelli in 1953. In it, Astaire portrays an over-the-hill movie musical star attempting to make a comeback with a Broadway show. The early numbers in the film reflect the influence of Kelly's self-conscious, complex character. The first number traces Astaire's dejection at the loss of his celebrity status ("I'll go my way by myself"). This is followed by the brilliant shoeshine number, in which Astaire and a portly bootblack, backed by the whir and flash of 42nd Street arcade machinery, perform an energetic routine for the awestruck passersby. This spontaneous song and dance is closer to what we would expect of Kelly than of Astaire. *The Band Wagon* eventually develops into a rather traditional stage-bound show musical, however, with the final numbers presented in an entertaining but unimaginative revue format which we associate with Astaire's earlier musicals.

Kelly's persona in the early 1950s

The Band Wagon was the only significant musical which Astaire did for the Freed unit during the 1950s. As far as MGM was concerned, the '50s belonged to Kelly, who starred in hit musicals directed by Minnelli (*An American in Paris*, 1951; *Brigadoon*, 1954), as well as a trio of masterpieces which he co-directed with Stanley Donen (*On the Town*, completed in late 1949; *Singin' in the Rain*, 1952; and *It's Always Fair Weather*, 1955). Of all the MGM postwar musicals, *On the Town* may have had the greatest impact on the genre. More than any other Freed production, it epitomizes the integrated musical romance. For this film, Freed combined Donen and Kelly's untried directorial talents with Leonard Bernstein's score, Cedric Gibbons' art direction, Comden and Green's script (adapted from their 1944 stage hit), and perhaps most significantly, Harold Rosson's location cinematography.

The film's plot line is simple enough: three sailors (Kelly, Frank Sinatra, and

Takin' it to the streets: Frank Sinatra, Jules Munshin, and Gene Kelly on location for the "New York, New York" number in On the Town. (Culver Pictures)

Jules Munshin) spend a twenty-four-hour liberty in New York City and team up with three women (Ann Miller, Vera Ellen, and Betty Garrett). The men play Svengali for the women, enabling them to express themselves musically and to forget their various problems—one is an overworked cabbie, another is belly-dancing to finance ballet lessons, and the third suffers loudly from war-induced sexual neglect. The general strategy of the film, in Donen's own words, was to show "how much juice there is in life that people weren't living, all crammed into those hours"[15] (Donen, 1977, p. 29).

What's remarkable and innovative about the film is that the principal performers—all *six* of them—enjoy life not only during the musical numbers but throughout the narrative. The film's utopian milieu is not a figment of historical revery (as in *Meet Me in St. Louis* and *Easter Parade*) or adolescent nostalgia (*Take Me Out to the Ball Game*), nor does it reside in some exotic fantasy land (*Yolanda and the Thief*, *The Pirate*). Instead it is discovered within a modern metropolis. The narrative traces the gradual transformation of the most familiar of cities into a vast arena of musical play and expression. New York City's familiarity is enhanced by the perpetual motion of the characters dancing through an array of urban locales, from museums to subways to skyscrapers. *On the Town* is also a convincing utopian manifesto because of the sheer vitality of its high-energy performances and of Kelly and Donen's dynamic direction, which inject a breath of musical life into the concrete and steel arena. As Donen himself has said of the film:

> It was only in *On the Town* that we tried something entirely new in the musical film. Live people get off a real ship in the Brooklyn Navy Yard and sing and dance down New York City. We did a lot of quick cutting—we'd be on the top of Radio City and then on the bottom—we'd cut from Mulberry Street to Third Avenue—and so the dissolve went out of style. This was one of the things that changed the history of the musical more than anything.[16] (Fordin, 1975, p. 269)

Thus *On the Town* adds another dimension to the integrated musical, celebrating the rhythms and romance of the lover/performers and also of their very milieu. MGM's consummate homage to postwar city life, though, came a year later with Vincente Minnelli's *An American in Paris.* From the opening words of Gene Kelly's voice-over introduction to that wondrous city ("this star called Paris"), we are ushered into a modern urban utopia, the ideal environment for sensitive romantics. Lovers, painters, composers, entertainers—even the folks in the street who've "got rhythm"—all are infected with the modern city's contagious musical atmosphere. The romantic conflict in *An American in Paris,* interestingly enough, pits Kelly's struggling painter ("If you can't paint in Paris . . .") against a Parisian version of Fred Astaire (French music-hall performer turned actor Georges Guetary), both of whom are in love with initiate Leslie Caron. This conflict is further complicated by Nina Foch, portraying an American art patron who finances Kelly's painting career in return for his reluctant attention. Kelly's occupational elitism (as painter) and Guetary's refined, stage-bound musical performances represent differing modes of artistic expression, and are ultimately juxtaposed with Kelly and Caron's more "natural" and spontaneous love/ballet duets. Their musical and emotional rapport grows steadily in secret, since Caron is committed to Guetary for aiding her family during the German occupation. Love conquers, and the Kelly-Caron coupling at the end reinforces the primacy of spontaneous musical expression over the refined but essentially static offering of the "serious artist."

The lovers' eventual embrace is realized in the brilliant "American in Paris Ballet," in which Kelly and Caron dance amidst lavish sets designed after the paintings of Dufy, Toulouse-Lautrec, Renoir, and other French masters. This climactic sequence also mediates Kelly's occupational conflicts: music and dance may be his primary means of personal and artistic expression, but they exist within an environment that integrates all art forms, elite and popular alike. Thus the film's two dominant oppositions—between Nina Foch and Leslie Caron as Kelly's ideal partner, and between Kelly's own conflicting impulses as painter and music man—are interrelated in the romantic resolution. If there is any real thematic opposition expressed in this most lighthearted and optimistic of musicals, it would seem to involve the film's attitude toward the hardened professionalism of art patron Nina Foch, who is capable of literally buying Kelly a reputation as a painter, and of Guetary, whose stage-bound musical persona seems increasingly unattractive as Kelly learns to articulate his own "natural" musical urges. Kelly's painterly inclinations are initially opposed by Guetary's musical disposition. Eventually, Kelly's more natural (i.e., non-professional) musical expression counters the calculated, well-rehearsed performances by Guetary onstage.

The film's celebration of personal and natural musical expression is reinforced by Caron's character. She is a graceful child-woman who never performs in public and never dances with Guetary during their courtship, although she does dance (clandestinely) with Kelly. It's significant that the climactic ballet sequence, certainly one of the most highly refined and well-rehearsed production numbers in the history of the musical genre, occurs within Kelly's *imagination* and thereby retains some semblance of the immediacy and spontaneity of the earlier Kelly-Caron numbers, all of which were of the simple *pas de deux* variety performed beneath a bridge on the Seine. Kelly's daydream ballet is not a romantic celebration; rather, it is initiated when Caron leaves the Art Students' Ball with Guetary. As the reverie ends, however, Guetary finally realizes Kelly and Caron's mutual attraction. He absolves her from her commitment so that she can pursue her natural inclinations with Kelly and so that the film can end with the predictable resolution-embrace.

Singin' in the Rain and *The Band Wagon:* **The professionals go natural**

While *An American in Paris* is an integrated romance musical, much of its dramatic tension revolves around Kelly coming to terms with himself, resolving his natural and professional urges. This narrative strategy recurs in *Singin' in the Rain*, in which the actor portrays a silent screen star caught up in the transition to sound films. As in *An American in Paris*, Kelly initially is out of sorts with himself and his professional career as a screen lover. His studio demands that he perpetuate his leading-man image and publicly court his co-star, the obnoxious, shrill-voiced Lina Lamont (Jean Hagen in a wonderfully abrasive performance). Just as Kelly's introduction to Leslie Caron had brought him in tune with his natural musical disposition in the earlier film, Kelly's relationship with initiate-lover/performer Debbie Reynolds instigates his musical reeducation. The barometer for both his professional development as well as the romance is Kelly and Hagen's new film, *The Duelling Cavaliers*. The film is Kelly's—and his studio's—first "talkie," a disastrous romantic melodrama, which Kelly and Reynolds, along with sidekick Donald O'Connor, magically turn into a hit musical comedy.

The transformation occurs only after Reynolds is convinced of the artistic integrity of moving pictures. Whereas Kelly had worked his way into the movie industry via vaudeville and stunt performance, Reynolds aspires to the "legitimate"

By the early 1950s, both Kelly (shown here in Singin' in the Rain) *and Astaire (in the shoeshine sequence from* The Band Wagon) *were discovering pretexts for song and dance literally everywhere.* Singin' in the Rain (Culver Pictures); The Band Wagon (Hoblitzelle Theater Arts Collection)

stage. She tells Kelly at their first meeting: "I don't go to the movies much—if you've seen one you've seen them all. Oh, they're all right for the masses." Her misgivings about silent film acting are shared by the typically insecure Kelly, although he refuses to admit it.

Eventually, not just the advent of sound but the development of the movie musical itself brings Kelly and Reynolds together and legitimates their professional activities. Kelly's "Singin' in the Rain" number celebrates both his embrace with Reynolds and also their brainstorm to salvage *The Duelling Cavaliers* by dubbing Reynolds' voice over Hagen's and by adding music and comic dialogue. The brainstorm and the Kelly-Reynolds coupling occur within the same sequence, motivating his delightful puddle-stomping routine outside Reynolds' apartment. Thus the central characters' adaptation to musical filmmaking seems as "natural" as their romantic embrace, and their shared spontaneous expression is underscored by the inability of Kelly's co-star to make the adjustment along with them.

The film ends with the successful premiere of *The Duelling Cavaliers* as a musical comedy. After the show, the audience demands that Lina Lamont give a live performance in front of the screen, but Kelly and O'Connor conspire to reveal Reynolds' talent—the real voice both on screen and onstage. Lina's inability to sing—or even to articulate herself verbally—is an extension of her attitude toward life itself. Like Nina Foch's dowager in *An American in Paris*, Lina Lamont is a professional in the worst way: greedy, self-centered, manipulative, insensitive, and out of touch with her own feelings. She has no capacity for love or genuine human contact, and by extension, no ability to express herself musically.

Lina's final fall from grace and Reynolds' ascent to a partnership with Kelly reinforce that musical expression is based in interpersonal contact and romantic love. In this and other integrated MGM musicals, especially Kelly's post-1950 films, musical talent and performance represent natural rather than cultivated qualities. After *On the Town*, the couple are rarely depicted as professional performers in the movie musical. They may be artists of some kind, but their musical success relies essentially on bringing their professional activities in line with their natural musical instincts.

Even in *The Band Wagon*, which finally adopts a revue format once Astaire has performed several integrated numbers, the romance is dependent on this "natural" musical expression. Astaire and his co-star (Cyd Charisse) steal away from a rehearsal for a doomed dramatic musical in order to find out if they can dance together as a team. Not only do they feel uneasy about performing in an ill-fated show, they have problems with their own abilities. Charisse is attempting to move from ballet to musicals, and Astaire is trying a musical comeback to salvage his sagging career. The couple's flight from rehearsal has romantic as well as professional connotations, of course, in that their capacity to relate musically is necessarily a function of their emotional and sexual relationship. Their coupling is assured when they break into a spontaneous *pas de deux* in the darkness and solitude of Central Park, recalling the nocturnal duets between Kelly and Caron in *An American in Paris*. The role of the woman as initiate is especially important in these films, as it both underscores the purity of attitude and uncompromised sexual-musical impulses of the "amateur" performer and also rekindles in the music man his own purity and spontaneity.

One of the remarkable features of MGM musicals is how convincing they really are—we do come away from the films believing that the characters are expressing natural inclinations rather than executing well-rehearsed routines. Our tendency to "believe" in the performer/lovers' purity of spirit and motivation is a tribute to the narrative sophistication of the Freed unit musicals, to their capacity to credibly integrate romance and musical performance. As it happens, our very presence in the theater indicates regard for the performers' professional competence and calculated artistry. But the internal narrative logic of these musicals—and of their backstage predecessors as well—effectively displaces common sense and plausibility. Whether the climactic show is the product of a stage-bound community of professionals or the "natural" expression of lovers within a utopian milieu, the show-making strategy *within* the films directs our response to the integrated narrative itself and away from our familiarity with the characters in their persona as professional entertainers.

As Jane Feuer has pointed out in her definitive study of the Hollywood musical, these films developed a system of narrative devices that effectively "humanized" the technically complex nature of Hollywood musical production—they disguised a commercial art as contemporary folk art. The seemingly spontaneous and effortless musical expressions of love, the passing off of polished performances as mere rehearsals, the success of the amateur-initiate, the backstage collective whose motives are communal and aesthetic rather than self-serving and materialistic— these narrative devices, argues Feuer, "erase" the alienating economic and industrial nature of musical filmmaking. This is particularly true in the integrated musical romances, because of their tendency to cast the principals as non-professionals. Even so, we never forget their star status for very long. The brilliant performances of Kelly, Astaire, Garland, Charisse, and their colleagues repeatedly remind us, not only in the story but in the integrated musical numbers as well, of the cumulative effects of the star system[17] (Feuer, 1978, pp. 10–61).

Characters, performers, and crises of identity

In the opening sequence of *An American in Paris*, we hear the familiar voice of Gene Kelly informing us that he is an American ex-GI and expatriate painter named Jerry Mulligan. This introduction leads into a delightful dance-comedy routine where we see Kelly/Mulligan gracefully transform his cramped apartment from bedroom to artist's studio. As the sequence closes, he examines a self-portrait he has sketched, the camera pulls in for a close-up on the portrait, and Mulligan takes a rag and erases his own image from the canvas/screen. This brilliant, concise opening effectively establishes the central character and his inherent conflicts: painting versus dance, work versus play, America versus Paris, reality versus utopia, war versus postwar, positive versus negative self-image. And these oppositions center upon one obvious and vitally important fact: this character who calls himself Jerry Mulligan clearly doesn't realize that he is actually Gene Kelly.

All of the Freed unit musicals, and particularly those featuring Kelly, deal to some extent with the central character's steady abandonment of his fictional identity and the gradual realization of his own transcendant musical star persona. Thus the conflict-to-resolution progression is a movement toward *self-recognition* as well as an effort to "get the show on the road." As the key performers of the musical genre and their distinctive musical abilities became more familiar to the public, the narrative concentrated more on the personal element. Earlier musicals, particularly the backstage films, also used this strategy, although the performers' new-found musical identities were "explained" and thus masked by the logic of putting on the stage-bound show. In the later musicals, this narrative technique is used to considerably more complex and engaging ends.

Self-consciousness almost becomes parody when the fictional show-within-a-show finally is equated with the musical movie itself, as in *Singin' in the Rain* and *The Band Wagon*. Each of these films ends with the successful production of a stage

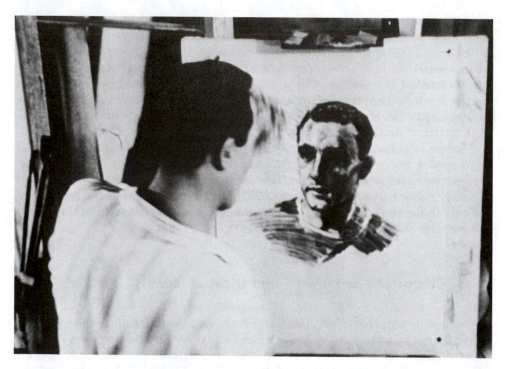

Frame enlargement from the opening sequence of An American in Paris: *painter Jerry Mulligan "erases" his self-portrait and sets off in search of his true identity as singer-dancer Gene Kelly.* (Private Collection)

musical whose title is the same as the film which contains it. And, in the closing sequence of *Singin' in the Rain,* we see Gene Kelly and Debbie Reynolds looking at their own images on a billboard that is promoting a show of the same title, a sort of narrative epilogue reaffirming the musical-marital coupling.

The narrative strategy in *An American in Paris* is actually a more conventional treatment of the progression toward self-recognition. Jerry Mulligan and his lover/partner finally dispense with their role playing, soul searching, and dramatic conflicts, and recognize the narrative for what it actually is: a showcase for their musical talents. This is not to suggest that the musical could do without its narrative-dramatic context, although many of MGM's revues and stage-bound theatrical adaptations—notably *Ziegfeld Follies, Annie Get Your Gun,* and *Show Boat*—were quite successful when they were released. These films have not worn well, however, because of their failure to exploit the formal and aesthetic qualities of weaving music and narrative together. The integrated musical, on the other hand, manipulates the tension between object and image, between reality and illusion, and is therefore among the most cinematic of Hollywood films. Because its performers constantly must shift their identities from being actors in a drama to entertainers addressing the audience directly, the integrated musical is also the most formally self-reflexive of Hollywood narratives.

These tensions between reality and illusion and between the couples' dramatic and performative identities often are developed *within the story itself.* The integrated musical plot frequently hinges on some character's mistaken or altered identity. Resolving this conflict generates the eventual recognition of the character's "real" identity as Hollywood star, as consummate musical performer.

In *The Pirate,* Judy Garland's Manuela must resolve her own confused sexual and imaginative identity, which she can only do by working out her fantasies regarding the legend of the pirate Macoco. Both of Garland's potential lovers, Kelly/Serafin and Slezak/Don Pedro, figure in her fantasy: Kelly is an entertainer and ladies' man who realizes that the only way to attract Garland's attention is to pretend to be the pirate; Slezak, the actual Macoco, has parlayed his pirate's booty into respectable citizenship within the community and so must conceal his identity. Garland's engagement to the unappealing Slezak is arranged by her family, although he obviously cannot fulfill her romantic fantasies of a pirate-lover. These fantasies are articulated most clearly in her daydream, "Saber-Dance Ballet," featuring Kelly as her idealized partner. Both Kelly and Slezak finally are unmasked at the end. Garland is liberated from her false reality—both dramatically in her commitment to Slezak and musically in her musical inhibitions—so that she can find musical and sexual fulfillment with Kelly. At the moment the mistaken identities are untangled, the screen erupts into the "Be a Clown" finale. Garland's transformation is depicted as altogether natural—despite her lack of professional training or experience—and her role onstage with Kelly at the film's end is logical within the realm of the integrated musical.

In *The Pirate,* then, the crisis of identity operates to integrate both the principal characters and the star performers. This also happens in *Yolanda and the Thief,* although not quite so neatly. Astaire is cast here as a con artist (Johnny Riggs) who masquerades as the guardian angel of an heiress (Lucille Bremer) in order to steal a few of her millions. Bremer's "real" guardian angel intervenes, unmasking Astaire and making him recognize his love for Bremer. Astaire's dual identity (as con man and guardian angel) works at the level of plot but this duality is only incidentally integral to the resolution/recognition of Astaire's dual identity on the larger narrative level (as character and performer).

In *Easter Parade, The Barkleys of Broadway,* and *The Band Wagon,* Astaire's transcendent musical persona is a narrative given—he portrays a professional entertainer in each film. The identity crisis concerns Astaire's initiate-partner: Garland in *Easter Parade* is transformed from naive Michiganite "Hanna" to partner "Juanita" and finally to performer-partner-lover Judy; Ginger Rogers in *The Barkleys* leaves Astaire for a career as a dramatic actress but eventually returns to a life of "fun set to music"; Charisse, Jack Buchanan, and the entire backstage community in *The Band Wagon* undergo a collective identity crisis, with Astaire himself resolving it by pulling together their musical version of *Faust* and making it into a hit revue. The closest Astaire himself comes to an identity crisis is in *The Band Wagon*, wherein the decline of his character's fictional career reflects Astaire's real-life decline due to his advancing age and the evolution of the genre away from the backstage formula. That decline leads Astaire/Hunter to go against his better instincts and take part in Buchanan's musical *Faust*. When the play bombs, Astaire recovers his temporarily skewed identity to lead the musical community back into more familiar territory.

In Kelly's musicals with the Freed unit, conversely, the fictional character's crisis invariably is integrated into the performance itself. Kelly's conflict may concern his role as professional entertainer (as in *The Pirate* and *Singin' in the Rain*), or it may be less self-reflexive, related to the split between his cultivated occupational self and his "natural" musical-sexual self. In the musicals in which Kelly does not portray a professional music man—as wartime sailor in *On the Town*, as silent film actor in *Singin' in the Rain*, and as gambler–fight promoter in *It's Always Fair Weather*—his social role initially is opposed but eventually subordinate to his role as singing, dancing lover. Whether the recognition of Kelly's transcendent musical persona is motivated occupationally or sexually, though, the narrative strategy is the same—he is transformed from character into performer, from actor to musical star. This recognition of the performer's musical identity serves three significant narrative functions: it integrates the story and performance into a cohesive whole, it allows the stars to do what they do best, and it celebrates the individual and communal value of the movie musical as a formal synthesis of art and experience, of word and music, of professional and amateur, of work and play.

Rites of integration/rites of entertainment

All of the Freed unit musicals function as veritable "apologies" for entertainment. This function may be incorporated into the story itself, as in *The Barkleys* and *The Band Wagon*, where the dramatic conflicts center upon the opposition between "serious art" and "mere entertainment." At the outset of *The Barkleys*, a stuffy highbrow stage director tempts Ginger Rogers, "You're wasted in musical comedy, you could be a great dramatic actress." Early in *The Band Wagon*, stage director/producer/actor Jack Buchanan dismisses "the artificial distinctions between musical comedy and drama," telling the dubious Astaire, "You've got a choice here between a nice little musical comedy and a modern musical morality play with meaning and stature." These stage-bound elitists with reactionary attitudes are clearly the villains of their respective pieces. As the performers' love-making and musical show-making transform the theater stage and the screen into a living canvas of dynamic human expression, we see just how lifeless is the elitist's art form.

We also see this tension in several of the integrated musical romances, particularly *An American in Paris* and *Singin' in the Rain*. Kelly's artistic but insecure charac-

Perhaps the genre's ultimate wedding of popular and elite art occurs in the "American in Paris Ballet," wherein Gershwin's music, French painting, Kelly's modern dance and ballet, and Minnelli's mise-en-scène coalesce into nearly twenty minutes of musical and visual perfection. (Private Collection)

ter is transformed in each film into a self-assured musical performer, a transformation which is motivated by his relationship with his initiate-partner. *Singin' in the Rain* acknowledges the values of the genre by tracing Kelly's transition from silent screen actor to movie musical performer, but the celebration of pure musical entertainment in *An American in Paris* is developed more subtly. Painter Jerry Mulligan is transformed into music man Gene Kelly when he rejects a professional career for a more natural and romantic (i.e., musical) means of expression. Once Kelly's character recognizes his transcendent persona through love and music, the issue of his—and Caron's—professional future is no longer a narrative issue. The climactic ballet and the lovers' embrace not only provide the anticipated show-finale, but also project their embrace into a timeless utopian realm.

Most post-1950 MGM musicals, in fact, created an integrated utopian community in which real-world concerns magically evaporated, in which performers and audience could mutually celebrate the liberating nature of romantic love and musical expression. The strategy of earlier backstage musicals had emphasized the viewers' collective participation in musical filmmaking, but it had also reinforced the distinction between music as a stage-bound professional activity and music as a spontaneous "natural" mode of expression.

The Freed unit musicals never stopped trying to erase that distinction, interweaving story and performance, character and performer, reality and fantasy. But perhaps most importantly, these films integrate the musical world with our own. The rhetoric of integration draws us not only into the *act* but also into the *world* of musical entertainment, and although we never forget the genre's primary show-making function, we are perfectly happy to lose ourselves in the world of the characters/performers we see on the screen.

ARTHUR FREED FILMOGRAPHY
(Listing includes productions only; dates indicate completion, not release, of film.)*

1939	*Babes in Arms*
1940	*Little Nellie Kelly; Strike Up the Band*
1941	*Babes on Broadway; Lady Be Good; Panama Hattie*
1942	*Cabin in the Sky; For Me and My Gal*
1943	*Best Foot Forward; DuBarry Was a Lady; Girl Crazy*
1944	*The Clock; Meet Me in St. Louis; Yolanda and the Thief; Ziegfeld Follies*
1945	*The Harvey Girls; Till the Clouds Roll By*
1946	*Summer Holiday*
1947	*Good News; The Pirate*
1948	*The Barkleys of Broadway; Easter Parade; Words and Music*
1949	*Annie Get Your Gun; Any Number Can Play; On the Town; Take Me Out to the Ball Game*
1950	*Crisis; Pagan Love Song; Royal Wedding*
1951	*An American in Paris; The Belle of New York; Show Boat; Singin' in the Rain*
1952	*Invitation to the Dance*
1953	*The Band Wagon*
1954	*Brigadoon*
1955	*It's Always Fair Weather; Kismet*
1957	*Gigi; Silk Stockings; The Subterraneans*
1959	*Bells Are Ringing*
1961	*Light in the Piazza*

* Dates throughout text are release dates.

The Family
Melodrama

*I am not an American; indeed I came to this folklore of American melo-
drama from a world crazily removed from it. But I was always fasci-
nated with the kind of picture which is called melodrama, in
America. . . . Melodrama in the American sense is rather the archetype
of a kind of cinema which connects with drama.*

—*Douglas Sirk*[1]

*"You're supposed to be making me fit for normal life. What's normal?
Yours? If it's a question of values, your values stink. Lousy, middle-class,
well-fed, smug existence. All you care about is a paycheck you didn't
earn and a beautiful thing to go home to every night."*

—*Patient to his psychiatrist in* The Cobweb *(1955)*

Melodrama as style and as genre

In a certain sense every Hollywood movie might be described as "melodramatic." In the strictest definition of the term, melodrama refers to those narrative forms which combine music (*melos*) with drama. Hollywood's use of
background music to provide a formal aural dimension and an emotional
punctuation to its dramas extends back even into the "silent" era. Live musi-

221

cal accompaniment (usually organ or piano) was standard from the earliest days of theatrical projection. As the Hollywood cinema and its narrative forms developed, though, and borrowed elements from pulp fiction, radio serials, romantic ballads, and other forms of popular romantic fiction, the term "romantic melodrama" assumed a more specialized meaning. Generally speaking, "melodrama" was applied to popular romances that depicted a virtuous individual (usually a woman) or couple (usually lovers) victimized by repressive and inequitable social circumstances, particularly those involving marriage, occupation, and the nuclear family.

Actually, the gradual development of the movie melodrama is quite similar to that of romantic and screwball comedy. "Comedy," in the early cinema, was a narrative filmic mode that evolved into the "romantic comedy" and then, as romantic conflicts began to be treated in terms of sociosexual and familial codes, into the screwball comedy genre. Similarly, the melodramatic mode of silent filmmaking gradually was adapted to romantic narratives and because of the coincidence of certain formal and ideological factors, it emerged as a distinct formula. We can extend this analogy by considering social melodrama as the inverse of social comedy: Whereas the characters of romantic or screwball comedies scoff at social decorum and propriety, in melodrama they are at the mercy of social conventions; whereas the comedies integrated the anarchic lovers into a self-sufficient marital unit distinct from their social milieu, the melodrama traces the ultimate *resignation* of the principals to the strictures of social and familial tradition.

The master of the silent melodrama was D. W. Griffith, who established its style, tone, and substance in films like *Hearts of the World* (1918), *Broken Blossoms*, *True-Heart Suzie* (1919), *Way Down East* (1920), and *Orphans of the Storm* (1922), in which the sociosexual trials and tribulations of the sisters Gish et al. were communicated in theatrical pantomime. The narrative strategies were calculated to enhance the victims' virtuous suffering: long camera takes, ponderous narrative pacing, frequent close-ups of the anxious heroine (usually with eyes cast heavenward), somber musical accompaniment, and so on. Griffith's heir apparent was Frank Borzage, who first directed silents (most notably *Seventh Heaven* in 1927) but is best remembered for his early sound melodramas—*A Farewell to Arms* (1932), *A Man's Castle* (1933), and *No Greater Glory* (1934). John Stahl also directed both silent and sound melodramas, although he had much greater success with his sound romances, particularly *Only Yesterday* (1933), *Imitation of Life* (1934), *Magnificent Obsession* (1935), *When Tomorrow Comes* (1939), and *Leave Her to Heaven* (1945).

By the 1940s, the plight of the star-crossed couple whose love conquered all had become familiar, although the notion of melodrama still applied as much to dramatic articulation and musical punctuation as to the narrative formula that the studios were in the process of refining. Not until after the war did Hollywood filmmakers really begin to test the range and emotional power of that narrative and with films showing the anxious lovers in a suffocating, highly stylized social environment. This period was dominated by Max Ophuls, an expatriate German filmmaker who directed three intense romantic melodramas—*Letter from an Un-*

known Woman (1948), *Caught* (1949), and *The Reckless Moment* (1949)—before leaving Hollywood and returning to Europe. Ophuls' fluid camerawork and elaborate sets enclosed his characters in a world where love is engulfed and overwhelmed by the material trappings of a repressive society.

Ophuls' work was complemented in the late 1940s by two novice Hollywood directors—another German expatriate, Douglas Sirk, and a set designer fresh from the Broadway musical stage, Vincente Minnelli. Minnelli's postwar melodramas (*The Clock*, 1945; *Undercurrent*, 1946; *Madame Bovary*, 1949; *The Bad and the Beautiful*, 1953), like Sirk's (*Summer Storm*, 1944; *Shockproof*, 1948; *Thunder on the Hill*, 1951; *All I Desire*, 1953), not only solidified the heightened visual style and somber tone of the Hollywood melodrama, but they fleshed out the narrative and thematic conventions that carried the genre into its most productive and fascinating period. It's interesting to note the concurrent development of the social melodrama and the integrated musical after the war, even though each represented radically different conceptions of contemporary social conditions—and in Minnelli's case, these different conceptions were realized by the same director.

1950s melodrama: The genre comes of age

It was in the mid-1950s that the Hollywood melodrama emerged as the kind of cinema that Sirk, Minnelli, Nicholas Ray, and other filmmakers could exploit successfully. Perhaps the most interesting aspect in the evolution of the genre is that its classical and mannerist periods are essentially indistinguishable from each other. Because of a variety of industry-based factors, as well as external cultural phenomena, the melodrama reached its equilibrium at the same time that certain filmmakers were beginning to subvert and counter the superficial prosocial thematics and clichéd romantic narratives that had previously identified the genre. No other genre films, not even the "anti-Westerns" of the same period, projected so complex and paradoxical a view of America, at once celebrating and severely questioning the basic values and attitudes of the mass audience. Among the more significant and successful of these melodramas are:

1954	*Young at Heart* (Gordon Douglas)
	Magnificent Obsession (Douglas Sirk)
1955	*Cobweb* (Vincente Minnelli)
	East of Eden (Elia Kazan)
	Rebel Without a Cause (Nicholas Ray)

1956	*There's Always Tomorrow* (Douglas Sirk)
	Picnic (Joshua Logan)
	All That Heaven Allows (Douglas Sirk)
	Giant (George Stevens)
	Bigger Than Life (Nicholas Ray)
	Tea and Sympathy (Vincente Minnelli)
1957	*Written on the Wind* (Douglas Sirk)
	The Long Hot Summer (Martin Ritt)
	Peyton Place (Mark Robson)
1958	*Cat on a Hot Tin Roof* (Richard Brooks)
	The Tarnished Angels (Douglas Sirk)
	Too Much, Too Soon (Art Napolean)
1959	*A Summer Place* (Delmer Daves)
	Some Came Running (Vincente Minnelli)
	Imitation of Life (Douglas Sirk)
1960	*From the Terrace* (Mark Robson)
	Home from the Hill (Vincente Minnelli)
	The Bramble Bush (Daniel Petrie)

Movie melodramas survived in the 1960s, but the formal and ideological effects of the New Hollywood and the Kennedy administration's New Frontier affected the genre's development. By the '60s, the melodrama had been co-opted by commercial television, not only in the "daytime drama" series (i.e., soap operas) but also in prime time domestic drama. The success of *Peyton Place* (as both a bestseller and a feature film) and its 1961 movie sequel *Return to Peyton Place* led to network television's first serialized prime time drama, also titled *Peyton Place*, which was on throughout the mid- to late-'60s and eventually ran in three half-hour installments per week.

The melodrama's narrative formula—its interrelated family of characters, its repressive small-town milieu, and its preoccupation with America's sociosexual mores—managed to live beyond the Eisenhower years and into the era of civil rights, Vietnam, the sexual revolution, and the Women's Movement. Still, the distinctive spirit of the '50s melodramas was lost in the transition. One of the more interesting aspects of this period of the genre is its paradoxical critical status: the "female weepies," "women's films," and "hankie pix" which were so popular with matinee crowds in the 1950s have become in recent years the filmic darlings of modernist, feminist, and Marxist critics. The initial success of romantic tearjerkers reflected their collective capacity to stroke the emotional sensibilities of suburban housewives, but recent analysts suggest that the '50s melodramas are actually among the most socially self-conscious and covertly "anti-American" films ever produced by the Hollywood studios. Thomas Elsaesser, for example, suggested recently that Hollywood's more effective melodramas "would seem to function either subversively or as escapism—categories which are always relative to the given historical and social context"[2] (Elsaesser, 1972, p. 4). His point is that Hollywood's postwar melodramas, following narrative and social conventions established in previous movies, in popular literature, on radio serials, and elsewhere, appeared on the surface to be something other than what they were. The audience was, on one level, shown formalized portrayals of virtuous, long-suffering heroines whose persistent faith in the American Dream finally was rewarded with romantic love and a house in the suburbs. Beneath this seemingly escapist fare, however, Elsaesser glimpses the genre's covert function "to formulate a devastating critique of the ideology that supports it"[3] (Elsaesser, 1972, p. 13).

Thus the critical response to the movie melodrama covers a wide and contradictory range. Depending upon the source and historical perspective, it is described on one extreme as prosocial pablum for passive, naive audiences, and on the other as subtle, self-conscious criticism of American values, attitudes, and behavior.

The widespread popularity and the surface-level naiveté of the melodrama usually discourage both viewer and critic from looking beyond its facade, its familiar technicolor community and predictable "happy ending." But in the hands of Hollywood's more perceptive filmmakers, particularly Sirk, Minnelli, and Nicholas Ray, the genre assumes an ironic, ambiguous perspective. As our previous analyses of postwar Westerns, musicals, and crime films already have indicated, the melodrama was not alone in subverting many of the ideological traditions that these genres had espoused earlier. Andrew Dowdy, in his *Films of the Fifties* (aptly subtitled "The American State of Mind"), has suggested that genre films, because of their familiarity and presumed prosocial function, could broach delicate social issues more effectively than could "serious" social dramas. He writes, "Themes that alienated a mass audience in a self-consciously *serious* movie were acceptable if discreetly employed within the familiar atmosphere of the Western or the thriller"[4] (Dowdy, 1973, p. 72).

Something does seem to be going on below the surface of '50s movies, and particularly in genre films. While current popular evocations of the '50s tend to wax nostalgic, projecting an era of stability, prosperity, and widespread optimism, those who look more closely at that period's cultural documents may see through the facile naiveté to an altogether bleaker reflection. As Dowdy observes, "If we had only movies by which to measure cultural change, those of the '50s would give us an image of an America darkly disturbed by its own cynical loss of innocence, an America prey to fears more pervasive and intense than anything admitted to during the war years"[5] (Dowdy, 1973, pp. 62–63).

Film critic-historian Michael Wood shares Dowdy's feelings about the movies of the 1950s, and devotes considerable attention to that period in *America in the Movies*. In describing his own changing impression of Joshua Logan and William Inge's 1956 masterpiece, *Picnic*, Wood suggests that the film's "persistent, insidious hysteria," its undercurrent of alienation and loneliness, went generally unnoticed when the film was released but now seem to "haunt" the narrative. During the '50s, these qualities were "muffled by other emphases we chose to give the film, but we did see its hopelessness and frantic gestures, we did hear its angry and embittered words, and this is precisely the function I am proposing for popular movies. They permit us to look without looking at things we can neither face fully nor entirely disavow"[6] (Wood, 1975, p. 163). What '50s audiences were trying to avoid was a radical upheaval in the nature and structure of American ideology. HUAC and McCarthy, Alger Hiss and the Rosenbergs, Korea and the Cold War, Sputnik and the threat of nuclear destruction, changing sociosexual norms and the postwar "baby boom"—these and other events brought our fundamental values under scrutiny. America's collective dream was showing signs of becoming a nightmare.

The family as narrative focus

The nuclear, middle-class family, the clearest representation of America's patriarchal and bourgeois social order, was undergoing its own transformation and became the focus of Hollywood's '50s melodramas. World War II and the "Korean Conflict" had sent men into the service and overseas and moved women out of the home and into the work force. By the mid-1950s, men had returned to increasingly alienating, bureaucratic jobs and women were caught between the labor market and the need to return home to raise families. Greater mobility, suburbanization, and improving educational opportunities uprooted families and put a strain on their nuclear coherence, which made the age-old "generation gap" a more immediate and pressing issue than it had ever been before. Among the dominant intellectual fashions of the postwar era were Freudian psychology and existential philosophy. Each stressed the alienation of the individual due to the inability of familial and societal institutions to fulfill his or her particular needs.

While these various cultural factors coalesced within the popular cinema, whose stage of narrative and technical evolution was ideally suited for the glossy, stylized world of the melodrama, the *family* melodrama began to take shape. As Geoffrey Nowell-Smith describes it, "The genre or form that has come to be known as melodrama arises from the conjunction of a formal history proper (development of tragedy, realism, etc.), a set of social determinations, which have to do with the rise of the bourgeoisie, and a set of psychic determinations, which take shape around the family"[7] (Nowell-Smith, 1977, p. 113). Because '50s melodramas centered upon the nuclear unit, and by extension, upon the home within a familiar (usually small-town) American community, both the constellation of characters and the setting are more highly conventionalized than in other genres of integration. That these familiar social structures are at once so very real to the viewer and yet so clearly stylized within the genre's artificial framework adds a unique dimension to the iconography of the family melodrama. This might explain the sparse attention the melodrama has received from critics, as a distinct narrative-cinematic formula.

The family unit seems to provide an ideal locus for the genre's principal characters and its milieu for two fundamental reasons. First, it is a preestablished constellation whose individual roles (mother, father, son, daughter; adult, adolescent, child, infant, and so on) carry with them large social significance. Second, it is bound to its community by social class (father's occupation and income, type and location of the family home, etc.). Ideally, the family represents a "natural" as well as a social collective, a self-contained society in and of itself. But in the melodrama this ideal is undercut by the family's status within a highly structured socioeconomic milieu, and therefore, its identity as an autonomous human community is denied—the family roles are determined by the larger social community. The American small town, with its acute class-consciousness, its gossip and judgment by appearances, and its reactionary commitment to fading values and mores, represents an extended but perverted family in which human elements (love, honesty, interpersonal contact, generosity) have either solidified into repressive social conventions or disappeared altogether.

The image of the American family as it evolves through the 1940s is very interesting in that even apparently optimistic films like *How Green Was My Valley* (1941), *Shadow of a Doubt* (1943), *It's a Wonderful Life,* and *The Best Years of Our Lives* (both 1946) rely for their impact on the gradual erosion of our cultural confidence in the nuclear family. Also *noir* thrillers like *Double Indemnity* (1944) and *Mildred Pierce* (1946) developed this thematic. These films exploited the changing roles of women in wartime and postwar America, and also showed how black-widow inclinations stemmed from dissatisfaction with a suffocating middle-class lifestyle. The heroine in each film—Barbara Stanwyck in the former, Joan Crawford in the latter—is bent upon escaping a tedious husband and tacky suburban home. Little motivation is given for her dissatisfaction, but none is necessary: middle-class claustrophobia and Mom's desire to escape it are simply taken for granted. But these are *noir* thrillers and the dissatisfaction is more difficult to explain in other films whose obvious aims are to uplift the audience and reaffirm their traditional values.

Consider *Meet Me in St. Louis* (1944) and *Father of the Bride* (1950), two of Hollywood's—and director Vincente Minnelli's—more successful and saccharine celebrations of small-town family life. Each film traces the courtship and betrothal of a naive heroine (Judy Garland and Elizabeth Taylor, respectively) which is complicated by their fathers' familial-occupational confusion. This conflict is animated in both films through a dynamic "nightmare" sequence, which momentarily points up the deep-seated doubts about family and community stability that the surface stories tend to repress.

In *Meet Me in St. Louis,* Margaret O'Brien (playing Garland's younger sister) is so distraught over her family's upward mobility and Dad's having been transferred to New York that she literally goes berserk at one point, running outside in an hysterical nocturnal frenzy to demolish a "family" of snowmen. In *Father of the Bride,*

Spencer Tracy's distress over his daughter's impending marriage brings on a surreal nightmare in which his role in the wedding is expressed in images of inadequacy, loneliness, and despair. This is accentuated by Minnelli's slow-motion camera, the severe visual angles, and the impressionistic set. Both of these films end happily enough, though. Not until the mid-1950s did Minnelli draw his cultural subversion out from under the cover of darkness and dream logic.

After the war, then, the traditional image of marriage, the home, and the family was undergoing more self-critical reflection. With the emergence of the family melodrama in the '50s, the American family moved out of its role as supporting player to achieve star billing. Films no longer simply used familial conflicts and interrelationships to enhance some external complication (a crime, the war, some social event) but focused on the social institution of the family itself as the basis for conflict. A rather interesting paradox emerged from this shift of concentration: on the one hand, the family crisis was the dominant narrative conflict; on the other hand, the resolution of that conflict had to be found within the existing social structure, i.e., the family. Unlike genres of order, the melodrama's social conflicts and contradictions could not be resolved by violently eliminating one of the opposing forces; unlike genres of integration, its social reality could not be magically transformed via music or screwball attitudes. In fact, those uninhibited types who ruled in the comedy-oriented films are often the more *angst*-ridden and oppressed members of the melodrama's community. The liberating quality of performance and individual expression of the musical and screwball comedy are simply means for establishing one's socioeconomic identity in the family melodrama.

Young at Heart and *Picnic:* The male intruder-redeemer in a world of women

The contrast is well demonstrated in the uneven and inadvertently ironic 1954 film, *Young at Heart,* a movie which shifts back and forth from a musical to a melodramatic stance. The Tuttle household is the focus of this film and contains a widowed professor of music who is raising three talented and eligible daughters (including Doris Day and Dorothy Malone—even the casting exhibits the film's generic schizophrenia). The film opens with Dad and two of his daughters playing classical music in the living room. The third daughter (Malone) enters and announces her engagement to a fellow named Bob, an overweight but available local businessman. This brings the issues of spinsterhood and marital compromise out into the open, and the remainder of the film traces the courtship and wedding of each of the daughters. Malone's home-grown fiancé is juxtaposed with a suave composer from the big city (Gig Young as Alex), who invades the Tuttle household—his father and Tuttle had once been close friends—to work on a musical.

Alex's refined wit and talent initially disrupt the Tuttle milieu, although as the narrative develops it becomes obvious that he is the heir apparent to the senior Tuttle, the hard-working and responsible but somewhat aloof patriarch.

Alex and Laurie (Day) eventually become engaged, but not before Alex brings in an old friend, Barney (Frank Sinatra), to help arrange the musical score. Barney is painfully antiheroic. He derides the middle-class environment ("It's homes like these that are the backbone of the nation—where's the spinning wheel?") and agonizes that "the resident fates" are keeping him from success as a songwriter. Even though Barney does little but slouch over a piano and whine interminably through the cigarette dangling from his lips, Laurie falls in love with him and eventually stands up Alex on their wedding day to elope with her ill-matched lover. (The wedding was to have taken place in the Tuttle house, further reinforcing its value as the locus for social-familial ritual.)

The narrative moves quickly after this. Alex hangs around the household as surrogate son and "good loser"; his musical is a hit while Barney's career is stuck at the piano-bar stage. Laurie plays the domesticator, renouncing her musical talents; and she becomes pregnant. Before she can tell Barney of their impending parenthood, he attempts suicide, but when he learns he's a prospective Daddy, a miraculous transformation takes place. Dissolve to one year later: Barney's unfinished song (which we first heard the day he met Laurie) is a hit and all's right in the family household.

Ultimately, no description of a film like *Young at Heart* can begin to convey the emotional and intellectual reversals that would have been necessary to sustain the narrative. The film's own internal schema—its inherent value system, characterization, and *mise-en-scène*—is so inconsistent, so filled with ruptures, and so illogical that the narrative is an amalgam of confused, self-contradictory impulses. The resolution is especially illogical: we have seen the central characters as either victimized by or utterly hostile to the existing social-familial-marital system, but somehow romantic love and parenthood magically transform familial anxiety and despair into domestic bliss. The unevenness is intensified by the casting—Doris Day's vibrant, naive enthusiast and Sinatra's emaciated, withdrawn sulker seem utterly incompatible. Their individual values and attitudes (as well as their established screen personalities) are so diametrically opposed that marriage, a hit tune, and kids in the house scarcely seem adequate to reconcile their differences. Director Gordon Douglas might have turned these drawbacks into assets by assuming a more ironic, distanced perspective, but he develops a straightforward, unselfconscious narrative that treats its material as "realistically" as possible.

Nevertheless, a number of generic elements converge in *Young at Heart*. They anticipate the more effective films that would turn logical inconsistencies into assets. The aging patriarch in a female-dominated household, the search for the father/lover/husband by the anxious offspring, the male intruder-redeemer who regenerates and stabilizes the family, the household itself as locus of social interaction, and the ambiguous function of the marital embrace as both sexually liberating and socially restricting—these qualities were refined through repeated usage and incorporated into melodramas that were at the same time coherent, consistent, and complex.

A direct narrative descendent of Douglas' film is *Picnic,* a 1956 adaptation of William Inge's Pulitzer Prize-winning drama which director Joshua Logan took from stage to screen with enormous success. Like its predecessor, *Picnic* involves a community of women whose preoccupations with marriage, spinsterhood, and morality are disrupted and intensified by a male intruder-redeemer. The plot traces a small Kansas town on Labor Day as it celebrates the harvest. The film follows the nomadic Hal (William Holden), who jumps the freight train on which he rode into town in search of an old college schoolmate, Alan (Cliff Robertson). Hal's search begins on "the wrong side of the tracks," where he happens upon and completely disarms a female collective. This group includes Madge (Kim Novak, whom we later learn is Alan's girl), her widowed mother and younger sister, an old maid schoolmarm (Rosalind Russell as Rosemary) who boards with them, and a wise old neighbor, Mrs. Potts (Verna Felton), whose invalid mother lives upstairs.

These four generations of unmarried women form a complex and fascinating configuration of characters and attitudes. Madge, the beauty queen, and her little sister (Susan Strasberg), the bookish tomboy, envy each other's distinct talents. While Madge repeatedly decries her reputation as "the pretty one," her mother encourages her to exploit her sexuality to snare Alan (a member of the local aristocracy), even if it means compromising her "virtue." Mrs. Potts, the stable matriarch who is too old and seasoned to let society's opinions dictate her judgment, continually calms the discord within the female collective. Peripheral to the group is Rosemary, the shrill neurotic spinster bent on snagging her long-standing beau, Howard (Arthur O'Connell). Rosemary's endless denials of her own sexual frustration and fear of spinsterhood affect the entire group, providing an almost hysterical subcurrent that touches each woman.

Madge is the central figure in this constellation. Each of the older women projects a different conception of sexuality and marriage to her: her mother (whose husband had deserted her years before) considers sex a commodity that can be exchanged for an improved social standing; Rosemary understands the spinster's social outcast status but seems even more concerned with marriage as a refuge against loneliness and an opportunity for natural human contact; Mrs. Potts, the one woman willing to admit she's pleased to have Hal ("a *real* man") around the house, is the most overtly romantic of the lot, suggesting that true love is—or should be—oblivious to social circumstances.

Madge's anticipated coronation as harvest queen at the Labor Day picnic is complemented by Alan's anticipated proposal of marriage—the holiday festival represents an initiation rite for the heroine in both a communal and a marital sense. Hal's arrival on the morning of the picnic, his obvious sexual rapport with Madge, and the fact that he's come to ask Alan for a job create a network of social and sexual tensions that intensify throughout the film. Both Hal and Madge are in a position to use Alan and thereby improve their social class, although their own

The constellation of characters in Picnic: *Madge (Kim Novak, in swing) and intruder-redeemer Hal Carter (William Holden, standing) shine at the center of this narrative universe, surrounded by (left to right) Madge's mother (Betty Field), her ardent, aristocratic suitor (Cliff Robertson, back to camera), her grandmotherly neighbor, Mrs. Potts (Verna Felton), the "old-maid schoolmarm" and her long-standing beau (Rosalind Russell and Arthur O'Connell), and Madge's younger sister (Susan Strasberg).* (Culver Pictures)

"natural" attraction to one another keeps them from becoming manipulative and self-serving.

At one point in the film, Hal leaves the women to see Alan at his family estate, and Alan takes him on a tour of the family's grain mills which are the economic and agricultural lifeblood of the community. Overlooking the Kansas wheatfields from the top of a huge grain elevator, an appropriate image of his father's domination of the milieu, Alan promises Hal a job, but makes clear his intentions regarding Madge. Alan also is planning to attend the Labor Day festivities, and thus is willing to cross the socioeconomic barrier in order to woo Madge and impress Hal.

The various narrative subcurrents surface at the picnic: Madge is crowned Queen of Neewollah (Halloween spelled backwards) and celebrates that rite of passage in a sensuous, moonlit dance with Hal. A drunken, panicky Rosemary interrupts their embrace as she tries to establish her own sexual and feminine identity, but she only causes an ugly scene that attracts the attention of the other picnickers. Hal is accused of disrupting the community's tranquility—he has clarified the myriad sociosexual tensions beneath the surreal glare of fireworks, Japanese lanterns and the full moon. At this point, director Logan and cinematographer James Wong Howe depart from naturalistic style and begin to use camera angles, movement, and lighting to create an artificial, stylized narrative-visual tone. The closing sequences take place in daylight on the following morning, once the community neuroses return to their subliminal realm, and this day/night break further stresses the importance of the picnic itself as the narrative and thematic core of the film.

Picnic is resolved with the promise of two weddings—one between Rosemary and Howard and the other between Madge and Hal. After the picnic, each couple had consummated their love in true Midwestern small-town fashion, driving into the Kansas night to the music of locusts and locomotive whistles. By now Rosemary and Howard's relationship takes up roughly the same amount of screen time as Madge and Hal's, and the viewer is able to contrast the two couples' radically different views of marriage, with the older pair sharing none of the romantic naiveté or sexual exhilaration of the initiate-lovers.

The film's closing sequences focus upon Madge, though, and upon the reactions of her mother and Mrs. Potts to the news of her impending marriage. Madge's mother warns her not to repeat the same mistakes she and Madge's father had made, whereas Mrs. Potts accepts the irrationality of romantic love. The film's closing image, in which the lovers are moving in the same direction but by different means (Hal has hopped a freight, and Madge promises to follow by bus), reinforces the ambiguity of their embrace. It represents an idealized sexual union, but it is also an impulsive flight into the same social traps which had ensnared their parents. Still, the possibility of escape from the repressive community and the obvious chemistry between Holden's and Novak's characters tends to enhance the "happy end" nature of this resolution, even though we cannot logically project that ending into the "ever after."

The widow-lover variation

Because the lovers in *Picnic* have managed to escape their milieu, it is possible for us to believe that their marriage might be a natural and human coupling as well as a social institution. This belief is reinforced by the intruder-redeemer Hal, a genuinely "natural man" whose character developed outside the community, seemingly in some timeless dimension. This is essentially the basis for his personal and sexual attraction. The prospect of a liberating marriage is actually quite rare in the '50s family melodrama, which usually depicts that social ritual as solidifying the couple's position within the community rather than providing them with an escape from it.

A more familiar narrative strategy traces the courtship of a widowed mother as well as—or perhaps in lieu of—that of the postadolescent daughter. *Magnificent Obsession, All That Heaven Allows, Peyton Place, Return to Peyton Place, A Summer Place, Imitation of Life*, and many other '50s films involve the courtship of an older woman, invariably a widow or divorcée, whose adult status and established familial role minimize the possibility for flight from her repressive environment. In *Picnic*, Madge, as yet unburdened by children, family home, or any significant community position, had a certain freedom denied to the women in these other films. In the family melodrama's puritanical moral climate, that freedom is closely related to the woman's virginity: Once she is literally and figuratively "taken" by a man, the heroine surrenders her initiative, her self-reliance, and in effect, her individual identity.

Her life is determined thereafter by the male—and by extension the male-oriented, patriarchal society—she commits herself to. The strategy of these films, generally speaking, is to counter the heroine's role as mother-domesticator with that of sexual partner. This opposition itself is intensified by the role of her daughter who is just reaching womanhood and whose romantic delusions are propelling her toward the same marital and social traps as her mother. Of the "weepies" just listed, only *Magnificent Obsession* lacks a mother-daughter opposition, although this film, like the others, does portray a woman in early middle age caught between her socially prescribed role as mother and her reawakened individual and sexual identity. As numerous critics have pointed out, the heroine's choice is scarcely viable: regardless of her ultimate commitment, which usually is to her lover-redeemer, the heroine merely exchanges one trap for another, allowing her individual destiny to be determined by the values of her new lover rather than her previous one.

The previous lover's ghost still haunts the heroine and impedes her romance, usually in the guise of her children and their class-bound family home. *All That Heaven Allows*, for example, shows a recently widowed mother-domesticator, Cary (Jane Wyman), whose postadolescent children, her friends from the club, and her middle-class home urge her to remarry a carbon copy of her dead husband (Conrad Nagel). Much to the community's consternation, she falls in love with her gardener, Ron (Rock Hudson), a younger man of somewhat lower social class. To intensify the conflict between true love and social conventions, director Douglas Sirk constructs an elaborate pattern of visual and thematic oppositions that contrast the lifestyles of her lover and her dead husband. But ultimately the heroine merely makes a choice between her stoic, Emersonian gardener and her dead bourgeois husband—one of these men will govern her life. Wyman makes the "right" choice, of course, opting for love and Rock Hudson, but only after a virtual act of God brings her to his aid when he is injured in an accident. Thus Sirk undermines the film's happy end on two levels. Only an arbitrary event within the logic of the narrative (Ron's accident) enables the heroine to break out of her assigned role; and on a broader thematic level, she manages to escape one dominating patriarch only to accept another.

We would have to assume that Cary's marriage to Ron would be less repressive and dehumanizing than her earlier, class-bound marriage had been, and so the resolution seems more positive than not. Like Hal in *Picnic,* Ron personifies the intruder-redeemer who somehow has fashioned his own value system outside the small-town community which has entrapped the heroine. But this does not alter his role as "breadwinner" and patriarch, nor is he any less "socialized" within his own community than was Cary's first husband.

The redeemer's ambiguous status, particularly in Sirk's films, is finally a function of the filmmaker's penchant for irony, as well as his capacity to depict the repressive middle-class environment so effectively. Like Vincente Minnelli, Sirk was a master of formal artifice and expressive decor. His filmic world—at once familiar and yet lavishly artificial and visually stylized—is inhabited by characters who are always emotionally at arm's length, operating in a social reality that clearly is once removed from our own. As Sirk and the other principal melodrama directors understood, any "realistic" narrative strategy in these glossy romances would be both aesthetically and ideologically counterproductive, and would undercut the films' obvious idealization of the viewer's social reality. Sirk's success is closely related to his use of music, camerawork, casting (Rock Hudson is ultimately nothing more than an evocative cardboard cut-out in Sirk's films), set design and costuming (especially in the use of color to "codify" the characters and their milieu), and other formal filmic devices.

Other directors chose the path of realism over stylization, and their films, straightforward paeans to the American middle class, generally have suffered critically in the long run. Mark Robson's *Peyton Place,* for example, relates much the same story as *All That Heaven Allows* but has not worn well over the years, mostly due to the fact that the viewer is supposed to take the subject matter seriously. Sirk never stooped to this level of insult—as Andrew Sarris has observed: "Even in his most dubious projects, Sirk never shrinks away from the ridiculous, but by a full-bodied formal development, his art transcends the ridiculous, as form comments on content"[8] (Sarris, 1968, p. 110). *Peyton Place* traces the romantic events in the lives of an unmarried woman and her daughter after an intruder-redeemer enters the community and courts the mother. Whereas *All That Heaven Allows* dealt primarily with America's socioeconomic and materialistic values, this film focuses upon its marital and sexual taboos. Whereas Ron's character was a synthesis of Thoreau and Marx, here the redeemer is an amalgam of Drs. Freud and Spock—in fact, the community crisis in the film results from the new high-school principal's efforts to initiate sex education classes. Cary's attempts to shed her materialistic value system are not similar to those of this heroine (Lana Turner as Constance McKenzie), a woman who is attempting to resolve the sexual hangups that resulted from her sordid past—adultery with a married man in the big city.

Constance has paid dearly (true to the melodrama's moral demand of absolute retribution), not only through a lifetime of guilt and sociosexual pathology, but through the very existence of her illegitimate daughter, Allison. Just as Sirk's film established a network of oppositions involving enlightened versus unenlightened capitalism, *Peyton Place* counters sexual inhibition with a more liberal (at least by '50s standards) attitude. The film suggests that the community can learn the error of its repressive ways and achieve the American Dream.

The film's utopian vision and neat happily-ever-after resolution are its undoing, however, since they create a rupture in narrative logic which cannot possibly be rationalized. While Sirk avoided this by resolving the plot with an arbitrary event (Ron's accident), in *Peyton Place*, Robson resorts to a ritual sequence—a sensationalized small-town trial—in which the community comes to its collective senses and renegotiates its system of values and beliefs. The climactic trial brings into the open the various acts of adultery, rape, incest, and other iniquities committed throughout the story. But the essentially benevolent citizenry is encouraged to appreciate the value of truth and understanding over retribution—that, in the local doctor's words, "we've all been prisoners of each other's gossip." The community realizes that in the past, "appearances counted more than feelings," but through honest human interaction they reach what Allison terms, "the season of love." If the forced, arbitrary nature of its resolution is not obvious in the original, one need only look to the sequel, *Return to Peyton Place*, to realize how easily this utopian community and the pat happy end could be undone.

The family aristocracy variation

At the narrative-thematic core of family melodramas is a metaphoric search for the ideal husband/lover/father who, as American mythology would have it, will stabilize the family and integrate it into the larger community. Hollywood mythology tends to portray the husband and the lover in essentially contradictory terms: the woman's dilemma is that she must opt for either socioeconomic security *or* emotional and sexual fulfillment. Her dilemma is intensified in what might be termed the family aristocracy variation of the '50s melodrama, which includes films like *Written on the Wind, The Long Hot Summer, Giant, Cat on a Hot Tin Roof, From the Terrace*, and *Home from the Hill*. These melodramas trace the behavioral and attitudinal traits of succeeding generations. The dramatic conflict is based on a contradictory view of marriage: it is a means of liberation from unreasonable familial demands and also the only way of perpetuating the family aristocracy.

The family's status is enhanced by its role within the community, whose economy and social climate it controls either directly or through benign neglect. This motif surfaces in *Picnic*—Alan will inherit the "family business," and thus the socioeconomic lifeblood of the community generates much of the tension surrounding his character. But the lovers' flight from Alan and from his father's wealth offers an option that is unavailable to the class-bound lovers in the family aristoc-

The aristocracy and the estate: the Benedict mansion dominates the landscape in Giant, providing an apt visual metaphor for the family's social and economic domination of the Texas community. (Museum of Modern Art/Film Stills Archive)

racy melodramas. The Varner family in *The Long Hot Summer,* the Hadley family in *Written on the Wind,* and the Benedict family in *Giant* are established as inescapable ideological givens; they create the socioeconomic climate that is around them. Significantly, these films usually are based in the South, where the conception of the landed gentry has survived into the twentieth century. The dramatic action may be confined exclusively to the family's mansion and estate, as in *Cat on a Hot Tin Roof,* or it may extend to the larger social community, as in *Written on the Wind, Giant,* and *The Long Hot Summer,* where the community is an extension of the family estate. In *Written on the Wind,* the town and the estate share the Hadley name, and the family insignia is everywhere—on automobiles, oil rigs, street signs—giving considerable weight to the actions and attitudes of the family members themselves.

The constellation of characters in this variation revolves around an aging patriarch (sometimes close to death), whose wife is either dead or else functions only as
a peripheral character who has produced inadequate male heirs and sexually frustrated daughters. The patriarch's search for an heir to his feudal monarchy usually
sets up the conflict between his own spoiled, ineffectual son and an intruder-redeemer figure who is equal to the patriarch in strength, intellect, and self-reliance.
The son's inability to negotiate the wealth and power of his legacy mirrors the
daughter's sexual confusion, although the idealized intruder invariably enables the
daughter to clarify her sexuality and develop an individual identity beyond familial context. (An interesting twist on this convention occurs in *Cat on a Hot Tin Roof*,
in which Paul Newman and Jack Carson are cast as the tormented, inadequate offspring of patriarch Burl Ives, with Elizabeth Taylor assuming the role of intruder-
redeemer, whose "true love" stabilizes Newman's sexual confusion and reaffirms
his role as heir apparent to "Big Daddy.")

Thus these films stress the patriarch's search for an heir and everything implied
by the handing down of power from one generation to the next. Operating in a
way similar to many of the screwball comedies, the redeemer figure often helps
the wealthy aristocrat to recover whatever values and attitudes had enabled him to
attain his wealth. His son's inadequacy demonstrates that these attributes have
been lost, and often the son, as well as the patriarch and the daughter, profits from
the intruder's redemptive powers. The role of the spoiled, whining offspring is one
of the more interesting in the aristocracy melodramas, and provided actors like
Jack Carson (*Cat on a Hot Tin Roof*), Tony Franciosa (*The Long Hot Summer*), and
Robert Stack (*Written on the Wind*) with some of the most intense and rewarding
roles in their film careers. As such, these melodramas are actually as much male
"weepies" as they are female ones.

Although the son's inadequacies are a function of his father's wealth, most of
these films stop short of an outright condemnation of wealth and the corrupting
influence of unchecked socioeconomic power. As in the screwball comedies, the
patriarch generally is reeducated and thus humanized by the redeemer figure. Ultimately, this progressive enlightenment resolves the various conflicts within the
family and returns the tormented son to the patriarch's favor. In *The Long Hot Summer*, for example, the aging and decadent Will Varner (Orson Welles) consistently
bemoans the lack of male heirs and "the establishment of my immortality." His
only son, Jody (Franciosa), is woefully insecure and inept, and at one point asks
his father, "Where do you go looking for it, Poppa, if you ain't got it in you?"
Intruder-redeemer Ben Quick (Paul Newman) eventually weds Varner's renegade
daughter (Joanne Woodward), promising Will many grandsons (i.e., real heirs
with more potential), and he also helps Jody discover his own worth, prompting
the patriarch's closing pronouncement, "Maybe I'll live forever."

The strain on internal narrative logic with such a pat ending is severe: The existing social and familial structures act as both the problem and its eventual solution, and the only significant motivation for the resolution is the influence of the
redeemer figure. But the problems themselves are so immediate, familiar, and in-

***The aging patriarch and the surrogate heir: Ben Quick (Paul Newman) and Will
Varner (Orson Welles) develop an antagonistic rapport in The Long Hot Summer,
where the stakes are the hand of Varner's daughter and the future of the family aristocracy.*** (Hoblitzelle Theatre Arts Collection)

tense, they scarcely can be resolved as easily as their narratives suggest. Generally
speaking, then, family melodramas might be seen as critical of American ideology
at the level of narrative exposition and complication, but their resolution invariably reaffirms, however implausibly, the cultural status quo.

Occasionally a film like *Written on the Wind* surfaces, however, where the subversion of familial and socioeconomic conventions is sustained throughout. In
Sirk's 1957 melodrama, the patriarch dies upon learning of his daughter's scandal-
ous sexual activities, she in turn loses the only man she ever loved, and the tormented son commits suicide. Sirk provides us with a moderately happy ending,
though. The redeemer (Rock Hudson) is finally cleared of the accusation that he
murdered the son (Stack), and he leaves the Hadleys' world with the dead son's
widow (Lauren Bacall). This arbitrary, ambiguous closure does little to resolve the
social and familial tensions that had destroyed the entire Hadley family, although
it provides the protagonists with a fortuitous escape hatch.

Nicholas Ray, Vincente Minnelli, and the male weepie

The aging patriarch and tormented, inadequate son appear most frequently in the aristocracy variation, although they occasionally are part of middle-class families as well. In films like *Rebel Without a Cause, Bigger Than Life, Tea and Sympathy, East of Eden,* and *The Cobweb,* the central conflict involves passing the role of middle-American "Dad" from one generation to the next. Here, the patriarch's anxieties and the son's tormented insecurities cannot be attributed to family wealth or a decadent aristocratic view of life. As a result, these films tend to be more directly critical of American middle-class ideology which both the characters and the majority of the audience know so well. The master of the tormented-son portrayal was James Dean. Whether encouraging his emasculated father (Jim Backus) to stand on his own in *Rebel Without a Cause* or simply trying to win his insensitive father's (Raymond Massey) love in *East of Eden,* Dean's soulful stare and agonized gestures projected the image of a son either unwilling or unable to accommodate society's expectation of male adulthood.

While Dean's films focus on the son, others like *The Cobweb* and *Bigger Than Life* are straightforward male "weepies," examining the plight of the middle-class husband/lover/father. Each of these melodramas is a sustained indictment of the social pressures which have reduced the well-meaning patriarch to a confused, helpless victim of his own good intentions. The heroes in Nicholas Ray's *Bigger Than Life* (James Mason as Ed Avery) and in Vincente Minnelli's *The Cobweb* (Richard Widmark as Stewart McIver) are both professional bureaucrats and community servants: Avery is a grade-school teacher, and McIver is the head of a psychiatric clinic. These films, like those of Douglas Sirk, develop artificial conflicts that are intensified and finally overwhelmed by the family conflicts they touch off.

In *Bigger Than Life,* we are introduced to the victimized hero as he is finishing his work day at school and slipping off to put in a few extra hours as a taxi dispatcher to "make ends meet." Ed is overworked and having dizzy spells but is too proud to tell his wife of his moonlighting or his illness. She, in turn, suspects that Ed's unaccounted extra hours mean that he's having an affair to escape the boring routine of their static life. Ed eventually collapses, and his physical illness is treated with a '50s wonder drug, cortisone. Ed abuses the drug because it gives him a sense of power, mission, and self-esteem that his familial and social roles do not. As the narrative develops, Ed becomes increasingly monomaniacal, loudly criticizing his family, his colleagues, and his social environment. Director Ray does not focus on cortisone as the cause of Ed's antisocial behavior and psychotic outbursts, and so, ultimately, we are interested in his character as a bizarre critique of American middle-class values and attitudes. Ed's tirade at a PTA meeting ("we're breeding a race of moral midgets") and his refusal to let his son eat until he catches a football properly are neuroses that any frustrated parent might exhibit under duress. They emphasize not only Dad's own past failures and lingering anxieties but also the social basis for those anxieties, as well as one man's impotence in effecting a change of the status quo.

While Ed's own family senses something is wrong—at one point his son whispers to Mom, "Isn't Daddy acting a little foolish?"—his lip service to social conventions prevents anyone else from recognizing the severity of his mental condition. This central apathy reinforces the film's subversive tone, in that those around Ed may look askance at his outbursts, but they accept his behavior as his way of "letting off a little steam." Ed's criticism of the American family, educational system, and class structure becomes more vocal and more intense, until he finally decides upon an Abraham/Isaac-style "sacrifice" to atone for his own failures and to save his son from the same class-bound fate. Over the protestations of his wife—"But God stopped Abraham," she pleads, to which Ed replies, "God was wrong!"—and with the television turned up to full volume in the background, Ed prepares for the ritual execution. A spectacular fistfight with the grade-school gym teacher (Walter Matthau), which devastates Ed's bourgeois home, prevents disaster as well as precipitating his return to the hospital and eventual recovery. In the film's ironic epilogue, the family is tearfully reunited in Ed's hospital room. The family doctor prescribes the same cortisone treatment but closer regulation of the dosage. Consider the narrative sleight-of-hand involved in this resolution: the real issue in the film is not the danger of wonder drugs but rather the kind of social-familial climate that Ed's drugged state permitted him to condemn. At the end, Ed's aberrant behavior is resolved but not the social conditions that motivated his behavior.

Ray's film recalls Sirk's in that it exploits a superficial plot device to camouflage its social criticism. Vincente Minnelli's male "weepies"—particularly *The Cobweb*, *Tea and Sympathy*, *Home from the Hill*, and *Two Weeks in Another Town*—also follow this narrative strategy. Whether Minnelli is examining the *angst*-ridden familial relationship in a mental hospital (*The Cobweb*), on a college campus (*Tea and Sympathy*), or even within a foreign-based Hollywood film unit (*Two Weeks in Another Town*), his melodramas trace the search for the ideal family. Usually, he contrasts the protagonist's "natural" family with an artificial group from his professional environment. In *The Cobweb*, for example, Richard Widmark portrays a clinical psychiatrist (Stewart McIver) torn between his domestic family (Gloria Grahame as his wife Karen and their two children) and the surrogate family that he cultivates in his psychiatric clinic with a staff worker, Meg (Lauren Bacall), and a disturbed adolescent artist, Stevie (John Kerr). Meg and McIver ask Stevie to design new drapes for the clinic's library as a therapeutic exercise, not realizing that Karen and a matronly bureaucrat at the clinic (Lillian Gish) already have assumed responsibility for doing it. This banal plot device generates an intricate network of familial, social, and professional conflicts, none of which is resolved satisfactorily—and at film's end the library is still without drapes.

The emphasis on family interaction is highlighted by the fact that McIver is a Freudian psychoanalyst. "Why don't you analyze my Oedipus complex or my lousy father?" Stevie asks McIver early in the film, to which the psychiatrist later

Life with Father: Two of director Nicholas Ray's "male weepies" shifted narrative focus to male roles within the American family. In Bigger Than Life (above), James Mason's abuse of cortisone treatment leads him to overindulge his paternal fantasies and terrorize his family; in Rebel Without a Cause, James Dean must literally drag his father (Jim Backus) from his knees to prompt him into action. Bigger Than Life (Museum of Modern Art/Film Stills Archive); Rebel Without a Cause (Culver Pictures)

responds, "I'm not your father, and I won't run out on you like your father did." As good a surrogate father as McIver is on the job, though, his domestic feelings are sorely lacking. He does not communicate with his wife either verbally or sexually and is a virtual stranger to his own children. We learn that when his daughter was asked at school what she wanted to be, she replied, "One of Daddy's patients."

McIver's role as professional father to the clinic's children clearly is more rewarding. He and Meg develop a camaraderie that is eventually consummated sexually—or at least Minnelli's well-timed fades imply as much within the limits of the Production Code. Their relationship is based on their shared devotion to Stevie. McIver eventually tells Meg: "If we make this work we may be able to show him we're different—good parents." Stevie does show signs of recovery at film's end, but these are not entirely due to the couple's ministrations.

Stevie, as Minnelli's spokesman against the "unbalanced" nature of contemporary society, assumes the role as principal social critic in the film. He has impeccable credentials for this job as both frustrated artist and deserted son. (Not only had his own father deserted him, but he confides in Meg midway through the film that his mother died the previous year, an event that triggered his breakdown.) Stevie's role as critic is established even before we learn that he's a patient at the clinic. When McIver's wife offers him a ride in the film's opening sequence, the two strike up a conversation about art and artists. With Leonard Rosenman's ominous, pulsating music in the background, Stevie laments: "Artists are better off dead—they're not so troublesome. . . . They said Van Gogh was crazy because he killed himself. He couldn't sell a painting when he was alive, and now they're worth thirty million dollars. They weren't that bad then and they're not that good now—so who's crazy?" As they pull onto the clinic grounds later, Stevie suggests that "everybody's tilted around here. That's why you didn't know who I was. You can't tell the patients from the doctors." "Yes, I can," replies Karen, "the patients get well."

This remark ultimately governs the narrative. Stevie's ability to "get well" and come to terms with himself is juxtaposed throughout with the essentially negative view of the community into which Stevie might hope to integrate himself. Although Stevie does emerge as a relatively "stable" individual, his insightful outbursts against McIver early in the film cast real doubts on the value of his "cure." In a psychiatric session early in the film, Stevie pours out a devastating critique of McIver and his lifestyle: "You're supposed to be making me fit for normal life. What's normal? Yours? If it's a question of values, your values stink. Lousy, middle-class, well-fed, smug existence. All you care about is a paycheck you didn't earn and a beautiful thing to go home to every night."

These are not the hysterical ravings of an unbalanced adolescent, since we can see that McIver's own deteriorating personal and professional competence lend credibility to these criticisms. We can also see that Stevie will be able to "recover" because he seems to understand that society itself is not well—an understanding that none of the "normal" characters exhibits.

McIver and Meg finally bow to the social impediments to their union, and he returns to his wife with the half-hearted pledge that he will work harder at their relationship. Minnelli himself accepted the arbitrary nature of his resolution, admitting, "It seemed dishonest, since we'd established extraordinary bonds between the doctor and the staff member, but the conclusion was very much within the existing movie code"[9] (Minnelli, 1974, p. 295). Which, of course, is a reflection of America's implicit moral code, and Minnelli clearly was sensitive to the need to resolve the issues raised in the film within an acceptable framework. McIver's decision to remain with the jealous, whining Karen rather than the stoic, supportive Meg scarcely represents a positive resolution, however, and *The Cobweb*'s end is more an act of resignation—for both McIver and Minnelli—than of integration.

Stylization, social reality, and critical values

The Cobweb is a typical Hollywood melodrama in that it traces the identity crisis of an individual whose divided domestic and occupational commitments provide a rational basis for confusion and anxiety. The more adept filmmakers learned to exploit these contradictions and ambiguities via plot and characterization and through heavy stylization as well. Although we have devoted most of our attention in this chapter to conventions of setting, plot, and character in the melodrama, ultimately their formal orchestration may well be the most significant quality in these films. In a 1959 review of Sirk's most successful and most overtly stylized melodrama, *Imitation of Life*, critic Moira Walsh described the film as a "pretentious, expensive, overstuffed Technicolor example of Hollywood at its worst," and she went on to condemn the film as "a perfect example of the tendency to confuse fantasy with reality which serious students of our mass culture are inclined to regard as most destructive of the human personality"[10] (Walsh, 1959, p. 314). This was written about the same film which German critic-filmmaker Rainer Werner Fassbinder, who himself has remade several of Sirk's films, recently termed "a great, crazy movie about life and about death. And about America." It is a film, argues Fassbinder, in which "nothing is natural. Ever. Not in the whole film"[11] (Fassbinder, 1975, p. 24).

In retrospect, the reviewers' highbrow myopia is not surprising—contemporary critics of Flaubert, Dickens, and D. W. Griffith often misunderstood what their melodramatists were doing. The huge success of *Imitation of Life*, and the renewed interest critics and scholars have in it, suggest that this and other film melodramas work on substantially different levels of viewer engagement. They range from transparent romantic fantasy to a severe indictment of the culture that perpetuates that fantasy. Moira Walsh was accurate about the confusion of fantasy with reality, but it is the characters within the melodrama, not the filmmaker, who are confused. In fact, Sirk's popularity seems closely related to his capacity to flesh out the *un*natural aspects of America's social reality, to articulate cinematically how that reality is itself a collective cultural fantasy.

Narrative rupture and the "happy end": frame enlargement from the final scene in Imitation of Life. *The obviously contrived resolution disturbed critics in 1959, and Sirk later suggested that the deus ex machina made the audience more aware of the social conditions that affected the characters' attitudes and actions.* (Private Collection)

In discussing *Imitation of Life* more than a decade after its release, Sirk compared his narrative strategy to classical Greek drama in which "there is no real solution of the predicament the people in the play are in, just the *deus ex machina*, which is now called 'the happy end' "[12] (Halliday, 1972, p. 132). Sirk's capacity to articulate society's cultural confusion encourages even the most naive viewer to reflect upon the nature of these social conditions that fashion our individual, familial, and social identities. He offers an ambiguous resolution, so, we in the audience can take it in a variety of ways.

One of the more fascinating aspects of the '50s melodramas is the breadth of emotional and intellectual response they elicit from viewers. Whether we regard the genre as a formula for prosocial pap or as a genuine critique of American ideology, however, depends upon our own attitudes, prejudices, and expectations. Unquestionably, the vast majority of Hollywood movie melodramas have been designed as transparent celebrations of the cultural status quo. But the family melodramas of the 1950s, particularly Sirk's, Minnelli's, and Ray's—with a nod toward Joshua Logan and Mark Robson—do seem to extend the genre into a stage of formal cinematic artistry and thematic sophistication not characteristic of other melodramas. The more effective of these films stand not only as works of considerable artistic merit, but also as cultural documents of Cold War America and, perhaps even more importantly, of Hollywood in its death throes. The repressive ideological climate, the false sense of sociopolitical security, and Hollywood's advanced stage of narrative and cinematic expression all coalesce in the family melodrama to produce a stylized and disturbing portrait of '50s America that, with each passing year, comes more clearly into focus.

Douglas Sirk and the family melodrama: Hollywood baroque

Time, if nothing else, will vindicate Douglas Sirk.

—Andrew Sarris, The American Cinema[13]

"It's funny how things turn out."

—Lora Meredith (Lana Turner) in Imitation of Life

It has taken students of the Hollywood cinema a while to recognize the peculiar, complex genius of Douglas Sirk. In fact, Andrew Sarris' prophetic anticipation of it, written some ten years after Sirk's retirement, flew in the face of the critical establishment. Sirk and his glossy, stylish melodramas were all but forgotten at that point. Although his fellow Europeans had been singing Sirk's praises since the late 1950s, few American critics even looked at the "impossible stories" (Sirk's term) that he was assigned to direct during his tenure with Universal studios from 1950 until 1959. (Sirk's filmography appears at the end of this chapter.) Critical reservations were intensified, predictably, by the tremendous popularity of Sirk's "weepies," particularly with the middle-aged, middle-class, middlebrow "women's matinee" crowd. But his talent is at last receiving its well-deserved acclaim—Sirk's critical stock has risen dramatically throughout the past decade.

Whatever he might owe to Sarris for his recognition by American critics, Sirk actually has been his own best critic and most persuasive advocate. In the tradition of many European filmmakers (Sirk is an expatriate German) and in contrast to most of his Hollywood colleagues, Sirk has a strong sense of aesthetics and dramatic theory, as well as a working knowledge of film history and criticism. Like François Truffaut, Jean-Luc Godard, Ingmar Bergman, Piero Paolo Pasolini, and Rainer Werner Fassbinder, Sirk's detailed analyses of his own work and of the cinema in general have enabled viewers and critics alike to understand the range and complexity of his films.

In his extended 1970 interview with Jon Halliday (more than a decade after Sirk's departure from Hollywood and America), Sirk describes how he was introduced to the subject of his final film, *Imitation of Life*. "As far as I remember," Sirk recalls, "[producer] Ross Hunter gave me the book, which I didn't read. After a few pages I had the feeling this kind of American novel would definitely disillusion me. The style, the words, the narrative attitude would be in the way of my getting enthusiastic"[14] (Halliday, 1972, pp. 134–135). If any single statement even begins to explain the fascination and critical confusion generated by Sirk's films over the years, it is this one. Sirk's interests as a film director, as the premiere narrator of female "weepies" in the '50s, were based on a style and attitude fundamentally at odds with many, if not most, of the other melodramatists. It certainly takes no more than a few pages of Fanny Hurst's tawdry 1933 bestseller to realize that in the novel, the narrator actually took the subject matter seriously, celebrating the American success ethic, romantic love, and the nuclear family. Sirk conceived of his subject quite differently than had Hurst—not as a celebration of the American Dream, but as an articulation and ultimately a criticism of it.

So refined was Sirk's "narrative attitude" in its balance of style and story that the very films that now seem most critical of American ideology—principally *Magnificent Obsession* (1953), *All That Heaven Allows* (1956), *Written on the Wind* (1957), and *Imitation of Life* (1959)—also were among Universal's biggest box-office hits of the decade. *Magnificent Obsession* put director Sirk and his discovery, Rock Hudson, on the industry map. The film pulled in the seventh largest profit among Hollywood releases of 1954 and solidified producer Ross Hunter's commitment to the slick, Technicolor "woman's picture." Hudson, who had been appearing in films for some five years without any real notice, became the biggest box-office star of the late '50s and early '60s, and Sirk emerged as Universal's star director. Sirk's last film, *Imitation of Life*, was Hollywood's fourth largest hit in 1959 and the studio's top moneymaker until then. Still, Sirk's work was overlooked except by the general audience. Few other Hollywood directors—Ford, Hawks, and Hitchcock are seemingly the only ones—have suffered so schizophrenic a critical reception as has Sirk through the years. Each of these directors made immensely popular genre films that have been consistently revaluated upward since their initial release and less-than-enthusiastic reviews. But one significant difference separates Sirk from these other directors: Whereas Ford, Hawks, and Hitchcock parlayed their popular (i.e., financial) success into independent productions and thus greater directorial control later in their careers, Sirk's films were assigned to him by studio bosses and he retired just at the point when he might have taken charge.

Conceivably, though, personal control over his projects might well have undermined Sirk's particular talents. He was one of those rare directors who thrived on adversity, whose best work was done with outrageous scripts and dehumanizing working conditions. Consider Sirk's own nostalgic recollection of the studio system: "There is the undeniable lure of this rotten place, Hollywood, the joy of being once again on the set, holding the reins of a picture, fighting circumstances and impossible stories, this strange lure of dreams dreamt up by cameras and men"[15] (Halliday, 1972, pp. 134–135). If we agree with Sarris that the *auteur* is one whose directorial personality—or in Sirk's terms his "narrative attitude"—emerges from the tension between the director and his material (script, cast, crew, etc.), then Douglas Sirk may be the consummate Hollywood *auteur*.

Because Sirk operated so successfully within the studio production system, however, any notion of "a Sirk film" must be qualified. There is a pattern of remarkable consistency in the credits of Sirk's "production unit" at Universal. For *Magnificent Obsession, All That Heaven Allows, Written on the Wind,* and *Imitation of Life,* Sirk used the same cinematographer (Russell Metty), musical director (Frank Skinner), set designer (Russell A. Gausman), art director (Alexander Golitzen), and costume designer (Bill Thomas). He also relied on a small repertory company of actors, principally Rock Hudson and Jane Wyman.

The distinctive style of Sirk's quality melodramas, then, was partly due to his collaboration with—his virtual "orchestration" of—the combined talents of a complex production unit whose capabilities Sirk understood. His unit was composed primarily of those craftsmen responsible not for the *story* (the writer composes the story and the editor assembles it after shooting), but rather for the *style* of

Interior framing as a thematic device: Sirk often portrayed his characters, particularly his women, as entrapped not only by social circumstances but by the material conditions of their lives as well. (Left) Jane Wyman (All That Heaven Allows) and (right) Susan Kohner (Imitation of Life) share similar frames of reference. (Private Collection)

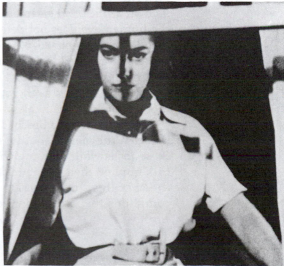

the film. The camerawork and lighting, the music, the sets, the art direction, and even the wardrobes contributed to the unique look and feel of Sirk's melodramas, and all of these filmmaking roles were organized, in each film except *Written on the Wind*, under the production supervision of Ross Hunter (Albert Zugsmith produced *Wind*).

Sirk as stylist

The distinction between story and style cannot be stressed strongly enough. Sirk's talent is a function of his storytelling, his stylization of the material, and his narrative attitude. Sirk was certainly aware that most film critics were of the (predominantly literary) disposition that "film art" was a function of subject matter and thematics, but as the creator of that art, he knew it was form and style which made the melodrama "work." As Sirk himself describes his early attraction to melodrama:

> Slowly in my mind I formed the idea of melodrama, a form I found to perfection in American pictures. They were naive, they were something completely different. They were completely Art-less. This tied in with my studies of the Elizabethan period, where you had *l'art pour l'art* ["art for art's sake"] and you had Shakespeare. He was a melodramatist, infusing all those melodramas with style, with signs and meaning. There is a tremendous similarity between this and the Hollywood system.[16] (Sirk, 1977–78, p. 30)

Fundamental to Sirk's style is his use of the camera and by extension his lighting, both of which were under the direct command of cinematographer Russell Metty. (Sirk on Metty: "We had just the same way of seeing things.") While most other filmmakers assumed that film melodramas, as a "reflection" or "representation" of existing social conditions, should be treated as realistically as possible, Sirk chose to shape his material in such a way that it repeatedly called attention to its own artifice. "The camera sees with its own eye," suggests Sirk. "It sees things the human eye does not detect. And ultimately you learn to trust your camera"[17] (Halliday, 1972, pp. 86–87). Sirk learned to accommodate the camera's unnatural, detached gaze. He also learned to light his sets and characters unusually: "Throughout my pictures I employ a lighting which is not naturalistic. . . . As [Bertolt] Brecht has said, you must never forget that this is not reality. This is a motion picture. It is a tale you are telling"[18] (Sirk, 1977–78, p. 33).

Sirk subscribed to Brecht's notion of audience "alienation," of creating distance between the viewer and the subject matter through stylization. Brecht developed these ideas while working within the tradition of Realist theater in Germany, and Sirk applied them to the realist tradition of social melodrama in Hollywood. The thrust of this strategy was to make the audience more acutely aware of the social conditions that are supported by the genre, and thus the tradition relies heavily upon the audience's expectations. Because the audience has learned to accept the melodrama's transparent, realistic celebration of romantic love and marriage (the cultural status quo), any calculated stylistic flourishes will cloud this perceptual transparency. As soon as the audience is reminded that they are watching a contrived reality, that only within this artificial world are "social problems" worked out so neatly, the prosocial fiction is cast in doubt.

Such a narrative strategy requires a delicate balance of story and style, of emotional engagement and intellectual distancing—a balance that Brecht himself never realized in his own brief Hollywood career. Sirk understood the degree of realism and emotional identification virtually built in to the film melodrama: "The camera is the main thing here, because there is *emotion* in motion pictures. Motion is emotion, in a way that it can never be in theater"[19] (Halliday, 1972, p. 43). Thus the camera became his two-edged sword: a device which records the world mechanically and encourages the audience to identify with the reality it reflects; and also a device that can be manipulated to distort, interpret, shade, and stylize the world, thus *re*creating reality to accommodate the filmmaker's vision.

Sirk manipulated not only camerawork and lighting in this way, but virtually every aspect of the filmmaking art: decor, costumes, sets, actors, and even the stories themselves. There is one basic narrative "tendency," as he terms it, operative in all his films, namely, romantic love, which is determined and controlled by social circumstances. Sirk found the melodrama an especially fertile ground for social commentary because one could depict "not just a love story, but one where the social circumstances condition the love. The structure of society in which this happening of love is embedded is just as important as the love itself"[20] (Halliday, 1972, p. 52). Sirk always resolved the immediate love story, but left unresolved the contradictory social conditions in which the story was "embedded" and that had prevented the lovers' embrace until some arbitrary event near the film's end. His resolution is ultimately unsatisfactory, challenging the viewer's expectations on virtually every level of engagement. Thus Sirk's "unhappy happy end," to encourage the audience to "think further, even after the curtain goes down."

All That Heaven Allows

Consider the narrative development in *All That Heaven Allows*. The film opens with a picture postcard panorama of a small town and introduces three of its inhabitants: Cary Scott (Jane Wyman), an attractive, middle-aged widow and mother; Sara (Agnes Moorhead), her neighbor and friend from "the Club"; and Ron Kirby (Rock Hudson), Cary's handsome young gardener. In the opening sequence, each of these characters wears clothing that is color-keyed to his or her immediate surroundings. Sara wears the same shade of blue as her station wagon in which she arrives; Cary and her two-story home wear a drab, neutral gray; Ron's khaki and tan reflect the "natural," earthy environment where he works. Sirk's color-coding of wardrobe indicates how material objects can become laden with thematic significance. This cumulative strategy develops along with the narrative and eventually provides as much information as the words and actions of the principal characters.

Cary is the antithesis of her self-assured gardener. While Ron's lifestyle is ridiculed among Cary's postadolescent children and her friends (he is cultivating his own nursery outside of town), it comes to represent his freedom from the social morass threatening to drown Cary. Hudson's Ron Kirby is the archetypal intruder-redeemer, alien to the repressive social environment, and thus an ideological reference for both the heroine and the audience. As Sirk observes, "In melodrama it's of advantage to have one immovable character against which you can put your more split ones," and Rock Hudson frequently portrayed that figure in Sirk's films. In effect, the exploitation of Hudson's beefcake charm and acting limitations is a prime example of Sirk's capacity to turn apparent debits into narrative assets. Sirk saw in Hudson similar qualities to those in John Wayne, an actor whose screen persona overwhelmed (and thus determined) his individual roles:

> Of course, there is always the danger of petrification, of sameness, of not reshaping your style. Because the only kind of style these actors have at their command is the one of their personality. But don't forget that petrification makes for greatness, sometimes. Petrification leads to being a statue of yourself. Wayne is a great actor because he has become petrified. He has become a statue. You need an *auteur* theory on this, too. Because he has a very consistent handwriting all his own. I enjoy seeing him: he has become a cipher, a sign in the cinema.[21] (Halliday, 1972, pp. 71–72)

While Sirk's description of Wayne is arguable (Wayne's range as an actor is certainly much greater than Hudson's), this statement does describe Hudson rather well, especially as his persona evolved within the melodrama. An "immovable" ideological figure, Hudson's Ron Kirby is little more than a thematic presence, an ideal of physical beauty and purely "natural" instincts. Unlike every other character, he understands exactly what he and the world are about. Hudson's character is the personification of the genre's version of American values. He is unaffected by immediate social circumstances and therefore is something of a mythic figure. Although Ron Kirby's narrative role is necessarily a static, one-dimensional pose, he is a narrative foil for all the "split" characters within the film, and *All That Heaven Allows* is overrun with them.

Ron and Cary fall in love, and even though their love offers Cary an escape from her oppressive world, she finds that the people in it whom she'd always taken for granted—her family and friends—protest when she decides to fashion an identity other than the one prescribed for her. Ron makes every effort to indoctrinate Cary in his "alternative" lifestyle, so their courtship becomes a tug of war between their respective value systems: Cary's naive, social-worker daughter quotes Freud while Ron quotes Thoreau; Cary attends a stifling cocktail party at the Club (where the drunken husband of a friend makes a pass at her) and later attends a joyous cele-

A different drummer: Cary Scott (Jane Wyman) is introduced to an "alternative" lifestyle (reading Thoreau's Walden) beyond her stifling bourgeois community by Alida (Virginia Grey), whose husband left Madison Avenue to live in the woods. (Private Collection)

bration of wine and song at the rustic home of Ron's congenial friends; Cary's son studies business at Princeton while Ron's closest friend has just quit the Madison Avenue rat race to live in the woods; Cary lives in a suffocating mausoleum filled with stained glass windows, overstuffed furniture, and marbled mirrors, whereas Ron makes his home in a refurbished mill, a spacious, wood-hewn retreat whose massive picture window looks out over his personal Walden.

The "alternative" lifestyle shown in *All That Heaven Allows* is scarcely a radical departure from the one Cary has known. The lovers are paralleled with Mick and Alida Anderson, an idealized pair who function as their role model. Mick finally listened to the "different drummer" who, as Alida tells Cary, had always played for Ron. He left the pressures and material trappings of New York City to find a more reasonable version of it in the country, raising trees and living in a simple home whose windowed roof opens to the stars. Alida is proof that indeed Cary can redefine her present lifestyle, although she is still the passive, subordinate, dutiful domesticator. Clearly hers is the preferable wifely role despite her conventional activities (it certainly must have seemed a more genuine alternative to '50s audiences). But as appealing as Ron and his disciples appear to Cary, she cannot break away from the life she has been conditioned to lead; she cannot erase the self-image fashioned over years of unconscious participation in the American Dream. The physical representation of Cary's entrapment is her bourgeois home, and she repeatedly is shown on the inside looking out—out of windows, out from behind room dividers, out from "inside" the mirrors that are everywhere. Sirk has said that his characters' "homes are their prisons," itself an indication that "they are imprisoned even by the tastes of the society in which they live"[22] (Sirk, 1977–78, p. 32).

The final resolution-embrace of *All That Heaven Allows* is motivated not by Cary's own initiative and self-awareness, but rather by an act of God. The immediate cause of Ron's accident is Cary's own indecision. Agonizing over whether to maintain appearances in the community and satisfy her narrow-minded children, Cary impulsively drives to Ron's mill, but she turns back at the last moment. Ron sees her from a distance, calls out, and falls from a hillside, striking his head. The injury accomplishes what Ron and true love had not: she promises the doctor she will stay and care for Ron. As empty and static as Cary's class-bound spinsterhood had become, she had to be forced into rejecting it. But even the freedom her final act implies is undercut in that Cary is going to Ron as a nurse and mother, not as a lover—his plight has rekindled her traditional maternal instincts.

Critic-filmmaker Rainer Werner Fassbinder has pointed out that one of the more engaging and unconventional aspects of Sirk's melodramas is that women actually think about their social conditioning, but that is all they do. Neither Cary's self-conscious introspection nor Ron's devotion is enough to motivate any radical redefinition of her identity. In the film's ironic resolution, then, Sirk brings the lovers together even as he acknowledges the pervasive, dehumanizing, and ultimately destructive power of American middle-class ideology, of those entrenched values and attitudes which both sustain and suppress the society's "silent majority."

Written on the Wind

Although *All That Heaven Allows* appears to us today as an obvious indictment of America's repressive, sexist, and materialistic middle class, indications are that its contemporary audiences and critics read the film as a straightforward love story. Sirk's heavy stylization of the material, intensified by the ironic happy ending, surely was there to see in 1956 just as it is now. But he, at least, was not surprised by the audience's response, because at the time "America was feeling safe and sure of herself, a society primly sheltering its comfortable achievements and institutions"[23] (Halliday, 1972, p. 98). However the audience responded to the subversive elements, though, there can be little question regarding Sirk's formal and thematic designs in his masterpiece of a year later, *Written on the Wind*. Sirk himself has compared the two films: "Just observe the difference between *All That Heaven Allows* and *Written on the Wind*. It's a different stratum of society in *All That Heaven Allows*, still untouched by the lengthening shadows of doubt. Here in *Written on the Wind*, a condition of life is being portrayed and, in many respects, anticipated, which is not unlike today's decaying and crumbling American society"[24] (Halliday, 1972, p. 116).

Written on the Wind is the consummate family aristocracy melodrama. The film employs the most complex constellation of characters of any Sirk film, involving the spoiled, decadent offspring of Texas oil tycoon Jasper Hadley (Robert Keith) who are juxtaposed with both a male and a female intruder-redeemer figure. The redeemer figures, Lauren Bacall as Lucy Moore (eventually Lucy Hadley) and Rock Hudson as Mitch Wayne, are the "unmovable" characters in the narrative. They have formulated their static self-reliance elsewhere, beyond the Hadley domain. Mitch has been with the Hadley family since his childhood, keeping the tormented male heir, Kyle Hadley (Robert Stack), out of trouble and continually refusing the sexual advances of libidinous daughter Marylee (Dorothy Malone, who won an Academy Award for her performance). Bacall's female redeemer, conversely, enters the Hadley constellation through her marriage to Kyle. Thus, she becomes the catalyst for family conflict and the eventual collapse of the Hadley aristocracy.

Written on the Wind is, in one sense, a bizarre detective story, with the audience as detective and America's corrupt ruling class as the heavy. The film begins with an enigmatic crime that sets the flashback narrative in motion. As the opening credits and musical theme ("A faithless lover's kiss/Is written on the wind") play, Mitch and Lucy (who is now Kyle's wife) are seen together through a bedroom window. The camera then moves to Marylee's window, where curtains and deep shadows hide all but her eyes. The scene then shifts to a severe low-angle on the mansion, which is obscured when Kyle's sportscar roars into the frame. Kyle staggers into the house, apparently drunk. A shot is fired (off-screen) and he staggers out, gun in hand, and falls dead to the pavement. Our attention is then directed back to the window, where the wind ruffles the curtains and turns back the pages on a desk calendar.

The majority of the remaining story relates, in flashback, the events leading to Kyle's death. A brief trial sequence follows (Mitch Wayne is accused of the murder), and then an epilogue. This plot structure is a brilliant stroke, in that it presents the death of the heir apparent to the Hadley family right at the beginning; consequently, Sirk can use his narrative to examine the basis for the Hadleys' decadence and the inevitability of Kyle's death. Not only does this technique inject "an underlying theme of hopelessness," as Sirk points out, but it also encourages the audience "to turn its attention to the *how* instead of the *what*—to structure instead of plot"[25] (Halliday, 1972, p. 119). The flashback has both narrative and formal advantages: it asks us to consider the social circumstances that led to an event we have already seen occur, and it frees Sirk to embellish these very circumstances stylistically.

As is typical in the family melodrama's portrayal of the big-business aristocrat, the senior Hadley is a fading scion whose individual capabilities once built an empire. Now they are in severe decline—and are all but nonexistent in his children. Mitch Wayne, the son of Hadley's boyhood friend, is a "natural" man, in the mold of Ron Kirby in *All That Heaven Allows,* magically oblivious to the class-bound social conditions that engulf him. Hadley's son Kyle is a playboy and amateur tycoon who cruises by plane across the country; sister Marylee's cruising is restricted to the bars and dingy hangouts in the town of Hadley, a tacky suburb of the sprawling oil fields. The flashback sequence opens with Kyle and Mitch flying to New York so that Kyle can buy a steak sandwich. There they meet Lucy Moore, a well-groomed, self-assured businesswoman who somehow falls for Kyle and marries him that night—but not until Mitch's desire for her is established. This gives us the first glimpse of the two men's Cain-and-Abel relationship.

Thus what Sirk has termed the characters' "unmerry-go-round" is set in motion: Marylee loves Mitch, Mitch loves Lucy, Lucy loves Kyle, and Kyle loves no one, not even himself. The plot's dramatic complications turn on sexual issues: Marylee's promiscuous behavior, which she uses to punish Mitch, Kyle's supposed sterility, Kyle's suspicions concerning Mitch and Lucy when she eventually becomes pregnant, and so on. Although Mitch and Lucy do gravitate toward one another as Kyle morally deteriorates, their inner stability enables them to maintain a respectable distance. As the nominal "star" in this constellation, Rock Hudson once again

The "secret owners" of Written on the Wind: *Kyle Hadley* **(Robert Stack, above),** **the inadequate and self-destructive male heir; and Marylee (Dorothy Malone), his** **libidinous little sister.** (Wisconsin Theater Arts Collection)

creates an appropriately static characterization which is complemented by Bacall's portrayal of willful, stoic Lucy Moore. In contrast, Kyle and Marylee, each plagued by insecurity, inadequacy, and overindulged passions, are the more dynamic and sympathetic characters—Sirk has actually dubbed them "the secret owners of the picture"[26] (Halliday, 1972, p. 98). In the melodrama's internalized dramatics, one-dimensional characters like Mitch and Lucy function as foils for the "split," multi-faceted figures, with the latter supplying most of the physical action and emotional engagement.

The only tension of the Mitch-Lucy pairing has to do with their disparate life-styles and backgrounds. While Mitch is quite close to Ron Kirby's Emersonian type, Lucy seems to want the same middle-class existence that Cary had been struggling to escape in *All That Heaven Allows.* Lucy even tells Kyle when she first meets him, "I'll probably walk down an aisle and wind up in a suburb with a husband, a mortgage, and children." Thus the Hadley aristocrats are countered by both middle-class (Lucy) and classless (Mitch) value systems, and the negative view of the decadent wealthy is reinforced at the film's end by placing Mitch and Lucy in different camps. In *Written on the Wind*, then, middle-class ideology assumes a more positive value, representing the "right" alternative for the corrupt, self-destructive Hadleys. Early in the flashback, for example, during Kyle and Lucy's whirlwind courtship, Lucy makes it obvious that she's a "good girl," not a one-night stand. She does eventually compromise her virtue that night, but not until Kyle pays the price with a marriage license. After the wedding, Kyle plays the model bourgeois husband, forgoing alcohol, staying home evenings, working regularly, planning his parenthood. Typical of Sirk's ironic vision, the transformation is only temporary. Kyle's ambivalent motives and the yin/yang depiction of the middle-class family show that Sirk's forte is not his capacity to reveal the ultimate truths of contemporary social conditions but rather demonstrate how ambiguous and relative any social truth is. Sirk wanted to articulate cultural contradictions and problems, all the while only *seeming* to deliver the solution. What lingers after viewing a Sirk film is less the conflict-to-resolution machinery (although Sirk's ability as a plot mechanic is remarkable) than the complex, unresolvable nature of conflicts which Sirk orchestrates. The conflicts in this film are so complex that even the stable characters exhibit a degree of ambiguity. Regardless of the purity of Lucy's motives, for instance, she sells herself in marriage to Kyle as a material possession, a sexual commodity. A similar ambivalence is evident in the Mitch-Marylee pairing, in that Mitch's morally upright rejection of his "little sister" drives her to acts of vengeful promiscuity and their disagreements frequently lead to violence. Ultimately Mitch's refusal to be her lover causes Marylee to lie to her brother about Mitch and Lucy, an act that culminates in Kyle's death.

Sirk has described *Written on the Wind* as "a piece of social criticism, of the rich and the spoiled and of the American family, really. And since the plot allowed for violence, it allowed for power of presentation also"[27] (Halliday, 1972, p. 116). This strategy is apparent from the opening sequence where Kyle is killed: the severe low-angle shot on the mansion in the unnatural dusk light; the doors to the vast funereal structure bursting open, letting a storm of beautiful, swirling, dead leaves into the foyer; the quick cuts from one character to another, building toward a crisis whose logic we do not yet understand. And just as the family mansion becomes a significant narrative arena after only the opening sequence, so the surrounding oil fields, which we see at either twilight or sunrise, serve as a visual expression of the film's internal dynamics. The barren Texas landscape, glutted with oil derricks pumping liquid wealth and power from deep beneath its surface, emerges as an apt metaphor for the Hadleys' confusion of money, influence, and sexuality. Unlike George Stevens' *Giant* (1956), where the realistic depiction of the Texas oil country provides merely a picturesque setting, the environment is itself an expression of the thematic conflicts.

Beginning the film with the death of Kyle Hadley and thus the fall of the Hadley aristocracy enables Sirk to manipulate characterization as well as the *mise-en-scène*. His manipulation is even more powerful because it is disguised behind the veneer of a murder mystery and takes the audience unawares. Once the flashback returns us to the opening confrontation between Kyle and Mitch over Lucy, the actual "crime" in this mystery story has been radically redefined. The dominant narrative issue is not who killed Kyle Hadley, but who killed the American Dream of unlimited wealth and power. Sirk's typically ironic happy ending involves a posttrial epilogue: Marylee's favorable testimony gets Mitch acquitted, he and Lucy leave the Hadley domain, and Marylee is left as sole survivor of the defunct Hadley empire.

Sirk's closing image of Marylee expresses the film's complex thematics. Apparently resigned to the loss of Mitch and her family, and to her new role as matriarch of a family business, the despondent Marylee sits at her father's desk beneath his huge portrait. She is wearing a conservative business suit similar to the one her father is wearing in the painting, and she is clutching the same miniature oil derrick that her father holds. Thus Marylee's role as the "secret owner" of *Written on the Wind* is reinforced: we now see her sexual aggression reoriented into a more acceptable social context (business), the oil rig replacing her feelings for Mitch and also for her dead father, and her confusion between Mitch as a stable father figure and as dynamic lover-redeemer. This evocative shot also suggests the steady decay of the familial and humanistic values in succeeding generations, and the implicit statement that a woman must assume a man's resolve and even his business uniform if she is to survive within his world.

Imitation of Life

Sirk's last Hollywood melodrama—and his last film—effectively extended this portrayal of an aggressive, self-reliant woman bent upon surviving in "a man's world." That film, *Imitation of Life* (filmed in 1958 and released in '59), centers upon Lora Meredith (Lana Turner), a widow, mother, and aspiring actress who takes her daughter and life savings to New York City for a stage career. *Imitation of Life* is a watershed film in the history of the family melodrama genre: It represents the ultimate woman's film with its success saga and widow/daughter opposition; yet, it foreshadows the "heavier" social issues—here racism and feminism—that would shortly displace the nuclear family as the genre's main focus. Evidently, Sirk was beginning to experience some displeasure with the melodrama's narrative limitations. Lana Turner's statuesque, long-suffering heroine is the least engaging and thus the least ambiguous of Sirk's victimized women—to the extent that several critics, Sarris included, tend to read the film as in the nature of a perverse social comedy.

(As if Turner's predictably histrionic performance is not enough, she does utter some of the most outlandish clichés in the genre's repertory. Lora to her agent: "You're trying to cheapen me, but you won't. Oh, I'll make it, Mr. Loomis, but it'll be my way." Lora on her early career setbacks: "Maybe I should see things as they are, and not as I want them to be." Lora on her fabulous rise to stardom: "Funny, isn't it? . . . You make it and find out it isn't worth it—something's missing." Lora on parenting: "Suzie's going to have everything I missed." Lora to daughter Suzie regarding Lora's fiancé: "If Steve is going to come between us I'll give him up, I'll never see him again.")

Sirk's depiction of Lora Meredith does push his characteristic irony dangerously close to parody, but *Imitation of Life* keeps its narrative balance through the film's "secret owners": Juanita Moore, the stoic, sturdy black woman who portrays widow-mother-maid Annie Johnson; and Susan Kohner as Sara Jane, Annie's fair-skinned daughter who eventually deserts her mother to pursue a show business career as a white woman. Widowhood has turned Annie, as it has Lora, into a working woman, although her being Lora's maid reaffirms her role as domesticator. Sara Jane, who even as a child is sensitive to her social-racial plight ("I don't want to live in the back—why do we always live in the back?"), refuses to accept her mother as a role model since her experiences as a black have only been painful. And it is through Sara Jane's criticism of her mother and of Lora that Sirk interweaves racial (woman as slave) and social-familial (woman as domesticator) motifs.

The story in *Imitation of Life* develops in two distinct movements. The first, set just after World War II, traces Lora and Annie's agreement to live together with their young daughters. Annie will be maid and "mammy" to the children while Lora struggles with her acting career. The second jumps in time to 1958 with the conventional success story montage (Lora's name in lights, taking bows before an enthusiastic audience, picture on magazine covers, etc.) and traces Lora's efforts to cope with both her success and her family. This is complicated by Sara Jane's flight from her mother and by Annie's eventual death from the strain that Lora and her own daughter had placed upon her. By the film's end, Lora and Sara Jane balance one another: Lora is convinced that success is worthless without love; Sara Jane is convinced that love is meaningless without success. Love to Lora means marriage and the compromising of her stage career; success to Sara Jane means denying her black heritage and thus mother-love. When Annie, the one character

Imitation of Life: *anticipating the Black Pride movement by a number of years, the wise and ever-stoic Annie (Juanita Moore) is unable to convince her fair-skinned daughter (Susan Kohner) to accept her racial identity.* (Private Collection)

capable of balancing her maternal and occupational roles, finally dies, both Lora's and Sara Jane's worlds collapse. The various survivors congregate at Annie's funeral—a reunion that is culminated when Sara Jane unexpectedly arrives and throws herself across her mother's coffin in a fit of hysteria—resolving to reestablish their family unity. But Annie was unable to sustain them while she was alive, and there is little indication that the family will survive now that she's dead. In Sirk's words:

> *Imitation of Life* and *Written on the Wind,* though so different, have something in common: it's the underlying element of hopelessness. In *Written on the Wind* the use of the flashback allows me to state the hopelessness right at the start, although the audience doesn't know the end. But it sets the mood. In *Imitation of Life,* you don't believe the happy end, and you're not really supposed to. . . . Everything seems to be OK, but you know well it isn't. By just drawing out the characters, you certainly could get a story—along the lines of hopelessness, of course. You could just go on. . . . But the point is you don't have to do this.[28] (Sirk, 1977–78, pp. 130–132)

Sirk's remarks recall the Brechtian notion of irony and formal distancing: the artificial happy ending (Sara Jane's appearance at her mother's funeral implying

258

that she's accepted her racial and familial identity; Lora's apparent resolve to forego her stage career for motherhood) is hardly convincing, particularly because we have seen that these characters' values and behavior are determined by unavoidable social conditions. The enforced resolution may provide an upbeat finale, but Sirk's "narrative attitude" encourages the viewer to consider the characters' plight after the curtain goes down. Sara Jane most certainly will continue to pass for white to avoid racial prejudice and to pursue her career, and Lora undoubtedly will return to acting, to the only role which provided her any personal satisfaction or significant social identity. Annie's very death is an ironic—if not pathetic—indication of the plight of the woman who devotes her life to her family.

The "family reunion" at film's end includes not only Lora, her own daughter Suzie (Sandra Dee), and her "foster" daughter Sara Jane, but also Steve Archer (John Gavin), an ardent suitor whose marriage proposals Lora had continually rejected to pursue her career. Gavin, a low-budget version of Rock Hudson, proves conclusively Sirk's thesis that the immovable macho hero in melodrama is nothing more than a statue. He is the "petrification" of that timeless image of honesty, integrity, and understanding. Lora actually comments on his perpetually stoic facade. The time-lapse montage depicting Lora's rise to fame and fortune follows the struggling Lora's rejection of Steve's marriage proposal, and immediately after the montage sequence Steve reappears in Lora's now successful life. On seeing him, Lora explains, "Steve, it's been so long—ten years—and you haven't changed a bit."

Actually, it had *not* been so very long (only about ten minutes of screen time) and, indeed, Archer/Gavin had not "changed a bit"—it does not even appear that his make-up has been adjusted. At moments like this the film borders on parody, but in context the line works well enough to sustain the logic of the surface plot.

As ever, Sirk strikes the delicate balance between internal narrative logic and real-world plausibility, occasionally skewing that balance to distance us but retaining our emotional engagement and identification. And when Sirk does choose to rupture the fictive realm, it is invariably to enhance the story's thematic impact. When we break out of our identification with the central character(s) and question his or her motives, behavior, and values, it enhances our sensitivity to the social conditions that have determined not only their ideology but inform our own lives. This narrative strategy distinguishes Sirk's films and makes his quality melodramas documents of both sophisticated cinematic narrativity and genuine social criticism.

In closing, I would suggest that Sirk understood, perhaps as well as any other American filmmaker, the peculiar workings not only of the melodrama but of the Hollywood movie itself. The Hollywood cinema, a dynamic narrative system within an ever-changing culture, has provided—and continues to provide even in the New Hollywood—an effective means for examining the evolving values and contradictions of American ideology. Even within the relatively inflexible realm of the family melodrama, Sirk refined a style, a narrative attitude, a self-conscious view of life that demands more from us than the passive consumption of escapist entertainment. Sirk demanded through his films that we actively negotiate and renegotiate our own social circumstances. He teaches us that we never really escape, not even in the slick, artificial realm he creates, the social and human conditions determining our own roles within the fascinating fiction of American life.

DOUGLAS SIRK FILMOGRAPHY

1935–37:	Credited for having directed nine films for Ufa, the German film studio, under the name Detlef Sierck.
1939	*Boefji* (filmed in Holland)

American films (Dates indicate completion, not release)

1942	*Hitler's Madman* (MGM)
1944	*Summer Storm* (United Artists)
1945	*A Scandal in Paris* (United Artists)
1946	*Lured* (United Artists)—retitled *Personal Column*
1947	*Sleep, My Love* (United Artists)
1948	*Slightly French* (Columbia)
	Shockproof (Columbia)
1950	*The First Legion* (United Artists)
	Mystery Submarine (this and all following produced by Universal)
1951	*Thunder on the Hill*
	The Lady Pays Off
	Weekend with Father
	Has Anybody Seen My Gal
1952	*No Room for the Groom*
	Meet Me at the Fair
	Take Me to Town
1953	*All I Desire*
	Taza, Son of Cochise
	Magnificent Obsession
1954	*Sign of the Pagan*
	Captain Lightfoot
1955	*All That Heaven Allows*
	There's Always Tomorrow
1956	*Written on the Wind*
	Battle Hymn
	Interlude
1957	*The Tarnished Angels*
	A Time to Love and a Time to Die
1958	*Imitation of Life*

Epilogue:

Hollywood Filmmaking and American Mythmaking

Throughout this study we have discussed Hollywood film genres as formal strategies for renegotiating and reinforcing American ideology. Thus genre can be seen as a form of social ritual. Implicit in this viewpoint is the notion that these ritual forms contribute to what might be called a contemporary American mythology. In a genuine "national cinema" like that developed in Hollywood, with its mass appeal and distribution, with its efforts to project an idealized cultural self-image, and with its reworking of popular stories, it seems not only reasonable but necessary that we seriously consider the status of commercial filmmaking as a form of contemporary mythmaking.

The relationship between a culture's cinema and its mythology has long been of interest to film critics and historians, particularly those genre critics who have noted the "repetition compulsion" and populist ideology of both folk tales and genre films. These notions have been applied most often to the Western, a genre whose mythic status was recognized long before its regeneration by commercial filmmakers. But studies of the Western have tended to treat the genre as an isolated phenomenon growing out of the pre-existing "myth of the West." In so doing, two significant factors usually were overlooked: the role of the commercial cinema in the development of the Western myth and also the Western's obvious kinship with other film genres. All of Hollywood's genres have been refined through the studios' cooperation with the mass audience, and all exhibit basic similarities of social function and narrative composition. As such, we should not restrict our inquiry into filmmaking and mythmaking to the Western genre alone.

But even some of the Western's most influential critics have hesitated to assign it mythic status. In the introduction to his evocative study of Western authorship entitled *Horizons West*, Jim Kitses states that, "In strict classical terms of definition myth has to do with the activity of the gods and as such the Western has no myth"[1] (Kitses, 1969, p. 13). Kitses' hesitation stems, I think, from a literary conception of myth that treats it in terms of *content* (traditional stories about the gods) rather than of *form* and *function*. Recent studies in anthropology and mythology suggest that myth should not be identified by its repetition of some classical content or "pantheistic" story. It should be perceived through its cultural function—a unique conceptual system that confronts and resolves immediate social and ideological conflicts.

This perception dates back to such pioneering anthropologists and cultural analysts as Bronislav Malinowski and Ernst Cassirer. Malinowski suggested that myth serves "an indispensible function: it expresses, enhances, and codifies belief; it safeguards and enforces morality; it vouches for the efficiency and contains practical rules for the guidance of man"[2] (Malinowski, 1926, p. 13). Although Malinowski was primarily interested in the myths of "primitive" cultures, Cassirer and others extended his ideas into a contemporary context. According to Cassirer, man's mythmaking impulse represents a distinct level of consciousness with its own conceptual and structural features. There is no unity of "subject matter" in myth, only a unity of function expressed in a unique mode of experience. In *Myth of the State*, Cassirer contends that this function is practical and social: it promotes a feeling of unity and harmony among the members of a society and also the whole of nature or life[3] (Bidney, 1955, pp. 379–392).

Even more significant are the more recent studies by Claude Lévi-Strauss, the proclaimed father of structural anthropology, and Roland Barthes, who has applied Lévi-Strauss' ideas to popular literature and other forms of mass-mediated culture. Lévi-Strauss' chief contribution to the study of anthropology and mythology is his insistence that any myth's cultural function is closely related to its *narrative structure*. In "The Structural Study of Myth," Lévi-Strauss states:

> A myth exhibits a "slated" structure which seeps to the surface, if one may say so, through the repetition process. However, the slates are not absolutely identical to each other. And since the purpose of myth is to provide a logical model capable of overcoming a contradiction (an impossible achievement if, as it happens, the contradiction is real), a theoretically infinite number of slates will be generated, each one slightly different from the others.[4] (Lévi-Strauss, in DeGeorge, 1972, p. 193)

Thus, mythmaking itself emerges as a basic human activity which structures human experience—whether social or personal, whether physical or metaphysical—in a distinct and consistent fashion. Lévi-Strauss defines mythical thought as "a whole system of reference which operates by means of a pair of cultural contrasts: between the general and the particular on the one hand and nature and culture on the other"[5] (Lévi-Strauss, 1962, p. 135). These "contrasts" are themselves reduced from the myriad ambiguities of human existence: life/death, good/evil, individual/community, and so on.

A culture's mythology, then, represents its society speaking to itself, developing a network of stories and images designed to animate and resolve the conflicts of everyday life. It is in the structure of these stories and images that we glimpse their mythic status. And as Lévi-Strauss suggests, "If there is meaning to be found in mythology, this cannot reside in the isolated elements which enter into the composition of a myth, but only in the way these elements are combined"[6] (Lévi-Strauss in DeGeorge, 1972, p. 174). Mythic elements are combined in what Lévi-Strauss terms "bundles of oppositions." Different mythologies are identified by the various ways in which these oppositions are combined, mediated, and resolved.

This "structuralist" approach to cultural storytelling provides a clear and accessible view of what might be termed man's mythmaking impulse, and one of the aims of this book has been to examine a contemporary manifestation of that impulse. In the final analysis, the relationship of genre filmmaking to cultural mythmaking seems to me to be significant and direct. Consider the basic similarities between those two activities: how the society at large participates in isolating and refining certain stories, the fact that those stories are essentially problem-solving strategies whose conflicts cannot be fully resolved (hence the infinite variations), the tendency for heroic types to mediate the opposing values inherent within the problem, and the attempt to resolve the problem in a fashion that reinforces the existing social and conceptual order. Genre films, much like the folk tales of primitive cultures, serve to defuse threats to the social order and thereby to provide some logical coherence to that order.

Roland Barthes, in his *Mythologies*, suggests that the internal logic of any mythical system functions to *naturalize* social experience. "The very principle of myth," contends Barthes, is that "it transforms history into nature"[7] (Barthes, 1957, p. 129). Like Lévi-Strauss, Barthes views mythmaking as a fundamental human activity, and he believes it is manifested today in our ideologies, in familiar belief systems like Christianity, democracy, capitalism, monogamy, and so on. Because the values that inform these systems are woven into the fabric of our everyday lives, these ideologies do indeed seem "natural," they appear to be virtually commonsensical or self-explanatory. When the Western celebrates rugged individualism or the musical celebrates romantic love and marriage, the genre forms act as myths—they are among the various stories our culture tells itself to purify and justify the values and beliefs which sustain it. Barthes might actually be describing a film genre in this description of mythic function: "In passing from history to nature, myth acts economically: it abolishes the complexity of human acts, it gives them the simplicity of essences, it does away with all dialectics, with any going back beyond what is immediately visible, it organizes a world which is without contradiction because it is without depth"[8] (Barthes, 1957, p. 145).

It is undeniably true that many genre films—whether a Ford Western or a Minnelli musical, a Chandler-scripted detective film or one of Douglas Sirk's melodramas—do seem to foreground ideological contradictions rather than do away with them, do seem to organize a world of depth and ambiguity. Our present concerns, however, are not with the artistic manipulation of a generic formula, but rather with the social and conceptual basis for the formula itself. An understanding of where genres come from and how they work both in and on our culture must precede our efforts to differentiate or single out individual genre films for their distinctive artistry.

Examining the various connections between genre filmmaking and cultural mythmaking provides us with a number of valuable insights. This approach encourages us to reconsider and reaffirm the essential, immediate social function of the commercial cinema and especially of genre filmmaking. It demands that we adjust our critical attitude and methods to the cinema's popular and industrial nature. Like the anthropologist studying folk tales, the genre analyst necessarily studies movies in order to glean the "form of their content"—that is, to consider the ways in which popular film narratives structure experience with their formulaic treatment of basic sociocultural issues.

There are, however, two significant considerations which qualify the genre-myth analogy. The first of these involves the role of the mass audience in genre filmmaking. Hollywood movies, unlike traditional folk tales, are not the immediate, spontaneous expression of the people; they are, instead, the calculated expression of professional filmmakers. A film genre develops when the audience encourages the repetition of a film narrative, but the original narrative—the generic prototype—is the product of collaborative artistry. Professional filmmakers are cut from the same cultural cloth as the members of the audience, of course, and we can assume that their response to human existence is substantially the same as the viewers'. There have always been technological, economic, and sociopolitical constraints in Hollywood filmmaking which do affect the nature and range of film stories available. But when considering these constraints, we should also consider a basic paradox of commercial filmmaking: movies are made by filmmakers, whereas genres are "made" by the collective response of the mass audience.

The second consideration involves generic evolution. In its evolutionary process, a genre's variation tends to render both filmmakers and audience more sensitive to the form as distinct from its social function. This increasing sensitivity to a genre's formal make-up—to its rules of expression and composition—leads to a number of interesting developments as the genre evolves: self-reflexive or formally self-conscious films, genre films which parody or subvert the genre's essentially prosocial stance, the tendency for foreign filmmakers to utilize a genre's formal features as aesthetic ends in themselves with little regard for their social function, and so on. But no matter how subversive or self-reflexive a genre film might appear to be, its success—like that of the genre—is necessarily a function of popular response. As I pointed out in the last chapter, even Douglas Sirk's most stylized and outrageous melodramas were among the most popular films of their particular era.

So for a number of reasons, Sirk's *Imitation of Life* is an appropriate finishing point for this book. The film heralds the end of the "classic age" of American cinema—the effective winding down of Hollywood's mythmaking function and the ultimate death of the Hollywood studio system. By the early 1960s, Hollywood's once-massive audience had dwindled to less than half its peak postwar size, movie "palaces" were being replaced by smaller and more economical theaters catering to more specialized audiences, foreign films were imported in record numbers, and commercial television (eating up the majority of the cinema's mass audience) emerged as America's principal means of collective cultural expression.

Actually, the American cinema passed into its mannerist or baroque age by the late '50s. The decade's "subversive" melodramas, along with its psychological Westerns, self-reflexive musicals, and manic crime thrillers, collectively represent a stage of narrative, technical, and thematic evolution that was light years beyond their classic prewar predecessors. By investigating the works of the formative prewar years, we can trace the lineage which produced the baroque masterpieces of Hollywood's final years. Many viewers and most critics have overlooked their distinctive artistry—and overlooked the expressive potential of their genres as well. But Westerns like *The Searchers* and *The Naked Spur*, musicals like *The Band Wagon* and *It's Always Fair Weather*, melodramas like *The Cobweb* and *Written on the Wind*, detective films like *Touch of Evil* and *The Big Heat*—these and many others represent a period of remarkable, and I think unparalleled, artistic achievement in modern American culture. If we temper our elitist biases long enough to look closely at these films, we notice that they do indeed exhibit those qualities generally associated with narrative artistry: irony, ambiguity, thematic complexity, formal self-consciousness. But what's so amazing about the American cinema is that this artistry emerged from such an overtly formulaic and socially immediate mass medium, from an industry whose steady evolution and direct audience contact enabled it to tap the flow of our cultural juices in an accessible yet formally sophisticated means of expression.

Hollywood's tradition of genres has survived, in one form or another, the death of the studio system of film production. Commercial television has been the primary vehicle for the regeneration and continuation of these popular formulas, having co-opted Hollywood's industrial and technological base as well as its mass audience and narrative formulas. Nonetheless, there are significant aspects of commercial television production which present a substantial departure from studio filmmaking. For one, television has yielded—quite willingly, it seems—to the demands of commerce and thus has severely compromised the aesthetic integrity of its texts. In fact, both the "commercial interruptions" and the continuous "flow" of television programming render it difficult even to isolate a television text. Furthermore, although the networks have developed elaborate methods of audience analysis and feedback (Nielsen and Arbitron ratings, etc.), their essential function is not to enable the audience to participate in program development but rather to determine advertising revenues. The cinema delivers stories to an audience, whereas television delivers the audience to advertisers.

The New Hollywood also provides a potentially productive but highly complex arena for further genre study. With the death of the studio system, the American cinema has evolved from a cohesive industry to a collection of loosely related business ventures; fewer films, most of them independently produced, are competing for increasingly higher revenues despite the substantial odds nowadays against a film even being released, let alone turning a profit. Movie "blockbusters"

(*The Godfather*, *The Exorcist*, *Jaws*, *Star Wars*, etc.) and the low-budget "exploitation" film (car-crash movies, mutilation thrillers, soft-core pornographic films) are flourishing, but that vast middle ground once dominated by the Hollywood studios is gone. And although virtually all the blockbusters of the '70s tapped directly into some established genre, their success seems to rely more on packaging, promotion, and other forms of media hype than on the movies' power as a form of collective cultural expression. Ultimately, genre analysis of current films might be best applied to the exploitation film rather than the blockbuster, mainly because the former has sustained the "formula factory" approach to film production and a certain regard for their consistent popular audience.

I am not suggesting, however, that our genre study of classic Hollywood can be applied wholesale to present-day forms. Genre study is of necessity a flexible critical method whose practice is contingent upon the system it investigates. Initial efforts to apply established literary genre theory to the cinema proved largely ineffectual, and so too, I think, would efforts to apply the critical theory developed here to the New Hollywood or to commercial television. Genre study assumes that there are certain inherent human impulses (primarily concerning narrativity and mythmaking) which are basic to humankind; it also assumes that these impulses are conditioned by—and must be studied in the context of—the specific cultural and industrial environment in which they are expressed.

It's worth suggesting that we can perceive and articulate those social conditions and any individual film's relation to them only from a considerable historical distance. It would seem that we most clearly recognize our culture's mythology in retrospect, and that at any given moment, we are in the process of formulating a mythology whose spirit and substance escape our conscious perception. In fact, our distanced viewpoint may do as much to distort as to clarify "historical reality." Hence the ambivalent conception of the term "myth" itself: a myth is both true and false, both a clarification and a distortion of real-world experience and the human condition. It is, finally, a formalized means to negotiate the present via concepts and images which are the residue of human history.

This might begin to account for the wide disparity of critical readings of '50s melodramas through time. Although we are now reading the same filmic text as viewers and critics did then, there is little question but that our historical perspective, compounded by our cultural and academic biases, renders our viewing of these films substantially different for us than it was for a '50s audience. We note now how the films anticipated certain social issues, how they accommodate our aesthetic biases regarding irony, ambiguity, and formal stylization, or how they comply with current intellectual interest in ideology and materialism. In each case, we can consider how these particular filmic narratives not only participate in but actually critique the complex workings of American mythology.

Basic to these considerations, however, both in the 1950s and today, is the immediate experience of the film itself. The ultimate value of studying cinema is a function of the depth and range of cultural insights—be they aesthetic, sociological, economic, political, mythological—which the movies afford us. The closer we examine the popular arts, the better we come to understand our culture and finally ourselves. What motivates and sustains that close study, though, is the elemental appeal of individual movies. Whatever my critical or academic investment in film study might be, I am secure in the knowledge that in the familiar darkness of a screening room or a nearby theater I once again can accompany the Westerner on his timeless search through Monument Valley, I once again might deny plausibility and the laws of gravity when Fred and Ginger turn to me and ask, "Shall we dance?"

Notes

Chapter 1

[1] The *Fortune* magazine excerpt is from a report on the Metro-Goldwyn-Mayer studio. Reprinted in Tino Balio, *The American Film Industry* (Madison: University of Wisconsin Press, 1976), p. 263.

[2] André Bazin's "La politique des auteurs" essay appeared originally as an editorial in *Cahiers du Cinema* in 1957, and is reprinted in Peter Graham's anthology, *The New Wave* (London: Secker and Warburg, 1968), p. 154.

[3] François Truffaut, "A Kind Word for Critics," *Harpers* (October 1972), p. 100.

[4] Descriptions and histories of the Hollywood studios' birth, development, and eventual death can be found in various sources, the most comprehensive being Balio, *The American Film Industry*.

[5] Distinctions among various levels of cultural expression (elite, popular, mass, folk, and so on) are treated most effectively in: Russell Nye, *The Unembarrassed Muse* (New York: Dial Press, 1970); George H. Lewis, *Side-Saddle on the Golden Calf* (Pacific Palisades, Cal.: Goodyear Publishing Co., Inc., 1972); and Stuart Hall and Paddy Whannel, *The Popular Arts* (Boston: Beacon Press, 1964). See also Dwight MacDonald's seminal essay, "A Theory of Mass Culture," in Bernard Rosenberg and David Manning White's anthology, *Mass Culture: The Popular Arts in America* (New York: The Free Press, 1964). See also Walter Benjamin's "Art in the Age of Mechanical Reproduction," in Gerald Mast and Marshall Cohen's anthology, *Film Theory and Criticism* (New York: Oxford University Press, 1974).

[6] Arnold Hauser, *The Social History of Art*, Vol. IV: *Naturalism, Impressionism, and the Film Age* (New York: Vintage Books, 1951), p. 250.

[7] Statistics on motion picture production, distribution, exhibition, and consumption are available in Christopher H. Sterling and Timothy R. Haight's invaluable source work, *The Mass Media: Aspen Institute Guide to Communication Industry Trends* (New York: Praeger Publishers, 1978).

[8] A reasonably comprehensive survey of the *auteur* policy can be gleaned from the following sources:

—Alexandre Astruc, "La camera stylo," and André Bazin, "La politique des auteurs," both of which are reprinted in Graham, *The New Wave*.

—special sections devoted to film authorship generally and the *auteur* theory specifically in three anthologies: Mast and Cohen's *Film Theory and Criticism* (op. cit.); *Movies and Methods*, Bill Nichols, ed. (Berkeley: University of California Press, 1976); *Awake in the Dark*, David Denby, ed. (New York: Vintage Books, 1977).

—of the countless studies devoted to individual directors, I find these particularly useful: Andrew Sarris, *The American Cinema* (New York: E. P. Dutton and Co., 1968); Georges Sadoul, *Dictionary of Film Makers* (Berkeley: University of California Press, 1972); several monographs in the "Cinema One" series published by the British Film Institute and *Sight and Sound* in conjunction with either Viking or the Indiana University Press, including Robin Wood's *Howard Hawks* (1968), Geoffrey Nowell-Smith's *Visconti* (1967), Jim Kitses' *Horizons West* (1969), Jon Halliday's *Sirk on Sirk* (1971), Joseph McBride's *Orson Welles* (1972). See also Robin Wood, *Hitchcock's Films* (New York: Castle Books, 1965); Joseph McBride and Michael Wilmington, *John Ford* (New York: De Capo Press, Inc., 1974), which nicely complements Peter Bogdanovich's analysis-cum-interview, also titled *John Ford* (Berkeley: University of California Press, 1968).

[9] Sadoul, *Dictionary of Film Makers*, p. 117.

[10] *Ibid.*, p. 89.

[11] Robert Warshow, *The Immediate Experience* (Garden City, N.Y.: Doubleday and Co., Inc., 1962), p. 130.

[12] Henry Nash Smith, *The Virgin Land* (Cambridge, Mass.: Harvard University Press, 1950), p. 91.

[13] Bazin, in Graham, *The New Wave*, pp. 142–143.

[14] Dwight MacDonald, *op. cit.*, p. 60.

[15] Warshow, *op. cit.*, p. 130.

Chapter 2

[1] Paul Rosenfield, "Lucas: Film-maker with the Force," *Los Angeles Times* (June 5, 1977), "Calendar" section, p. 43.

[2] Robin Wood, "Ideology, Genre, Auteur," *Film Comment* (Jan-Feb 1977), p. 47.

[3] The portion of Ferdinand de Saussure's *Course in General Linguistics*, first published in Paris in 1916, in which Saussure proposes the study of semiology, "a science that studies the life of signs within a society," and also outlines the general principles of semiology (*langue/parole*, signifier/signified, etc.), is reprinted in *The Structuralists: From Marx to Lévi-Strauss*, Richard and Fernande DeGeorge, editors (Garden City, N.Y.: Doubleday and Co., Inc., 1972), pp. 58–79. The reference in the text appears on page 62 of DeGeorge.

[4] For Chomsky's clearest description of this distinction, see *Current Issues in Linguistic Theory* (The Hague: Mouton Publishers, 1964).

[5] Molly Haskell, *From Reverence to Rape* (New York: Penguin Books, 1974), p. 124.

[6] Robert Warshow, *The Immediate Experience* (Garden City, N.Y.: Doubleday and Co., Inc., 1962), p. 147.

[7] Christian Metz, *Language and Cinema* (The Hague: Mouton Publishers), pp. 148–161.

[8] Henri Focillon, *Life of Forms in Art* (New York: George Wittenborn, Inc., 1942), p. 10.

[9] Leo Braudy, *The World in a Frame* (Garden City, N.Y.: Anchor Press/Doubleday, 1976), p. 179.

[10] For a more detailed treatment of the evolution of the musical genre, see Jane Feuer, *The Hollywood Musical: The Aesthetics of Spectator Involvement in an Entertainment Form* (Iowa City: University of Iowa, 1978), unpublished doctoral dissertation.

Chapter 3

[1] It is in this capacity that the Western genre's mythic function is most apparent. As Roland Barthes suggests, myth serves to transform history into nature and thus to make cultural conditions seem "natural." (For a more detailed treatment of this idea, see the last chapter.)

[2] Peter Bogdanovich, *John Ford* (Berkeley: University of California Press, 1968), pp. 99–100.

[3] Joseph McBride and Michael Wilmington, *John Ford* (London: Secker and Warburg, 1974), p. 181.

[4] Andrew Sarris, *The American Cinema* (New York: E. P. Dutton and Co., 1968), pp. 46–47.

[5] Bogdanovich, *John Ford*, pp. 94–95.

Chapter 4

[1] Robert Warshow, *The Immediate Experience* (Garden City, N.Y.: Doubleday and Co., Inc., 1962), p. 131.

[2] *Ibid.*, p. 133.

[3] Colin McArthur, *Underworld USA* (New York: The Viking Press, 1972), p. 55.

[4] Stephen Louis Karpf, *The Gangster Film, 1930–1940* (New York: The Arno Press, 1973), pp. 59–60.

[5] Cobbett Steinberg, "The Codes and Regulations," *Reel Facts* (New York: Vintage Books, 1978), pp. 460–461.

[6] *Ibid.*, pp. 450–460.

[7] *Ibid.*, p. 460.

[8] *Ibid.*, pp. 464–467.

[9] *Ibid.*, p. 469.

Chapter 5

[1] Siegfried Kracauer, *Theory of Film* (New York: Oxford University Press, 1960).

[2] Michael Wood, *America in the Movies* (New York: Basic Books, 1975), p. 51.

[3] Paul Schrader, "Notes on *Film Noir*," *Film Comment* (Spring 1972), p. 13.

[4] Raymond Chandler, *The Atlantic Monthly* (December 1944), p. 59.

[5] *Ibid.*, p. 58.

[6] Dorothy Gardiner and Kathrine Sorley Walker, *Raymond Chandler Speaking* (Boston: Houghton Mifflin Company, 1977), p. 52.

[7] Comments appear in Gardiner and Walker, *op. cit.*, and in Maurice Zolotow's *Billy Wilder in Hollywood*. Quoted in John Henley's CinemaTexas Program Notes on *Double Indemnity*, February 1, 1978.

[8] James Agee, *Agee on Film*, Vol. I (Boston: The Beacon Press, 1958), p. 119.

[9] Gardiner and Walker, *op. cit.*, p. 130.

[10] Georges Sadoul, *Dictionary of Films* (Berkeley: University of California Press, 1972), p. 178.

[11] *Ibid.*

Chapter 6

[1] Georges Sadoul, *Dictionary of Films* (Berkeley: University of California Press, 1972), p. 160.

[2] Molly Haskell, *From Reverence to Rape* (New York: Penguin Books, 1974), p. 93.

[3] Quoted in Louis Black's CinemaTexas Program Notes on *Meet John Doe*, October 24, 1977, p. 75.

[4] Frank Capra, *The Name Above the Title* (New York: Macmillan Co., 1971).

[5] Frank Capra, " 'One Man, One Film'—The Capra Contention," *Los Angeles Times* (June 21, 1977), p. 12.

[6] See the remarkable exchange between Capra and David W. Rintels, president of Writers Guild of America, West, in the *Los Angeles Times* "Calendar" section. Rintels initiated the exchange on June 5, 1977, with a blast at the *auteur* theory and at Capra in a piece entitled "Someone's Been Sitting in His Chair." He concludes the piece with these assertions: "Today Capra's name is widely known and Riskin's name is widely not. It might have turned out differently if the critics and film schools and French wine snobs had willed it, but they didn't. It might even have turned out differently if Riskin had written his autobiography and promoted it all over the place, but he didn't. Capra did, though. He wrote the story of his life and called it 'The Name Above the Title.' The final Capra touch."

Capra replied in the June 28 "Calendar" with " 'One Man, One Film'—The Capra Contention," which Rintels answered in the same issue with " 'Someone Else's Guts'—The Rintels Rebuttal." Whereas Rintels' tone in the earlier piece was somewhat jocular, he's deadly serious this time around. He asserts that Capra's so-called touch actually came from someone else's (i.e., Riskin's) guts. Capra himself was no less ungracious: "Yes, Robert Riskin was a giant among screenwriters—at least when he worked with me. He got his reputation on my films." Capra closes his argument with his own version of the *auteur* theory: "Regardless of where the original material came from, or what writers worked on my scripts, *all* my films—good, bad, and stinko, all were Capra films, stamped with my own kind of humor, my own philosophies and ideals. They expressed dreams, hopes, and angsts that came out of my guts, for better or worse. With me, as with many other filmmakers, it is 'one man, one film.' "

[7] Andrew Sarris, *The American Cinema* (New York: E. P. Dutton and Co., 1968), p. 87.

[8] Stephen Handzo, "Under Capracorn," *Film Comment* (November–December 1972), p. 12.

[9] Bosley Crowther, review of *Meet John Doe* in *The New York Times* (March 13, 1941), p. 25.

Chapter 7

[1] I am deeply indebted to Charles F. (Rick) Altman and to Jane Feuer for their contributions to the conception and development of the essays in this chapter on the musical. My basic understanding of the musical genre evolved out of studies with Altman and Feuer at the University of Iowa in 1975 and 1976, and both of them provided valuable editorial advice in the preparation of this manuscript.

[2] Michael Wood, *America in the Movies* (New York: Basic Books, 1975), p. 152.

[3] Vincente Minnelli, *I Remember It Well* (Garden City, N.Y.: Doubleday and Co., 1974), p. 117.

[4] John Belton, "The Backstage Musical," *Movie* (Spring 1977), p. 36.

[5] Interview with Stanley Donen," *Movie* (Spring 1977), p. 28.

[6] *Ibid.*, p. 27.

[7] Wood, *op. cit.*, p. 154.

[8] Hugh Fordin, *The World of Entertainment: Hollywood's Greatest Musicals* (New York: Avon Books, 1975), p. 73.

[9] Charles F. Altman, "Hollywood Genre: A Semantic/Syntactic Approach," *Semiotexte,* forthcoming.

[10] Fordin, *op. cit.*, p. 153.

[11] Minnelli, *op. cit.*, p. 115.

[12] Quoted in Fordin, *op. cit.*, p. 525.

[13] "Interview with Stanley Donen," *op. cit.*, p. 29.

[14] Leo Braudy, *The World in a Frame* (Garden City, N.Y.: Anchor Press/Doubleday, 1972), pp. 147, 148–149.

[15] "Interview with Stanley Donen," *loc. cit.*

[16] Quoted in Fordin, *op. cit.*, p. 269.

[17] See "The Relationship of the Spectator to the Spectacle" in Jane Feuer, *The Hollywood Musical.* Unpublished Ph.D. dissertation (Iowa City: University of Iowa, 1978), pp. 10–61.

Chapter 8

[1] Jon Halliday, *Sirk on Sirk* (New York: The Viking Press, 1972), p. 93.

[2] Thomas Elsaesser, "Tales of Sound and Fury: Observations on the Family Melodrama," *Monogram* #4 (1972), p. 4.

[3] *Ibid.*, p. 13.

[4] Andrew Dowdy, *Films of the Fifties* (New York: William Morrow and Co., 1973), p. 72.

[5] *Ibid.*, pp. 62–63.

[6] Michael Wood, *America in the Movies* (New York: Basic Books, 1975), p. 163.

[7] Geoffrey Nowell-Smith, "Minnelli and Melodrama," *Screen* (Summer 1977), p. 113.

[8] Andrew Sarris, *The American Cinema* (New York: E.P. Dutton, 1968), p. 110.

[9] Vincente Minnelli, *I Remember It Well* (Garden City, N.Y.: Doubleday and Co., 1974), p. 295.

[10] Moira Walsh, review of *Imitation of Life, America* (May 9, 1959), p. 314.

[11] Rainer Werner Fassbinder, "Fassbinder on Sirk," *Film Comment* (November–December 1975), p. 24.

[12] Halliday, *op. cit.*, p. 132.

[13] Sarris, *op. cit.*, p. 109.

[14] Halliday, *op. cit.*, p. 129.

[15] *Ibid.*, pp. 134–135.

[16] "Interview with Douglas Sirk," *Bright Lights* (Winter 1977–78), p. 30.

[17] Halliday, *op. cit.*, pp. 86–87.

[18] "Interview with Douglas Sirk," *op. cit.*, p. 33.

[19] Halliday, *op. cit.*, p. 43.

[20] *Ibid.*, p. 52.

[21] *Ibid.*, pp. 71–72.

[22] "Interview with Douglas Sirk," *op. cit.*, p. 32.

[23] Halliday, *op. cit.*, p. 98.

[24] *Ibid.*, p. 116.

[25] *Ibid.*, p. 119.

[26] *Ibid.*, p. 98.

[27] *Ibid.*, p. 116.

[28] *Ibid.*, pp. 130–132.

Epilogue

[1] Jim Kitses, *Horizons West*, (Indiana University Press: Bloomington, 1969), p. 13.

[2] Bronislav Malinowski, *Myth in Primitive Psychology* (New York: W. W. Norton and Co., 1926), p. 13. See also his *Freedom and Civilization* (New York: Roy Publishers, Inc., 1944).

[3] See David Bidney's analysis of Cassirer's work in "Myth, Symbolism, and Truth," *Journal of American Folklore* LXVIII (October–December 1955), pp. 379–392. See also Ernst Cassirer, *An Essay on Man* (New Haven: Yale University Press, 1944), *The Myth of the State* (New Haven: Yale University Press, 1946), and *The Philosophy of Symbolic Forms* (New Haven: Yale University Press, 1955).

[4] Claude Lévi-Strauss, *The Structuralists.* (Richard and Fernande DeGeorge, eds. New York: Doubleday, 1972), p. 193.

[5] Claude Lévi-Strauss, *The Savage Mind* (Chicago: University of Chicago Press, 1962), p. 135.

[6] Lévi-Strauss, *The Structuralists*, p. 174.

[7] Roland Barthes, *Mythologies* (New York: Hill and Wang, 1957), p. 129.

[8] *Ibid.*, p. 145.

References

ACKERMAN, DAN. "The Structure of the Preston Sturges Film," CinemaTexas Program Notes, April 6, 1976.

AGEE, JAMES. *Agee on Film: Reviews and Comments*. Boston: The Beacon Press, 1958.

ALLOWAY, LAWRENCE. *Violent America: The Movies 1946–1964*. New York: The Museum of Modern Art, 1971.

ALMENDAREZ, VALENTIN. CinemaTexas Program Notes on *Imitation of Life*, November 26, 1975.

ALTMAN, CHARLES F. "The American Film Musical: Paradigmatic Structure and Mediatory Function," *Wide Angle*, II (January 1978).

————. "Toward a Theory of Film Genre," *Film: Historical-Theoretical Speculations (The 1972 Film Studies Annual: Part Two)*.

ANDREW, J. DUDLEY. *The Major Film Theories: An Introduction*. New York: Oxford University Press, 1976.

ANOBILE, RICHARD J. *John Ford's Stagecoach*. New York: Avon Books, 1975.

ARNHEIM, RUDOLPH. *Film as Art*. Berkeley: University of California Press, 1957.

BALIO, TINO, ed. *The American Film Industry*. Madison: The University of Wisconsin Press, 1976.

BARTHES, ROLAND. *Mythologies*. New York: Hill and Wang, 1957.

————. *S/Z*. New York: Hill and Wang, 1970.

————. *Writing Degree Zero/Elements of Semiology*. Boston: Beacon Press, 1968.

BASINGER, JEANINE. "The Lure of the Guilded Cage," *Bright Lights* (Winter 1977–78).

BAXTER, JOHN. *The Cinema of John Ford*. New York: A. S. Barnes, 1971.

————. *The Gangster Film*. New York: A. S. Barnes, 1970.

BAZIN, ANDRÉ. "The Western, or The American Film *par excellence*," *What Is Cinema?*, Vol. II. Berkeley: University of California Press, 1971.

————. *What Is Cinema?*, Vols. I and II. Translated by Hugh Gray. Berkeley: University of California Press, 1971.

BELTON, JOHN. "The Backstage Musical," *Movie* (Spring 1977).

BERGMAN, ANDREW. "Frank Capra and the Screwball Comedy," in *We're in the Money: Depression America and Its Films.* Evanston: Harper and Row, 1971.

————. *We're in the Money: Depression America and Its Films.* Evanston: Harper and Row, 1971.

BIDNEY, DAVID. "Myth, Symbolism, and Truth," *Journal of American Folklore*, LXVIII (October–December 1955).

BLACK, LOUIS. CinemaTexas Program Notes on *Meet John Doe*, October 24, 1977.

BOGDANOVICH, PETER. *The Cinema of Orson Welles.* New York: The Museum of Modern Art, 1961.

————. "The Evolution of the Western," *What Is Cinema?*, Vol. II. Berkeley: University of California Press, 1971.

————. *John Ford.* Berkeley: University of California Press, 1968.

BOOTH, WAYNE. *The Rhetoric of Fiction.* Chicago: University of Chicago Press, 1961.

BORDE, RAYMOND, and ETIENNE CHAUMETON. "The Sources of Film Noir," *Film Reader 3* (1978).

BORDWELL, DAVID, and KRISTIN THOMPSON. *Film Art: An Introduction.* Reading, Mass.: Addison-Wesley, 1979.

BOURGET, JEAN-LOUP. "God Is Dead, or Through a Glass Darkly," *Bright Lights* (Winter 1977–78).

————. "Sirk and the Critics," *Bright Lights* (Winter 1977–78).

BRAUDY, LEO. "Musicals and the Energy from Within," *The World in a Frame.* Garden City, N.Y.: Anchor/Doubleday, 1977.

————. *The World in a Frame.* Garden City, N.Y.: Anchor Press/Doubleday, 1976.

BRECHT, BERTOLT. *Brecht on Theater.* New York: Hill and Wang, 1964.

BROOKS, PETER. *The Melodramatic Imagination.* New Haven: Yale University Press, 1976.

BROWNE, NICK. "The Spectator and the Text: The Rhetoric of *Stagecoach*," *Film Quarterly* (Winter 1975–76).

BURCH, NOEL. *The Theory of Film Practice.* New York: Praeger, 1973.

BUSCOMBE, EDWARD. "The Idea of Genre in the American Cinema," *Screen* 11 (March–April 1970).

BYARS, JACKIE. "Three Films by Douglas Sirk: Subversion or Participation?" Seminar paper, Austin: University of Texas, 1978.

CASSIRER, ERNST. *An Essay on Man.* New Haven: Yale University Press, 1944.

———. *The Myth of the State.* New Haven: Yale University Press, 1946.

———. *The Philosophy of Symbolic Forms.* New Haven: Yale University Press, 1955.

CAVELL, STANLEY. "Leopards in Connecticut," *The Georgia Review* (Summer, 1976).

———. *The World Viewed.* New York: The Viking Press, 1971.

CAWELTI, JOHN G. *Adventure, Mystery, and Romance.* Chicago: The University of Chicago Press, 1976.

———. *The Six-Gun Mystique.* Bowling Green, Ohio: Bowling Green University Press, 1971.

CHAFE, WILLIAM H. *The American Woman.* New York: The Oxford University Press, 1972.

CHANDLER, RAYMOND. "The Simple Art of Murder," *Atlantic Monthly* (December 1944).

CHOMSKY, NOAM. *Current Issues in Linguistic Theory.* The Hague: Mouton, 1964.

COHEN, MITCHELL S. "Villains and Victims," *Film Comment* (November–December 1974).

CORLISS, RICHARD. "Preston Sturges," *Cinema* (Spring 1972).

CROWTHER, BOSLEY. "Meet John Doe," *New York Times*, March 13, 1941.

CULLER, JONATHAN. *Structuralist Poetics.* Ithaca: Cornell University Press, 1975.

CUTTS, JOHN. "Oriental Eye," *Films and Filming* (August 1957).

DAMICO, JAMES. "Film Noir: A Modest Proposal," *Film Reader 3* (1978).

DEGEORGE, RICHARD and FERNANDE, eds. *The Structuralists: From Marx to Levi-Strauss.* Garden City, N.Y.: Doubleday and Co., Inc., 1972.

DONEN, STANLEY. "Interview with Stanley Donen," *Movie* (Spring 1977).

DOWDY, ANDREW. *Films of the Fifties.* New York: William Morrow and Co., 1973.

DURGNAT, RAYMOND. "The Family Tree of Film Noir," *Film Comment* (November–December 1974).

DYER, JOHN PETER. "The Murderers Among Us," *Films and Filming* (December 1958).

DYER, RICHARD. "Entertainment and Utopia," *Movie* (Spring 1977).

ECO, UMBERTO. *A Theory of Semiotics.* Bloomington: University of Indiana Press, 1976.

EIDSVIK, CHARLES. *Cineliteracy: Film Among the Arts.* New York: Random House, Inc., 1978.

EISENSTEIN, SERGEI. *Film Form.* New York: Harcourt, Brace, and World, 1949.

ELSAESSER, THOMAS. "Tales of Sound and Fury: Observations on the Family Melodrama," *Monogram* no. 4 (1972).

ENGLE, GARY. "*McCabe and Mrs. Miller:* Robert Altman's Anti-Western," *Journal of Popular Film* (Fall 1972).

EVERSON, WILLIAM K. *The Detective in Film.* Secaucus, N.J.: The Citadel Press, 1972.

FASSBINDER, RAINER WERNER. "Fassbinder on Sirk," *Film Comment* (November–December 1975).

FELL, JOHN. *Film and the Narrative Tradition.* Norman, Oklahoma: University of Oklahoma Press, 1974.

FENIN, GEORGE, and WILLIAM K. EVERSON. *The Westerns: From Silents to Cinerama.* New York: The Orion Press, 1962.

————. "The Western—Old and New," *Film Culture*, Vol. 2, No. 2 (1956).

FEUER, JANE. *The Hollywood Musical: The Aesthetics of Spectator Involvement in an Entertainment Form.* Ph.D. dissertation, Iowa City: University of Iowa, 1978. MacMillan/British Film Institute, forthcoming.

————. "The Self-Reflective Musical and the Myth of Entertainment," *Quarterly Review of Film Studies* (August 1977).

————. "The Theme of Popular versus Elite Art in the Hollywood Musical," *Journal of Popular Culture* (Winter 1978).

FOCILLON, HENRI. *Life of Forms in Art.* New York: George Wittenborn, Inc., 1942.

FORDIN, HUGH. *The World of Entertainment: Hollywood's Greatest Musicals.* New York: Avon Books, 1975.

FRENCH, PHILIP. "Incitement against Violence," *Sight and Sound* (Winter 1967–68).

————. *Westerns: Aspects of a Movie Genre.* New York: The Viking Press, 1973.

FRYE, NORTHROP. *Anatomy of Criticism.* Princeton: Princeton University Press, 1957.

GABREE, JOHN. *Gangsters: From Little Caesar to the Godfather.* New York: Gallahad Books, 1973.

GARDNER, DOROTHY, and KATHRINE SORLEY WALKER, eds. *Raymond Chandler Speaking.* Boston: Houghton Mifflin Co., 1977.

GILES, DENNIS. "Show-Making," *Movie* (Spring 1977).

GRAHAM, PETER, ed. *The New Wave.* London: Secker and Warburg, 1968.

GREGORY, CHARLES. "Knight without Meaning? Marlowe on the Screen," *Sight and Sound* (Summer 1973).

GROSS, LARRY. "*Après Film Noir:* Alienation in a Dark Alley," *Film Comment* (July–August, 1976).

GUBACK, THOMAS H. *The International Film Industry.* Bloomington: Indiana University Press, 1969.

HALL, STUART, and PADDY WHANNELL. *The Popular Arts.* Boston: Beacon Press, 1964.

HALLIDAY, JON. *Sirk on Sirk.* New York: The Viking Press, 1972.

HAMPTON, BENJAMIN. *History of the American Film Industry.* New York: Dover Press, 1970.

HANDZO, STEPHEN. "Imitations of Lifelessness: Sirk's Ironic Tearjerker," *Bright Lights* (Spring 1977).

————. "Under Capricorn," *Film Comment* (November–December 1972).

HARCOURT-SMITH, SIMON. "Vincente Minnelli," *Sight and Sound* (January–March, 1952).

HASKELL, MOLLY. *From Reverence to Rape.* New York: Penguin Books, 1974.

HAUSER, ARNOLD. *The Social History of Art,* Vol. IV, *Naturalism, Impressionism, and The Film Age.* New York: Vintage Books, 1951.

HERNADI, PAUL. *Beyond Genre.* Ithaca: Cornell University Press, 1972.

HIRSCH, E. D. *Validity in Interpretation.* New Haven: Yale University Press, 1967.

HOUSTON, PENELOPE. "The Private Eye," *Sight and Sound* (Summer 1956).

JACOBS, LEWIS. *The Rise of the American Film.* New York: Teachers College, 1968.

JACOBS, NORMAN, ed. *Culture for the Millions? Mass Media in Modern Society.* Princeton, N. J.: D. Van Nostrand Co., Inc., 1959.

JAKOBSON, ROMAN. *Selected Writings.* Vol. I, *Phonological Studies;* Vol. II, *Word and Language,* The Hague: Mouton, 1962; 1971.

JAMESON, FREDERIC. *The Prison-House of Language.* Princeton: Princeton University Press, 1972.

JENSEN, PAUL. "Raymond Chandler: The World You Live In," *Film Comment* (November–December 1974).

————. "The Return of Dr. Caligari," *Film Comment* (Winter 1971–72).

JOHNSON, ALBERT. "The Films of Vincente Minnelli," *Film Quarterly.* Part One (Winter 1958); Part Two (Spring 1959).

JOWETT, GARTH. *Film: The Democratic Art.* Boston: Little, Brown, and Co., 1976.

KAMINSKY, STUART M. *American Film Genres.* Chicago: Pflaum Publishers, 1974.

————. "*Little Caesar* and Its Place in the Gangster Film Genre," *Journal of Popular Film* (Summer 1972).

KARPF, STEPHEN LOUIS. *The Gangster Film: 1930–1940.* New York: The Arno Press, 1973.

KAUFFMAN, STANLEY, ed. *American Film Criticism: From the Beginnings to Citizen Kane.* New York: Liveright Press, 1972.

KIDD, MICHAEL. "The Camera and the Dance," *Films and Filming* (January 1956).

KITSES, JIM. *Horizons West: Anthony Mann, Budd Boetticher, Sam Peckinpah: Stud-*

ies of Authorship within the Western. Bloomington: Indiana University Press, 1969.

KNIGHT, ARTHUR. *The Liveliest Art*. New York: New American Library, 1957.

KRACAUER, SIEGFRIED. *Theory of Film*. New York: Oxford University Press, 1960.

LANGER, SUSANNE K. *Problems in Art*. New York: Charles Scribner's Sons, 1957.

LEACH, EDMUND. *Levi-Strauss*. New York: The Viking Press, 1970.

LEMON, LEE T., and M. J. REIS. *Russian Formalist Criticism*. Lincoln: University of Nebraska Press, 1965.

LEPSCHY, G. C. *A Survey of Structural Linguistics*. London: Farber and Farber, 1970.

LEVI-STRAUSS, CLAUDE. *Myth and Meaning*. Toronto: University of Toronto Press, 1978.

————. *The Raw and the Cooked: Introduction to a Science of Mythology*. Evanston: Harper and Row, 1964.

————. *The Savage Mind*. Chicago: University of Chicago Press, 1962.

————. "The Structural Study of Myth." *Journal of American Folklore* LXVVIII (October–December 1955).

LEWIS, GEORGE H. *Side-Saddle on the Golden Calf*. Pacific Palisades, Calif.: Goodyear Publishing Co., Inc., 1972.

LOWRY, ED. *Art and Artifice in Six Musicals Directed by Vincente Minnelli*. Masters thesis, Austin: University of Texas, 1977.

————. Notes on *Ride the High Country*. CinemaTexas Program, October, 23, 1975.

MALAND, CHARLES J. *American Visions: The Films of Chaplin, Ford, Capra, and Welles, 1936–1941*. New York: The Arno Press, 1977.

MALINOWSKI, BRONISLAV. *Freedom and Civilization*. New York: Roy Publishers, 1944.

————. *Myth in Primitive Psychology*. New York: W. W. Norton and Co., 1926.

MAST, GERALD, and MARSHALL COHEN, eds. *Film Theory and Criticism*. New York: Oxford University Press, 1974.

MCARTHUR, COLIN. *Underworld USA*. New York: The Viking Press, 1972.

MCBRIDE, JOSEPH, and MICHAEL WILMINGTON. *John Ford*. London: Secker and Warburg, 1974.

MCCARTY, JOHN ALAN. "Sam Peckinpah and *The Wild Bunch*," *Film Heritage* (Winter 1969–70).

MCCONNELL, FRANK. *The Spoken Seen*. Baltimore: Johns Hopkins University Press, 1976.

MCCOURT, JAMES. "Douglas Sirk: Melo Maestro," *Film Comment* (November–December 1975).

McBride, Joseph, and Michael Wilmington. "The Private Life of Billy Wilder," *Film Quarterly* (Summer 1970).

McLean, Albert F. *American Vaudeville as Ritual.* Lexington: University of Kentucky Press, 1965.

McVay, Douglas. "Minnelli and *The Pirate,*" *Velvet Light Trap* (Spring 1978).

Metz, Christian. *Language and Cinema.* New York: Praeger, 1975.

Meyer, Leonard B. *Music, The Arts, and Ideas.* Chicago: University of Chicago Press, 1967.

Minnelli, Vincente. *I Remember It Well.* Garden City, N.Y.: Doubleday and Co., Inc., 1974.

———. "The Rise and Fall of the Musical," *Films and Filming* (January 1962).

Mitry, Jean. "John Ford," *Interviews with Film Directors.* Andrew Sarris, ed. New York: Bobbs-Merrill, 1967.

Nachbar, Jack, ed. *Focus on the Western.* Englewood Cliffs, N.J.: Prentice-Hall, 1974.

Nichols, Bill. *Movies and Methods.* Berkeley: University of California Press, 1976.

Nowell-Smith, Geoffrey. "Minnelli and Melodrama," *Screen* (Summer 1977).

Nye, Russell. *The Unembarrassed Muse.* New York: Dial Press, 1970.

Oliver, Bill. "*The Long Goodbye* and *Chinatown:* Debunking the Private Eye Tradition," *Literature/Film Quarterly* (Summer 1975).

Pechter, William. "Movie Musicals," *Commentary* (May 1972).

Perkins, V. F. *Film as Film.* Middlesex, England: Penguin Books, 1972.

Place, J. A. *The Western Films of John Ford.* Secaucus, N.J.: The Citadel Press, 1974.

———, and L. S. Peterson. "Some Visual Motifs in Film Noir," *Movies and Methods.* Berkeley: University of California Press, 1976.

Poague, Leland. *The Cinema of Frank Capra.* New York: A. S. Barnes & Co., 1975.

———. "A Short Defense of the Screwball Comedy," *Film Quarterly* (Summer 1976).

Propp, Vladimir. *Morphology of the Folktale.* Bloomington: University of Indiana Press, 1958.

Rahill, Frank. *The World of Melodrama.* University Park: Pennsylvania State University Press, 1967.

Reichert, John F. "Organizing Principles and Genre Theory," *Genre* (January 1968).

Richards, Jeffrey. "Frank Capra and the Cinema of Populism," *Film Society Review.* Part One (February–March 1972); Part Two (April–May 1972).

RICOEUR, PAUL. *Interpretation Theory.* Fort Worth: The Texas Christian University Press, 1978.

RODOWICK, DAVID. CinemaTexas Program Notes on *Bigger Than Life,* November 6, 1978.

ROSENBAUM, JONATHAN. "Circle of Pain: The Cinema of Nicholas Ray," *Sight and Sound* (Autumn 1973).

ROSENBERG, BERNARD, and DAVID MANNING WHITE, eds. *Mass Culture: The Popular Arts in America.* New York: The Free Press, 1964.

ROSS, LILLIAN. *Picture.* New York: Discus Books, 1952.

ROSTEN, LEO. Hollywood: *The Movie Colony and the Movie Makers.* New York: Harcourt, Brace, and Co., 1941.

ROTH, MARK. "Some Warner's Musicals and the Spirit of the New Deal," *Velvet Light Trap* (June 1971).

RYALL, TOM. "The Notion of Genre," *Screen* (March–April 1970).

SACKS, ARTHUR. "An Analysis of the Gangster Movies of the Early Thirties," *Velvet Light Trap* (June 1971).

SADOUL, GEORGES. *Dictionary of Film Makers.* Berkeley: University of California Press, 1972.

———. *Dictionary of Films.* Berkeley: University of California Press, 1972.

SALT, BARRY. "Film Style and Technology in the Forties." *Film Quarterly* (Fall 1977).

———. "Film Style and Technology in the Thirties." *Film Quarterly* (Fall 1976).

SAN JUAN, E., JR. "Notes Toward a Classification of Organizing Principles and Genre Theory," *Genre* (October 1968).

SARRIS, ANDREW. *The American Cinema.* New York: E.P. Dutton, 1968.

———. "Max Ophuls: An Introduction," *Film Comment* (Summer 1971).

———. "Sarris on Sirk," *Bright Lights* (Spring 1977).

SCHEURER, TIMOTHY E. "The Aesthetics of Form and Convention in the Movie Musical," *Journal of Popular Film* (Fall 1974).

SCHOLES, ROBERT. *Structuralism in Literature: An Introduction.* New Haven: Yale University Press, 1974.

SCHRADER, PAUL. "Notes on Film Noir," *Film Comment* (Spring 1972).

SEBEOK, THOMAS, ed. *Approaches to Semiotics.* The Hague: Mouton, 1964.

SIDNEY, GEORGE. "The Three Ages of the Musical," *Films and Filming* (June 1968).

SIMMONS, GARNER. "The Generic Origins of the Bandit-Gangster Sub-genre in the American Cinema," *Film Reader 3* (1978).

SIODMAK, ROBERT, and RICHARD WILSON. "Hoodlums: The Myth and the Reality," *Films and Filming* (June 1959).

SKLAR, ROBERT. *Movie-Made America.* New York: Vintage Books, 1975.

SMITH, HENRY NASH. *The Virgin Land.* Cambridge: Harvard University Press, 1950.

SMITH, JAMES L. *Melodrama.* London: Methuen and Co., Ltd., 1973.

SMITH, ROBERT E. "Love Affairs That Always Fade," *Bright Lights* (Spring 1977).

SOBCHACK, THOMAS. "Genre Films: A Classical Experience." *Literature/Film Quarterly* (Summer 1975).

SOLOMON, STANLEY J. *Beyond Formula: American Film Genres.* New York: Harcourt, Brace and Jovanovich, 1976.

SONTAG, SUSAN. *Against Interpretation.* New York: Dell Publishers, 1966.

STEINBERG, COBBETT. *Reel Facts.* New York: Vintage Books, 1978.

STERLING, CHRISTOPHER H., and TIMOTHY R. HAIGHT. *The Mass Media: Aspen Institute Guide to Communication Industry Trends.* New York: Praeger Publishers, 1978.

STERN, JANE. "Two Weeks in Another Town," *Bright Lights* (Spring 1977).

STERN, LEE, E. *The Movie Musical.* New York: Pyramid Books, 1974.

STERN, MICHAEL. "Interview with Douglas Sirk," *Bright Lights* (Spring 1977).

————. "Patterns of Power and Potency, Repression and Violence: Sirk's Films of the 1950s," *Velvet Light Trap* (Fall 1976).

TAYLOR, JOHN RUSSELL, and ARTHUR JACKSON. *The Hollywood Musical.* New York: McGraw-Hill, 1971.

TODOROV, TSVETAN. *The Fantastic: A Structural Approach to a Literary Genre.* Ithaca: Cornell University Press, 1970.

————. *The Poetics of Prose.* Ithaca: Cornell University Press, 1977.

TRUFFAUT, FRANCOIS. "A Kind Word for Critics." *Harpers* (October 1972).

TUSCA, JOHN. *The Filming of the West.* Garden City, N.Y.: Doubleday and Co., Inc., 1976.

TYLER, PARKER. *The Hollywood Hallucination.* New York: Simon and Schuster, 1944.

URSINI, JAMES. *The Fabulous Life and Times of Preston Sturges—An American Dreamer.* New York: Curtis Books, 1973.

VIVAS, ELISEO. "Literary Classes: Some Problems," *Genre* (April 1968).

WARSHOW, ROBERT. "The Gangster as Tragic Hero," *Partisan Review* (February 1948). Reprinted in *The Immediate Experience.* Garden City, N.Y.: Doubleday and Co., Inc., 1962.

————. *The Immediate Experience.* Garden City, N.Y.: Doubleday and Co., Inc., 1962.

WHITEHALL, RICHARD. "Crime, Inc.: A Three-Part Dossier on the American Gangster Film," *Films and Filming* (January, February, March, 1964).

————. "The Heroes Are Tired," *Film Quarterly* (Winter 1966–67).

WHITNEY, JOHN S. "A Filmography of Film Noir," *Journal of Popular Film*, Nos. 3, 4 (1976).

WILLIAMS, FORREST. "The Mastery of Movement: An Appreciation of Max Ophuls," *Film Comment* (Winter 1969).

WOLLEN, PETER. *Signs and Meaning in the Cinema*. Bloomington: University of Indiana Press, 1969.

WOOD, MICHAEL. *America in the Movies*. New York: Basic Books, 1975.

————. "Darkness in the Dance," *America in the Movies*. New York: Basic Books, 1975.

WOOD, ROBIN. "Film Favorites: *Bigger Than Life*," *Film Comment* (September–October 1972).

————. "Ideology, Genre, Auteur." *Film Comment* (January–February 1977).

————. "Shall We Gather at the River?" *Film Comment* (Fall 1971).

WRIGHT, WILL. *Six Guns and Society: A Structural Study of the Western*. Berkeley: University of California Press, 1975.

ZOLOTOW, MAURICE. *Billy Wilder in Hollywood*. New York: G.P. Putnam's Sons, 1977.

ZUCKERMAN, GEORGE. "George Zuckerman on Sirk," *Bright Lights* (Spring 1977).

ZUGSMITH, ALBERT. "Albert Zugsmith on Sirk," *Bright Lights* (Spring 1977).

Index

Page numbers in italics refer to illustrations.